LITTLE GARDENS
OF WORDS

LITTLE GARDENS OF WORDS: BOOKSEED'S STORIES OF TRAVEL AND SERVICE

Tim Deppe

LITWIN BOOKS
SACRAMENTO, CA

Copyright 2018

Published in 2018 by Litwin Bookss

Litwin Books
PO Box 188784
Sacramento, CA 95822

http://litwinbooks.com/

This book is printed on acid-free paper.

Library of Congress Cataloging-in-Publication Data

Names: Deppe, Tim, author.
Title: Little gardens of words : Bookseed's stories of travel and service / Tim Deppe.
Description: Sacramento, CA : Litwin Bookss, 2018.
Identifiers: LCCN 2017032882 | ISBN 9781634000192 (alk. paper)
Subjects: LCSH: Central America--Description and travel. | South America--Description and travel. | Deppe, Tim--Travel.
Classification: LCC F1433.2 .D47 2017 | DDC 917.2804--dc23
LC record available at https://lccn.loc.gov/2017032882

Contents

Introduction ... 1

PART ONE: MEXICO

Chapter 1 - Mani: "We Burned Them All" ... 11

Chapter 2 - Mitontic: Coloring Outside the Lines ... 21

Chapter 3 - Acteal ... 27

PART TWO: DOMINICA AND CUBA

Chapter 4 - Deep Doo Doo on the Hot Potato or An Ant in the Ear of an Elephant ... 53

Chapter 5 - Cuba, The Forbidden Island ... 75

PART THREE: GUATEMALA, HONDURAS AND NICARAGUA

Chapter 6 - The Chorti Maya: In Memory of Cándido Amador ... 99

Chapter 7 - Deconstructing Chachauate ... 107

Chapter 8 - The Sliver ... 129

Chapter 9 - Yes, We Have No Bananas ... 135

Chapter 10 - The Rama of Nicaragua ... 149

PART FOUR: PANAMA

Chapter 11 - Darién and a Goat towards the Gap   165

Chapter 12 - Houses without Walls   195

Chapter 13 - The King of Poverty   211

Chapter 14 - The Ngäbe-Buglé Indians   247

PART FIVE: PERU

Chapter 15 - From the Devil's Curve to the Land of Laughter   271

Chapter 16 - Huancavelica and a Lacuna of Literacy   307

Chapter 17 - Olleros to Chavin   315

Chapter 18 - Pisco Sour   323

Chapter 19 - The Amazing Amazon Again and Again...   331

Chapter 20 - "Ya Vari Nice, Mista"   379

PART SIX: BOLIVIA AND CHILE

Chapter 21 - Bookends without Books   413

Chapter 22 - In the Navel of Chuquisaca   421

Introduction

Books and seeds are encapsulated forms of energy waiting to sprout and bear fruit. Both are forms of nourishment, one for the body and the other for the mind and soul. Books, like seeds, hopefully germinate a foliage of thoughts and flowerings of ideas. A book is the fruit of one person's knowledge containing a seed for others, and the seed carries the coded story of its past as well as hope for the future. Without books, life would be an unimaginably limited intellectual existence; without seeds, there would simply be no existence.

Thomas Moore once wrote: "Education is not the piling on of learning, information, data, facts, or abilities—that's training or instruction—but is rather a making visible what is hidden as a seed." The philosopher Voltaire, who said, "Nothing enfranchises like education," also said that "to cultivate one's garden is the best thing we can do on earth." His book *Candide* ends with the title character saying, "Let us cultivate our garden." But how can one cultivate a garden without seeds, or learn how to read and write without books, notebooks, and pens?

In reality it is the children who are the real "Little Gardens of Words," waiting to be cultivated. For their sake, Bookseed, a 501(c)3 non-profit non-governmental organization (NGO), works to donate children's books, school supplies, and seeds to remote impoverished indigenous and marginalized schools and communities. Our purpose in donating children's books and school supplies is to instill an early interest in and love of reading and education. And by donating seeds we hope to enhance people's nutrition and their micro-agrarian economy. There can never be gardens without seeds, and there can never be literacy without books.

The present state of education among indigenous and marginalized children around the world can be depicted by some statues. The first statue is that of the 16th century pope, Julius II. "What do I know of books, make it a sword," the Pope complained to Michelangelo in 1508, after seeing his new marble statue with a book in hand. "What do I know of books, make it a sword," pretty much sums up the world's historical priorities and educational values. In Peru, more money has been spent on gilded statues of defeated generals than on school children's books. Even in the US, far more has been spent on bombs than ever has been spent on books.

Another statue in Izamal Yucatan is of the 1660s Maya book burner, Diego de Landa. He seems very much alive and is still covered with centuries of bronzed lies and "the violence of the letter" of his auto-da-fé. A patronizing plaque proclaims Bishop Landa, with a staff in hand, to be the "Good Shepherd" of his faithful Mayan flock. Yet this flock has not only had virtually all of its written records burned, but has been prevented access to education.

In Panama's San Blas Islands, on Muletupo, beneath the colorfully painted statue of the 1920s Kuna Indian leader Ina Paquina is his powerful quote: "Education must never go against the culture of the people." He knew firsthand how nation-states often abuse education as a weapon to control and acculturate rather than to enhance and liberate. Too often the book has been turned into a weapon against the people.

It is the indigenous and marginalized children who are caught in the vicious cycle of poverty perpetuated by illiteracy and poor nutrition. Young lives are formed very differently depending upon whether one grows up with books in hand, or as a child soldier, or as a vendor of things whose labels one can't even read. In much of the world there are more guns than children's books. In parts of Central America many children can barely count or recite the alphabet, yet they know the number 18 and the letters MS, because they are the marks of gangs. It was blood from guns which gave those numbers and letters significance, not the power of the pen.

Indigenous and marginalized schools are virtually always lacking books and materials, just as their communities often lack seeds. Is a school a school without books and writing materials, or can a garden grow without seeds? Just as with soil, if schools are missing certain elements, then there will be no growth. Children's books and school supplies are vital educational elements, like nitrogen-phosphorus-potassium fertilizer for a garden. Nitrogen-like paper and potassium-like print for growth and phosphorous-like pens and paints for flowering are indispensible. Without them there will be no harvest. Unfortunately there are often more letters in a can of alphabet soup than in most indigenous and marginalized schools.

Having previously worked in a problematic Palestinian school in 1982, Bookseed's official work started unexpectedly in 1994 with the Garifuna, Black Caribs in Honduras. There it sprouted in the thorny grounds of threatened indigenous lands and squalid squatters' communities on unused Honduran military land. In the Garifuna island of Chachauate and the squatters' community named after the murdered American priest, Guadalupe Carne, children's books helped thwart soldiers. The words of children's books, and pencils, paper, paints, and seeds, became some of our tools and weapons to show support for these impoverished and jeopardized communities. Soon other village leaders were asking, "When will you help our school with a little library and bring seeds to our community?" So for two decades I have brought seeds, books, and school supplies to hundreds of remote indigenous and marginalized communities in Latin America, Africa, and Asia.

In South America, where I have done most of my work and which is the focus of this book, the written word is often hard to find and there is still a gentle acceptance of illiteracy. After all, it was a book of all things, either a Bible or a breviary, which triggered the capture of Inca Atahualpa in Cajamarca, Peru in 1532 and started the conquest of the Incas.

The stories here are about some of these remote indigenous and marginalized peoples, and the places where I have brought books and seeds. These are stories about how children's libraries need planting just like gardens need seeds.

The story "Deconstructing Chachauate" is about the start of my NGO work and the life and afterlife of a provocative little children's library, the Biblioteca Satuye. Like a pink mushroom beside the crystal Caribbean, a children's library suddenly sprouted on the spot for a desired Honduran military post. It is a story in which books defeated bullets, and it shows how some snotty-nosed little Garifuna kids won the day against the Honduran military and the Smithsonian Institute.

Others stories, like "The Sliver," "Mitontic," and "Acteal," reveal the problems, controversies, and educational emptiness the indigenous and marginalized face. Another called "Cuba: The Forbidden Island," although applauding the 1961 Literacy Campaign, questions that nation-state's leaders. I was arrested there once while giving away books in a school. It seems that when Fidel Castro said, "Our words are our weapons," he actually meant that the nation-state is the only one allowed to use those weapons.

Using various modes of transportation from donkeys to dugout canoes, from bicycles to airplanes, I have visited many places not on many maps and where few people care to go. During these decades of nearly constant journeys with books and seeds, I have been fortunate to have visited many hundreds of remote primary schools. Most of these were among more than fifty different indigenous tribes throughout remote parts of Latin America.

Little snapshots can sometimes relate a lot and it is impossible to hide surprised joy. Once after helping a bookless school in Huancavalica, Peru, thirty ecstatic school kids blocked the dirt road beside their school to prevent my vehicle from leaving. In Bolivia, a wide-eyed teacher once told me, "We have heard of encyclopedias, but we have never seen any. Thank-you!" And a tiny Shipibo Indian girl in an Amazon school suddenly looked up from behind one of the new books and gave me a thumbs up. In Panama's Darien, the whole Waounan Indian village of Cemaco walked over barefoot to see the seeds I had brought and their school's first books. To show their appreciation, three women's dance groups performed for an hour. Then people gave me gifts of fine basketry and wood carvings, which their poverty prevented me from taking.

My work has been criticized by some people who say, "You are just making museums. You should give computers and not books and school supplies. After some time the books will be ruined, the notebooks will be full, and the pens will be empty. What then?"

To this, I respond, "Yes, I know! But in the places I go to, most kids have never even had a notebook. And pushing a button on a computer will never teach them to write. Yes, I could supply things forever, but for them it is like a miracle to suddenly receive a little something. Remember that when Christ fed loaves and fishes to the thousands, he didn't feed them forever."

Another man once criticized my work in Guatemala by telling me that I don't give enough books to the schools. "We have 30,000 books in our library in Panajachel," he bragged.

"Well, that's great, but with that amount I could help 300 bookless small schools with one-hundred books each. I prefer to spread the 'jam' around to many of those dry crusts of bread called schools, rather than helping just one community," I replied.

I am not an ethnologist, nor a teacher, nor a literacy scholar. I consider myself something of a pedagogical delivery boy, with perhaps a gene of Don Quixote, Johnny Appleseed, and hopefully a touch of Paulo Freire. In all my work, I have never been to a community not excited to receive seeds and a little garden of words.

PART ONE: MEXICO

Chapter 1

Mani: "We Burned Them All"

> "Wherever they burn books they ultimately burn people."—Heinrich Heine

When I arrived in Merida, I found a hotel with high ceilings near the central market, whose old adobe walls had large steel rings for hammocks. An overhead fan kept the mosaic tile floor cool despite the heat. I was waiting there for a shipment of children's books from Mexico City. By the next day, the floor was covered with stacks of books. A couple of days later, I boarded a bus to the Yucatec Maya village of Mani, which is as small and empty as a peanut shell, a mani. Though the nut has long since been consumed, the mnemonic shell remains. Some of the books were for the primary school there and some were for other villages, including Ticun, the ancient Maya capital of Mayapan, and three other empty shells.

A few cars may show up on Sundays, but on the whole, Mani attracts few visitors. The only reason it's remembered at all is for Friar Diego de Landa's infamous auto-da-fé in 1561. That occurred next to the massive old stone church, where the good and holy friar incinerated every treasured Mayan writing he could find and tortured Xui leaders to death. Massacres and book burnings received even greater infamy in 1562. Landa's "cleansing," which horrified even calloused conquistadors, hastened the end of the Mexican Conquest.

Traveling about fifty miles southwest into the vast, flat countryside of northern Yucatan, the old bus I was riding in passed dozens of small villages. Sitting amid plots of henequen, corn, sugarcane, and beans, they seemed to have been etched from the scrubby savannah ages ago. In a village square I spotted a small but intact pyramid that had escaped destruction after the Papal bull of 1535. One of the few left in the area, it seemed like a sad caged animal at the zoo, wondering how it had come to be there.

Signs appeared periodically along the road reading, "Route of the Monasteries." They refer to the huge limestone monasteries that exist in many villages which are made out of stones taken from pyramids and usually tower high above surrounding dwellings and shops.

According to a map drawn in 1556 that John Lloyd Stevens was shown at Mani in 1842, one can count fourteen monasteries in a small area. He reportedly called Mani "a miserable little place." Supposedly the large monastery at Mani was built in seven months, thanks to the labor of six thousand Xui Maya. Nearly all of these monasteries have long been deserted, but they stand as eerie memories of the Conquest. Like the peanut, only their shell remains.

Mani is the historic home of the Yucatec Xiu Maya. Pottery found there has been dated to the third millennium BC. It is an ancient place, because of its reliable cenote providing clean water, but Mani somehow never developed like its neighbors. It never had glorious filigree stonework like Uxmal, or the organizing power of Mayapan, or pyramids and a ball court like Chichen Itza. No, unfortunately, Mani's fame came as a result of loss, not gain. It was remembered for horror and holocaust rather than for its physical or intellectual accomplishment.

The Xiu were in Mani long before the legendary Kukulkan (Quetzalcoatl) came into the area, built Mayapan, and formed an alliance. It only became the center for Xiu culture after 1451, when a civil war destroyed Mayapan and shattered the Triple Alliance of the city-states of Mayapan, Uxmal, and Chichen Itsa. For unknown reasons, the Xiu abandoned the elegant city of Uxmal and made "the miserable little place" Mani their capital.

Mani controlled a ring of villages and became the first Yucatan town to succumb to the Spanish conquest. Perhaps they were influenced by the words of a seventh-century savant named Chilam Balam of Mani, who had predicted the the arrival of the Spanish in the sixteenth century. For whatever reason, in front of thousands the governor of Mani, Tutul-Xiu, threw down his bow and arrows and surprised the conquistadors by accepting the Spanish state and church. Soon thereafter, he was baptized Francisco Montoya.

No one ever changed the historical landscape of the Maya more, though, than Diego de Landa, the sixteenth century Franciscan friar—not Kukulkan, and certainly not the builders of modern day Cancun. The Spanish chronicler Eligio Ancona del Castillo complained in his *History of the Yucatan* that Landa and the Franciscans had "turned the whole country into a Franciscan monastery, effectively independent and superior to the regular Church authorities."

Following the arrival of the Franciscans in 1545, many villages were razed and the subjugated Xiu were forced to coexist with the new monasteries. Far more deaths resulted from reshaping stones into churches than had ever resulted from building pyramids.

During this period, Landa used a young man from an influential Xiu family in Mani, Gaspar Antonio Chi, as his interpreter. Chi's father was one of approximately forty Xiu nobles murdered by the Cocomes, rival Mayan dynastic leaders, for having peacefully received the Spanish. Many more people languished and died in monastery jails and torture chambers. Dogs, fire, hot wax, and mass hangings consumed countless others. Like a catalogue of horrors, new forms of murder were continually being thought up.

Saint Francis fed the birds and established a religious order that somehow morphed into one that fed the vultures. This was all part of Landa's auto-da-fé, which he zealously used to "cleanse the land" of idolatry. Strangely, Landa is not remembered as much for the killings that resulted as he is for burning books at Mani. It was of Mani that he famously wrote, "We found a great number of books and since they contained nothing but superstitions and falsehoods of the devil WE BURNED THEM ALL, which they took most grievously, and which gave them great anguish."

The "violence of the letter" resulted in eyes that were burned by wax and tongues that were pulled out for reading their texts. Ironically, Landa was both the destroyer and the preserver of Xiu culture. By burning the writings at Mani, he destroyed virtually all record of their written knowledge and history, but by writing his book, *Relación de las cosas de Yucatán* (*An Account of the Things in the Yucatan*), he personally saved a remnant through his own permanent record. The fact that his book languished in an archive in Madrid for some three hundred years (until 1863) adds a further touch of strangeness. How odd that a man can have such profoundly contradictory effects on a culture and the world. William Gates, an English scholar and the translator of Landa's book, states in the introduction that: "...he burned ninety-nine times as much knowledge of Maya history and sciences as he has given us in his book." It almost seems that Landa wanted to be the only voice for the Maya.

An erudite Jesuit priest named Jose de Acosta commented on Landa's iconoclasm with disgust, writing that: "This follows from some stupid zeal, when without knowing or wishing to know the things of the Indies, they that say that in a sealed package everything is sorcery...the ones who have wished earnestly to be informed of these found many things worthy of interest."

Therefore, it is because of Landa that we have nothing left, and it is also because of Landa that we have something left. His translator tells us that it was Landa's superior, Bishop Francisco Toral, to whom we owe thanks for Landa's writing. For when Landa wrote the book as a defense of his auto-da-fé, it was Toral who sent him to Spain to face trial for his actions before the Council of the Indies. He was accused of torturing to death 4,500 Maya. Toral wrote to the king of Spain that, "when Mayas knew a friar was going to the village everyone absented themselves from it and ran off to the bush to hide, and others hanged themselves from fear of the friars."

Prior to his departure for Spain, Landa had the foresight to have a series of form letters written in transliterated Yucatec. More "violence of the letter"! Ten of these letters remain, nine of which were signed by many of the Maya caciques. Nearly all of the signatures appear to have been written by the same hand. So, not only did he burn their writings, he also forged their approval of it. These letters were sent to the Spanish King Phillip II in support of Landa. They pleaded for his return to shepherd his "faithful flock" in the Yucatan. The ruse worked, because when Bishop Toral died in 1573, Landa replaced him, and with the help of well-placed friends, was able to return to the Yucatan.

From letter nine, we know that the Maya privately loathed Landa. The 1567 Xiu-Pecab petition missive was signed by four Mayan batabo'ob (governors). It states that 1562 brought "a persecution of the worst that can be imagined from the religious of San Francisco, who had taken us to indoctrinate us; but instead of doing that, they began to torture us, from which many of us died or were maimed…Only to hear them named (Landa and company) and our entrails revolt." In other words, he literally scared the shit out of them.

To show how Landa was subverting the Spanish crown, they wrote that he had told them that, "your Majesty has approved the killings, robberies, tortures, slaveries, and other cruelties done to us…." Other conquistadors and settlers, including Francisco de Montejo, denounced Landa and his fellow clergy and asked for their expulsion. Considering Montejo's reputation, however, that may have been done more out of greed than goodwill. Las Casas records show that Montejo once took a baby from its mother, sliced it up with his sword, and fed it to dogs. Landa himself, perhaps to assuage his guilt, told of how one conquistador, "hanged from the branches of a great tree near one village many Indian women; and hanged their infant children from the mothers feet," like Christmas tree ornaments.

When John Lloyd Stevens and the artist Frederick Catherwood visited Mani in 1842, they were shown an old manuscript, "an object of great reverence among the Indians of Mani." This was the Chilam Balam of Mani, a text from the early seventh century written by a prophet (chilam) living there. Among all the writings of the Maya, it is auspicious that the Chilam Balam of Mani was one of the few that survived, since it predicts the conquest of the Maya and their Gods. It states that, "...within a short time a white and bearded race will come from where the sun rises and that they will bear on high a sign like this †, which their gods could not approach and before which they would flee, and that this people would rule the land...and the natives of the country will abandon their idols and worship a single god...." Would Landa have claimed this to be a work of the devil too? Stevens mentions that:

> it was the first and only instance in which we met with any memorial in the hands of the Indians, tending to keep alive the memory of any event in their history; but this must not be imputed with reproach. History, dark as it is on other points, shows clearly enough that this now abject and degraded race did cling with desperate and fatal tenacity to the memory of those ancestors whom they know not know; the records of their conquerors show the ruthless savage policy pursued by the Spaniards to root this memory from their minds; and here, in this very town of Mani, we have a dark and memorable instance.

Before the actual book burning, Landa had his friars perform a petit auto-da-fé weekly beside the church in Mani. Landa chose Mani for the site because some of its people had secretly continued to worship their traditional deities. After the fall of Mayapan in 1451, Mani became the site of the annual (secret)

Kukulkan ceremony. Landa had forty important Xiu elders from Mani arrested, including their leader Francisco de Montoya Xiu, for taking part in cult-like rituals and (claims of) human sacrifice. Stevens writes:

> Some who had died obstinately in the secret practice of idolatrous rites had been buried in sacred ground; he (Landa) ordered their bodies to be dug up, and their bones thrown into the fields; and, in order to strike terror into the minds of the Indians, and root out the memory of ancient rites, on a day appointed for that purpose, attended by the principal of the Spanish nobility, and in the presence of a great multitude of Indians, he (Landa) made them bring together all their books and ancient characters, and publicly burned them, thus destroying at once the history of their antiquities." According to a line from the book of Chilam Balam of Chumayel, "This was the Antichrist here on earth....

Ground zero for the Mayan literary holocaust was somewhere near the massive Parroquia y Exconvento de San Miguel Arcangel (San Miguel the Archangel Church) in Mani, probably in the grassy parking area. According to the Chilam Balam of Mani, it was attended by Governor Quijada, a not too willing supporter of Landa, but unwilling to oppose him.

I walked the grounds one Sunday afternoon looking for a plaque or some mention of the act, but found nothing. Only in a restaurant down the road could any record of the genocide and book burning be found. A striking painting in orange and black hangs there of a silhouetted figure in a cowl, tossing a scroll into a fire. Landa, though, is memorialized by a bronze statue in the village square of Izamal where he once lived. He holds a staff and is likened to a good shepherd.

For me, going into the huge church was nothing less than entering into a place of holocaust. The lovely garden in the back was the only area that didn't feel like a place of violation. I was surprised when a velvety spike-horned deer calmly walked over and licked my salty hand. Once, deer were favored as Mayan pets. Landa wrote how some Yucatec women would "let the deer suck their breasts by which means they raise them and make them so tame that they will never go into the woods, although, they take them and carry them through the woods and raise them there." Thank you, Landa!

Though Landa's book-burning crusade at Mani was perhaps the most zealous, it was not the area's first. Over thirty years before, in 1529, Frey Juan de Zumarraga, Mexico's first Bishop, had initiated the burning of thousands of hieroglyphic books from the royal Aztec library of Texcoco. He had his monks collect the books and bring them to the market place at Tlateloco, where they were set ablaze. As Von Hagan notes, the "spiritual assault on the conquered people began with the destruction of their learning." What Zumarraga did to the Aztecs, Landa did to the Maya, and both iconoclastic conflagrations signaled the destruction of their respective cultures. Landa's work was so complete that there are only four known remaining Mayan writings. "Thus in the fires of Tlateloco and Mani was destroyed almost the whole of the physical evidence of the paper of the Aztec and the Maya," Von Hagan laments. One of the only comparable events in world history was the burning of the great Ancient Library of Alexandria, the Serapeum, in 391 AD. Through his inquisitional fervor, Landa purposely destroyed an irreplaceable wealth of astronomical, medical, historical, and other knowledge.

It should be remembered that, hundreds of years before the eighteenth century when Linnaeus devised an ordered classification of botanical nomenclature, both the Aztecs and the Maya had an excellent system of taxonomy. Perhaps in some hidden place or other, Mayan hieroglyphic writings will be rediscovered. In 1696, a studious friar named Avendano, who spoke the Mayan language, recorded seeing some in the village of Tayasal in the Peten, but nothing since has been noted.

The Mani primary school was right on the main road through the village. They have their own Xiu people teaching there and they all wear traditional, finely-stitched blouses. The school was in better shape than many others I have seen, but even so, they still had no children's books. I was happy to visit there as a symbolic act, if nothing more.

One morning, I took another box of books by local bus to the dusty rural ruins in the community of Mayapan. Like Mani, Ticul, and all of the rest of rural indigenous village schools, Mayapan had no books. It seemed incredible that a place that had once taken such pride in its written words would now be so empty of them. Sadly, I realized that the box of books I brought were certainly some of the few to enter Mayapan since it fell to rival Mayan armies in 1441. I could sense that the teachers were embarrassed by their lack of books, but also joyful to be somewhat replenished.

It was here that the famed Kukulkan had built his capital of the Yucatan around 987. The site was chosen for its geography of control. Landa related how "the whole land appeared to be one town." About two hundred years after its founding, Kukulkan defeated Chichen Itza, where it is said that he introduced idolatry to the Itzas. For the next two hundred years, Mayapan ruled the ever degenerating Triple Alliance. Before its destruction in 1451, it was so well-organized that they "even have a system to care for the socially unfit," according to Von Hagen. From Landa we know that, "It was the custom to seek in the towns for the maimed and the blind and there they supplied their needs." Now, though, the little primary school was as handicapped as its ruinous community. A five-mile long rock wall once circled an area where some fifteen thousand people lived. The entrances were narrow so they would be easier to defend. As its wall was being built, bridges of trust were being burnt. The city had quarters where nobles from the league were required to keep a house. One certain date in Mayan history is the destruction of Mayapan and the Triple Alliance in 1451. Internecine rivalry tore the Triple Alliance apart. The heavy-handed hegemony of the Cocoms was overthrown. Xiu nobles massacred all but one member of the

Cocom dynasty. This was in direct retaliation for an attack by Hunac Ceel on Chichen Itza where a revolt was being planned. The Xiu had long contended that they were oppressed by the Nachi Cocom and there were stories of them selling Yucatec slaves. With the fall of Mayapan, a whole new story of Mayan history was set to unfold—an independence movement of local powers. Civil war dismantled the tyranny of the central government, but in so doing, gave birth to over a dozen statelet offspring. Led by Landa's auto-da-fé in nearby Mani, the importance of Mayapan for Mayan history became its destruction. It was at this point that the Xiu evacuated lovely Uxmal, the Itzas left for the Peten, and the Cocomes fled to the northeast. Mani emerged then as the leading regional town after the fall of Mayapan. Perhaps it was awareness of his crime that led Landa to later write, "The most important thing that the chiefs who stripped Mayapan took away to their own countries were the books of their sciences...."

Chapter 2

MITONTIC: COLORING OUTSIDE THE LINES

"Nine tenths of education is encouragement."—Anatole France

The Tzotzil Maya village of Mitontic rests high on the mountainside above the Chenalho Valley in the central highlands of Chiapas, Mexico. From there one can see far down the palisading slopes of the rugged range. It seems that the twists and turns, risings and fallings of its horizons are no different than its undulating history. The Tzotzil Maya number about 370,000 and together with their cousins, the Tzeltal, numbering some 350,000, make up most of the indigenous population of Chiapas. The Tzotzil are sometimes referred to as the "bat people," as bats were once a revered totem. Nearly every family still hand tills the cool fertile soil, and they have a few scraggly sheep whose wool the women use to weave.

Not having a vehicle that year, I hired taxis or used buses to take me around to different village schools. This particular day, I used the proprietor of the pension I stayed at in San Cristobal de Las Casas to drive me and my old friend Manuel to Mitontic. Manuel had been a friend for years and had helped me before. He spoke Tzotzil, which was very beneficial. Previously, he had worked with a Mexican government family planning group for the indigenous in Chiapas. He would put on workshops and show them how to put on condoms. Once, a Chol Indian man returned after some days and asked Manuel if it was alright to take off the condom now. So besides being a good helper, he was also good for a laugh.

Intrigue, mistrust, and suspicion then plagued Chiapas and it was an uncertain time. Ultra right-wing elements opposing any indigenous autonomy increased their campaign of intimidation and fear. The year before, in 1997, a grisly massacre of over forty peaceful Tzotzils occurred in the church at Acteal. The faltering San Andreas Peace Accord cast uncertain dark shadows over the area, and convoys of Mexican military Humvees were as ubiquitous as barefoot Indians. At several select places along the road, razor wire was swirled on top of sandbags, enclosing little military camps.

After more than an hour of driving, we finally saw Mitontic in the distance. Far in the distance, small white dwellings stood out on a slope like a flock of grazing sheep above the valley below. We were going to the primary school, which was just beside the road at the beginning of the village. It was enclosed by a whitewashed adobe wall. The few scribbles of Zapatista EZLN graffiti on the outside amounted to more than all the written material inside. We drove right up and parked beside a large closed gate. Inside was a cement courtyard, with two small buildings facing each other, each with three classrooms.

The driver stayed beside his car as Manuel and I entered with some boxes. We soon found the principal, a middle-aged Tzotzil woman, in her open office. She was surprised by our unannounced visit and pleasantly shocked by the books. Though I knew what she would answer, I asked her anyway: "Do you have any children's story books here?"

"No!" she said, "We have no books like these. We have only some old textbooks." Wanting to show the books and other things to the entire school, she had us go into the courtyard and display them on a large table. Each class was amped with an electrified excitement as they filed out. Manuel and a teacher handed out a notebook and pen to every child. Meanwhile, the principal addressed them, telling them things like, "Now we have some encyclopedias and dictionaries and many interesting books. Each classroom will receive some. The books are for you to help you learn, but are not to be taken home. So use them, but take care of them."

Then she asked me to say a few words in Spanish. At every school I always ask the kids some of the same things and always get the same responses. Having them hold up their new notebooks and pens, the first for many, I asked, "Children, do you like notebooks and pens?" Like a thunder bolt they responded in unison with a loud, "Sí!" And knowing that perhaps none of them have ever held a children's book before, I then asked, "Who likes storybooks?" It was as if those words lit a fuse; there was an immediate explosion from the two hundred Tzotzil kids shouting, "Sí, sí ..." which resounded beyond the walls of the school.

Ironically, it was pen and paper via the "violence of the letter" that had stolen more indigenous land than the pistol and gun. So, the kids holding up two hundred pens and notebooks as weapons perhaps offered some hope against the pestilence of the gun. The illiterate gun has never really changed anything for long, except adding more names to graveyards. It only knows how to write in blood, the blood of others, and its loud voice of violence always tries to shout over the silent reasoning of the thoughtful pen. Without education, though, the indigenous were forced to choose the gun, although they don't really want that. They would rather not have to fight at all. These humble people would rather tend their crops and the few sheep they have than fight to defend their rights. But the reality of the world dictates differently. Perhaps in holding up those pens and books, the children here showed hope that the living ink of the pen will defeat the bloodsucking gun.

After awhile, the principal had the kids express their appreciation with an emphatic "Gracias," the intensity of which matched the intensity of their desire to learn, but also echoed in the emptiness of the place.

Tzotzil is their Native language, but unfortunately they have only a couple of children's books available in that language. The Mexican government prints a limited number of books in the languages of each of the country's fifty-two indigenous groups. Despite good intentions, two books are insufficient and largely symbolic. This means that everyone must learn some Spanish, the dominant language, but they often learn just enough to barely function. Many kids do not continue on to secondary school and thus remain only semi-literate.

The exuberant response of those two hundred Tzotzil kids not only drew attention to their bookless existence, but also drew the attention of some of the other villagers. As we opened the gate amid friendly farewells, we saw four men approaching the car. The first thing I noticed was that they were drunk. One had a pistol stuck in his waist. Another, wearing a long black woolen chuuk, approached the driver and said something in Spanish. Though almost unintelligible, I could make out the word "cacique," meaning chief. I realized immediately that he was the cacique. But clearer than the words for me was the alarm in the driver's eyes. Continuing to speak, the cacique slurred and mumbled more drunken words, which I could not understand, but which seemed to cause the driver even more concern. Manuel whispered to me that the cacique had told the driver that he was going to impound his car. Stealing cars was not an uncommon occurrence in Chiapas in those years. The police would do nothing, except sometimes help sell the cannibalized parts.

It turned out that the cacique was angry because we had broken protocol by not asking his permission to visit the school first. He felt snubbed. So not only was he drunk and armed, he was also irate. At that point, drawn by the ruckus, the principal and a teacher walked over. Perceiving the cacique's demeanor, they were reluctant to get involved but felt obligated. The Tzotzil principal told the cacique that we were helping the village by giving books to the school and notebooks and pens to the kids, but the cacique told her "Shut up!" Continuing a fusillade of denunciations, he tapped his index finger on his chest and said that he was the cacique and she should listen to him. She then appeared very worried as well. These men could not be reasoned with and were completely drunk and belligerent. As we stood there, we wondered where all this was going to lead. But right then, just as things were on their way to possibly getting much worse, Manuel said to me, "Let's give them some seeds."

"Good idea!" I answered.

Getting a box out of the car, I placed it on the hood and started to take out an assortment of small bags of various vegetable seeds.

"Would you like some seeds?" Manuel cleverly asked them in Tzotzil.

"Seeds, what seeds?" the drunken cacique brusquely questioned.

"Oh, we have all kinds of seeds, what would you like? What do you want to plant?" Manuel asked.

Then the men all started naming different vegetables in Tzotzil. Suddenly, within seconds, things changed. It seemed that the farmer inside all of them came out and plowed over new ground. Manuel looked at me, gave a wink, and started writing the names of the vegetables in Tzotzil and Spanish on some little coin envelopes. Meanwhile, I began to spoon in the seeds.

By that time, a crowd of curious school kids were peeking through the partially open gate. The cacique, no doubt wanting to impress them with his chirographic talents, decided that he should take over the writing from Manuel. His major disability, though, was that he was too drunk off the local booze. He soon gave up, handed the pen over to the principal, and ordered her to do it.

After finishing with the seeds, the cacique then wanted us to go with them, for some drinks of course. To their chagrin (and to the driver's relief), Manuel excused us, saying that we had to get back. So, before there were any more complications, we drove off amid a forest of waving hands and shouts of "Adiós, adiós!" Soon we were shaking our heads in laughter and disbelief. With a big smile Manuel then told me in English, "Look, the driver was so scared he pissed in his pants!"

Chapter 3

ACTEAL

"The great aim of education is not knowledge but action."
—Herbert Spencer

"Every action beyond ordinary limits is subject to evil interpretation..."—Montaigne

When Manuel, asked me what other villages I wanted to take books and seeds to, I said, "Let's go to Acteal!"

"Well, if there's a place that deserves help, it's Acteal," he responded, slowly nodding his head.

"But can we get there?" I wondered.

"Only one way to find out. Let's just try," he answered. "Oh, I'll take Violeta! I know that she wants to go." He said this proudly, referring to his twelve-year-old daughter.

A few days later, we put a couple boxes of books and a box of seeds in the back of my old flatbed truck. With my dog, Mr. Jeb, riding in the back, the three of us started off early one foggy February morning from their house in San Cristobal de Las Casas, in Chiapas, Mexico.

Although thirteen months had passed since the grizzly December 22, 1997 massacre of forty-five Tzotzil people inside the church in Acteal, the tension in the area remained high. Over four thousand indigenous had fled the vicinity, and Mexico's new President Zedillo had ordered thousands of more troops into the area.

The Acteal massacre were the result of three years of intense social unrest in Chiapas, which began on January 1, 1994. This date marked the beginning of the North American Free Trade Agreement (NAFTA) and the waging of an economic war against Mexico's indigenous. In reaction, on the same day the Zapatista Army of National Liberation (EZLN) and thousands of independent indigenes captured San Cristobal de Las Casa and parts of the Chiapas highlands.

The pacifist Abejas sided with the EZLN in opposing the neo-liberal policies of NAFTA, but they chose another means of resistance than the gun. As a pacifist group, they chose to resist NAFTA via non-violent direct action, including fasting and praying for their enemies. They believed that the gun, though it can bring change, will never bring a lasting change. It will never change the vital component of people's hearts, and the Mexican government has far more guns than the EZLN will ever have. Though the peaceful Abejas, the bees, made the sweetest honey, they were exterminated like insects by the bitterness of NAFTA's neo-liberal lackeys. Their bodies ended up being discarded like trash, dumped in a cave in the ravine below the church.

Of the forty-five pacifist Tzotzil people murdered, nine were men, fifteen were children, and twenty-one were women, four of whom were pregnant. The Perez family lost fourteen members and the Luna family lost ten. It seems that these people's prayers, fasting, and non-violent actions were more threatening than the guns of the EZLN. "Who are those so terrified of this dream?" a Mexican human rights activist questioned.

So Acteal, though a tiny Tzotzil Maya hamlet built on a remote ridge in the Chiapas highlands, became a very significant place. Besides affecting the families involved, the massacre there changed the political and social landscape of Mexico.

During that time, as the serpentine knot of events was being untied, it was proven that the vehicles, dark uniforms, AK-47s, and all the other materials used, were paid for by SEDESOL,

Mexico's Department of Social Development. Thus the name "Social Development" became a euphemism for slaughter. This group was accountable to the Institutional Revolutionary Party (PRI) which governed Mexico for six decades, which only inflamed the situation more.

It was later proven that over forty indigenous paramilitary and at least a dozen state police officers were responsible for massacring those poor, peace-seeking Tzotzil people. But while about forty of the culprits went to jail for eight years, others did not. And of course the men who made the plans and gave the orders were never found out.

Because of poor education, most indigenous youth have very few opportunities to improve their lives. As a result, some become convinced to join right-wing paramilitaries. Many of the murderers at Acteal came from such life circumstances. This makes no excuse for their crimes, yet it puts the events into their social context. When faced with the hardships and shame of perpetual poverty on one side and prestige and promise of an income on the other, they chose the militias. Because of lack of education they are even more susceptible to indoctrination. This is not unlike some soldiers coming from minorities and marginalized backgrounds in the US military today. Prior to the Acteal massacre these indigenous militia members also had the "right" to extract both a "war tax" from villagers and loot the houses and fields of those indigenous people who fled. So the spoils of war were also used as carrots to entice them on.

Two evangelical church groups, The Wings of Eagles and God's Army, helped pay for the legal aid of the culprits. Their evangelical "good news" really encouraged and preached a militant gospel of murder against those who prayed for peace and justice inside the Acteal church.

It is more than a three-hour drive from San Cristobal de Las Casas to Acteal. But because of the military checkpoints at that time, it took us even longer. Driving uphill towards San Juan

Chamula, the whole area becomes a patchwork of small plots of vegetables, orchards, and pasture among the highland forest. This is the land of the "bat people," as the Tzotzil Maya were once referred to. "Tzotz" means "bat" in their language. There are some 350,000 Tzotzil Maya living in small villages and hamlets, mostly concentrated in that part of the Chiapas highlands.

The vast majority of Tzotzil are agriculturists and still use planting sticks to plant maize and other crops in their milpa clearings. Most families also have a few sheep that provide wool. These animals are considered almost holy and thus are rarely eaten. The women, timid around strangers but jovial by nature, love to weave. They can sometimes be seen weaving under trees beside their waddle and daub or rough wooden homes.

Every now and then a couple of barefooted Tzotzil or Tzeltal Maya women would appear walking along the road carrying heavy loads of firewood. Cords tethered them to their heavy loads just as poverty tied them to their lives. This heavy work is considered women's labor, while the men cut and split logs in the ever-shrinking forests. Sometimes military humvees would growl by. After all, the road was paved for them rather than for the hundreds of thousands of indigenous.

Those were the days of the mask in Chiapas. The mask gave face to the faceless, dignity to the dispossessed. It became their face not out of fear, but rather as a way of protesting against injustice. By becoming faceless they were saying that they never counted, were never recognized. On certain days thousands of masked indigenous marched the streets of San Cristobal in protest. Only then were they seen and the whole world took notice. Sometimes it takes a mask to show the truth.

The Tzotzil people, especially those in San Juan Chamula, have been famously fierce about their independence since the time of the Conquest. They have a long history of raiding San Cristobal de Las Casas. Many Chamulans led the anti-NAFTA uprising in which the Zapatistas took over San Cristobal de Las Casas. As in old times, hundreds stealthily descended on the town through the pine forests.

Ruins of the original Catholic church, bordered by a neglected, centuries-old cemetery, could just be seen as we passed by the turnoff to Chamula. A couple of years before, in 1996, Manuel and I took books to three schools around this village and several other villages in the area. Parts of the old church stood like a giant gravestone, seemingly wanting to bury its history. The Dominicans who built it were referred to as "God's hounds," i.e. domini canus; some had been sent to the eternal humane society. This was because the priests took away some "talking stones," probably pieces of meteorites, which Chamulan shamans claimed fell from heaven and used for divination. It was here at the old church where the Chamulans crucified one of those first Catholic priests. After doing so and sacking the church, they built their own and Rome never sent any more priests. Even the admirable Bartholomew de Las Casas, the great Dominican defender of the indigenous, would not venture to Chamula.

Now the huge whitewashed church is a tourist trap destination. But Chamula has always had its limits and its own ways of doing things. To break them could still be deadly, even for their own people. Back in the 1980s, an Italian man was chased down and murdered for disobeying the strict protocol of not taking photographs inside the church. And with the recent advance of evangelicalism, religious strife led to thousands of Chamulans fleeing from their villages' intolerance. They lost their houses and land and formed new makeshift communities here, carved out of the forest.

Despite the huge white-washed church standing so proudly, many local worshippers lay passed out inside, prostrate in holy bliss from too much sacramental posh. If a little is good then more must be better. Beside them their holy grail Coca-Cola bottles filled with posh lined the blue tiled floor. Among scented pine needles, smoke from copal, and colored votive candles, walls of saintly statues looked on in syncretic wonder.

Continuing on towards Acteal, we passed a marker made of four cement crosses draped in corn stalks. These designate indigenous boundary lines and are a Mayan symbol of pre-Christian cosmology.

But other boundary lines, especially those written ones of ink and paper, have been changed. The white collar pen and paper have stolen more land than the sword and the gun. Just like in the 1910 Mexican Revolution, land was the main issue sparking the 1994 Zapatista uprising. It is crucial to understand NAFTA's methodology in order to understand the rage it provoked and which eventually led to the twisted road to Acteal.

As a classic example of white-collar crime against the indigenous, NAFTA insisted that Mexico modify Articles 4 and 27 of its Constitution. These articles referred to their long standing ejido program. The ejidos were basically co-ops in which a group of the landless poor could farm land themselves. Though actually an ancient Aztec and also a medieval Spanish practice, they were initiated nearly a century earlier, during the Mexican Revolution. The self-effacing Emiliano Zapata expropriated huge latifundias "acquired" by Mexico's rich, and allotted them back to the indigenous and landless peasants. Most of the land had been granted long before to wealthy people through the slave-based encomienda system. Zapata and others turned this ruthless land-grabbing system on its head and replaced it with the justice of ejidos. Though it had its ups and downs the ejido policy, imperfect though it was, was central to helping eliminate the degrading dialectic between Mexico's rich and poor which was destroying the nation's social fabric.

Like the archangel in the Garden of Eden, Zapata basically evicted the Adam Smith belief that the owners had the right to eat all of the fruits. Though the ejido members were still under the human curse of eking out a living by the sweat of their brow, at least they could do it on land they could freely use, even though they did not own it.

NAFTA demanded the dismantlement of Article 27 in Mexico's 1917 Constitution, and by this, the US, Canadian, and Mexican neo-liberals waged war against Mexico's indigenous and other poor. NAFTA turned the ejido system into a giant fraudulent real-estate business. Suddenly the ejidos could be sold and even corporations could be become ejidos. Deconstructing the ejidos through the Constitution made it possible and profitable for NAFTA backers such as Monsanto, DuPont, Syngenta, and others to enact their pernicious plans. After the neo-liberals modified Mexico's Constitution, they then started planting their genetically modified seeds.

Everything Zapata and others accomplished in the Mexican Revolution through the sword, NAFTA reversed with the power of the pen. NAFTA reinstated Adam Smith's ideas into "paradise lost" and started feeding the planet with the forbidden GMO fruits from their scientific tree of knowledge.

The consolidation of small ejidos into giant corporate NAFTA farms has disenfranchised untold numbers of families. Now over half of Mexico's two and a half million small farmers, who once worked on Mexico's 28,000 ejidos, have been banished to the slums by NAFTA. They simply could not compete. They now eke out a futureless living and see their sad reflections in the shiny shoes that they polish.

Continuing on our way, we soon saw breathtaking views of rugged ridges and canyons in the distance and crops in nearby milpas. Patches of arnica, like large yellow poultices, covered hillsides among slopes of pines and oaks in that wounded land. Descending into the steep and narrow Chenalho Valley we passed the village of Mitontic. Then San Pedro Chenalho could be seen far in the distance, at the confluence of two streams. Two years earlier. we had brought books to four schools in this area. Like most of Chiapas, the Chenalho district had a literacy rate of less than fifty percent, and most children didn't progress beyond third or fourth grade.

Like nearly all indigenous highland Maya villages, San Pedro Chenalho suffered from political division. An outspoken French priest, who for twenty-eight years had worked openly and tirelessly for indigenous rights and justice, had been deported by Mexico's government just weeks before. For some years the Red Badge death squad operated there with impunity. It was proven that the vehicles driving the death squad to Acteal started from San Pedro Chenalho, and for months members of Mexico's covert Human Intelligence Team (HUMINT) were located in Chenalho. They spied on people like the priest and others involved in EZLN activity. Yet the schools were so empty that they seemed totally incapable of producing any human intelligence.

At the other side of San Pedro Chenalho, the road forks and at a military checkpoint every vehicle is stopped and searched by soldiers. This was one of twenty military checkpoints that Mexico's President Ernesto Zedillo had ordered set up just around that area. When we pulled up to the makeshift gate, a Mexican soldier politely told us to get out. Then he asked to see our identification and the papers for my vehicle. He also asked me where we were going to. I answered, "Acteal."

"Why do you want go to Acteal? This is a restricted area. You cannot go to Acteal," he flatly stated. At that point I reached into my briefcase and silently handed him an envelope containing a letter. Some months before I had received this letter from President Ernesto Zedillo's office. Seeing the Mexican seal and the presidential stationary from Los Pinos raised his eyebrows.

"You must wait here, please," he told us, and he proceeded to the office to inquire about what to do. In the tiny guardhouse I saw him hand the envelope to his commanding officer. After reading the short letter the man made a telephone call, most likely to the military headquarters in San Cristobal.

While we waited the soldier returned and searched through my truck. It seemed that he was most likely looking for guns. The old saying that guns go south and drugs go north is no rumor. Seeing the boxes of books and seeds in the back of the truck he wanted to open them. But with Mr. Jeb's large body dozing nearby he would not step inside. So I entered and placed the boxes in front of him.

When he opened one of the boxes, he was surprised to find the children's books. I could see that his attention was immediately diverted. Standing there he leafed through a couple of the books. I watched him read a few words softly to himself. His lips moved, slowly, unsteadily, revealing his own para-literacy. Then, sensing that this was his only opportunity, he turned to me and with a real innocence which didn't seem fitting to a hardened soldier, he meekly said, "Please, Señor, give me some books!"

Suddenly the father, the parent inside of him, seemed to forget that he was a soldier. Even his uniform couldn't camouflage his humanity.

I was pleasantly shocked, but in this game at the gate, I teased, "Don't you think you are kind of big to be reading children's books? What grade are you in anyway, third?"

"Oh, no Señor, I don't want them for me. Please, I want some for my children. I have five children and they have no books. I want them to learn. So please, can you give me some books to help them read better?"

Then he went on to tell me their names and ages, hoping it would help his cause.

Usually I am no fan of soldiers, especially the type stopping me with guns. But I found myself touched by his humble sincerity and his persistent desire to help his children. He was so human despite the olive green uniform, which always tries to make the man inside into its own image. He saw his chance and knew enough to take advantage of it. Though I abhorred his military mindset, I admired that. How could I not?

So, I told him, "Okay, I'll give you five books."

Imagine, I thought, some simple kids' books had just won over my ideological enemy, some stupid soldier, but yet "the other." What else besides children's books could have caused the same reaction, I wondered?

Then seeing that other soldiers were coming over, probably to ask for some books too, I shoved the box close to my dog. After some minutes the officer came out and told us, "Okay, you can go to Acteal, but you must return before dark." We assured him that we would only be there for a few hours.

"Besides, my dog has a date with a beautiful *perra* tonight, so we have to get back," I joked.

After driving a short way, Manuel and I turned to each other and broke out in laughter.

"I'm so glad that I brought that bullshit letter. I can't believe it worked, because it doesn't say anything!" I told Manuel. "Look, read it, all it does is acknowledge my work and thank me for helping schools in Chiapas."

"Well, it worked. It got us through," he said with a smile.

Mexico's ex-President Ernesto Zedillo's office had responded twice the summer before to a protest letter I sent regarding Acteal. Besides mentioning my work in Chiapas as a concerned NGO, I had given some suggestions. I wrote that providing 70,000 children's books will do more for peace in Chiapas than 70,000 soldiers will ever do. Ultimately it comes down to either backing the book or backing the gun. If there is no chance for education, then the gun will win, which means that everyone will lose. Like a pen the gun is an instrument of expression, but it writes in blood rather than ink. Denying books and education invariably invites the bloody script of the gun. And if school kids have no hope through education, then what? Then we find the gun coming along and giving a false hope. Then we find drugs, crimes, and prostitution doing the same thing. Besides, how many potential Garcia Marquezes, Nerudas, or Einsteins are out there who will never get a chance to develop because of poverty and a failed school system?

When writing Zedillo about the empty conditions of all the schools I visited, I mentioned that they always have a basketball court but rarely any books. I realized my words would not score a basket. The double-dribbling Mexican government has built many nice new schools in indigenous villages, but there is always next to nothing inside them. They are like shoe boxes with no shoes inside. This kind of mis-education is only meant to keep the status quo and its modern feudalism intact.

"Is this the future you want for Mexico?" I had asked. I tried to sensitively shame them a little by ending the letter saying, "It's too bad a gringo has given books to more indigenous primary schools in the Chiapas Highlands than the Mexican government has."

After a long uphill climb from San Pedro Chenalho we finally came to Pol Ho, a few turns away along the narrow road before Acteal. Greeting us as we entered were a row of boarded up wooden kiosks, a silent statement of the status of Acteal. It seemed like a ghost town after the gruesome massacre the year before.

In a wide parking area beside the closed kiosks I pulled over and parked my old truck. It had been a tiring and taxing drive and we all needed to get out, especially Mr. Jeb. But there was nothing open and no one in sight. An eerie feeling clung to the place. The only face we saw was a large mural of Zapata staring sternly from the wooden wall of a house. Below this his slogan, "Tierra y Libertad" (Land and Freedom) screamed out. It seemed as relevant then as it was one hundred years ago, but as controversial also.

While we sat there Manuel, who loved Zapata, proudly said, "Of all the world's revolutions, only the Mexican gave priority to land. Not the American, not the French, not the Russian, none of them, only the Mexican! Zapata divided up the haciendas to give to the landless poor. But then the rich corrupted his agrarian reforms and stole the Indian's land again. What Mexico needs is another revolution, another Zapata! Viva Zapata!" Manuel called out.

Perhaps because he had heard this, a young Tzotzil man walked over to us. Greeting him in Tzotzil, Manuel asked him about the school. He told us it was still closed. But really, the whole village seemed closed and abandoned, not just the school. This was the first time that anyone had given us any reliable information. Even the military at the Chenalho checkpoint didn't know.

While we were talking an old white-haired couple showed up, but stopped and stayed some distance away. The diminutive man wearing a typical Tzotzil conical straw hat with dangling red ribbons stood there looking at us inquisitively. He was holding hands with his even tinier wife. There was something very charming about them, like two colorful lovebirds. Sensing their uncertainty, Manuel called out a greeting to them in Tzotzil. Then he told them not to fear the big dog, and that we had seeds to give them if they liked.

Trusting Manuel, perhaps because he spoke their language or perhaps because they saw the innocence of young Violeta, they slowly walked over. They were both in their eighties, but still worked the land. Manuel asked them about their need for seeds and listed some of the different ones we had. The little old man and his wife said they wanted some beans. I found a bag containing a variety called Jacob's Cattle, a white and brown speckled bean, which I thought they might like. I placed a few of the smooth beans into the man's calloused hand and he scrutinized them with a smile.

Just then the young man talking with us ran off, disappearing over the hillside among some houses. The top of the church where the massacre happened could be seen sticking out there like the top of a gravestone. A couple of minutes later he returned, followed by some curious villagers who all wanted seeds. Then even more people showed up as the word got out. All of a sudden a small crowd of Tzotzil men and women had gathered around my truck, all wanting to see what we had. Manuel listed off the names in their language. Having seen the beans we had given the old couple, everyone wanted some. Beans are a main staple there; together with corn they are one of the most important crops.

The market in San Cristobal de Las Casas boasts more than twenty-five local varieties of beans, perhaps the most in the world. All are colorfully displayed and sold from cubical wooden bins; the shopkeepers know each and every variety.

We did not have enough beans with us to supply everyone, but we gave out all we had, trying to distribute to different families. They also wanted the other vegetable seeds we had, for it was planting time and they grow many things.

We had already captured their curiosity with the beans and because I knew of their respect for corn, I took a few kernels of a variety called Anazazi Blue from a seed bag. As with the beans, I placed a few kernels into the open palm of one man. Though the beans had brought joy and smiles, the corn caused a reaction that was almost reverent. The man held them as if they were gemstones, blue sapphires. Soon a kernel was passed around from one person's hands to the next. These people know seeds and to see them dote over them reveals the profound respect for and understanding of the symbiotic relationship they share. Maize is commonly classified by color and this diversity has a direct relationship to people's ethnolinguistic diversity. Perhaps the converse is also true of a monoculture.

The metaphor of maize permeates Maya cosmology to such an extent that very few comparisons with seeds in other cultures equal it. The Wakah Chan, the Mayan celestial world tree which is our Milky Way, is often depicted as a maize plant. In Palenque at the Temple of the Foliated Cross, an intricately carved maize tree has ears of corn for branches. Each of the kernels has a human face. As Shele and Freidel wrote in their seminal book *Maya Cosmos*, "maize was an ultimate symbol of Mayan social existence in communion with nature." Because corn needed human intervention, one relied on the other.

In the four or five books left of Maya writings, both the Popul Vul and the Chilam Balam state that mankind is made from maize. In one account handfuls of kernels, which their maize god Hun-Nal-Ye scattered from his seed bag, sprouted to life as human beings. In another, "The first Mother shed her blood, causing maize—the raw material of humanity—to sprout from the waters of the Otherworld...."

A prophetic verse in the Chilam Balam of Chumayal can be seen as a reference to Monsanto and the "Lords of the Underworld" who adulterate maize with genetic engineering. It states, "the justice of our Lord Dios shall descend everywhere in the world, straight from Dios upon Ah-Kantenal, he who adulterates maize...." This will lead to the worms and disease consuming Hun-Nal-Ye. Another reference states, "But it shall still come to pass when tears shall come to the eyes of our Lord Dios, the justice of our Lord Dios shall descend everywhere in the world, straight from Dios upon Ah Kantenal (he who adulterates maize)...."

So these demonic "Lords of the Underworld" and their myrmidons like Monsanto will finally be defeated, the Mayan prophecies state. According to the ancient narrative in the Popol Vuh, the twins Hunahpu and Xbalanque are the cultural heroes who maintain the corn plants lives through their successes against the Lords of the Underworld. The world is left with little more than this hopeful verse because of the seventeenth-century Catholic Church's destruction of Mayan texts.

For more than an hour we made up seed packets. Manuel wrote the names of the seeds in Tzotzil and Spanish on manila coin envelops, I spooned seeds into them, and Violeta sealed them shut. Then she placed the envelopes into zip-lock bags and handed them to the people.

Hopefully the seeds provided a harvest. Thousands of people had become dislocated from their land and unable to plant. San Cristobal became inundated with such people. Not planting one year often means having no seeds to plant the next year and thus no crops to sell.

But if NAFTA has its way all the traditional markets will give way to supermarkets, and all the milpas will give way to the corporate monoculture. Wall Street prefers WalMarts and their packaged imports rather than the open air markets where poor peasants can come and sell their local items.

NAFTA and Monsanto prefer monoculture plantations of biotech corn with titan-like tractors. Subsistence farms and milpas, where planting sticks are still used and seeds are still saved for the next year's planting, do not fit into this program. NAFTA and Monsanto wish they would all be sprayed with Roundup or Agent Orange. It prefers that the Mayas' thousands of ancient strains of corn be infected with their biotech varieties and lost forever. Then the world will only be able to buy their seeds. This pits the milpa mode of production against Monsanto, and the calloused hands of indigent indigenous farmers against the executives.

The milpa was for thousands of years the locus and caretaker of communities and unified everyone involved. "Most Mayan communities originated as a milpero, which later developed into a community. For the peasant the milpa is the ideological text in which his or her culture is inscribed" wrote Alicia Re Cruz. These subsistence economies were based on adequacy and dispensation, while market economies are based on inadequacy and deprivation.

La fagina is the ancient Mayan institution of communal labor, wherein every adult Maya has to serve in community projects periodically. Now many people pay someone else to do the work so that they can work a job in Cancun or some big city. The dialectic of community versus the culture of things, and of subsistence versus the city has eroded their culture.

Now in many places what Alicia Re Cruz calls "the new urban milpa of the mall" acculturates Mayan culture and eats away at it like the worms eating their ancient corn god Hun-Nal-Ye.

Like old Adam, Monsanto chooses to believe that the rights of possession of the fruits of the world garden are theirs to do with as they please. What NAFTA's creators caused to happen in the church at Acteal they also want to do to the temple of the world.

NAFTA is basically destroying culture through agriculture. Monsanto and others with a genetically modified menu of seeds and social engineering have taken the culture out of agriculture. Certainly the ancient stone glyphs of the Maya corn god being bound with ropes and eaten by worms reflects what they are doing.

Having finished dispensing all the seeds and knowing that Acteal's little primary school was closed, we wondered what to do with the books we had. The best thing to do we decided was to give them and the school supplies to a primary school in neighboring Pol Ho. So we left Acteal and drove the short way to the larger community of Pol Ho.

After we had just found the school, we were shocked to be suddenly accosted in front of it by a group of masked Zapatistas, all heavily armed. They all appeared to be young, like their unmasked leader, who was no more than twenty. I turned to Manuel and saw a look of alarm on his face. He knew this was going to lead to a confrontation, so he stayed seated in the truck with Violeta while I got out to talk with them.

The young leader immediately wanted to know what we were doing there. I told him that we had just given seeds away in Acteal, and because their school was closed we wanted to give the books and school supplies we had to the primary school in Pol Ho.

"Show me the books," he demanded.

Ah, another soldier interested in children's books, I first thought, thinking that he too probably wanted some just like the government soldier in Chenalho. So I took a box from the truck and opened it in front of him. Reaching in, he took out a book.

"Are all these books in Spanish?" he wanted to know.

"Yes, they are all in Spanish."

Immediately I knew where this was leading.

"Why don't you have any books in Tzotzil?"

"Because there are no children's books in Tzotzil. If I could get books in Tzotzil, I would bring them. But there are just a couple, which the government prints. The Zapatistas should print children's books in Tzotzil," I told him.

Then, as if to justify his words, he kept insisting, "Spanish is bad, Spanish is bad! Spanish destroyed Indian culture! No Spanish books! Spanish is bad!"

Though it only angered him more, I told him, "But you are speaking to me in Spanish. You can read Spanish, so why don't want the children to be able to?"

Glaring at me he said something in Tzotzil, which I took to be derogatory by the tone of it. So I told him, "Look, the schools all teach Spanish and Tzotzil. They are bi-lingual. I bring these books to help the children learn how to read Spanish better. They must learn Tzotzil, but they must learn Spanish, too. Some of these children will become lawyers and doctors. But you don't want them to learn Spanish? Besides, I have given these same kinds of books to many Zapatista schools." Then I started listing some of the many schools I had been to, such as Oxchuc, Huistan, Chenalho, and Mitontic. I also told him, "I even gave lots of books to the Zapatista library in Joventic. They loved these books. All of the places did. This is the first time anybody has told me that the books are bad. Why don't you ask the children if they want the books?"

He suddenly changed his approach and blurted out, "Where are your permission papers?"

"What permission papers? From whom?"

"From Subcomandante Marcos!" he stated.

Now it was obvious that he was just playing a power game.

"No, I don't have written permission from Marcos. I never needed it before. But he knows of my work. He knows that I gave books to the Zapatista library in Joventic and to over twenty other indigenous schools."

Then with some force in his voice he said, "If you have no permission papers then you must go! You cannot go to this school!"

Shocked at his hardness, I shot back in protest, "OK, I will go, but then you will be the reason this school has no books."

His eyes stared at me as if through they were the sites of a rifle. Not wanting to cause a physical response, I decided to concede; I shoved the box of books back further into my flatbed truck. Without saying anything I turned and stared at him for a couple seconds, revealing my disgust. Then I got into my truck and drove off, leaving the group of young Zapatistas coddling their automatic weapons in the middle of the road.

After rounding the first corner Manuel and I looked at each other and we each let out a heavy sigh, shaking our heads. Realizing that Pol Ho was quite large, I said to Manuel, "Don't you think there must be another primary school here in Pol Ho? Let's take the books to another school! Screw those guys!"

"Let's ask somebody," he suggested with a sneaky smile. He spotted a man just ahead and said, "Let's ask him."

Not only did the man say, "Yes, there is a school just up ahead," but he offered to go there with us. It turned out that he was a person of some power in Pol Ho, a councilman and a decent man it seemed. So after just a couple of turns in the road away from the young Zapatistas, we were getting out of my truck. I parked right along the road beside a new one-room school built just below.

My dog was the first to get out and he ran down by the basketball court to sniff some bushes. Seeing us, a teacher stood in the doorway with a very questioning and suspicious look on her face. She wasn't sure what to think; it seemed she thought it might not be good, whatever it was we were doing there.

She was alarmed to see a bearded gringo with a big dog and other people she didn't know, including the councilman. Even after we called out to her that we had books and supplies for the school, she still seemed suspicious and didn't reply. So we walked down with a couple of boxes and placed them on the floor of the little school. Her paranoia affected the classroom and everyone sat completely silent when the four of us entered. For a few seconds there was an uncomfortable feeling and an awkward silence.

Manuel and I thought the councilman might introduce us and say something, but he did not.

Quickly sensing the students' nervousness, young Violeta smartly took the lead and greeted them in Tzotzil. Reaching down, she grabbed a box of pencils and started handing them out. Some of the kids were her age and for them to be greeted by her in their native language was like the sun breaking through the Chiapas fog. Immediately the teacher's eyes lit up. Everyone's uneasiness was suddenly transformed into smiles, which gave way to laughter and soon after to shouts of sheer joy. Manuel grabbed the notebooks and followed his daughter, giving them out. Meanwhile I opened a box of children's books and displayed them on a table for all to see. Another box containing a set of children's encyclopedias amazed the teacher who told me, "The children have never seen any encyclopedias."

So within a few seconds that one-room school transformed from its questioning silence into a place of shouts and excited commotion from thirty Tzotzil children.

As had happened at other times, Mr. Jeb heard the jubilant noise inside the school and romped in with his tail waving and a big grin, having decided to steal the show. The sight of a large gentle dog, bigger than most of the kids, suddenly appearing unannounced in the small crowded classroom set off a pandemonium of uncontrollable laughter and joy. When the clown-like canine joined in with some celebratory bellowing barks, the elated kids could not contain themselves. Try as she might, the teacher could hardly control the academic anarchy. To get both books and barks all at the same time satisfied the students on many levels.

Wondering if the noise might have reached the nearby Zapatista soldiers, we thought it best not to linger too long. So off we went as quickly as we came, back towards Chenalho. On the way, I turned towards Violeta and remarked that her quick-witted assertiveness had won the day.

We found our way back down the narrow ravine towards Chenalo, until we could finally see the military checkpoint far in the distance. But the closer we got to the closed gate, the more it felt like a fishbone stuck in my throat. Though the same shift of soldiers greeted us as they had a few hours before, something had changed. One told us to get out of the truck and go inside the checkpoint. Something was different, though I wasn't yet sure what. The man who I had given the books to a few hours before was no longer smiling. From inside the tiny building I watched as some soldiers searched the cab of my truck again.

Soon it became clear that while we were in Acteal, the officer in charge had contacted his headquarters about me. Getting up from his desk the officer handed me an official looking envelope. I opened it and took out the letter inside. It ordered me to appear at the immigration office in San Cristobal de las Casas within forty-eight hours.

"Oh, first I give you a letter from your government and now you give me one. It's almost like we are exchanging presents," I sarcastically joked. We left the checkpoint as quickly as we could, before they could manufacture some other entrapment. In the spirit of a true Mexican, Manuel yelled out, "Viva Zapata!" to the soldiers as we drove off.

I was convinced by friends that not showing up at the immigration office would ultimately be worse than showing up, so I went there two mornings later. The office was in a new complex on the edge of town by the Coca-Cola plant, which people complained hogged all the city's water. Perhaps the immigration office purposely built their new offices there. Being next to the holy ground where the sacramental bottles of the cult of Coca-Cola of the Chamula church are produced would perhaps provide them with divine protection and keep them safe from any attacks.

Once I presented myself to the secretary, I sat for barely a minute before a thirty-five-year-old man overdressed in a three piece suit came out of his office to greet me. He looked more like some dapper investment banker than the new head of immigration for San Cristobal. In perfect English he told me to come in and offered me a chair in his large carpeted office.

Straight away he asked me if I would like some coffee. I guess he realized that I would be needing it, because for the next two and a half hours he asked me dozens and dozens of questions. Everything was typed up by another man on a new computer. I was shocked to find out how much he already knew about me. I suspected that the military officer at the Chenalho checkpoint must have given him my website address, which was printed on the back bumper of my truck.

I soon learned that he came from a northern Mexican city, like nearly all of the immigration officers and soldiers in Chiapas. Because of the problems in Chiapas they use people from other parts of the country to do the soldiering and administrating. Countries have done this for millenniums. Perhaps because Chiapas had been a separate Central American nation until 1836 was a part of the reason. Though in a different context Chiapanecos now repeat the famous Mexican dictum, "Nothing good comes from the north."

One of the dozens of questions the immigration boss asked me was, "Where did the books come from?"

I clearly shocked him by saying, "Mostly from S.E.P. (Mexico's Secretary of Educational Publications). Fillipi Garido, the Minister, donated ten boxes containing several hundred books. Others came from several publishers in Mexico City who gave me huge discounts, and there were also some donations."

Since he let me continue, I went on: "I was just in Fillipi Garrido's office last month and he asked me what I hoped to do this year. I told him that I wanted to go to ten more schools in Chiapas and then more in Guatemala and Honduras, so he even let me choose what books I wanted. Naturally I then picked the best ones. They were expensive books. And he gave me ten copies of his newest book. But I only wish I would have said that I was going to twenty or thirty schools in Chiapas, not just ten. He would have given me more."

To hear that S.E.P. donated most of the books seemed to unsettle the immigration officer. He knew of Fillipi Garrido, both as a Mexican government minister and an author.

The immigration boss paused in thought, as if my answer put him a bit off balance and he was trying to decide his next move. So I took the opportunity to state my case further and said, "I have known Fillipi for a few years and he always gives me books. Call him if you want and ask him. Just like in my letter to President Zedillo I remember telling Fillipi once that it's too bad that a gringo is supplying more indigenous primary schools in Chiapas with S.E.P.'s books than they are. But just last month in his office he told me that S.E.P. has plans to start thousands of children's libraries in schools throughout Mexico. He said that my work helped inspire him, but now you claim that I did something wrong. Oh, Fillipi will love to hear about this."

After more than two hours and a few secretarial visits with coffee and cookies, the immigration officer told me, "Listen, we like what you are doing, but you broke Mexican law. I have no choice but to deport you. You must leave Mexico within seventy-two hours. I am very sorry! If you want to do more work in Chiapas you are welcome, but you must first come here to my office. We will send a soldier with you."

Expecting as much, I told him, "So because the Mexican Army allowed me to go into a restricted area and bring my seeds and books, now you blame me. What logic! That doesn't seem fair. That's a type of entrapment. You should blame the Army then, not me."

After a few seconds of silence, as if to consult his own council and personal feelings, or perhaps realizing the absurdity of it all, he said with a tinge of hope, "But you can appeal!"

I was as surprised by his offer as he was by my answer. For I said, "No, thank you! Maybe next time. I'll save my appeal for next time. And no way would I ever go with a soldier to indigenous schools."

He looked at me in disbelief, as if I hadn't learned my lesson, or as if his words hadn't sunk in. It seemed that he didn't know whether to pat me on the back, or kick me in the ass. I guess that he did a bit of both.

PART TWO:
DOMINICA AND CUBA

Chapter 4

DEEP DOO DOO ON THE HOT POTATO
OR
AN ANT IN THE EAR OF AN ELEPHANT

"Strive not to be a success, but rather to be of value."—Albert Einstein

I entered Cuba at midnight of the day George W. Bush was re-elected in 2004; it was a day of infamy. Nobody in Cuba was in a good mood. I was told that a lot of school kids cried when they found out that Bush won again. It seemed that Cuban kids had more political savvy than most adult Americans.

I had flown in from the lovely island of Dominica to avoid being arrested by their very repressive government, because I had been giving away seeds to Carib Indians, Rasta farmers, and other subsistence families. A few weeks before, the personal secretary of the Dominican Minister of Agriculture had shaken his finger at me sternly, warning me not to give away any seeds to the people. Instead, the Ministry wanted me to give all the seeds to them. When they asked me if I had given any seeds away to any farmers, I was forced to I lie or suffer some undesirable consequences such as being deported, or worse. So I left the Minister's fancy office in Roseau and I never returned as I was expected to do.

Instead, I continued giving seeds away. I still had about sixty pounds left after having spent over two weeks going around to selected subsistence farmers and supplying them with the best organic open-pollinated seeds available, all well-suited to their tropical climate.

I had corresponded with the Dominican Ministry of Agriculture a couple of months before and they had sent me a letter expressing interest. Little did I know then that they had a very different agenda from mine. I clearly stated that the seeds were meant for Carib Indians and the island's subsistence farmers. With no email contact, letters slow, and winter on the way, I wanted to go. Since I had the letter from the Ministry of Agriculture, I expected them to overlook my lack of a phytosanitary permit from the USDA. Fortunately, I was right, since it would have been difficult to get it from my rural location in northern California, especially after my truck's transmission went out. Nonetheless, it later became a very problematic mistake as this story will reveal.

When I flew to Dominica's small, scenic airport in a prop plane from Puerto Rico, their Customs naturally wanted to know what I had in the three small plastic barrels. "Seeds," I said, and handed them the letter from their Ministry of Agriculture. They let me through with no problem; the phytosanitary permit was not an issue for them.

I rented a car near the airport and drove to Portsmouth in the north of Dominica. Much to my favor, I soon met an island Rasta named Jacoweh. He told his name translated to "God is laughing," and the name suited him well. His dreadlocks were so long that he would stick them in his back pocket; and his smile was a rainbow so big it could cover life's storm clouds. I had a car and Jacoweh knew the island, so we spent over two weeks traveling around with the seeds. The select ganja seeds I secretly brought were especially appreciated by the very amiable Rastas of Dominica. Together with his beautiful little half-French daughter and another Rasta man, we went to eighty poor family farms as well as to the Carib Indian Reserve.

It was Jacoweh and other Rastas who convinced me not to give any seeds to the government. The stories about corruption, nepotism, and past oppression sprouted like weeds in my mind. Nevertheless, after two weeks I kept an appointment with the Ministry of Agriculture. That was when I received the threats.

Most people in Dominica grow only enough crops to meet their own needs. What surplus they have they will sometimes sell in the surprisingly bare markets of Portsmouth and Roseau. It is nearly impossible for people there to get certain seeds to plant, so the news of a white guy giving away seeds to family farmers spread rapidly. Before long I had small time farmers and gardeners searching me out from across the island, all hoping for a gift of seeds. None ever went away empty-handed, but the news had also reached the office of the Ministry of Agriculture. Luckily they did not know where I was staying, as I had been told to tell them a wrong address.

My purpose in coming to Dominica was to help some of the last remaining Carib Indians. They are related to the Garifunas of Honduras, with whom I had worked for years. The Caribs of Dominica refer to themselves as Carinagu and the correct plural name for Garifuna is Garinagu. The Carib language is basically the same as that of the Garinagu.

Around the eleventh century, Carib Indians started migrating up into the Caribbean from the Orinoco River area, gradually taking over and replacing the previously predominate peaceful Arawak culture. With the advent of Spanish, English, and French colonialism in the sixteenth and seventeenth centuries, their domination came to an end. But for two centuries the name "Carib," which is the root of the word cannibal, caused many a ship to steer clear of their waters.

Today the remaining Caribs in Dominica are quite acculturated and live mostly along the narrow ocean side road that borders their 2,500 acre Carib Reserve. All of them have small garden plots beside their simple cane-sided homes, where some also make baskets to sell to the occasional tourist.

One afternoon the four of us drove up to the Carib tribal offices, where we happened to meet their current chief, Mr. Charles Stevens. Chiefs are elected for five years and are normally replaced at the end of their term. In his suit and tie, though, Mr. Stevens seemed more like a slick businessman than anything else, and one with a taste for fine things at that. He suggested I stay at his private hotel, but seemed put off when I told him I couldn't afford the seventy dollars per night.

"I spent more than that on a tie in a duty-free shop in a European airport," he told me.

"Good for you, but I don't wear ties," I answered.

He obviously did not like us and the feeling was mutual. Jacoweh tried to embarrass him by asking him why he had parted with the Carib tradition of wearing his hair long. He got no answer except for a dirty look, while I tried to hold back my laughter. Many Carib men still wear their hair long and live a life close to the earth and sea.

I brought seeds there twice within one week, and they were much appreciated. Like everyone on the island, they grow many different yams, but not much else, so they were especially grateful to get seeds of different melons, squashes, tomatoes, cucumbers, and peppers.

When we returned a week later, we somehow forgot to give Charles Stevens some seeds. He actually hid from us when we came; we eventually found him cowering in an empty room. Again Jacoweh laughed and asked him if he was playing hide and seek.

Though I ignored the Ministry's ridiculous order and kept giving seeds away, I knew it was just a matter of time until I had a problem. Having heard rumors that the Ministry had been tipped off, I decided to leave before they found me, for it was just a matter of time.

I decided to buy a ticket to Honduras, where I had given seeds away a few times before. There, too, the lack of a phytosanitary permit was not an issue. Then, because I had been invited the year before by the Cuban Institute for Friendship with the People (ICAP), I decided to stop in Cuba on the way. Little did I know that I was stepping out of the frying pan and into the fire.

ICAP wanted me to return to Cuba and bring more open-pollinated seeds. On my last trip, I had been taken out of a primary school by the police for donating books. Problematically, I also had some seeds. The remaining ones I brought over to the ICAP office and the people there had been very pleased and invited me to come back with more. Since my situation in Dominica had been compromised, it seemed like a good idea to give some of the remaining fifty pounds of seeds to ICAP. They had certainly been very keen on receiving seeds the year before. Some of their staff had even given me their cards and telephone numbers. Despite not having a pytosanitary permit, I believed that my relationship with ICAP would trump some certificate from the USDA. After all, if Cuba couldn't trust the US government, why should they trust the USDA? As it turned out, because of a change of staff at ICAP, I was wrong.

I arrived in Havana at the José Martí Airport just before midnight and was asked by a Cuban customs officer, "What is in these containers?"

"Seeds, about fifty pounds of seeds," I answered.

"What kind of seeds?" she then pressed.

"They are open-pollinated vegetable, fruit, and flower seeds."

"Show me your phytosanitary permit," she then demanded.

"Señora, last year ICAP invited me to return here with seeds. Half of the seeds are for ICAP and the other half are for poor farmers in Honduras. I do not have the phytosanitary permit because I originally brought them to the Ministry of Agriculture in Dominica. But here are the cards of the people from ICAP who invited me."

I then handed the officer two business cards from the people at ICAP who had invited me. She took them and wrote down the names and telephone numbers. For the next two and a half hours two Customs officers opened every bag of seeds and everything else I had. Their lack of care set off an immediate alarm in my head. I had to re-seal the packages correctly myself after they went through them because seeds were leaking out everywhere. I was finally given a formal document with a stamp, but they would not release the seeds to me.

By that time, it was almost three o'clock in the morning and there was no way to leave the airport. I looked for a quiet corner to lay down in, with the words of my Dominican friend Jacoweh echoing in my mind: "I don't think you should go to Cuba." Unable to sleep, I rose exhausted at dawn from the airport floor.

Soon the taxis were running again and I had one take me to a private house in the Vedado section of Havana where I rented a room. After a few hours rest, I walked down a few tree-lined blocks to the ICAP office on 19th Street. I was concerned about my seeds and wanted to straighten things out as soon as I could. The office was in an old house that I had visited a couple of times the year before.

I was hoping to see one or both of the two people who had earlier given me their cards and invited me to come back with seeds. The previous year I hadn't had to convince them that agriculture in Cuba, though perhaps the most organic of all countries in the world, lacked variety. Cuban watermelons, for example, are the size of grapefruits, there are no zucchinis, and they have just two types of tomatoes. It seems as if the authorities there don't want variety. What they do have is of excellent quality, but they lack variety

As it turned out, both of the people I had been hoping to find no longer worked with ICAP. One had just had a baby, and the other had been transferred. I soon found out that not only were my allies gone, but their replacement was purposely unhelpful.

After explaining my situation to the new staff member, I asked for her help in retrieving my seeds from Customs. After all, half of them were a gift for ICAP. Though not pleased, she finally agreed to check on it, telling me to come back in a couple of days. When

I returned in a few days, she told me that she needed more time and to return after the weekend. When I met her the next Monday, she smiled and told me with pleasure in her voice that "Your seeds have been burned!" Because of her smile I thought she was kidding, but she wasn't. I was stunned! "Customs keeps seeds for only seventy-two hours and then they burn them," she stated flatly. It had been five days since I had entered Cuba. I later discovered that she had never gone to the Customs office.

I realized then that I had really messed up and should have had the phytosanitary permit. However, I was also told that even with the permit, the Cuban authorities still might have done the same thing. They could easily have examined the seeds, or quarantined them until they were satisfied. But no, shoot first and ask questions later, that was their way. All of this happened despite the fact that the seeds were a gift, a gift that ICAP had asked me for.

Not willing to accept this as the fate of my seeds, or at least not willing to go down without a fight, I asked some Cuban friends for advice.

"You should go to the Attención de Población Office," they suggested.

A People's Attention Office can be found in every Cuban city and town. After finding the number in the phone book, I called and made an appointment for the next day. I had no idea yet where I was going, but my Cuban friends all did.

"You're going to Fidel's office," one of them gleefully stated.

She was basically right, for to my surprise, the main Attención de Población's office was right next to Fidel's office. In fact, the two offices shared the same entrance and the same secretaries. The entrance door for the two offices is inside a short stone tunnel adjacent to a front corner of the massive stone Consejo de Ministeros (Council of Ministers) building.

In order to enter the grounds, everyone had to pass through a security checkpoint where a soldier looked at one's identification and then called to verify one's appointment. In the course of the next month I passed through there at least eight or nine times. At first, a guard would escort me to the tunneled entrance, but after a while I became familiar to them and some of the guards let me walk alone.

Very few foreigners, especially Americans, have ever set foot in this nerve center of Cuba. I remember thinking what a pity it was that for over fifty years no US Presidents or members of Congress had bothered to visit there due to American pride and arrogance. The first time I entered the Attención de Población office was after I had walked for several kilometers and I was terribly hot and thirsty. Noticing a water dispenser I asked a secretary if I could have a glass of cold water. Watching me quickly finish the glass, he realized I wanted more and made two more trips, each time with a smile. I was impressed by his polite sincerity and wondered if I would have been treated so well at a government office in the US. Surely they rarely got foreign visitors, but nonetheless he was genuinely very nice.

Also waiting there was a very poor-looking couple. Whatever their problem was, they too were treated very kindly by the office staff. It was a great touch to have Fidel's private office right there, with his door just a step or two away from the Attención de Población office. It shows an attempt to be close enough to hear the people's problems, which is a very positive thing, even though it may be more symbolic than anything else. Can one imagine having a People's Attention Office right next to the President's office in the White House? Though I doubt that any Cuban human rights activists frequented the office, where in the US is there anything to compare? I can't imagine a foreigner coming into the US with a problem such as mine and gaining access to the political powers that be, or even a cold glass of water from a presidential secretary.

Once I was refreshed, the secretary sent me to an adjacent waiting room. It seemed like it would be more suited to a down-at-the-heels dentist's office than a room next to the office of the president of a country. The linoleum was buckling, the upholstery was ripped, the paint was peeling, and the curtains were all faded; still, the human contact was five stars.

After a few minutes a very kindly man in his seventies walked in and greeted me in English. His name was Roger and he was assigned to help me. Already somewhat familiar with my situation he assured me that my seeds had not been burned. His kind words gave me hope and I wanted to believe that he was right. During those same days a good friend in Havana introduced me to a leader in the Union of Cuban Writers and Artists (UNEAC). He had contacts working in the Customs office and agreed to personally investigate the fate of my seeds. By that time I wasn't sure who to believe. I feared, however, that the obnoxious woman from ICAP was right and kind-hearted Roger from Attención de Población was wrong.

One of them had to be wrong and the man from UNEAC was going to find out. I met with him two days later in a lovely garden cafe beside the elegant old mansion they used for their offices. Apologizing sincerely, he told me that my seeds had indeed been burned. He felt ashamed and told me so, agreeing that the Cuban Customs could have handled the situation better and blaming it on the new woman from ICAP.

At that point I returned to the Attención de Población Office to tell Roger what I had found out. He seemed surprised and embarrassed when I told him that a leader from UNEAC had investigated and told me without a doubt that my seeds had been burned. It did seem odd to be telling this to Roger, rather than him telling me.

Then I said, "Now that I know the truth, sir, I protest this abuse! ICAP invited me here and now Customs has burned my gift for them. My seeds were not just intended for Cuba, but for poor farmers in Honduras as well. If Cuban Customs wants to burn my gift for your country that is one thing; but when they burn my gift for poor Honduran farmers that is something else. That isn't right! I was never even given an opportunity to leave with the seeds. They could have quarantined them, if they were worried about some contamination. If I had known this would happen, I would never have come back here. They should have at least given me the opportunity to leave the country in order to save the seeds. I have a ticket to Honduras, but because Customs destroyed my seeds, I no longer have a reason to go. Roger, I want to speak with the Minister of Agriculture. I think Cuba owes me some compensation and maybe he can do something. So please, will you make an appointment for me?"

A sad look clouded Roger's face. "Alright, I will call the Minister," he sighed. "I'll call your house when I have an appointment."

A couple of days later, Roger called the old colonial house where I was staying in Vedado and told me, "The Minister can't see you for ten days. The President of China is coming. Take a break! Go snorkeling like you told me you enjoy!"

"OK, Roger. I've been wanting to go to the Oriente anyway. I'm tired of all my problems in Havana. I'll go see some friends in Chivirico."

"Good, do that," he said. "Call me in about a week."

So I took Cuba's Cruz Azul bus line to Santiago and then caught a jeep ride to tiny Chivirico. Close to the shore a bit before Chivarico is a nameless old Spanish naval vessel from the 1898 Spanish American War. Refusing to entirely sink, it remains in the sea, an unsalvageable memory. The coastline there is slightly drier, as the Sierra Maestra mountain range blocks much of the rain. In the distance, Pico Torquino, Cuba's highest peak, and the rest of the Sierras form a dog-toothed silhouette as they stare out to sea. There in Chivarico I looked up a diving friend and once again stayed illegally in a private house. The owner had me stay out of sight a couple of times to avoid suspicion when a snoopy cop wandered by.

A week later, I called Roger. He said that I should return to Havana because he had made an appointment for me with the Minister of Agriculture. So the next day I went to Santiago by truck and then caught the night bus to Havana. I had a layover in

Santiago for a few hours, so I decided to go to San Juan Hill, which for decades has been a war memorial. There the United States made an imperial mountain out of a mole hill. The war started with the false flag sinking of the USS Maine and didn't end until the US had dismantled the last of the Spanish Empire and started one of its own. Though pulled out to sea and sunk, it was later proven that the Maine had been blown up from the inside. Two hundred and sixty dead sailors became the *casus belli* for the war that gave birth to the American empire.

Under the pretext of liberation, the US took over Cuba, Puerto Rico, the Philippines, and Guam. Thus began the US quest for empire, whereby the so-called liberators became the oppressors. The US-built war memorial at San Juan Hill, commemorating Teddy Roosevelt's charge, was left intact after the Cuban Revolution but has an historical/poetical commentary beside it. For some years now, a permanent carnival with a rickety Ferris wheel has been situated right next to the memorial. It is fitting, because it memorializes the start of the dark carnival of US global positioning which Mark Twain and the Anti-Imperialist League protested against as treason and lies.

On the long return bus ride back to Havana I sat next to a Cuban woman, about sixty years old, who had spent six years living in the US. Unable to adjust to life there, she had recently returned to Cuba. It occurred to me that one rarely hears about people like this.

Once I was back in Havana, I decided to change my lodging to save some money, since it seemed that I would be there for a while. All legal private houses, "casa particulars," are Cuba's B&B alternative to hotels. Though junior partners with the government, they are taxed monthly, whether they have profits or not, and are therefore somewhat expensive. The only way to get a cheap room in Cuba is to find an illegal place, and the owner is subject to a stiff fine if caught. But I soon found an illegal room on the roof of a building just in front of the old Havana Hilton. I was almost close enough for room service. An elegant old lady owned the building and was happy to accept the twelve dollars per day that I gladly paid her.

While walking on the street beside my building one day, I was surprised to hear an elderly neighbor invite me over in perfect English. This is how I met Pablo. He was enchanted with his country, but disenchanted with the way things had become. He had lived in the same house for over fifty years. Like many Cubans he was very gregarious. We talked and I told him about my situation.

On another day, with half a bottle of Havana Club in front of him, he said to me, "You know, you are like an ant against an elephant. The state, of course, is the elephant. But how does an ant fight an elephant? I'll tell you how! In your weakness there is strength. So your strength is your seeming weakness, your non-existence and insignificance. For you are seemingly no physical threat."

"But for an ant to affect an elephant it must do something its size permits. It must enter an orifice. But surely if it enters the trunk the elephant will spray it out like a fire hose. And if you have ever seen an elephant shit then you know not to enter its ass. So that leaves the ears. Yes, an ant in the ear of the elephant can do something. The ant must crawl in and grab hold. The elephant may shake his head sideways and spray water in his ear, but that will only send the ant further in. Finally, the ant will go in and attach itself to the tympanum. Then the elephant will go crazy and wish he never saw that ant. Then the ant must shout, 'Okay Mr. Elephant, though I am just a tiny ant and you are a giant elephant don't deny me my rights. For in denying the rights of tiny others you end up denying yourself. For are you not the other also? And Mr. Elephant, just remember that someday you will die and we will eat you and you will become us. Then your law of the big will be usurped by the law of the small.'"

Pablo's analogy gave me some strength to continue my "fight" with the Cuban government. Five different Cuban agencies were now involved, and it wasn't over.

One day I took a taxi to the Consejo de Ministeros to pick up my seed catalogues, which I had left with Roger. I wanted to show them to the Minister of Agriculture. On the way over, the inquisitive taxi driver asked me, "What is the name of your country?" This question, ubiquitous in Cuba, often presents an opportunity to joke a bit with the curious questioner and perhaps get some insight into a clever mind.

"My country is the same as that of José Martí," I answered.

The old man paused in thought for a moment. I could see that my answer had thrown him a curve ball. Neither expecting nor accepting my answer, he then replied, "Well, you surely are not from Cuba, like José Martí."

"Sir," I responded with a smile, "have you never read Martí? He calls humanity (humanidad) his country."

My play with the philosophical Martí humored him and he turned to me with a silent smiling nod. But it did not satisfy him; it only made him all the more inquisitive.

"But where were you born?" he rephrased his question.

I sensed an invitation to play some more. "OK, I will give you some clues. My country is like this," I said while rubbing my bony elbow into my thigh. He gave me a quick pensive glance. Then, raising my nose high with pride, I said, "My country is like this!" Realizing that he surely must now know, I joked one last time by saying, "OK, I am from Los Estados Perdidos (The Lost States)."

"Oh, no es Unidos (is United), es Perdidos (is Lost)," he laughed.

From the Council of Ministries, near the Plaza of the Revolution, it's only about a kilometer to the Ministry of Agriculture (MINAGRI), so I decided to walk. There is a large wooded area across the road from the huge Ministry complex, where I entered in a short ways in order to urinate. It seemed to have been a favorite place for passing people to defecateas well, because there were land mines of human detritus everywhere. Unknowingly, I stepped on one. The main problem was that I didn't realize it until I was checking in with the receptionist inside the MINAGRI building. Having a cold and being outside kept me from smelling the human shit on my shoe.

Once I told the receptionist my name, she made a brief telephone call. With a smile she said, "Just wait here, sir, someone is coming down right now to meet you."

Then and there, in the still air of the crowded office building, I caught the scent. I vainly hoped it was not my sandal that I smelled, but someone else's. Unfortunately, I quickly had to abandon that thought. What to do? I ducked into a janitor's tiny dark bathroom, but I was at a loss to get the doo doo out of the deep tread of my sandals. There was no soap, no brush, no nothing to use, only a large sink. Try as I might, nothing worked to completely rid my sandal of the stink. With a curse of my country's blockade on my lips, I hurried back to my appointment, only to realize I had still missed some shit.

"Someone is on the way down to see you!" the receptionist told me. By then it was too late to return to the distant bathroom. Within a few seconds a middle-aged man in blue jeans and a red flannel shirt approached me.

"Are you Señor Tim Deppe?" he asked.

"Yes, sir," I answered.

Thinking he was some Ministry employee to take me to the Minister's office, I said to clarify, "I am here to meet the Minister of Agriculture, Señor Antonio Lopez."

Very humbly the man said, "I am Antonio Lopez."

I had been expecting to meet a man in a suit and tie, so I was a bit embarrassed to realize that I had given in to stereotyping. I never would have thought that the Minister himself would walk down from the fourth floor to personally meet me.

Warmly shaking my hand, he said, "Come, let's go to my office."

As I followed him we passed through an identification checkpoint and then walked up the stairwell to his fourth-floor office. In typical Cuban style there was nothing at all pretentious about it. No carpet, no easy chair, just an ordinary office with an older model computer on a plain steel desk. Waiting inside was his secretary and a hot-shot lawyer.

I doubt that I made a very good impression when I entered the room, with the smell I brought with me. What I should have done, but didn't, was to just leave my soiled sandals outside his door. The Minister sat at his desk, and the lawyer and I sat facing him on metal folding chairs. After just a few seconds I noticed their noses twitching. Then both of them, almost in unison, pushed their chairs back a couple of feet on the tiled floor. They never said a word while I was there, though I am sure that they were glad when I left and no doubt commented on it.

It was the lawyer, after being introduced by the Minister, who started off our forty-five minute discussion. He basically checkmated me in one move by saying that I had broken Cuban law, which prohibits foreigners from bringing seeds into the country. To add some weight to his words, he also said that I could be fined. I then got a little lecture about Cuban law. Finally, he asked me why I had come to Cuba with seeds.

Eager to answer, I took this opportunity to say, "Sir, I didn't just come here, I was invited by ICAP to bring seeds here last year." Reaching into my briefcase, I pulled out a couple of the seed catalogs and handed the Minister the 2004 copy of the Seeds of Change catalog, opened to the tomato section.

"Please, let me show you what seeds I brought," I said.

I could see that the Minister enjoyed looking at the catalog and also perhaps appreciated my diversion from the legal lecture. "Cuba, I believe, has only two types of tomatoes. They are very good tomatoes, but I brought you ten more varieties. Look here," I explained, pointing to a colored photo of some yellow cherry tomatoes. "These are the sweetest!"

While the Minister continued paging though the catalog, I handed another one from Johnny's Select Seeds to the lawyer. It seemed that vegetables, fruits, and flowers were not his thing and he promptly handed it to the secretary. His suit somehow didn't seem to side with the seeds, unlike the red flannel shirt of the Minister.

Perhaps I should show him the receipts, I thought, so I handed him four or five different bills listing all the seeds I had bought from the different seed companies.

"You can see that I paid over $3,000 for the seeds," I told the lawyer.

I glanced over at the Minister and watched as he continued paging through the catalog's contents with interest. Then, using a friendly respectful appellative, I said, "Don Antonio, do you know that I brought Cuba more varieties of vegetable, fruit, and flower seeds than exist here?"

Raising his eyes from the catalog, a gentle smile was his silent response.

"I brought seeds here because Cuba has excellent quality, but not much variety. You have three types of lettuce, but I brought eight or nine more. I brought five types of melons, different types of zucchini, summer squash, red okra, and many other things which are not found here, but would grow well. Not only that, I brought a couple of pounds of different cut flower seeds. I brought them because they could be raised by co-operatives to sell to tourists in Veradero."

Raising his eyes from the colored photos in the catalog, the Minister looked at me calmly and said, "Cuba has more reasons than most countries to be very cautious regarding agriculture!"

He didn't have to elaborate, for I knew that he was referring to more than fifty years of the US government's agro-terrorism. I knew many of the things that our government had done to try to hurt their agriculture, such as sowing "tares" amongst Cuba's farms, as in Christ's parable of the wheat and tares. Paradoxically, the US blockade denied Cuba fertilizer and forced them into organic farming, which has been a blessing in disguise. It is doubtful that they would have done it otherwise. Cuba is now a leading country in organic gardening and has won UNESCO prizes for it. Even so it lacks variety, the spice of life. Cuba's history with the mono-culture sugarcane industry fits right into that. But not having certain basic fruits and vegetables when one easily could is like not having certain colors or tastes. There is really no excuse other than a political one.

"Yes, sir," I said, answering the Minister. "I understand that, but at the same time your Customs officials foolishly burned a treasure. Those were the best organic seeds I could find! None of them were trans-genetic, which I know Cuba outlaws. And, Señor, I brought seeds here to show solidarity with you against the blockade and the things my country has done. But imagine, now Cuba threatens to fine me for bringing them a valuable gift. George W. Bush has already threatened to fine people like me and take away their passports for even coming to this country." Invoking the name of the noble Cuban revolutionary, I said, "I wonder what José Martí would say about all this? What bothers me most, more than losing the $3000 dollars I spent on the seeds, or even the problems I am having now, is that now I have no seeds to give to poor farmers in Honduras. I had clearly told Customs that half of the seeds were going to Honduras. They burnt them anyway! Now I have no work to do there. I have a ticket, but by burning my seeds they destroyed my work and the work of many others. They could have given me an ultimatum, or quarantined the seeds, but they just stupidly burned them. If you burn my gift for yourselves that is one thing, but burning my gift for poor farmers in Honduras is something else. I do not think either is right, but you had no right to burn my gift for the poor Honduran farmers. I protest that especially. So I think that I should be compensated, especially seeing that I was invited here by ICAP." Having been told by Cuban friends that I was unlikely to have my money reimbursed, I said, "I think Cuba should give me some seeds to replace the ones which Customs has burned."

The Agricultural Minister, who by that time I had a good feeling about, seemed to be caught off guard by my demand. He wasn't overly pleased.

"That is not possible!" he quickly said. "Look, if Cuba gives you seeds, then we are partly responsible for your work. We do not operate like this!"

"But you would not be responsible for anything," I responded. "Why would you be? I just need some seeds replaced. Honduras has no seeds to buy. I realize you can never replace these same seeds. Mine were better than anything you can replace them with, but you should give me something."

Despite my efforts to convince him, he would not budge. That pretty much put an end to our meeting, that one anyway. Realizing that there was not much more that I could do, I thanked the Minister for talking to me, shook his hand, and left. The smell of human excrement followed me out of his office like a septic truck. They must be glad to get rid of me, I snickered to myself, feeling somewhat like what I had mistakenly stepped in.

Frustrated and not wanting to have it all just end like that, I decided I needed to do something more. For as Comandante Fidel once said, "Our words are our weapons!" And as my neighbor old Pablo had told me, "Be the ant in the ear of the elephant." So over the next couple of days I wrote a five-page letter that I titled "Cuba Burns Seeds for Poor Honduran Farmers." It was written like a newspaper article from a third-person perspective. I wrote it in printed English on some stationery with my Bookseed logo. In addition to being able to express myself better, I was told that my letter might receive more attention in English. For one thing, they would have to translate it. Without being judgmental or blaming anyone, I simply related the unfortunate story of my seeds.

I took the letter to one of the very few photocopy places in all of Havana and made five copies. Each one I placed in a different envelope, envelopes which I knew would "push the envelope."

After all, "a man's gotta do what a man's gotta do," and this was my last ditch chance.

One letter I addressed to Fidel Castro Ruz, who was then recovering from broken bones after a terrible fall. Another was for his brother, Raul. The third went to Carlos Lage Dávila, a politician. The fourth was for Antonio Lopez, the Minister of Agriculture, and the last was for Roger at the Attención de Población.

In order to get into the Consejo de Ministeros, I had to make another appointment. I called Roger's office once again, but I was told that he wasn't there. After telling the always helpful secretary that I wanted to deliver a letter to him, I was told that I could come over. The taxi I took let me out directly beside the security post in front of the gated complex. Though the soldier recognized me, having dealt with me a few times before, he still checked my passport. Then, calling to confirm my meeting, he let me walk without an escort the short distance to the tunnel and Fidel's office door. The drive was lined with towering royal palms and the well-kept grounds were elegant. I had been there so many times that I thought of asking for a gardening job. After dropping off the two letters, one for Roger and the other for Fidel, with Fidel's secretary, I exited back into the tunneled entrance. Since I was just out of sight of a nearby soldier, I decided to take the rare opportunity and freely enter the inner halls of Cuba's political nerve center. Carlos Lage's office was just inside the large front doors and I waited for only a few minutes in order to give his secretary the letter.

In order to hand deliver my letter to Raul's office, I had to exit and circle the large stone building, and come back in from another entrance. Several people were waiting in a large front room. The feeling was very relaxed and more comfortable than the furniture. After I had been told to take a seat, a man came by the door with some watermelons, one of Cuba's most desired, though least impressive fruits. Immediately people got up and the tiny melons were sliced and the pieces passed around. They gave me a couple and I spit the seeds into my hand. I wondered what their response would have been to see the watermelons that would have come from the seeds I had brought.

Raul Castro's secretary proved to be exceptionally responsive. Telling me not to apologize for having written the letter in English, she told me that she would translate it that same night. "Come back the day after tomorrow, in the afternoon," she suggested. I was impressed! I couldn't imagine that many governments, surely not Washington's, would react like that. And I didn't in the least get the feeling that it was because I was a Yuma, an American. I'm fairly certain, though, that receiving hand-delivered letters from Americans was a rare occurrence in those offices.

The only letter I had left was the one for the Agricultural Secretary. So I walked down the road a kilometer to the MINAGRI building. The receptionist in the Ministry building recognized me with a smile; I told her that I had a letter for "Don Antonio."

While I was out the next morning, I received a telephone call at the place where I was staying. It was from the Minister's secretary, I was told. "The Minister wants to see you tomorrow afternoon in his office," my landlady said. It was obvious that the Minister had talked to Raul Castro's office about me, because my appointments were back to back.

I again returned to the Consejo complex and entered the waiting room of Raul Castro's office. One of his secretaries told me apologetically that there was nothing their office could do. They knew of my appointment with the Minister of Agriculture and told me, "You have to settle it with him." Those words, though sympathetic, did not encourage me about my situation.

I was sure that the Agriculture Minister had thought that the matter was finished when I left his office before. And I was sure that he didn't think that I would try to rally the support of his superiors to have Cuba reimburse me with some of their own seeds, especially after he had told me an emphatic, "No!" I had found him concerned and friendly, but because I gotten nowhere with him, I had decided to "push the envelope" with the letter. It seemed to me that, since I had already climbed quite high up the Cuban political ladder, I might as well go up the rest of the way, even if I lost again.

After making sure that I didn't track any more human excrement into the MINAGRI building, I checked in with the receptionist. Someone soon came to bring me up to the fourth floor office of the Minister. The Minister greeted me with a friendly handshake. Waiting with him was the same lawyer from before and another man, who he introduced as the head of Cuban Customs. It was on the orders of the Customs man that my seeds had been burned. He spent the next several minutes justifying his actions and repeating many of the same reasons the Minister had used before. Though he spoke in general terms, I knew that a couple of times he was referring to the US government's acts of agro-terrorism against Cuban agriculture.

Then the Minister spoke. He referred to the letter that I had written and asked with concern, "What are you going to do with this? Are you going to send it to the *New York Times*?"

"Sir, I consider myself to be, as you have called me, 'a friend of Cuba,'" I replied. "I have no plans to send this letter to any newspaper or magazine. I wrote it out of a feeling of frustration and helplessness. What would you have done? I realize that I made a very costly mistake bringing seeds to Cuba. I don't blame you for doing what you did, though it is a shame, because you burned a treasure. You ended up hurting me, yourselves, and many poor farmers in Honduras. Everybody lost! That is the truth! I know seeds are very problematic, but this was uncalled for. The Customs did not have to burn the seeds. I will never bring seeds to Cuba again."

"No," interjected the Minister. "If you want to bring Cuba seeds, you are welcome! You just have to go through the proper procedures." He then explained to me how to do that. Continuing, he told me with a wry smile, "You have gone from office to office for some weeks now. Perhaps you think no one wanted to handle your problem, but that is not true! We did what we had to do; I hope you understand that." Then, just before wishing me good luck and a fast return to Cuba, he said with a smile, "You know, you have been a papa caliente (a hot potato) here."

Chapter 5

CUBA, THE FORBIDDEN ISLAND

> "We write for children because it is they who know how to love, because it is children who are the hope of the world."—José Martí

On previous visit to "The Forbidden Island," a Cuban family I know asked me to help their daughter's school in Vedado, in central Havana. Returning a year later I did so. Luckily Cuban Customs somehow neglected to check my two large bags at José Martí Airport. As they were too heavy to carry, I dragged them over the polished tile floor and out the door, where I found a taxi. I went straight to my friends' house and surprised them. I had brought enough books (bought in Mexico) for three primary schools. Surprisingly, despite Cubans' love of books, Cuban schools turned out to be as short of books as the government "stores" were of shampoo, soap, and toothpaste. A few days later my friends and I took some of the books and visited one of the schools. Just as I was told, though it was a very caring school, they had no books for children.

The school was in a nice section of town, with many old mansions now divided into multi-family dwellings. But my friends' apartment building, built in 1846, seemed ready to fall down like thousands of others in Havana. The National Ballet School was just a block away as were some big hotels like the famous old Tropicana. For decades it had been a mafia playpen, but one of the first things done in Havana after the 1959 Revolution was to destroy and dump all the gambling machines from these mafia-owned hotels onto the streets outside. Now it seems that the only slot machines left are the prostitutes, who ply their entrepreneurial enterprise anywhere in Havana's "free trade" zone. There, making money with what is between one's legs is accepted and even encouraged, but doing it with what is between one's ears is not. They stand around in groups like unemployed assembly line workers in the US. But though sexual liberties are allowed, other civil liberties are denied.

While waiting to go to the east with the rest of the books, I spent some time walking around Vedado. Near my friends' house along the pleasant shady streets are several embassies. I passed the French and German, next to each other with just a one-man guard house serving them both. The Chinese embassy close by also had only one guard. But some blocks down by the oceanside Malecón Boulevard, I was shocked to see some one-hundred armed guards around the six-story blue glass US Interest Section. In classic Cuban style, they built an outside concert area just beside it.

I wanted to take the other books I had to Eastern Cuba, because it is the poorest area and has many small remote schools. A friend of the family in Vedado was from Guisa; he convinced me to go to a primary school there and to another in the nearby village of Victorino. So, a few days later I took a taxi to Havana's train station with over two hundred books. In front of the station was a row of vintage 1950s American cars. All the taxis, just like the one I was in, were lined up like an old car show. In cities in Eastern Cuba like Bayamo, Baracoa, Santiago, and others, however, there are lines of old horse-drawn carriages working as taxis. Cuba is one of the only places in the world like this; there is a real charm to it. Some horse shit on the road is far better than car exhaust in the air, but that is an index of the economic difference between poor Havana and the poorer east.

Though my work is usually with the indigenous, they had all been killed off centuries ago in Cuba. The Taínos of Cuba, the Bahamas, Haiti, and the Dominican Republic were the first to be discovered and the first to suffer genocide in the New World. Though Cuba says there are some Taínos left, that is basically for publicity to cover any feelings of guilt. None of the good deeds of the friendly Taínos went unpunished. By 1548 there were only five hundred left in Cuba. Ironically, "Cuba" is a Taíno word meaning "great place." Havana, Bayamo, Baracoa, and a host of other Cuban towns are Taíno names, too. Guisa, where I was headed, took its name from the naked Taíno group called Guis. It's so typical, just like in the US, Canada, and elsewhere: first kill all the Natives and then name cities and parks after them.

Columbus, who first met the Taínos in the Bahamas, wrote to the Spanish king Fernando: "...they took great delight in pleasing us. They are very gentle and without knowledge of what evil is; nor do they murder or steal...Your highness may believe that in all the world there can be no better people...They love their neighbors as themselves, and have the sweetest talk in the world, and are gentle and always laughing."

Then, just a few years later, Bartolomé de las Casas recorded that between "1494 and 1508 over three million Taínos had perished from war, slavery and the mines. Who in future generations will believe this?"

The first indigenous chief to revolt against New World imperialism was Cuba's honorable Taíno chief Hatuey. After witnessing the slaughter, rape, and ill treatment by the foreign Spanish he formed a rainbow coalition of tribal people and runaway slaves. They returned by boats from Haiti and made guerilla attacks against the Spanish. In 1512, he was betrayed and burned to death in Baracoa. While bound and ready to be burned alive, a compassionate Franciscan priest offered Hatuey an opportunity to avoid a second burning in the fires of hell. He invited him to an other-worldly paradise if he would only accept his words. But after finding out that paradise was full of murdering Spanish imperialists, Hatuey opted for hell.

In its own twisted way, history repeated itself some 450 years later. Fidel Castro and his band of freedom fighters returned to Cuba by boat and fought a guerilla war against the US imperialists. But unlike Hatuey, they won. After five centuries Cuba was more than tired of imperialism. When the US threatened to economically "burn" Cuba with their blockade unless they accepted the paradise of capitalism, Fidel's Cuba, like Hatuey, also chose hell. They could not bear to share paradise with the US imperialists and are still paying dearly for it. They decided that it was better to be free and poor than better off but a slave. Just like Hatuey and the Taínos with the gold-seeking Spanish, Fidel and the Cubans knew well the sins of the Mafia, the corporations, the US military, and their puppet politicians.

In Securities and Exchange Commission documents, Cuba is listed as one of the few countries in the world not to be a corporation. Unlike the US, which is registered as a corporation in Puerto Rico of all places, at least Cuba keeps it balance sheet at home. Thankfully, though the state is the corporation, it is not controlled anymore by United Fruit, AT&T, or the Mafia. Even so, Patrick Henry's "Give me liberty or give me death" has no time or space today in repressive post-revolutionary Cuba. Instead, Fidel's coined phrase is "Fatherland or Death," which misses one thing: liberty. It's a pity that, rather than advocating universal paradigms to bring humanity to new heights, he opted for a narrow nationalist slogan, which has done good social things but kept liberty in chains. Though the melody may be the same, somehow the song of a bird in a cage does not have the same sweetness as one in the forest.

I boarded an old Czech train and found a place on one of the hard seats. My destination of Bayamo was an overnight ride. Though warned about thieves, I doubted anyone would try to carry off the heavy bag of books beside me. As the endless fields of mono-culture sugarcane drifted by across the level landscape, so did my thoughts. Perhaps Cuba relies so much on sugar in order to sweeten the bitterness of poverty. The saccharine schlock of Walmart capitalism does no better, although there are more material goods in one Walmart than in all of Havana. Cuba, the land of dialectical materialism is without material and without any popular dialectic, and the land of literacy is without many books. Though Cubans love books and have an annual book fair in Havana each February, books are not readily available. Ocean Books is one of the only foreign-founded bookstores in the whole country. The government has some bookstores that have a very inexpensive but very limited stock. It is a place to bite one's tongue, because the social political menu of the state is inedible. It is also a good place to go on a fast, because its obese northern neighbor refuses it even a cracker.

On a previous journey, I had bought 675 kids books for $110, although they were not of good quality in either content or printing. I was taking them to Honduras. At José Martí Airport, customs officials made me take out all 675 books, fifteen copies each of forty-five titles. I even had fifteen copies of a children's book written by Fidel. They looked at each book and mixed them all up, leaving me with a big mess to repack. They almost made me miss my flight until I told them I would make an official complaint if they did.

Though Cuba succeeded in accomplishing near universal literacy, it failed by excluding from its national lexicon, social syntax, and philosophical semantics the most human of words: freedom. Though perhaps every Cuban can now read, they still cannot speak, except the politically accepted phonology dictated by the state. Instead of leading a movement against the imperialism of control, Cuba has become a deaf mute. Its people cannot listen to, read, or speak of anything but the accepted words and rhetoric of the state. Most pay lip-service, but their tongues are tied. Basically, they have padlocks bored through their lips. The Council for the

Defense of the Revolution will throw away the key if a word out of place is heard. Much of Cuba's analysis of the world is correct, yet to delete any and all opposition creates an intellectual slavery.

The juxtaposition of Fidel's public displays of well-oiled verbosity to his people's collective fear of free speech has no justification. Just as the US embargo is wrong, so too is Cuba's embargo on free speech and other human rights. Cuba itself has put an embargo on its people's freedom. Not the false capitalist freedom to exploit, but rather the human rights to travel, free speech, and the pursuit of happiness. If the Revolution is so right, why then are they so opposed to basic freedoms that have been championed since the Magna Carta and the Rights of Man?

While the leading Communist party members and government workers have nice apartments and cars, most people walk, or take buses or trucks, and live in bohios or shabby apartments. This two-tiered reality has irked many Cubans.

What way is left between capitalism's gas-guzzling freeway of greed and Cuba's path of total state control? As one Cuban man told me, "The only option left between the failures of both neoliberalism and communism is the reasonable anarchy of Diogenes, William Godwin, Bakunin, and Kropotkin."

When the night train finally arrived in Bayamo, the capital of Granma Province, horse carriages were waiting beside the station. It was here that Carlos Manuel de Céspedes was born, who became the Father of Cuba. In 1868 he wrote *El Grito de Yara*, *The Cry of Yara*, declaring independence from Spain. Six years later the Spanish killed him, but he had lit the fuse for independence. This fine man was also the first to liberate Black slaves from his own plantation. That was 355 years after Bayamo became the first place in the New World to have a slave revolt, in 1533. It was the bitterness and suffering of slavery that produced many sweet and enjoyable things for the rest of the world, from sugar to rum. Cuba didn't end slavery until the 1870s because former slave masters from the US wanted to maintain a slave state where they could perpetuate their crimes.

To get to Guisa, some twenty kilometers away from Bayamo, I travelled in a multi-passenger taxi. Unlike a couple of other times, the car was not stopped by police and the driver fined because a foreigner was inside. In Guisa, carrying a heavy bag of books, I walked to the only accommodation, a hilltop hotel in a pine forest with a great view. On one side were flat fields of vegetables and sugarcane, which stretched out far beyond the small town like bristles of a toothbrush. On the other side, Mount Torquino, Mount Martí, and the other rebellious peaks of the Sierra Maestra mountain range proudly stared down.

The next day I went over to one of the village's primary schools with the books. As always in bookless schools, the kids went nuts. But unlike in a lot of para-literate indigenous communities, where no one has ever seen a children's book, here they were treated like gold. Afterwards I took photos of the smiling kids outside beside a bust of José Martí. It was a pleasure to make them happy, and they reciprocated with a song. Cuban kids are some of the sharpest and most exuberant that I have encountered. Afterwards, they returned to their classroom and I returned to my $1 hotel room.

I had one box of books left and they were destined for Victorino, I thought. About fifteen miles above the bucolic village of Guisa, a famous revolutionary place, is the humble hamlet of Victorino. I was riding in the back of an overcrowded old Willy's jeep as it wound its way up into the heart of the lush Sierra Maestra towards Mount Martí. At 1630 meters, it is the second highest peak in that mountain range. Here, the northern slopes of the Sierra catch most of the rain, like a favored child receiving most of the inheritance. Though the Guisa valley is a vast agricultural area, the soil and moist fresh climate up in Victorino are the best for growing. Very tidy little farms—cooperatives—were carved out of the dense dripping jungle along the meandering road. Manicured beds of lettuce, onions, and tomatoes tenderly hugged each side of peasant homes—dirt floored bohios made from scraps of wood, thatch, and whatever else was available. Though the people were very poor, there was still a sense of nobility.

The poor in Cuba often show more dignity than the poor on nearby continents, or perhaps lack of dignity is just a characteristic of the poverty of capitalism. Cuban poverty is more stoic, perhaps resigned to the fact that things won't change. Because of this, everything is in order, in its place. When anything is broken, it is patched, fixed, and reused. Because of the blockade and poverty, rags are cut into strips and used for toilet paper. Things are clean and virtually no trash is thrown away, because there is very little to buy. That has a simple beauty, but there is a beast lurking inside of it. The Cuban community in Miami probably consumes more and sends more stuff to the local dump than all of the eleven million people of Cuba combined. As in all of Cuba, there were no barking watchdogs, because people have nothing for dogs to guard.

A welcoming garland of flowers was wrapped around the sides of a clear stream, which seemed to play tag with the continually crisscrossing road. "What a beautiful part of Cuba," I thought. Then suddenly, at the entrance to Victorino, the driver pointed out the little primary school and stopped beside it. The entrance had a flower garden gracing its turquoise walls. A sense of care emanated from the grounds. I knew before entering that it would be a good school to visit, it just had that feel. Unannounced, I entered the three-room school with a big box of over a hundred books.

I introduced myself to the principal and told her that I had some story books for the school. As Baudelaire once wrote, "Next to the pleasure of feeling surprise, there is none greater than to cause a surprise." And that I did! When I opened the box and handed her a couple of the books, her eyes widened with awe.

"Do you have any kids' books here?" I always ask; the inevitable response, "No, none," was also hers. As Cicero once said, "A room without books is like a body without a soul."

This remote school in the rainforest of the Sierra Maestra was as empty of kids' books as the one in Vedado in central Havana. It seems odd that a country known for education and literacy, which spends ten percent of its GNP on education, has no children's books in their schools. The great Martí, who knew "the entrails of the beast," might have been proud of Cuba's "bread of literacy" but he would have been saddened by the moldy condition the loaf was now in. He had criticized the elitist education of Cuba in the 1890s and said, "I want to cast my lot with the poor of the earth." Today he would criticize Cuba's state control of print and the internet. Nevertheless, the state uses Martí as a poster boy, which he no doubt would dislike. Despite having one of the highest literacy rates of any country, Cuba has some of the fewest books and only one newspaper to read. As Cabrera Infante wrote, "Cubans can read, but read what? Only the diet sanctioned by Fidel."

Fidel and company, with all their ingenuity, brought literacy, education, healthcare, and other positive changes to Cuba, but one wonders why the written word is so controlled and discouraged. If their social calculus is correct, then what are they worried about? With one dominant newspaper, the *Granma* (no want ads, of course), the State wants no alternative voice. The *Granma* took its name after the boat used by Fidel, Raúl, Che and company on their voyage to free Cuba from US imperialism. Yet their totally controlled *Granma* newspaper reveals how shipwrecked things have become. It's as unreadable as the boat it was named after was unseaworthy; it belongs in a museum, just like the boat. Having once censured parts of *Moby Dick*, Fidel seems like Captain Ahab whaling against the rights of freedom of the press.

Orwell's *Animal Farm* was once added to the list of what the "big brother" state decided was fitting to read at the zoo. The Bible, of course, is considered profane. Perhaps the Sermon on the Mount is thought to compete with Fidel's sermons at Revolution Plaza. Martin Luther King's "I Have a Dream" speech was censored because it might remind Cubans of what a nightmare they live in. Now several people are in jail for disseminating books not on the state's menu.

Yet the great 1961 Cuban National Literacy Campaign, with the slogan "Yes I Can" (which may have influenced Obama's "Yes We Can"), was the most successful in history. It makes the US government's No Child Left Behind policy and the forty-seven percent illiteracy rate in Detroit look like a broken down jalopy. As Malcom X once said, "Without education you are not going anywhere in this world." Perhaps purposeful neglect is actually the US policy. But in one year, some eight-hundred thousand illiterate Cubans were taught to read. This campaign was Cuba's "epic poem" and opened the way to mass participation in education.

Though Cuba is known for its educational system and is full of very educated people, it is not a land of bookstores and internet cafes. On the contrary! Education there is caught in the maze of state control. As Jonathan Kozol wrote, "education which is financed, governed, and dirtied by the state will logically seek to propagate the values of that state." Of course the US does the same thing, as do other countries.

Like the US, the Cuban military has eaten up most of the money; they opted for the same means of change, through violence. Though the US wanted to destroy their revolution, Cuba kept exporting their ideology. Angola is just one example of past military nightmares Cuba was involved in. And now look at Angola. It's booming! Perhaps it should come and rescue poor Cuba from itself. Prior to the Revolution, Cuba had a population of haves and have nots, with high levels of disparity between urban and rural populations. Now everyone graduates, but only prostitutes, taxi drivers, and musicians benefit financially.

After seeing the books, the principal at the school in the Victorino smiled and said to me, "Come meet the students." There were about seventy or eighty children divided into three classrooms. Like all primary students in Cuba, they were dressed in burgundy uniforms with white shirts. Cuba has some of the happiest school children anywhere and these were no different. Like nature, poverty asks for very little but appreciates positive attention. In each of the three classrooms, the books brought such exuberant shouts of joy that the walls could hardly contain the excitement and applause.

Perhaps one good surprise deserved another, for after displaying the books in each classroom, they surprised me by reciting a poem. One student in each class was asked to come forward and recite in front of the class. I was impressed by their high degree of elocution. They each recited the same poem about dignity, sacrifice, and conscience. It was about the "new man" and a time when people will live in harmony rather than in opposition; when they will selflessly help each other and share rather than selfishly compete. Of all the hundreds of schools I have visited this was the only one where each class recited a poem. They were speaking more than words and one could sense their true belief in the high ideals described. After reciting the poem, the chosen student in each class also offered a short thank-you speech for the books.

In the third classroom, an eleven- or twelve-year-old girl was chosen to stand in front of the class and recite the poem. As I stood beside the principal, I could tell how proud she was of this girl as she made her presentation, and rightly so, for she was an impressive speaker. As with the others, it was obvious that her words were not just memorized rhetoric but that she really meant and believed what she was saying. For me, it is in children like this that the beauty of Cuba's revolution can be found.

Suddenly something changed, for just as the word "dignity" rolled off this student's lips, she gasped and placed a hand over her mouth in astonishment. Her eyes grew saucer-like and expressed a bewildered fear. I turned around to where she was staring and saw two uniformed police officers entering a side door. The whole class sat in frozen silence, shocked by the sudden intrusion. Like two grimacing gangsters, these anti-pedagogical police sent shock waves through the classroom. They walked directly towards me, and one asked me if these were my books. I answered that I had given them to the school. Then he ordered me to pack up the books and take them out of the school. When I asked why, I received no answer, only a cold stare. The students watched with dismay and disbelief as I followed the two policemen out. Their dejection and sense of violation was as profound as their joy had been just a few minutes earlier. Reaching the door, I turned when I heard the principal sternly say in protest, "Incredible!" Our eyes met in a mutual sadness and disgust, never to meet again.

The taller of the two policemen had a very unfriendly way about him. He seemed to take delight in what he just did. But all of the children were horrified and would probably never forget it. As I walked beside them, struggling with the box of books, the shiny silver spurs on his highly polished black boots clinked with every step. I can just imagine his poor horse feeling those large spurs. He seemed to me like an arrogant Cuban gamecock that had just defeated his foe. His hair was slicked back almost feather-like and his large nose curved to a point like a beak. He seemed ready to crow, but remained arrogantly silent. They led me to the tiny Victorino jail. It seemed more like a birdcage, the *gallero* of the rooster-like cop. Once inside, I demanded to know the reason for their actions.

"Why did you take the books from the children?" I asked, but I received no answer.

Inflating his chest and preening back his hair, the cop told me that I would soon be taken to the police station in Guisa.

Before the 1959 Cuban Revolution, only half of the children were enrolled in school and about a quarter of the island's population was illiterate. Forty percent of the population lived in rural areas, mostly in the area called El Oriente, the east, where Victorino is located. First the Spanish and then the US used illiteracy and the "violence of the letter" as a means to keep the status quo intact. As Fidel Castro once said, "The lack of education is the best index of the state of political oppression, social backwardness, and exploitation in which a country finds itself."

One of the most brilliant and beautiful aspects of the 1959 Revolution was incorporating children into its country-wide literacy campaign, for that turned the pen into a sword. These were not in the hands of adults, but children. Most of them came from cities and taught the poor peasants, guajiros, in the countryside. If the kids who recited the poem in the Victorino school were the same age in 1961, they would have been teachers, not students. There were over 100,000 young people in Cuba's literacy army, some forty percent of them between the ages of ten and fourteen. Another forty-five percent were age fifteen to nineteen. They became part of the Conrado Benitez Brigades, named for an eighteen-year-old black youth murdered while teaching people how to read. "Operation Mongoose," part of The Cuba Project run by the CIA, was thought to be responsible for his murder and helped organize various counter-revolutionary actions against the literacy campaign.

In 1961, two days after Cuba launched its literacy campaign, the US launched the Bay of Pigs Invasion. An invading army of counter-revolutionaries used boats from United Fruit Company's docks in Puerto Cabeza, Nicaragua. An army of Cuban soldiers with US weapons, when juxtaposed next to an army of Cuban teachers and children armed with pens and primers, is striking. But while the Cuban insurgents were abandoned and failed, the child literacy teachers became successful heroes. "We shall read and we shall conquer" became their motto, and they soon conquered the illiteracy demons keeping over 800,000 people from reading.

After I'd been sitting for about an hour in the tiny Victorino jailhouse, a Jeep stopped in front. The other cop transported me down the mountain to the much larger police station in Guisa, where several people were silently waiting inside. I joined them on a long bench placed against a wall. Rarely do any foreigners visit Guisa and far fewer, I'm sure, visit its police station. So all eyes were on me: Cuban country people often stare with no shame.

Within a few minutes I was led down a hallway and through some doors to a large office where the police chief and several others sat at their desks. The chief was a short stocky man with particularly piercing eyes, about forty years old. Though not as physically Kafkaesque as the gamecock cop in Victorino, he definitely found pleasure interrogating me. For the next two hours he asked me countless questions. He started off with, "Did the teachers ask for the books? Why did you decide to go to Victorino? Where are you staying? Did you pay in pesos or dollars? How did you pass customs with the books? What work do you do in the United States?" He went on and on like a cat playing with a captured rat. I barely finished answering one question and he would immediately ask another.

It seemed like a lot of this was done to impress the other cops in the room, who were all curiously trying to listen. They don't often get to play with a "Yuma," as Americans are known in Cuba. This symbolic appellative is taken from the gunslinger Johnny Yuma character in the 1959 spaghetti western TV series called *The Rebel*.

In the course of interrogating me, the police chief proudly disclosed that it was he who had ordered the cops in Victorino to seize me and the books. I figured as much. He already knew that I had given books to the primary school in Guisa the day before, and he knew that I had taken pictures of smiling students holding some books beside the statue of José Martí. When he bragged about his order to take the books, I decided to let him know what I thought, since by that time I was quite put off by this self-inflated small-town cop. When I compared his anti-bibliophile abrasive demeanor to the joy of the children, it made a Johnny Yuma out of me. I had the taste of gun powder on my tongue and a verbal shootout was coming. I asked myself, "What kind of man am I if I don't tell him what I think?" So I spoke my mind, and the mind of every kid and teacher in that school who had been offended by the police action.

As everyone knows, free speech in Cuba is free only for the leaders, but very costly for the people. All of Fidel's elegance couldn't find words to justify silencing the most fundamental human right: free speech. He could speak nonstop for hours about the abuses perpetrated by the Yankees against his state. But if a poor Cuban so much as says one word about the abuses of the Cuban state, he will go to jail. It was of course Fidel who said, "Our words are our weapons."

So when the police chief paused in thought for his next question, I used Fidel's dictum, loaded my tongue, and surprised him like I was Johnny Yuma's sawed-off shotgun. I unloaded with, "Then you are the one responsible for robbing the school children in Victorino of their gift of books! Now we know who to blame! Imagine, the police chief of Guisa stealing books from children. What a big man you are! What, you have nothing better to do than to take books away from school kids? Are you happy now?" I sneeringly mocked, "Qué vergüenza! What shame!" I had decided that there was no way that I wasn't going to tell him what I thought, regardless of the consequences.

By then I believed that I would be deported anyway, because he had already called the Immigration Office in Bayamo. I knew that he didn't dare to lay a finger on me, since I was a foreigner, despite being angered by my words. And even if he did, I didn't care. Just as I could see that he found pleasure in interrogating me, I too found some pleasure in unleashing my watchdog tongue on him. Without letting him interrupt me, I continued my tirade. I pointed to the ubiquitous picture of Che Guevara on the wall behind his desk. For all to hear and much to his displeasure, I said, "If Che Guevara was alive he would put you in a re-education camp on the Island of Youth. He'd have your head! You're a counter-revolutionary by taking books away from children."

Though displeased with me, he had been stoic until then. I was getting him angry now, but I wasn't going to let that stop me. I decided to throw Cuba's mother of all insults at him, as I launched one last vitriolic verbal assault. All of my previous salvos didn't faze his reptilian skin like my final last word: "You're a Fascista!" I said, pointing my finger at him.

This immediately triggered an emotional meltdown. He was seething! He wanted to beat me, but he didn't dare because he knew that he would be in trouble with Cuban law. In total frustration he yelled, "Get him out of here!" to one of the other cops. I felt immediate satisfaction in getting him as livid as I was. The rat had bitten the cat on the nose. I had seen a dark side of Cuba and perhaps a shadow of my own.

Another cop calmly came over and escorted me out of the room. He took me back to the bench in the waiting room where I had been a couple of hours before. Immediately, a dozen people waiting there fixed their stares on me. They had heard everything. On a few faces I sensed silent smirks. It seemed that some had found humor in my denunciation of the police chief, although they didn't dare crack a smile.

In general, the police are disliked by the Cuban people and they are famous for asking for bribes. Certainly a Cubano could never get away with denouncing a chief of police without being severely punished. Only a Yuma or some other foreigner could get away with such hubris. But what a shame that cops in Cuba would take a gift of children's books away from a school. For the people waiting there, the guajiros, I was surely a version of the gunslinger Johnny Yuma. They had all witnessed the verbal shootout with flesh-cutting words used against their feared sheriff.

After that, the police chief wanted to get rid of me as soon as possible, so he had another cop go get my luggage from the hotel. The chief had asked me in what currency I had paid for my room at that hotel. I told him the truth: twenty-five Cuban pesos. However, it is illegal for foreigners to use Cuban pesos. They must use Cuban convertible dollars instead, whose value ironically floats with the US dollar. So I had actually paid one dollar for a twenty-five dollar room. Now this would spill over onto the amiable hotel manager, who had accepted my twenty-five Cuban pesos. But if I had told the police chief that I had paid twenty-five dollars, they would have asked to see the registry and then accused the owner of theft.

Within minutes I was waiting beside the road with my police escort. Also standing there were about twenty guajiros all waiting for a ride. The next vehicle to approach was flagged down. It was a large old flatbed Russian truck. There must have been at least forty people in it already, all standing up in the back. The cop politely offered to carry my bag, but I declined and placed it on the high bed of the truck myself. While we were boarding, the police chief came out to make sure that I was gone. He wanted to display to the crowd of gawking guajiros his captured Yuma prize. The sheriff had won and Johnny Yuma was done. But to the amazement of everyone, I found a couple more bullet-like words with which I shot the sheriff, from the back of the crowded Russian truck. I was going to make sure everyone there knew what had happened in Victorino. So as the old truck started to pull slowly away, I called out again, "What kind of man are you to rob the children in Victorino of their books? Qué vergüenza!" And then to further stir his ire, one last time I called out the trigger word, "Fascista!" For a few seconds I thought that he was going to stop the truck to take his revenge. But no, he just stood there as still as a statue, though I knew that he was seething inside. As for me, I was off to the Cuban Immigration Office with a police escort to face more problems.

As I rode the twenty kilometers back to Bayamo, I thought about Cuba and felt disgusted with the regimented control that the government placed over the lives of its people and even my own. I certainly wasn't out to browbeat Cuba, but I also wasn't going to agree with them. I realized that if I had told that chief of police how impressed I was with the principal in Victorino, I probably would have gotten that woman into trouble, too. The two Victorino policemen already knew that they had really angered her. Certainly, both she and the hotel manager would later be questioned.

I knew that what I had told the Guisa police chief about being sent to a re-education camp would surely have applied to me, if I was Cuban. For Che, though he laid down his life for the dispossessed, also locked up thousands of gay people, writers, dissidents, and other non-conformists. "Work will make men out of you," was written on signs at the entrances, not unlike the Nazi concentration camp signs that read, "Work will make you free." How could such contradictions exist? This was not about the politics of left and right, but about right and wrong. It was an ethical concern, which transcends politics.

Che also burned the private library of an older writer who opposed communism. It happened just two blocks away from my friends' apartment in Vedado. Che had lived for a while on the same street in the corner apartment.

There are more horror stories about what happened when he was in charge of both Principe and La Cabana prisons. It is alleged, though hard to prove, that he had a penchant for watching executions. The same is true for allegations that he bled prisoners before executing them and profited by selling the blood to North Vietnam. I wonder how many Che t-shirts Cuba could sell if this was proven true. The irony is that Fidel abandoned Che Guevara in La Higuera, Bolivia, and that Miguel Cienfuegos' airplane conveniently disappeared, too. I guess that dead heroes are worth more than living ones.

Why does the Cuban government hold back the people it claims to have freed? They had a marvelous Revolution, but why hold the people down? That is counter-revolutionary.

Once we arrived in Bayamo, the policeman walked me several blocks to the Immigration Office. It was a Friday afternoon and the office was already closed. Within a short time though, three official-looking men came and unlocked the door. I was handed over to their custody and followed them up a stairwell a few floors to a large, windowless room. It was unfurnished except for four folding chairs and a table. For the next three hours I sat answering questions. While one man questioned me another wrote down my answers in longhand. There was no computer.

The first thing I was asked was, "Did you call the police chief of Guisa a fascist?"

"Yes, that's right," I told them.

"That is a very bad name here!" he somberly replied.

"Well, I also told him that if Che Guevara was still alive, that he would put him in a re-education camp on the Island of Youth."

Invoking the almost sacred name of Che Guevara seemed to be enough to make him drop the subject and move on. Though they repeated many of the same questions that the police chief in Guisa had asked, their demeanor was very different. While two men concentrated on me, the third sat in a corner silently paging through every one of the more than a hundred children's books. He seemed to think that they might contain some encrypted code or a top secret military document. Once, though, I noticed a smile enliven his serious face when he found a little book titled, *A Flea Named Cecelia*. He was looking for anything subversive, either political or religious. Finally, something caught his eye. It was a little storybook about animals with a picture of Noah's Ark on the cover. Thinking that he had found some corrupting evidence, he held it up for the other two men to see. All of us then turned to see the tiny book in his hand. It all seemed so absurd that I let out a hiss and rolled my eyes, as the other man turned back to me to continue his questioning.

Their examination of every book as if it was a top secret file made alphabet soup out of logic. "Yes, these books are highly classified material," I mocked, and before he could ask me the next question, I asked him, "Why are you authorities so upset with these kids' books when the students and teachers were so happy with them? I find that quite strange, for José Martí wrote *The Age of Gold* (*El Edad de Oro*) and even Fidel wrote a children's book. The schools I went to had so little, but the cops took away the books I gave them like thieves. What, don't you want them to read? Don't you trust the teachers enough to be able to judge the material? So what are you going to do with my books then?" I demanded. "You must give them back to the Victorino primary school. And I'll tell you, the Victorino police made every school kid there dislike the police when they took away the books. It's true! Taking me is one thing, but why take the books?"

Unmoved by my analysis, he told me, "Look, you broke Cuban law! No foreigner can come here alone and do what you did. You are not authorized by the government. Period! You have to work in conjunction with the Cuban organization, Institute of Friendship for Cuban Villages (ICAP)." Then, after writing out a long document, the head Immigration officer said, "We want you to sign this paper." It stated that I acknowledged that I was guilty of breaking Cuban law number 153.

"If you sign it you are free to go," he told me.

"And if I don't sign it?" I questioned.

Looking me in the eye, he sternly said, "If you don't sign it, you will be deported to Mexico!"

"Okay, of course I will sign it," I told him with a bit of a laugh, "but you know that I was only trying to help those schools."

"That's not the point!" he insisted.

So I signed the paper. Then he said to me, "You are free to leave. Where are you going from here?"

"I am going to find a cheap room and then drink a tall mojito" I told him. He smiled, we shook hands, and I left.

PART THREE: GUATEMALA, HONDURAS, AND NICARAGUA

Chapter 6

THE CHORTI MAYA: IN MEMORY OF CÁNDIDO AMADOR

"Education can be dangerous. It is very difficult to make it not dangerous. In fact, it is almost impossible."—Robert Hutchins

It was not until 2002 that the road near Chiquimula, Guatemala, going up to the Honduran border at Copan was paved. Up until that time it was a rocky dirt road. It hadn't changed much since the days when the explorer John Lloyd Stephens and his very talented artist companion Frederick Catherwood traveled it on foot in 1839, except for getting wider.

Now the road bypasses villages like San Juan Ermita (St. John the Hermit), whereas before it passed through a shallow streambed and up a shady wooded hillside and into the old village square. There the village's ornate white adobe church stood out like a luminous full moon. And there the White Hand death squad acted with impunity against the brown hands of the Chorti.

Before the road was paved there was very little traffic, but now large semi-trailers roar dangerously by at breakneck speed. It saves them considerable time from going the old way down to the border at Esquipulas.

The road bisects Chorti land, where some of the most abused people in Central America live. Much of the way the road follows the Motagua River, one of Galeano's "Open Veins of Latin America."

It irrigates tobacco fields, sugar cane, and cattle ranches, all now owned by rich Ladinos.

The Motagua is the river which General Jorge Ubico, president of Guatemala from 1931-1944, once compared to the Potomac on a state visit to Washington, D.C. Having never seen an ice flow before, the general said, "We have a river in Guatemala like this, but it is not clogged with ice, but rather bodies." He was callously referring to the genocide of untold thousands of Chorti Mayas, whose bodies were tossed into the Motagua River. His successful mosquito eradication program against yellow fever seemed to be a model for his actions designed to eradicate the impoverished Chorti.

Ubico, educated in the U.S., was also the one who allowed the United Fruit Company, "the Octopus," to spread its tentacles from the Caribbean Coast across Guatemala to the Pacific Ocean. He was a devout disciple of Mussolini and compared himself to Napoleon. He even affected a Bonaparte hairstyle and was called the "Little Napoleon of the Tropics." Ubico also had Guatemalan school children, at least those lucky enough to attend, dress in military uniforms.

In 2003 I brought Spanish language children's books to four Chorti primary schools, and organic, open-pollinated vegetable and fruit seeds for some impoverished Chorti farmers. This tribe has one of the highest illiteracy rates in the world. In Guatemala, where the Chorti number at least 52,000, the illiteracy rate is nearly 92%. On the Honduran side, the government desperately worked to acculturate the 4,500 Chorti living there. Though the illiteracy rate is not as high among the Chorti in Honduras, they are treated as badly.

Because of circumstances and other commitments it took me several years to fulfill a promise of bringing books to Chorti schools. I was asked to do so and to be accompanied by a Chorti activist, Cándido Amador. But in 1997, two Chorti Maya leaders were murdered outside of Copán in Honduras. One of them was

Cándido (Sandy) Amador, this same young charismatic activist. Just weeks before, we had sat together in my truck in Copán talking about the conditions of his impoverished people.

With a wry sense of humor Sandy had told me, "The Chorti have the largest book in the world, but few people can read and no one can read it."

He was referring to a site not far from where we were sitting in the Copán ruins. Ironically, it was the now bookless, semi-literate Chorti who once wrote the largest book in the world. Across from the Great Plaza and behind the magnificent ball court is the incredible Hieroglyphic Stairway. Carved into the sixty-foot wide stone risers with some thirty steps on this ancient Mayan pyramid are hundreds of undecipherable glyphs.

Their semiotic stares seem to say that we are the illiterate ones, because our culture is the one that destroyed all the Mayan writings. Now their history is as mute as this book. The exposed gnarled roots of a giant old ceiba tree growing out of the pyramid reach around and clutch the massive staircase, like huge hands gripping the book.

It is only because this book was written in stone, and not on paper made from strangler fig trees, that it is still preserved. Otherwise it too would have been burned by anti-bibliophiles like Bishop Diego de Landa in his auto-da-fé at Mani in 1562.

Thanks to Landa virtually every Mayan book is now lost.

Sandy Amador was at Copán organizing a non-violent Chorti protest at the ruins. This, and associated unresolved land issues, were why he was murdered soon afterwards. Sandy's death is emblematic of the plight of the Chorti people.

At the famous Copán ruins, once purchased by John Lloyd Stevens for $23, the Chorti don't benefit from the entrance fees, nor do they benefit from the million dollar museum built with money from Harvard University and the Japanese. Though every tourist pays $10 to enter the archeological site and museum, the Chorti don't receive a penny. The Honduran government and foreign universities admire it much and benefit greatly, but they don't compensate the poor Chorti, whose ancestors built everything in Copán.

When sitting in my truck, Sandy also talked about the sad state of affairs of his people's education on both sides of the border. I remember him saying, "Especially in Guatemala, only a minority of Chorti kids have access to primary schools. Most adults still harbor deep suspicions about the educational motives of Guatemala and Honduras. We voice complaints that our ancient Maya book, the Popul Vuh, is never taught."

"The insensitive educational systems of these countries have little relevance to our lives. For the most part we consider their education systems to be anti-Chorti. They don't respect our language or history and this just adds to our feeling of abandonment and distrust. They have already killed our rainmakers, now they are suppressing our healers and midwives, and destroying our language, dress, and religious *cofradías* (brotherhoods). They stole all our land and left our children and elderly malnourished. Like our common chagras disease, this is exploding our collective heart."

It wasn't until years later that I was finally able to take books and seeds to some Chorti communities. I got these books in Mexico City and Guadalajara and they filled the back of my old, one-ton, flat-bed truck. Leaving Chuquimula and driving towards Honduras along the newly paved road, I followed the Motagua River. The small river seems to come from springs of tears. Its memories of the atrocities it has witnessed remain forever in its quiet pools.

The first place I visited was an orphanage school not far outside of Jocotán. The fact that the UN has a food program in Jocotán reveals the socio-political state of affairs. Because most of the good farming land was given away decades ago by Jorge Ubico to Ladinos, the Chorti have become dispossessed and impoverished.

The grateful Belgian priests who ran the orphanage have a history of opposing Guatemala's state-sponsored oppression against the Chorti. They loved the books and added them to the little library they set up for the Chorti orphans. Some priests once had to flee for their lives to the Petén district in the north, and others were exiled after leading a small Chorti uprising against land-robbing Ladino ranchers. The juxtaposition of these selfless Belgium priests to the local Ladino death squads like the White Hand, and others with virtuous names such as the "Guerillas of Christ the King," is shocking. While one group sacrifices their lives for the Chorti's "politics of recognition," the other sacrifices the lives of the Chorti.

Historically, the only political dawning light for the Chorti was with the progressive land reform, education, and voting rights policies of Guatemala's President Jacobo Árbenz in the early 1950s. Completely different from Ubico, Árbenz included his own vast land holdings in his agrarian reform. The noble Árbenz did more to help and gain the trust of the Chorti than any other Guatemalan leader. His agrarian reform policies gave landless indigenous and Ladino peasants some of the unused land of several large companies.

The US government and the United Fruit Company considered him too radical and too communistic. He angered United Fruit by paying them compensation in government bonds for their lands' book value price, based on the company's tax-evading, under-declared value of their lands. During this time United Fruit appointed itself the disseminator of information to US and other international news agencies. In 1954 this led to "Operation Success," the first US-staged coup d'état in Latin America.

"The Revenge," as it came to be known, happened when Howard Hunt's CIA-trained counter-revolutionary forces entered Guatemala. They came from Honduras through the Chorti region. They had the support of local Ladinos, including the 400 horsemen who fought in San Juan Ermita. The White Hand death squad ran wild after Árbenz fled the country to Czechoslovakia.

It was at this time that Che Guevara took refuge in the Argentine embassy in Guatemala City before going to Mexico, where he met the Castro brothers. Later Guevara explained the 1954 coup by saying, "Árbenz didn't execute enough people."

It is said that more than 200,000 Guatemalan people were killed between the late 1960s and the 1980s. Some tens of thousands were Chorti in eastern Guatemala. The cultural and social consequences and ramifications of thirty years of civil war are still taking their toll.

Because the Chorti were the only Mayan tribe to be a minority in their traditional lands, they supported the rebel movement more than any other Mayan group when full-blown civil war erupted in the 1960s. As a result several Chorti hamlets were strafed with aerial bombardments by the US-backed Guatemalan military. Those suspected of aiding the guerillas were gruesomely tortured and killed. Ironically, some twenty-thousand fled to the US, the source of the weapons used against them and the backer of their murders.

After giving away the books and talking with some of the monks, I supplied several local subsistence farmers with seeds. Then after spending the night I continued on towards the Honduran border.

Along the way vast tracts of sugarcane waved in the breeze. While new model 4x4s from nearby ranches drove proudly by, blasting their much loved "ranchero" music, Chorti with trumplines carrying heavy loads around their heads, walked barefoot, in meek silence. They no doubt just came from their milpas, where they would use their traditional planting sticks to plant maize and beans. Not having even a donkey to help carry their meager harvests, they relied on their bodies. Meanwhile brand new John Deere tractors were parked on the best land, which not long ago belonged to the Chorti.

According to Metz, "Ubico also declared that sugarcane production, the principle source of Chorti income, be licensed at a prohibitive cost." This cast many into abject poverty. Having no work, many were forced to eke out a living on their milpas and land far back in the pine forested hills.

To make matters much worse, during Ubico's twelve-year tyranny he initiated a much despised vagrancy law. "All able bodied 'underemployed' men were forced to work without pay or provisions" on both private and state projects, according to Metz. It was local Ladinos who forced the Chorti to work; they actually hunted down those who had no land to work on anymore, or those who were considered intransigent. This "violence of the letter" through the laws of the nation-state, was an alphabet the illiterate Chorti knew well, and it fertilized the seeds of revolution.

Continuing on towards Camotán, I soon found a little primary school just beside the road. I parked in the shade of an almond tree next to the school, and was surprised to find that the Guatemalan government had built a new one-room bi-lingual school.

Though Chorti children's lexical acculturation to the dominant Spanish language is certainly taking place through government schools, there has been a growing demand to learn in their own language. Organizations like the Academy of Mayan Languages and CONALFA, the National Institute for Literacy, help assist in reading and learning this endangered language.

But language loss continues and the Ladino "culture of condescension" has so intimidated the Chorti that many are afraid to speak their language in Ladino towns. Rather than consider Chorti Maya as a distinct language similar to Chol Maya, it is commonly denigrated as a dialect by many Ladinos. This is particularly unfortunate because the Chorti language is the "Rosetta Stone" of the Mayan languages; it is the closest of all their languages to the hieroglyphics found at Copán.

I knew that I had brought only books in the dominant Spanish language, which is taught in their schools. Nearly all of the kids already spoke some Spanish, but few could read or write it very well. The problem is not just that they lack books, but that there are virtually no books available in indigenous languages.

Hopefully Spanish will not completely replace their native tongue, which is what often happens in indigenous communities.

But it is also true that if they are not able to learn to read and write in the dominant Spanish language, they are condemned to be chained to the abuses of the past.

After introducing myself to the principal, I placed a box of children's books and a box of notebooks and pens on a large wooden table in the single classroom. Like every other rural indigenous school, it was nearly empty of materials.

Then, much to the delight of everyone, we passed the books around for the kids to hold. It was the first time any of those Chorti youngsters had ever held any children's books. After a while, to show their appreciation the teacher had the thirty-some students sing a song for me in their Chorti language. The books and school supplies for the barren classroom were just as eagerly received as the fresh organic seeds for their milpas were received by the farmers. The only difference was the exuberance of the children.

As always I entered the school with my large furry companion, Mr. Jeb. He would sit calmly beside me as I spoke to the children about the books. His ninety-five pounds dwarfed most of them. Like in scores of other schools he ended up stealing the show. I told them that he was an educated golden retriever dog in the fourth grade, the grade in which many Chorti kids drop out so that they can work on their family farms.

After they finished their song and another round of applause, Mr. Jeb let out a series of happy barks, as if applauding their applause. Though some of the kids were intimidated by his size and bass-like bellows, it was an ever so tiny girl who surprised me by coming over and asking if she could pet him. She then ran her tiny fingers freely through the thick hair on his neck. Having satisfied her desire, she then excitedly ran off with bragging rights. A little while later I drove off, as everyone stood outside waving good-bye and making a joyful noise.

Chapter 7

DECONSTRUCTING CHACHAUATE

> "In reality every reader is, while he is reading, the reader of his own self."—Marcel Proust

"Next time, bring me a big television," Suyapa demanded, stretching her arms out wide to emphasize her desired size.

"Oh, sí, sí," I smiled and nodded, as much in jest as she was serious. "Black and white, that's okay, right?" I teased.

"No, no, color. I want color!" she insisted.

Suyapa and her husband Henry, both Garifuna (Black Carib), were the proud new owners of a tiny twelve-volt television. Though not the last, it was the first to infect the diminutive cay of Chachauate, in the Hog Islands of Honduras in 1997. From that point on, a group of Garifuna women would gather each day at noon to watch a romantic Mexican or Venezuelan soap opera, and each evening, an even larger crowd of men, women, and children would sit on the sand fixated, watching either a football game or some game show. It didn't take long until the conversations of the women started to revolve more and more around the names of the people in the soap opera, revealing just how magnetic the power of television really is. Sitting in their paradise of poverty, they could dream themselves into fantasy roles. Soon, it had cult status, and Henry and Suyapa could use TV as bait to attract people and sell them sodas, alcohol, and snacks. Thanks to the new TV their sales skyrocketed. None of these poor fisher families had ever owned a television, so it was easy to lure them to the shiny screen. It became a daily ritual, a profitable venture for Henry and Suyapa.

Some months later, when I returned, they had an even larger TV. The only problem was that it was powered by a solar panel and battery donated by Cultural Rescue, a UN program, that someone had stolen at Henry's request. In fact, they were taken from the roof of the neighboring children's library, the tiny seaside Biblioteca Satuye, which we had constructed a few years before. The power generated must have turned on a light bulb over Henry's head, because he had an epiphany: hook the battery to his new TV. Before that theft, however, the solar panel and battery had powered the only two light bulbs on the football field sized cay. Kids and adults would sit together at night, just six meters from the crystalline Caribbean—reading, joking, and painting. Like moths before a flame, people would gather each night around the two naked bulbs. The little library soon became more popular than Henry's first diminutive television.

But envious Henry put an end to all that. To complicate matters, I had known Henry and Suyapa for a few years, and I was like a son to Mama Kalika, Henry's mother. Nonetheless, I had to say something to him because it was such an abuse. So one day I asked him to return the solar panel to its rightful place on the roof of the children's library. We found out that it had been Joel, Suyapa's brother, who had stolen it some months before. How strange to have a TV, of all things, stealing the show, I thought—the spoken word dominating the written. That TV literally turned the lights out on any reading done at night. When I confronted Henry about it, he didn't even hear me. I picked a bad time—he was watching football and totally absorbed in the game. He knew what I wanted but he never took his eyes off the screen. I was interrupting his show and the electronic images unplugged his mind to any other reality. Henry was disheartened that his favorite team lost, but he was happy because his TV won.

I had been visiting the Hog islands off and on for several years. During that time, nearly all of the social politics had changed. "The Foundation," as everyone called it, had come and set up The Hog Islands National Park, which restricted diving for lobster and conch. A member of their inner circle, a Honduran colonel named Kiki Morales, wanted to expropriate the tiny cay of Chachauate. He dreamed of making the bug-less cay his own and building a hotel. It is indigenous land, though, and has been used by the Garifuna as a fishing outpost for generations. Because Honduras is a signatory to the International Labor Organization Convention 169, it had to respect the Garifuna claim to Chachauate. But in the murder capital of the world, things like signatures are erased as easily as lives, and agreements are regularly drown in a sea of ink. As with all indigenes, losing their land is the biggest problem confronting the Garifuna. They have been divided and manipulated by land-lusting outsiders, and it has devastated their community like a virus of real-estate AIDS.

In the early 1990s, Stephan Schmidheiny, a billionaire Swiss businessman, purchased the smaller of the two Hog Islands for one million dollars. He bought it from a Honduran named Bobby Griffith, who inherited it from his grandfather. It has a small airport, which was used for years by drug traffickers. That all changed when Schmidheiny and his Coral Reel Foundation built a twenty million dollar facility there for marine research. The Smithsonian Institute was invited to operate it, which they did from 1994 to 1997, during which time the Hog Islands National Park was established on behalf of the Honduran government. The Smithsonian came there after having been evicted by the indigenous Kuna in Panama's San Blas Islands, where for years they had operated the Smithsonian Tropical Research Institute. They became very unpopular with the Kuna because of their perceived heavy-handed treatment and were asked to leave. In the Hog Islands, they used eighteen soldiers from the Honduran navy to patrol the waters and enforce the new regulations regarding diving and fishing.

All of these groups wanted the Garifuna off of Chachauate and moved back to the coast. Most of them had come from Nueva Armenia, a perennially poverty-stricken village ten kilometers away. The Foundation blamed the Garifuna fishermen in their tiny dugouts for the depletion of lobster, conch, and fish, yet the rich owners of large fishing trawlers were never accused. This was even after a Honduran named McNabb was nabbed and jailed in the US for selling thousands of pounds of undersized lobster. These Honduran boats supply millions of pounds of lobster each year to chain seafood restaurants in the US.

They even tried to fix blame on the Garifuna for the death of coral reefs. I once heard Hector Guzman, the head biologist for the Smithsonian, say that the coral was dying because "the Garifuna shit in the sea." Chachauate had two outhouses perched like pelicans at the end of some rickety docks. The Smithsonian built two septic system outhouses on top of a massive seven meter long cement tank to replace them. On the door of one of the little plywood outhouses was printed WURI, the Garifuna word for man, and on the other WAGURI, woman. The septic system needed fresh water to work properly, however, which Chachauate doesn't have, so the tank was soon a smelly, vile health risk. It also became a breeding ground for mosquitos, which had never been a problem before. Perhaps that was the plan. At about the same time, they also built a large red brick incinerator next to the outhouses to burn waste. That never worked either, because the flue was designed improperly. Both are now dilapidated ruins, monuments to the Smithsonian's mismanagement.

All the while, they were scheming with the land-lusting colonel to get the Garifuna off of Chachauate. They began a campaign of pressure and threats against the eighty or so Garifuna residents, who lacked title to the land, but were there by virtue of a right of possession agreement.

In order to facilitate their expropriation, they planned to set up a military post to house four soldiers and in so doing, crossed a red line. When Captain Martinez from the military and Guzman from the Smithsonian came over and told of their plans for a "posta" for four soldiers, no one, except one mestizo quisling named Betin, wanted any part of it. "No way!" was the people's response, but what could they do? For them, a military post there would be disastrous. Apart from the existential threat to the island's Garifuna inhabitants, all the fishermen hated the thought of not being able to smoke their marijuana openly anymore. Being caught with just a few grams would land them in a terrible jail for a few years. In addition, the women feared abuse from the soldiers. Most importantly, though, everyone suspected that a military post would mean their eviction.

Things heated up further when a young Garifuna diver was shot in the leg by a park guard working with the Smithsonian. The diver was trying to flee after they caught him with a couple of lobsters. He had been diving there for years, and as an indigene, was within his rights according to the UN Declaration of the Rights of Indigenous. Unfortunately, this didn't seem to matter to either the Smithsonian or the Honduran military.

The Committee for the Defense of Human Rights in Honduras (CODEH, a Honduran human rights organization) and OFRANEH (the Black Fraternal Organization of Honduras, a Garifuna NGO) later took both the Honduran military and the Smithsonian to court in La Ceiba, a very brave thing to do in Honduras. The judge threw the case out of court, but to avoid a scandal the injured man was paid off with $1500 and he got to keep the bullet in his leg as a permanent souvenir. On occasion, Captain Martinez was known to use far-off fishermen in dugouts for target practice with his M16 when drunk. Fortunately, since he was drunk and a bad shot, no one was ever hit.

One day, Captain Martinez and Guzman came to the cay in a Boston Whaler. It always meant trouble when the two showed up together. I stood by with some Garifuna and watched from a distance, figuring they were up to no good. They took out a tape measure and staked out an eight by twelve meter area, one of the few vacant spots available on the overcrowded little cay. It was here they planned to put a small block building for their "posta" and house the four soldiers. The land actually belonged to an old Garifuna man named Siriyakov, who was Mama Kalika's older brother. The dilapidated thatched champa where he had lived for years had been torn down some time before, and since he lacked money to build a new one, the ground sat empty. So, not only were they going to build a military post, but they were prepared to rob an old man of his property in order to do it.

We all knew the ramifications of this act, so as soon as they left and the arrogant wake of their departing speed boat had stilled, the stakes and string somehow disappeared. But what to do now was the question? A meeting was quickly called, at which sixty or seventy raggedy Garifuna sat, perplexed and wondering. From white-haired old women smoking pipes to muscular fishermen with calloused hands, everyone agreed that the proposed military site was unwelcome. It was a threat to their freedom and life on the cay. No one, though, knew what to do about it.

But finally C suggested, "Let's build a children's library."

"Brilliant! What can they do to against that?" I responded. "It wouldn't look good if the Smithsonian and the Honduran military took over and destroyed a children's library would it?"

Everyone agreed that building a children's library on the same spot was the best weapon to destroy the plans of an unwanted military post, but it was just a dream.

"Who is going to do it?" the people asked.

"No one has any money to do this," a Garifuna man remarked.

He was right—they barely had a dollar between them. Suddenly, a crowd of eyes turned and focused on me. I knew what those looks meant.

Then the elderly matriarch, Mama Kalika, turned to me with a sad look and pleaded, "Please Timo, help us!"

I was put on the spot, as other pleas followed. How could I not help them? What kind of person would I be if I ignored their need and told them I couldn't help? For the Smithsonian, the spoiled child of my own government, to be doing this filled me with disgust. The Honduran military followed orders. It was those who gave them who were to blame.

So, without any idea where it would lead, I dove in head first and said, "OK, let's do it!" I joked later with C about how he had set me up, knowing full well my serendipitous relationship with books and my willingness to help. We all knew, though, that this was our only hope to save Chachauate. It would either save the little cay for the Garifuna, or hasten its demise. Maybe it would work, or maybe we would only get ourselves into trouble. What we knew for sure was that if we didn't do something quick, the cay would be lost. Neither the Honduran military nor the Smithsonian wanted to respect the Garifuna claim to Chachauate, and they would soon be back with materials to start building.

There was no time to lose. I left early the next morning with a couple of Garifuna men in a motorized dugout bound for Nueva Armenia on the coast. From there we would go to La Ceiba and buy materials for the proposed children's library. As we left before dawn, the two Hog Islands were silhouetted against the darker sky. Sunrise found us searching for the narrow mouth of the Papaloteca River, which from a distance can barely be seen as it slowly spills from a lagoon into the Caribbean.

Pushing the dugout over a shallow bar in the mouth of the Papaloteca, we entered the swollen estuary. In a few minutes we came alongside the muddy banks of Nueva Armenia. This pitifully poor village is nearest to the Hog Islands and is where most of the inhabitants of Chachauate come from.

By late afternoon we returned by truck from La Ceiba with a load of building materials. That meant staying a night in the falling star Hotel ChiChi, whose birdcage-sized rooms had signs posted saying, "Don't Kill the Mosquitos" on the walls. Early the next morning, after filling a large dugout with lumber and other materials, we left.

Embossed on the horizon like two dark breasts, the Hog Islands slowly changed from dark gray to green as we drew nearer. Turning coastward, the striking dog-toothed Name of God Mountains rose abruptly from the narrow coastal plane. Pico Bonito, at 2200 meters, is the highest point along the entire coast of the Caribbean in Central America. From its heights, countless cold and clear streams rapidly descend, as if they were in a hurry to taste the salty warm waters of the Caribbean. Like the ineffable name of God, these mountains are still unknown; their steep granite peaks, often shrouded in clouds, seem to forbid entrance. Only twice has the granite-faced Pico Bonito been climbed. Like Jewish high priests armed with the secret name of God, those climbers managed to enter this forbidding holy place. The sanctity of the wild Name of God Mountains is accentuated when juxtaposed against names like United Fruit, Standard Fruit, and Dole, all of which had ruled below at one time, making Honduras a classic banana republic.

Far down the coast I could almost discern where the Garifuna village of Sambo Creek lay. Far above, in the hills, a plume of steam rose from one of the world's most awesome hot springs. But from a distance, one has no idea that Sambo Creek is really like an oozing sore on the lip of a beauty queen. AIDS has ravaged the place, leaving indigent orphans like bouquets of flowers at a cemetery.

Finally, Chachauate poked over the horizon. The nearer we came, the more colorful the once reef-rich waters became. It looked like clear liquid malachite. The corals are bleaching, but it's not the fault of seventy Garifuna shitting in the ocean as claimed by Guzman.

Many children were waiting for us on the beach and they greeted us with shouts. More than a dozen men and women helped unload the lumber and other building materials from the dugout.

We counted every board and piled them at the new building site. Siriyakov, who owned the parcel, came by and seemed pleased to learn that it would become a children's library rather than expropriated for a military post. To celebrate, I bought him a small bottle of gifiti, Garifuna rum mixed with medicinal herbs.

The next day, seven or eight of us worked together digging twenty holes in the sand for the pilings. The night before some wily Garifuna "liberated" them from the Smithsonian's dock project. By the second afternoon the foundation, floor, and walls were all in place. We knew that we had to work fast. We wanted to get as much done as possible before Captain Martinez and Guzman returned. While we worked on the building, other Garifuna men went to the big Hog Island and cut manaca palm thatch for the roofing.

Four days later Martinez and Guzman returned. This time they came with a few soldiers with M16s slung over their shoulders. Martinez and Guzman were furious when they realized that we had purposely taken their spot. They walked over to confront us.

"Who gave you permission to build this?" Captain Martinez demanded of me.

"Oh, the children wanted a library, so we're building a library," I told him matter-of-factly.

Then Martinez firmly told Jose Huelto, a Garifuna leader, to call a group meeting to talk about our actions. Nearly everyone on the cay showed up except C. Captain Martinez had a particular dislike for him and that might have further poisoned the atmosphere. As it was, Martinez and Guzman both lectured us about the inappropriate and illegal nature of our activity.

"How dare you defy the Honduran military?" Captain Martinez spouted. "You have purposely defied us. You cannot build this building. This spot belongs to the Honduran military. You must stop building." He carried on some more and then let Guzman put his two cents' worth in.

Finally old Mama Kalika got up and spoke with a voice of authority: "Basta, basta (Enough, enough)! We should let the children decide—this is getting us nowhere." Turning to the group of raggedy, half-naked children, she slyly asked, "Children, what would you rather have here—a military post, or a children's library?"

Glancing over at the captain and the director, I could see frustration written all over their faces. Adding to their unease, little voices united like a rising storm shouting "Biblioteca, biblioteca (library, library)!" Quickly realizing how much this pleased us and how much it upset Martinez and Guzman, they continued their defiant chant, "Biblioteca, biblioteca!" We could hardly contain our laughter watching little children assert a collective voice against the military post. "Out of the mouth of babes…"

Unable to cope with such relentless opposition, Martinez, Guzman, and the four soldiers returned to their Boston Whaler and sped off. Exultant laughter drowned out the roar of their boat as they left in frustrated anger. C appeared soon after from within one of the thatched huts.

"I guess counter-insurgency training at the School of the Americas never included how to deal with children's libraries," he joked.

Knowing the propensity of Captain Martinez to take revenge, the Garifuna recommended that both C and I make ourselves scarce for a while. It was nearly Easter, so we went to Copán for a while, then on to Santiago de Atitlan in Guatemala. I returned after a couple of weeks, loaded down with children's books for the new Biblioteca Satuye. I bought them from bookstores in Guatemala City, San Pedro Sula, and Tegucigalpa. Few places sell children's books, since few families can afford to buy them. I didn't know it then, but this was just the first of several times I would stock it with books.

The building project we had left behind remained much as we had left, it so we set about adding the roof, windows, and door that were still lacking. Finally, in true Caribbean style, we painted it a provocative bright pink. It clearly stood out next to the thatched huts, as well as from the Foundation's twenty-million dollar facilities a mile away. The Garifuna named the library after their hero Satuye, an eighteenth-century warrior chief from St. Vincent.

The Garifuna came to the area after a slave ship wrecked off the Carib Indian island of St Vincent in 1630. The freed Africans were soon integrated into the island's Carib tribe; as the years passed, they began to dominate. In the 1760s, Satuye led an insurgency against the invading British, who were encroaching on the island and wanted to grow cotton there. Satuye's guerilla war continued for thirty years. He actually used chemical weapons against the imperialists. His archers would shoot burning canisters of chili pepper at the British troops, blinding them and setting them up for easy slaughter. Satuye died in battle in 1796. The British claimed they found the *Rights of Man* from the French Revolution on his body, but it is likely that Satuye was illiterate. After his death, over 2,000 Garifuna were deported to the island of Roatán, off the Honduran coast. The British separated lighter-skinned people (with more Carib blood) from those with darker skin and more African features, shipping the latter to Roatán. They did this to rid St. Vincent of these freedom-loving people, dumping them for the Spanish to deal with. From Roatán, the Garifuna spread quickly to the Honduran coast, Belize, Guatemala, and even to places in Nicaragua. Today, their population exceeds 200,000. They are considered indigenes by the UN due to their Indian blood and language ties to the Caribs. Thus, they are considered one of only four hybrid African/Native American cultures—along with the Miskito, Rama, and Seminole Indians.

Once we finished the wooden library structure and placed the books inside, it was time to celebrate our victory. We didn't invite Martinez or Guzman; instead, the children battered a piñata as if it was their effigy. From its inception, tiny Biblioteca Satuye was constantly crowded with kids. It was the only place on the tiny cay that they could call their own. Most had never heard the word library (biblioteca) before and none of them had ever held a book, much less a children's book. They would sit for hours—drawing and practicing their reading around a couple of brightly-painted tables we had made. These were placed under the thatched roof of the long porch. Just a few meters away, gentle waves lapped like thirsty dogs against the sugar-sand shore.

C soon convinced Cultural Rescue, the UN program, to donate a solar panel and the Biblioteca Satuye became crowded with kids and adults in the night as well as the daytime, since it was the only place on the cay with electricity. I remember the delight I felt watching a table full of children reading simple stories to an illiterate old Garifuna man named Katacho. He told me he was eighty, and he loved to sit and listen to the children read. I still have a photo of him sitting with a group of kids at a table. He is holding a book upside down (he couldn't tell the difference until he saw the pictures). Like many elderly Garifuna he came from an oral tradition that had never embraced reading. Each evening at dusk, before he paddled out to fish all night, the kids would read to him. The children became his textual community. They made the pages talk for him. One night, though, old Katacho went out fishing but never came back. He was never seen again. His empty dugout was found washed ashore on a beach near the Smithsonian's facility. We always wondered about his mysterious disappearance. This was a time (mid-1990s) when the Honduran military would sometimes shoot at Chachauate fishermen. Chachauate was embroiled in a multi-layered conflict and the Biblioteca Satuye was right in the middle of things.

When I returned the following winter, 1997-98, I found that nearly every book had disappeared. Who knows where they had gone? Reportedly, many were taken by soldiers, probably more to keep as presents for their kids than out of spite. The kids of the cay probably walked off with some, too. Just as educated, sophisticated people love to display their books as a sign of their intelligence, so too, perhaps, do poor uneducated children like those of Chachauate. But instead of placing them on a shelf, which none of their thatched huts have, they put them in a box under the family bed as if they were a prized possession. Several turned up that way. So once again, I restocked the library with books that I had driven down from Mexico. The sad truth is that book loss is just a fact of life for any library. Biblioteca Satuye didn't have many to lose, though, and Honduras has only a couple of publishers and a limited number of places to buy more. Plus, books are expensive. A problem was that there was no formal control, so things just disappeared sometimes. For that reason, the library was locked up at night by some women, who were usually more trustworthy than the men.

I heard that a surly group of Garifuna men had taken over the library's tables for gambling some months before, which could have also contributed to the deconstruction of the little Biblioteca Satuye. One of the leading culprits was said to have been Gito, a large, fifty-something Garifuna—a cyclopean character who was blind in one eye. At some point in 1996, he managed to get control of the key to the library by intimidating one of the women who took care of the place. Gito was not interested in the kids or the books—he was interested in the building. It was during his tenure, so to speak, when the theft of the solar panel and battery took place. As a result, there was no longer light at night to read by. Instead, there was Henry and Suyapa's entrepreneurial pride and joy a few doors away. Just buy a soda, beer, or snack and you can watch TV all night—never mind that the library no longer has any lights.

During this same time I had a very revealing encounter with a friend of Gito, an illiterate Garifuna man named Didi. Not known for his honesty, Didi was more pirate than fisherman. One morning I was waiting to use one of the cay's little outhouses perched so precariously at the end of a short rickety dock, directly over the sea. People washed their dishes on the calm, leeward side of the cay; on the other side are the two outhouses. I was waiting on the beach for the occupant to finish and it was Didi who exited.

Though he must have known I was there from the cracks in the walls, he didn't acknowledge me when passing and ignored my greeting. He stepped off the dock and he turned his face away from me and tossed some soiled papers onto an adjacent refuse heap. As I stepped onto the dock, my eye caught sight of his discarded toilet paper. Though crinkled and stained with his excrement, I couldn't help but notice that they appeared to be some vestigial remnants of a torn up children's book. "You've got to be kidding!" I said to myself. Stepping back off the dock I bent over for a better look. Yes, I was right! I was unwilling to pretend that I didn't notice or didn't care, so I said to him, "Didi, why did you use a kid's book from the Biblioteca for toilet paper? Listen, I bought this book to help kids learn how to read, not for you to wipe your dirty ass with." Taking offence that I was deriding his hygiene, he gave me a dirty look and cursed me in Garifuna as he walked away. I later found out that it was Didi, the classic bibulous anti-bibliophile, who had stolen and sold a nice wooden chair from the Biblioteca too. Needless to say, I wasn't surprised. His loutish life was a complete literary lacuna. The only printed material he had any respect for was money—or a lottery ticket. There was not much he wouldn't do for money; his picaresque behavior was devoid of any idealism.

Didi was basically the lackey of Rene Arzu and his brother Johnny, who ran cargo out to the cays in dugouts (tuk-tuks) from Nueva Armenia. Rene was smart, though a sell-out to his people. Johnny, though, was missing more than just his front teeth. Later that day I spoke to a few of the five-man "directivo" (directors), who are the power base on Chachauate. One was Johnny. Each one represents one of the five main families from Nueva Armenia. They are mostly partners in crime. I asked them to take the key to the Biblioteca away from Gito and return it to the women, since he refused to do it for me. Though reluctant for reasons I found out later, they did have the key returned. Not long after that I left the cay again.

I returned again at the end of December in 1999. This was two months after the horrendous Hurricane Mitch had devastated the region—especially Honduras. At least 10,000 people were killed, most from along the north coast and many from Garifuna villages. For two days the hurricane had stagnated over the island of Guanaja, one of the nearby Bay Islands. The coastal beaches for over 150 miles became choked with piles of wood flushed out from the flooded rivers.

The few dozen Garifuna left on the meter high Chachauate sought refuge at the Foundation but were refused. The Smithsonian had left the year before, after having spent three years there, and were replaced by an organization from Miami called AVINA. They didn't want to be bothered with giving refuge to the Garifuna. Instead, they told the desperate people to go to the one-room primary school over on the big island, at a place called East End. This one-room school was another one I had supplied with books, and that was where all the kids went to school during the week, in a dugout.

After the hurricane it was Julian, a fisherman with calloused hands, who was the subject of much discussion. He had spent a couple of days marooned on Chachauate in a coconut palm. Julian had been too drunk to leave the cay and remained there. He told me that he shimmied up into the heart of the tree and tied himself to it when waves began washing from one side to the other over the tiny cay. An untold number of people and animals on the coast and inland were washed away by flooding rivers. A Garifuna woman from Santa Rosa de Aguan was found alive in the sea, after six days clinging to a tree. She had been swept for miles into the Caribbean by the raging Aguan River. I asked friends in Nueva Armenia who spent days in the rafters of houses what they ate. "Meat, lots of meat from floating cows," one told me. Several people on the coast told me that they ate toucans that sought shelter in villages. These people were the lucky ones. Chachauate was hit hard—Mitch took the roof off of the Biblioteca Satuye.

That was the first thing I noticed approaching Chachauate by boat after Mitch—the roofless Biblioteca. Because of its wooden walls, it fared better than most of the thatched champas. Nonetheless, Mother Nature proved to be far more destructive than any of her wayward sons like Didi. For a few weeks, the library had become home to four or five young Garifuna men. It was in ruins, a complete mess. I called it El Palacio de los Pescadores Perdidos (The Palace of the Lost Fishermen). One of the squatters, a twenty-year-old named Wilmar, seemed to be in charge so I approached him with a request. I said, "Wilmar, listen, you guys have been living here for some weeks now, right?"

"Sí," he answered.

"Okay then, the children of Chachauate and I would like you guys to help me put the two roofs back on. Will you do it?"

Immediately he assured me, "Sure, sure, we will help!"

So, a few days later, I took Wilmar and another man with me to La Ceiba to buy materials. I convinced myself that I had to roof it myself. I just couldn't leave the place to ruin, not after everything we had gone through.

"We'll put a metal roof on it this time. That way it can collect water also. What do you think, Wilmar?" I asked.

"Yes, it will be good, because Chachauate has no water. People have to go by boat way over to the big island and fill containers just to have drinking water." Lacking water, Chachauate also lacked mosquitos and sand flies. A trade-off, I guess—at least until the Smithsonian built their scatological monument.

In the course of our journey, Wilmar watched as I wrote down a list of materials we needed. Humbly, and with some embarrassment, he quietly asked me, "Will you teach me how to write my name?" That was when I realized that Wilmar was illiterate. Strangely, he only wanted to know how to write his name—nothing more.

"Sure, Wilmar," I told him. "I'll teach you how to write your name, but wait till tomorrow back in the cay."

The next afternoon he walked briskly into my sand-floored champa, eager as a child to learn. He was holding a notebook and pen, which he bought with some of the money he earned from helping me. He was excited! "Finally, I will learn how to write my name," he said, reiterating that he only wanted to learn to write his name, nothing more. He told me that he hadn't gone beyond the third grade in the primary school in Nueva Armenia. I asked him why. Poverty, he replied, and he told me how his family had no money for books, notebooks, and pencils, so he could never learn. When he was nine, he dropped out of school to work.

The world is full of people like Wilmar. In Honduras alone there are multitudes of children selling products on the streets whose labels they will never even be able to read. Poverty feeds off of illiteracy like an ouroboros eating its tail. In Honduras' big cities especially, kids are often recruited into gangs like MS and 18, which originate in L.A. For some, like Wilmar, those are the only letters and numbers they recognize. They learn these through the power of the gun, not the power of the pen. Handicapped by poverty and cheated out of a way to learn to read and write, young lives can all the more easily be bent and twisted by forces that be. Barry Sanders wrote brilliantly about this in his book *A is for Ox*.

Wilmar reminded me of Sanders' analysis of Huck Finn, stuck between worlds of literacy and orality. He will never read a book or write a sentence. The world of chirography is alluring, but also threatening to him. His family was swindled out of some land because they were illiterate and he was swindled out of education because of their poverty.

In Nueva Armenia, Wilmar grew up speaking Garifuna, and most kids still speak it there. The language he was weaned on, though, is not considered a valid form of expression in the Spanish- and English-speaking worlds. Accordingly, the mother-tongue becomes a badge of shame for some, and schools unfortunately often contribute to this. Illiteracy and his own language keep Wilmar and his people separate and distant from much of the outer world.

When he came for his first lesson we put a table in the doorway of my sand-floored champa where the best light was. I then wrote out the alphabet in his copy book, but Wilmar knew what he wanted and didn't want. He quickly reminded me that it was his name and not the alphabet that he wanted to learn. Like Sanders' perception of Huck Finn, it seems that a search for "self" was behind Wilmar's desire to learn to write his name, which is what state-sponsored poverty had stolen from him. Thus he reasoned that "the power of the name" could be brought to life by the "talking letters."

"Listen, Wilmar," I told him, "I think you should learn all the letters, not just those in your name. What if you learn the wrong letters? Suppose you show someone you can write your name and write Donkey instead of Wilmar? It has six letters too! Would you want your friends laughing at you when you write Donkey for your name?"

He agreed to learn the whole alphabet.

One day, while I was sitting with Wilmar at the table, a teenage girl walked by and asked Wilmar what he was doing. She had a twinkle in her eye.

"Oh, I am leaning how to write my name," he proudly told her.

"Why do you want to know how to write your name, if you can't even read?"

Unfazed, he told her proudly, "Because my name is beautiful!"

He proceeded to show her his writing, at which point she laughed and left. Wilmar's full name is Wilmar Alexander Barrios. He copied it over and over below where I had written it in his notebook. This was his first attempt at writing since he was a child. At first, none of his letters were the same. It seemed he was creating a new orthography, but after a couple of days I began to notice a difference.

One of the only times Wilmar had previously tried to write something was when he tattooed a large, almost illegible letter D on his upper left arm. It was more like a brand or an intaglio than a tattoo. He told me that D stood for Daisy, an old but never forgotten girlfriend. It was to impress her, I realized, that explained his eagerness to learn how to write his name. He wanted to show Daisy that he was halfway educated.

It took three days before Wilmar decided he was ready to graduate, whereupon he immediately left for the coast to find Daisy. Wilmar left as suddenly as Huck Finn, and like Huck, he would never become literate. As Barry Sanders observed about Huck Finn, Wilmar also "can't make the transition from orality to serious reading and writing." The letters, though alluring, probably scared him more than sailing his little dugout through a storm. He was drawn to them, but afraid of them—like a non-swimmer fears a wave. Wilmar would never learn to swim the sea of letters. He knew that! He knew that he would never learn to dive deep and bring up intellectual food, like he does with lobster and conch. But if he could just learn how to write his name, he reasoned, he would be satisfied and feel more complete. Then maybe he could float on the sea of letters without sinking, and maybe even impress Daisy.

By the time I left that spring, the Biblioteca Satuye had a shiny new zinc roof and new thatch over the front porch. Kiki Morales must have wondered about it each time he flew over in a helicopter on his way to the Foundation. For several months until it oxidized, it could be seen reflecting the sun from far away, making it a constant reminder to those at the Foundation on the smaller Hog Island. Kids that had been tiny when the Biblioteca was first built were now old enough to read. They had grown with the word biblioteca as part of their lexicon, but they gave new meaning to it. For them it was the biblioteca, with or without books, since they would soon disappear again. I had given them fifty books, but for these kids the biblioteca was more like a clubhouse. They all remembered the books, though, and having known me and my dog Mister Jeb for years, they always petitioned me for more. I drove down that year with many books, along with some watercolor paints, brushes, and paper. Some of the books from Harcourt Brace were large format. They were so big they nearly hid the reader. The rest of the books that year went to schools in over a dozen other rural villages still devastated by Hurricane Mitch, such as Santa Rosa Aguan, Puerto Castillo, and Nueva Armenia.

A year and a half elapsed before I returned to Chachauate again; I had been working in Bolivia. My friends in OFRANEH told me that many things had changed there. During my absence, almost every coconut tree along the north coast had died from a disease called lethal yellowing. It kills the heart of the tree and they die within months. Hurricane Mitch spread the pestilence, though others claimed that they saw planes, crop dusters, flying low along the coast and spraying something.

"Why would they do that?" I asked.

"To get the niggers off the beach," I was told by a Garifuna friend. "Developers drool over our land. And we rely so much on coconuts to survive."

So Chachauate, like most of the coast, had no more coconut trees to grace and shade its shores—nowhere to hang a hammock, the lover of the coco palm, and no more coconut bread or spoon meat. Everything looked so bare without them. At that time the trunks were still standing like long, hurtful memories, giving the place an eerie feeling. A few of the cays had become thick forests of trunks, where a single pelican would sometimes perch. Gradually, they all fell or were cut down. This was the second disaster in three years for the Garifuna and the third worst, after AIDS and Hurricane Mitch.

It was almost as shocking to find that a television had replaced the books in the biblioteca. It sat on a bookshelf like an idol in its new sanctuary—how perfectly imperfect! The directivo leadership had wanted their own TV and now Henry's had company. As I was forewarned, the biblioteca had been taken over by the five members of the directivo and become a private consumo (store). They were selling some basic dry goods and had sacks of rice, flour, and beans stacked against the back wall. The word was that the (now retired) Colonel Kiki Morales gave them money to start the store. He had hated the little library ever since it prevented his planned military post years before. It was the Foundation, AVINA, which had taken over when the Smithsonian left that had so thoughtfully donated the TV, solar panel, and battery.

They closed the open door of literacy and replaced it with a television. Ironically, the TV was paid for with US tax dollars by way of a $200,000 grant the Miami-based 501(c)(3) received for marine research. When the grant money ran out the next year, the WWF took over the facility, but the tiny pink library had already been subverted by television—courtesy of US taxpayers. I could hardly believe it and there was nothing I could do. Where the local kids could once be heard reading aloud or seen painting, people now sat like zombies, spellbound by the shining screen. Where once there were books, paper, pencils and paints for children, there was now the magnetic screen. Great! Once, the library sparked protests over indigenous rights for the Garifuna; now it was a catalyst for mind control and a dream box for consumerism. Once it was a public space, especially for the children; now it was a private business for five greedy men.

With characters like Didi and Gito still around, I could only imagine what had happened to the books—a year of toilet paper perhaps? Once again, tiny Chachauate felt like a stage. The Foundation was buying off the directivo, and how I wanted to monkey-wrench it—but they would know it was me and besides, I convinced myself that the TV wouldn't work for long anyway. Sand or storm or perhaps a clumsy hand would take care of it. Anyway, that would make me just like Didi. The TV had been more bait than gift. It certainly wasn't given to make up for AVINA's refusal to shelter dozens of desperate Garifuna families during Hurricane Mitch. No chance! Rather, the Foundation was following a policy to prevent the Garifuna from obtaining title to Chachauate, something that OFRANEH had tried to accomplish for years, but the directivo had purposely avoided. After all, they were being compensated to do nothing. Eventually, some years later, OFRANEH managed to get the municipality of Roatán to issue a collective title. The books, though, which had once exploded like knowledge bombs and defeated unwanted guns, were now defused by television. Nonetheless, though a pedagogical failure, the provocatively pink little Biblioteca Satuye was a political success.

Chapter 8

THE SLIVER

> "What could be more important than to live and work with the oppressed, with the rejects of life, with the wretched of the earth?"
> —Paulo Freire

> "Thought has meaning only when generated by action upon the world."—Paulo Freire

The Sliver, what a name for a village! But this appellative for a tiny remote Honduran community is apt. Something has penetrated into the collective flesh of the community and embedded itself there. Some foreign object has implanted itself, causing a festering, infected wound. A professor friend from La Ceiba suggested that we take some of the books I had to the school there. So, along with a couple of human rights workers and my dog Mr. Jeb, we drove east one morning along the North Coast highway. Just before the bridge to Masica, we turned off onto a lonely dirt road. Seventy years before, this bridge was the site where some seventy Honduran banana planters were murdered by the army. They had been marching to La Ceiba in a protest against the theft of their land titles by Standard Fruit. Standard had burned down the city office in La Ceiba where all the records were kept. Then, because Honduran law accepts the testimony of three people as the gospel truth, they would hire three men to testify in court that the land belonged to Standard. This enabled Standard to rapidly expand their enterprise. But while the Standard Fruit Company built an economic paradise for itself, it also created a hell for the subsistence farmers whose *Musa × paradisiaca* they stole. Any semblance of justice slipped on the peels, with a little push from the Monroe Doctrine.

It was April and it was hot. Clouds of choking dust from occasional vehicles formed contrails like those from jet planes. For more than an hour we drove down the back road, crossing and re-crossing the bridgeless San Juan River. Three times my friends got out to wade and guided me towards the shallows. Then the road became flanked on both sides by endless rows of young African palms. At one point the trees were so small that we could see over the top of them. They stretched far into the distance beyond sight to a point where the plantation ended. It was huge! I saw some men up ahead and slowed down, to avoid engulfing them in a cloud of dust. The three men, one with a rifle, stared inquisitively at us as we slowly drove by the large, gated entrance they stood beside. Turning to my friend the professor, I said, "Those guys look scary!"

"They should," he answered, "they're Miguel Facusse's hired killers." Pointing, he snickered in disgust, "All of this land now belongs to Facusse, and this is only a tiny part of what he owns. All of it he got with threats or murder. If people wouldn't sell him their land, they ended up in a shallow grave."

Finally, one side of the road became free of the African palms and little shacks began to appear in the shade of large trees. A few goats searched for food in a makeshift corral and new corn was coming up in little fenced-in gardens.

A short distance down the road, we came to a rustic hamlet. The ubiquitous Coca-Cola sign painted on the side of a building suggested that we had probably arrived. Yes, we were in the downtown section of The Sliver, amongst its eight or ten haphazardly built structures. This community had been home to the six poor peasants Facusse's murderous thugs had killed when they refused to sell their land.

"He is the richest man in Honduras, but he is never satisfied. Nothing is enough! He feeds off the poor!" my friend Raul complained. "He's like the Biblical king Ahab, who had the poor man Naboth killed because he wouldn't sell him his garden."

We asked for directions to the school and a man pointed to a small building in a field off in the distance. Though shaded from the incandescent sun by a large mango tree, the two-room schoolhouse had been withered by poverty. Large patches of plaster had crumbled off the walls and the barred windows had shards of glass hanging like icicles. Driving up and parking under the tree, we caused an instant commotion. We could see a group of curious little faces staring at us from the open door of a classroom.

It is rare for The Sliver to receive visitors, and even rarer for the school. The sight of a bearded Gringo with a large dog and three other men suddenly driving up caused a stir. As we got out, a teacher greeted us and took us around the building to meet the principal, who also served as a teacher.

Happy to be out of the truck, Mr. Jeb lingered by the tree. My friend the professor introduced us to the class and told them that we had books and school supplies. This immediately evoked an uproar of applause, shouts, and screams. Hearing the noise from around the building, Mr. Jeb ran to investigate and entered the jubilant room with a big bellowing bark. At that point, uncontrollable laughter broke loose. The more the kids screamed and laughed in unbridled horseplay, the more Mr. Jeb happily barked. He loved to go to schools and always managed to steal the show. One moment there was pedagogy and then the next there was pandemonium. It was easy to see that everyone was loving every howling minute of it.

Once things calmed down, Raul opened the boxes of books which caused another salvo of shouts. At that point, someone remembered the kids in the other room. They had been there the whole time and must have been wondering what was going on, but they were too obedient to leave their own classroom.

Their teacher brought them over, which added another thirty-five screaming voices to the cacophony. Then suddenly a group of parents showed up, concerned after hearing the noise and shouting. Within a few minutes there were more than a dozen curious people huddled together, talking and smiling in the open doorway. Then Raul pulled out a poster that Mexico's Secretary of Educational Publications had given me a couple of months before. It was a beautiful poster that depicted a Mayan tale about a turtle. Unrolling it for all to see, he held it up and asked, "Who would like to read this?" He picked out a little girl whose smile seemed too big for her diminutive face. She read the poster with a clear voice until she faltered on an unfamiliar word. Then, after Raul helped her pronounce each syllable, she continued to the end and was rewarded with the applause of all the kids and parents.

It was obvious that this school was particularly needy, but it wasn't until I asked the teacher for a written receipt that I discovered the depth of their poverty. She told me to wait for a minute and left the room. She returned a short time later holding a half sheet of torn paper. Embarrassed, she said, "This is all the paper we have!" Then, on the school's last piece of paper, she wrote a receipt acknowledging the gift.

When she had finished, an inquisitive local man came over and invited the four of us visitors to lunch. He was a white-haired old man named Don Claudio, whose physiognomy reflected a life of much suffering. Don Claudio rode back with us to his rustic little ranch which barely supported his family. It turned out that he was one of the only men alive who had dared to stand up to Miguel Facusse. Refusing to sell one's land to Facusse had been a death sentence, but Don Claudio was somehow still alive.

When we later asked about Facusse, Don Claudio said, "All he does is take! He never gives! He takes our land and he takes our lives; but he has never given our community anything. He leaves us with nothing but bad memories and graves. Look at the school—it's a disgrace! How can our children learn with nothing inside?

We are all ashamed, but we are too poor to do anything about it. There is no place to buy books like the ones that you men have brought. Even if there was, we couldn't afford them. You saw how many of the kids were barefoot. Facusse, the richest man in Honduras, could bless us with a better school, but all we get are his curses and bullets. By the way, have you seen the memorial for the six dead men?" he asked.

"It's big and tall," he said, stretching out his arms. "There are six arching cement pillars, symbolic of the men Facusse had murdered. They rise up twenty feet, and then come together and form a single column that binds them in unity."

As he spoke, we heard automatic gunfire in the distance. Raul immediately asked, "What was that?"

"Oh," Don Claudio answered, "Those are the thugs of Facusse. They do that a lot to try to intimidate us. They think that guns and weapons are signs of power and strength. To me they are signs of fear and weakness. True power, true strength, is when children's voices explode into shouts of laughter and joy, like I heard when you men brought the books."

Chapter 9

YES, WE HAVE NO BANANAS

On his fourth voyage, in 1502, Columbus set foot for the first time on land in the area of what is now Honduras. After he departed, the area remained virtually undisturbed for the next twenty years. Later it became the first place in the "New World" to be embroiled in a multi-sided land grab. Though Honduras lacked the golden glow of Mexico or Panama and offered little hope of riches from plundering or mining, it soon proved to have one important asset—its peoples. Its ethnic diversity was astounding, although by now all but a handful have been "disappeared." Honduras was described by a sixteenth-century Spanish priest as having "more tribes than hair on a deer." Thus it was humans who were mined and harvested, as Honduras soon became the center of the Native American slave trade.

In 1522, Gil Gonzáles Dávila sailed up the Pacific coast from Panama to Nicaragua and then traveled overland into Honduras. Later, he returned to Panama for more support from his backer, Pedro Arias de Ávila or "Pedrarias the Cruel," then governor of Panama. Both Pedrarias and Hernán Cortés in Mexico wanted Honduras. Thanks to its location halfway between Mexico and Panama, it was soon invaded from both the north and the south. Cortés dispatched Cristóbal de Olid to claim Honduras, which he did—for himself. At that point, Cortés sent soldiers to arrest Olid. When they failed to do so, he made the journey from Mexico himself, a trip that was ultimately disastrous for him...but that is another story. By 1524, five different factions were trying to carve Honduras up, like five fingers of a hand trying to take it for their own. Though battles threatened, in the end the parties involved divided it between themselves. There were enough land and enough natives to enslave for everyone, they reasoned.

Modern Honduras is not too different, with fruit companies, other multi-national conquistadors, and the mega-rich all seeking to claim it as their own. But in the end, they all simply agree to divide it amongst themselves.

OFRANEH (the Black Fraternal Organization of Honduras) represents the interests of the Garifuna, indigenous people with mixed African ancestry. At one time, they had an office on the second floor of an old Caribbean-style wooden house close to Central Park in downtown La Ceiba. As with the ceiba trees that lend the town their name, most of these comfortable old houses with wide porches on three sides are gone.

Early one Saturday morning I went to the OFRANEH office to meet C, as we had plans to go to the Garifuna village of San Juan near Tela. Just a few minutes after I arrived at the office, someone knocked on the door. Who would come by at such an hour we wondered? C opened the door to a courier, who was hand-delivering a letter from the New York office of the Organization of American States (OAS).

Quickly reading the letter, C became ecstatic. "We won!" he shouted. "We actually won! Finally, some justice in Honduras! This is the first good news for San Juan in years!"

The letter revealed the outcome of an OAS decision concerning a sixteen-year-old land dispute in a tiny coastal Garifuna village not far from Tela. I had brought books to two schools there just a couple of years before.

C was going to San Juan to film a play written by a young Garifuna man, who had formed a theater troupe there. Over a year before I had given this group a seventy-watt radio transmitter.

C asked me to come along and help him film and I quickly accepted. The play was based on the 1936 massacre of eighteen Garifuna, seventeen men and one woman, by Honduran soldiers. This happened because a local Garifuna man falsely reported to the dictatorial government of Tiburcio Carías Andino that these people were armed and dangerous insurrectionists. The men and the woman were rounded up by the police and ordered to dig a large pit in the sandy soil, not far from the sea. When they finished digging, they were told to stand for a group photograph. Lined up in front of the pit for their photograph, the Garifuna were executed by the soldiers and tumbled back into their mass grave.

The memory of this incident has endured for more than seventy-five years. Nearly every local Garifuna school child knows the story.

Now, though, C had some really good news to share. So within minutes we made several photocopies and were out the door to get a taxi to the bus station. By the time we had walked half a block, C spotted his "watcher." For over a year he had been followed by a man or two every time he left the office. Sometimes it would be a black car with tinted windows, or it was a different car, a motorcycle, a bicycle, or a man on foot. This man was standing alone, which probably meant that he didn't have a vehicle that day. We quickly hailed a taxi to elude his pursuit and we had the driver take a back way to the bus station.

C recognized the man as the same one that he had baited one day and led into a trap. He purposely led the man toward some gang-banger friends in La Ceiba's notorious Barrio Inglés. After C quickly told them about him, they pounced on the man like dogs on a cat.

In the taxi C said, "It's ironic that we are going today."

"Why is that?" I asked.

"Because we're on our way to film a play about a massacre, on the anniversary of another massacre. It's August 16th, the same day as back in 1920, when the Standard Fruit Company had Honduran soldiers massacre several dozen poor banana farmers. It happened in front of the Hotel Paris on Eighth Street, right in the middle of town. And nothing was ever done."

"It seems that this park is still the locus for planned shootings," I commented. "Wasn't Goya shot right on the opposite corner of the park in front of San Isidro church?"

"Yeah, she was shot crossing in front of the church. It was a drive-by assassination team—two men on a motorcycle. She was lucky they missed and only got her in the shoulder."

Goya, a larger-than-life Garifuna activist, had worked for OFRANEH before she was shot in 2004. Fearing for her life, she left Honduras and moved to the United States after being given political asylum.

During the day, the poor people in La Ceiba's Central Park cling to embowered benches like the bromeliads cling to the trees above. At sunset obnoxious zanates, black birds, flock and gather in the trees like noisy carnivalistas. Unlike La Ceiba's better-heeled, who find relief from the searing sun in La Ceiba's air-conditioned mall, the poor go to the park.

In the taxi, C started talking about the Standard Fruit Company. "The names 'Standard Fruit' and 'La Ceiba' were once almost synonymous—bananas got into people's blood and blood got into their bananas."

Starting in the late 1890s, the Sicilian-American Vaccaro brothers made La Ceiba the capital of their own little banana republic. This became the inspiration for Coralio, capital of Anchuria, in O. Henry's novel, *Cabbages and Kings*. In real life, it became the home of men like Christmas Humphreys, an American soldier who, as second in command of the army, had once set up a machine gun in the Barrio Inglés cemetery just off the beach.

At first they only shipped other farmers' bananas to the US, but before long they started acquiring land and began to grow and ship their own. Within a few years they had built a cardboard box factory and their own railway, whose tracks still lay along the boulevard leading to an old wooden pier. During the first two decades of the twentieth century, Standard Fruit tightened its grip on La Ceiba. The 1924 civil war in Honduras was essentially a struggle between liberals and conservatives vying for patronage and support from various North American fruit companies.

Standard was already at work, however—they wanted to control the banana market, not just be a player, and decided that the best way to do that would be to eliminate the competition from the many small banana farms along the north coast. To accomplish this, they burned down the building that held all the land titles in La Ceiba.

The Vaccaro brothers knew that, in Honduras, the law required the word of only three witnesses to reclaim land when the records have disappeared. Standard had plenty of perjuring witnesses on its payroll to do that, so before long they had disenfranchised a host of small farmers. Lacking any other recourse, hundreds of these poor disenfranchised Honduran banana farmers marched to Standard's offices in La Ceiba to protest. They came from all along the north coast. At the bridge over the San Juan River in Masica, sixty kilometers to the west of La Ceiba, the Honduran army came and killed many of them, perhaps more than they had in La Ceiba. Near La Ceiba's Central Park, the soldiers shot dead at least seventy impoverished farmers who had also lost their land to Standard.

Soon, thanks to Standard, the world began consuming its soon-to-be favorite fruit, the *Musa x paradisiaca*. But the true owners of this Edenic land, where the fruit of knowledge of good and evil grew, were being robbed of their lands by Standard. No fruit has ever been used to assault the common respect for human rights and values more than what occurred through the commercialization of bananas.

Honduras was the first country (but not the last) to fall to the multi-national fruit companies. The American Navy showed its support by anchoring the USS Sacramento ("the sacrament") just offshore. Like a burly thug, it served as body guard for the rich thieves. From that point on, Standard was never challenged. The devastated farmers learned that challenging Standard meant challenging the United States. Such is the free enterprise of imperialism. But the strange thing is that, according to C, the local people never speak badly against Standard.

"That's probably because they all have a family member who works or has worked there," I said. "It's the classic company town."

"That's true; some families have worked there for generations. Talking to them about Standard's killings, theft, or pollution is an insult to many of them. It's almost like talking bad about their family. Strange, huh?"

"Perhaps it's as Paulo Freire said, 'The oppressor is housed in the oppressed.' I think that there is a lot of that in Honduras."

"Yes," C nodded, "it's called Standardization."

We had no sooner gotten out of our taxi at the bus station when we saw a friend of C—a local newspaper reporter. He was immediately handed one of the photocopies about the OAS decision. It pleased the reporter, who was left reading it as we got on our crowded bus.

I knew it was C's habit to take a slow bus, or "the milk truck" as he called it, and we boarded one just as it was leaving.

"It takes an hour longer to get to Tela, but at least you know it won't be robbed. No thief is foolish enough to rob these people, for only the poor are passengers," C stated.

Taking a video-camera with a tripod and other gear could be quite inviting to thieves, so in an abundance of caution, we had placed our equipment inside of a white grain sack.

Since 1990, Jaime Rosenthal, the second richest man in Honduras and once perennial presidential candidate, had tried to lay claim to two hundred acres of beachfront property on beautiful Tela Bay in San Juan. In Honduras, people say that what Miguel Faccuse doesn't own, Jaime Rosenthal does. Rosenthal's problem was that some three hundred squatters also laid claim to the seaside land and had built their humble homes there while the dispute made its way through the courts.

Nuevo San Juan, as it is known, is adjacent to San Juan and has always been considered a part of it. It is village land and a natural place for expanding families to build.

Somehow, though, Rosenthal had acquired a title for it. In Honduras, it is not uncommon for more than one person to hold title to the same land, so having some papers doesn't necessarily prove anything. But papers or no papers, legal or illegal, Rosenthal was determined to build a multi-million dollar resort hotel right there on Tela Bay. And papers or no papers, the three hundred poor Garifuna and mestizo families were not going to leave their shacks in the sun-soaked seaside fields of Nuevo San Juan.

It seemed that Rosenthal had anticipated the OAS ruling and planned for it. He knew that his days were numbered unless he made a new move. This, we were to discover, was the never out-of-fashion bribe.

A couple of years before, in 2000, I had brought children's books for some primary schools in San Juan. The people there had asked me if I could help them acquire a seventy-watt radio transmitter, suitable for a pirate radio station. So on my next journey there, I brought two sets with me. One was for San Juan, and the other was for the Garifuna village of Punta Piedra, along the Garifuna Coast. I bought them in Berkeley and hid them among the books and other things I was carrying, and managed to cross two borders with them in an old Dodge van.

At the Copán border, the OFRANEH accountant was waiting for me in case I had problems. Though children's books had once defeated a military post on the Garifuna cay Chachahuate, the situation in San Juan was different. With a seventy-watt transmitter they could wage a war of words against Rosenthal for fifty kilometers down the flat coast. And that is exactly what the young Garifuna theater troupe did.

Arriving in Tela, we took a taxi to travel the seven kilometers to San Juan. It was a hot and dry summer, and the taxi driver drove so fast that he left a trail of dust eclipsing any roadside pedestrians. After he dropped us off next to the Catholic Church in San Juan, I paused to look at the small memorial plaque that listed the names of the eighteen victims of the 1936 massacre.

There, just in front of us, was the caressing Caribbean. Like two pelagic pincers, Punta Sal and Punta Izapo stretched out like the claws of a giant crab, forming Tela Bay. Not far away was the Jeannette Kawas National Park, named for the ex-mayor of Tela, a very fine woman who in 1995 was gunned down in her home because of her environmental activism.

"People don't read, but they listen," a young Garifuna man told me one day in San Juan, bragging about how good the radio was. He was part of the Garifuna theater troupe we had come to film. He was comparing the radio I brought them to the books which I had brought to San Juan's seaside primary school a couple of years before. And he was right! In bookless countries, and even in the US and Europe, people don't read much. In a place like Honduras, where there is hardly anything to read anyway, the written word is muffled by the spoken. The quiet, inner thoughts formed by a book are drowned out by boom-boxes. Most people would rather listen to a TV, radio, or CD, for many of them are not comfortable reading.

I responded to him, saying "Yes, but I gave those books to children to help improve their reading skills, not to some anti-bibliophile adults. I wouldn't waste my time bringing books to adults, unless they were for jails. The only printed materials you guys care about are money, cards, and lottery tickets. You would rather listen to yourselves talk. It seems that books scare you," I teased.

To put pressure on the situation in Nuevo San Juan, Rosenthal had paid judges to issue eviction notices. But no one left. Then he paid some thugs to burn down the house of a Garifuna leader. He also arranged for the Honduran military to send foot patrols to intimidate the villagers. Then he had his conservative newspaper, *El Tiempo*, print articles against the people of Nuevo San Juan, calling them "the invaders."

Things reached a boiling point when two Garifuna boys were found dead near San Juan. The villagers blamed the soldiers. Perhaps the boys had witnessed soldiers transporting drugs and were killed because of it, but it could also have been a revenge killing over the land. Honduras has the highest homicide rate in the world and "any stick will do to beat a dog." Perhaps it was learning of these murders, as well as the mysterious rape of a local Garifuna girl (also blamed on soldiers), that prompted the OAS to finally act after sixteen years.

All the while OFRANEH had been quietly reporting Rosenthal's abuses to the OAS. I remember how OFRANEH's two Italian lawyers used to joke about who would be killed first by Rosenthal. Both knew that it was no joke, though, for both were followed by shadowy characters every time they left the office. But it got even worse: Goya was shot. Not long after that, OFRANEH's office was raided and their computer hard drives and data were confiscated by the police.

We arrived in San Juan at that time of day when the sun bakes the beach sands and they were screaming hot; the faint whispers of a breeze offered no relief from the torrid tropical heat of the Honduran sun. It was time for a swim, but C was anxious to bring the news and photocopies of the OAS letter to the village leaders so we didn't linger long in the sea.

We walked a short distance and stopped at a tiny cinderblock house belonging to a Garifuna woman named Margarit. She lived there with her three children. Like the vast majority of the three hundred families in Nuevo San Juan, Margarit and her children were portraits of poverty. Only a few of the homes there could be considered adequate, and they were no doubt built with remittance money from relatives in the Bronx.

There she was, sitting in a broken chair in the shade of an Indian almond tree with her two sleeping pigs snoring beside her. Like all of the people of Nuevo San Juan, Margarit lived in constant uncertainty and fear of eviction because of Rosenthal's threats. She offered us food, but we told her "Later," and stayed just long enough to tell her the news.

We walked on, toward the burned-out house of our friend Will. C and I passed through a rickety gate that broke the barrier of a long hedgerow that bordered the property. C walked up, smiling as he excitedly waved the OAS letter. There in the shade of a large mango tree sat six Garifuna men, some quite elderly. Will, the owner, virtually lived under the mango tree ever since Rosenthal paid someone to torch his house. Its charred remains were a reminder of Rosenthal's burning greed.

"Bidi bnafi'" (good-morning), the men welcomed us in their native Garifuna language, as C proudly began to read the OAS letter aloud. He read it slowly and clearly, so that the older men would have no trouble understanding. The letter explicitly stated that the land belonged to the families living there and was not the property of Jaime Rosenthal. It also warned against any retribution on Rosenthal's part. Then, after parts the letter were re-read, it was passed around. One of the men then took several of the photocopies to post around the village. This was the best news that Nuevo San Juan had heard in many years! They all hoped that perhaps now the threats, intimidations, arsons, rapes, shootings, and murders would end. Some, knowing that Rosenthal's revenge respected no law, said they would continue to pack a pistol.

Some hours later, we returned to Margarit's house to eat the meal she had prepared for us. Her two pigs had just returned from foraging, but still snorted shamelessly for a handout. They only left when Margarit's little dog jealously chased them away.

Knowing that I had only a sheet for bedding, C asked me where I wanted to sleep for the night. I said I didn't know. He had a little piece of foam he slept on in the building that housed the radio.

We decided I would stay in one of the cane cabins down on the beach, which was owned by a man named Tongo. I had heard many bad stories about Tongo, but we had never met. He hated C, who concocted a little plan that he asked me to help with.

On past visits to San Juan, C and I would drive to Lancetilla, the nearby botanical gardens. We would stay in a bungalow there and swim in the river. "Too bad the van isn't working," I told him, "because it would sure be nice to sleep in a bamboo bed in Lancetilla again."

"Yeah, I'd like to see the poisonous plant section again, too," he responded with a laugh.

Lancetilla is the largest botanical garden in Central America. It is nestled by a river in a jungle valley which means that it is always a bit cooler there. Its many varieties of bamboo, rare tropical trees from all over the world, and the orchard house are all very impressive. It was created under the direction of William Popenoe, a gifted research botanist who worked for the Standard Fruit Company in the 1930s. He was also was the person who developed the Hass avocado. There in the poisonous plant section, Popenoe's wife is buried beside a fenced-in Aki tree. She had eaten the famously seductive forbidden fruit and it had killed her. "Perhaps he gave it to her," C sinisterly conjectured.

Instead of this tropical paradise, it was to Tongo's I would go. It didn't take much for C to convince me to play with Tongo's mind, because that was actually my main reason for agreeing to sleep there.

To understand Tongo one must first know that it was his father who lied to the Honduran military in 1936, leading to the massacre of the eighteen Garifuna in San Juan. Then, to further understand Tongo, one must know that he is the lackey, the myrmidon of Jaime Rosenthal—his eyes and ears in San Juan. And to really understand Tongo, one must know that his son Kiki was a leader in the theater troupe until he tried to take it over and they kicked him out.

"Why don't you tell that quisling Tongo that you work for Condoleezza Rice?" C suggested. "That will make him very paranoid. Tongo knows that the US State Department knows about the problems in San Juan. He doesn't know you though and he'll probably believe you if you do it right. And even if he doesn't believe you, he'll wonder what is going on."

So just before dark, I walked down the beach to Tongo's group of cane-walled and thatch-roofed cabins. They were built as a community tourist project in the late 1980s using money from USAID. Within a couple years, the crafty and irascible Tongo had taken control of the facilities and chased out the other co-op members.

I got a cabin with a sand floor and decided to have dinner at the restaurant Tongo has next to his cabins. I sat down at a table on the deck where I could see him sitting alone at a table inside, accompanied only by several empty beer bottles. A few minutes after a worker took my order, Tongo approached my table. He was drunk! C was completely correct when he had told me that Tongo would want to know what I was doing in San Juan.

I told him that I was waiting for my dinner and he asked if I would like a beer. I knew that wasn't why he had come over, but I agreed. He then took a seat at the table and started asking me questions like, "Is this the first time you have visited San Juan?" and "How do you like it?" Then with very little tact, he asked, "Well, what brings you to San Juan then?" I was purposely baiting him by being evasive, which I knew would make him even more suspicious and curious.

"Oh, I'm just having a look around," I said.

Sipping his beer, he asked me, "Well, what kind of work do you do?"

Pausing, I knew that I had him. Looking him straight in the eyes, I quietly answered, "Let's just say that my boss is Condoleezza Rice. Do you know who she is?"

Just then the woman came with my dinner, giving Tongo the perfect opportunity to leave. My answer had made him nervous—it wasn't the answer he that wanted to hear. I only saw him once more. The next day we passed each other at a short distance, but he pretended not to see me. I just laughed to myself and kept walking.

That same day, as I left the small block building which housed the radio station, I noticed Tongo's son Kiki watching me. He remembered me from my prior visit and my involvement in bringing the seventy-watt radio. Kiki was becoming more like his father and undoubtedly informed Tongo about me. I had been told about how Kiki had tried to take control of the radio station. He had been a leader of the theatrical troupe which controlled the radio, their new weapon against Rosenthal. No doubt Tongo knew of this plan. After an argument some months earlier, Kiki took the transmitter and kept it at his house for several weeks.

When the theater troupe planned to perform the play about the 1936 massacre, Kiki reacted with opposition and resentment. He was embarrassed and ashamed because it had been his own grandfather who had informed the military. For Kiki, the play was an attack on his family. It was when the troupe refused to give up their plan to perform the play that he had taken the transmitter. "The sins of the fathers visited upon the children..."

Unknown to us at the time, Rosenthal had made one last desperate attempt to get control of the land by bribing Jessica, the president of Nuevo San Juan village. She was a Garifuna single mother of three daughters and had accepted the bribe. She was so poor that she couldn't resist. All of this occurred just a few days before the OAS decision, and Rosenthal must have felt some hope of victory. He had certainly anticipated the OAS ruling and had tried to counter it by getting Jessica's signature on the land title. These stealthy actions once again involved the prevaricator Tongo, who informed Jessica that money had been transferred into her bank account. Once she received it, she was obligated to turn over the signed title to Nuevo San Juan to Rosenthal.

But the plan started to unravel fast when OFRANEH found out. Not only could they prove that Jessica had betrayed her community, but they could also prove that Rosenthal was the source of the bribe. When OFRANEH leaders pressed her for information, Jessica broke down in tears. She told them that one of Rosenthal's thugs had put a gun to her head to make her sign. Everyone knew, though, that her incentive was the money. There had been no gun to her head, at least not yet.

Bribery is a problem throughout Honduras, and especially in Garifuna villages. Men like Rosenthal prey on people's poverty and try to conquer them by division. The easiest way to do that is to tempt a village leader with money. Honor, integrity, fealty, and even their communities can all be for sale—it is just a matter of price.

What frightened Jessica was not what the people of Nuevo San Juan would do when they found out. She knew the passivity of the Garifuna; they would do nothing, just talk. No, what frightened her was what Rosenthal would do when he found out that she had spent all the bribe money and he still didn't have the title. Her tears of fear were mostly for her daughters. Perhaps Rosenthal would do something to them; maybe they would suffer for her dishonesty. She spoke of fleeing to Belize. After all, that's how things work in Honduras.

Chapter 10

THE RAMA OF NICARAGUA

"We'll make real men out of Indians [through schooling]"—Caesar Sandino

On my way from Managua's airport to Granada, my amiable taxi driver proudly told me, "Look at the volcanoes!"

"Yes," I said, "They are really something! But we have a much larger volcano in the United States."

"Oh really, what is its name?" he asked.

"Its name is Washington, DC!" I answered, which prompted an eruption of laughter from the elderly driver.

"Oh, yes, señor, and it is very active," he added with another laugh.

Such was my entry into this charming and sometimes disarming land. I had returned to Granada, Nicaragua for its annual book fair. It was February 2013, just before Valentine's Day. All government leaders gave a red rose away on that day of lovers.

"Too bad they don't give even a pencil away to most schools," I thought.

Granada, one of the oldest colonial cities on tierra firma, still has a grace about it. Though its people may stumble over the prose of its history, they walk or run with its poetry. But in this land of many riches, nearly everyone is poor. Nicaragua is a land with the most beautiful wicker rocking-chairs, but very few people have time to sit in one and even fewer can afford to buy one. The mangoes are cheap, though, and the coffee strong and determined, like the people's will.

Unlike Costa Rica and Panama, which have become more Americanized, the Nicaraguan people have retained more of their traditional culture. Despite once having been the bread basket of Central America, it has now become a basket case, although it is still is a nice country. Now, as in Panama and Costa Rica, foreign land speculators circle overhead like vultures in search of opportunities. Very few of the children there will have an opportunity to buy a piece of their own country's land, because rising prices keep it forever out of reach. But what can one expect from a revolution in which the Sandinista leaders claimed the mansions of Somoza?

Contrary to my experiences in 2011, the book fair of 2013 turned out to be quite disappointing. Everything was priced in dollars and there was very little selection. Plus, I did not get my discount. In 2011, I had bought enough books and supplies for ten schools in the Solentiname archipelago, Monkey Point, and some Garifuna and Miskito villages along the Caribbean. But in 2013 there weren't enough good books for ten schools, so I ended up only getting enough books for a couple of schools and calling it quits. These books were going to some Rama communities in the Indio Maíze Biological Reserve, which is located just off the Caribbean coast in the extreme southeastern part of Nicaragua. I had wanted to go there in 2011, but had run out of books at that time.

The book fair happens in conjunction with Granada's annual poetry fair, held every February since 2004. Nicaragua's revolutionary ex-priest and poet, Ernesto Cardinal, helped start it. At night one could hear the registered poets recite to a dressed-up audience seated on Granada's plaza. For me, though, the real meter of the place came from the cadence of passionate street poets reciting on tiny stages at closed-off intersections.

Lovely colonial Granada was one of the first casualties of the Monroe Doctrine. It was once burned by William Walker in the 1850s, after he declared himself president. He was recognized as such by the US government, but by no one else, especially not in Nicaragua.

I returned from the book fair to my market-side hotel with a few boxes. Outside of that walled-in oasis, it's a different world—throngs of Granada's poor walk through the detritus of the streets. A flattened dead rat revealed that it had been in the lane for some time. But the wide smile on the old woman nearby, who sells me seeds, revealed that she was happy to see me.

Two of the ten schools that I had brought books to in 2011 are worth noting. One is on the Solentiname Archipelago in Lake Nicaragua, and the other is at Monkey Point along the Caribbean coast.

One morning I had traveled by boat to visit two schools, along with Señora Guevara. Her two brothers had been killed by Anastasio Somoza and now had an island named after them. One of the schools was on Mancarron, only a half mile away in a quiet little cove. It was just fifty meters from the pebble beach, set back in the scrub forest.

We were spotted approaching by a group of twelve kids, who wondered who we were and waited anxiously for our arrival. We tied the boat to a tree and I carried a big box up the trail to the school, where a flower-bed of faces greeted us. The tiny room had a back wall of cinder block, and on the other three sides the walls went up only about a meter. Cyclone fencing enclosed everything. The school seemed more like an aviary than anything. A wide overhang kept out most of the weather, but a tarp was rolled up along one side. In the middle of the small room was a large wooden table with benches placed around it.

There, like a group of half-starved chickens, the kids picked at the very few pedagogical grains that existed. I was shocked by the emptiness of the place. Ironically, I donated a couple of Ernesto Cardinal's children's books, which I had purchased from the Nicaraguan publisher, Libros para Niños (Books for Kids). I remember wondering why there was such a dearth of books, and even such a lack of paper and pencils, especially since it was so close to the Solentiname artists community.

It seemed that Cardinal's version of liberation theology was unfortunately more interested in restoring the revolutionary church than in the education of the island's youth. Later, I let my feelings be known, after finding out that the community had received a grant for $40,000 to repair the old adobe church. Something was surely wrong with this picture! I told Señora Guevara that I thought God would prefer that the Archipelago's kids get the $40,000 for their schools, rather than the church. I must say, my thoughts did not receive a welcome response. The adobe building blocks of the church seemed more important than the building blocks of the nation—the kids.

Monkey Point has been a flash point in recent years. Although it is in the autonomous indigenous zone of the Región Autónoma del Atlántico Norte (RAAN), the Nicaraguan government has plans to make it a container port, contrary to the will of the Rama people. Monkey Point is the best deep-water port along Nicaragua's Caribbean coast. Because of its remoteness and the opposition to the government's plans, several soldiers were posted in Monkey Point by the Nicaraguan government.

From Bluefields, I traveled with Alan Duncan and several other Rama and Creole leaders in a panga with a seventy-five-horsepower motor south along the coast to Monkey Point. Having passed Rama Cay, the main population center of the Rama, we soon exited Bluefields Lagoon and entered the open Caribbean. The nearer we got to Monkey Point, the hillier the land became. All along the way, the coastal forest showed signs of repeated storm damage. After about an hour, we landed on a white sand beach, which is one of several bordered by finger-like points that stick out into the blue Caribbean. Separated by thickly forested hills are the thirty or so wood-frame homes of Monkey Point.

After we landed at this lovely beach, the soldiers came and asked me to show my passport. They scrutinized it and seemed suspicious of my assertion that I was there to help the school. Their office, which was right on the beach, had once been the home of an elderly woman villager. They had expropriated it when she was in Managua.

I spent a few days at lovely Monkey Point, sleeping on the floor of Alan Duncan's family home. He was a Creole-Rama indigenous leader who was working in the Rama's office in Bluefields. One of his sisters was the teacher at the local school.

As with almost every indigenous school, there were no books and hardly any of the twenty kids had a pen or notebook. That's what passes for normal. As in Cuba, Nicaragua had also had a literacy project. Without any materials or books, though, the kids seemed bored, as did the teacher. Since they never had even one book to read, they hungrily took the ones I had brought like food. One boy who seemed somewhat educationally challenged was not interested, however. He had been kept back two or three years due to academic and disciplinary problems, and stood head and shoulders above the other kids. The books and writing materials did not interest him. While the others looked through the books, he sat unhappily apart.

I had wanted to give the books and writing materials first, but I also had art supplies, which no one knew about yet. Watching him sit there, I unpacked the art supplies and saw an immediate change in his demeanor. That is what interested him, for he could barely read or write. He felt frustrated and was looking for a way to express himself. The pen was not the tool for him, but the brush was! Of course the art supplies caught everyone else's attention too, but he was fixated. Just as none of them had ever held a children's book before, none of them had ever held a paint brush or colored pencil, either.

Clara, the teacher, suggested that I hand out some paper from the ream for the kids to paint. So, after pushing the desks together and placing the paints in the middle, everyone started to work. Suddenly the boy seemed very interested and his attention became focused. For half an hour or more, all of them drew and painted together in silence. Meanwhile, I talked with Alan's sister, the teacher. She, of course, noticed the effect on the boy even more than I had. When the time came to a close, the boy did not want to stop painting.

For the next couple of days, after going by boat down to the Rama "school" at Eagle Point, I gave away seeds. People came by Alan's home to receive them. Everyone had gardens, but they had few varieties of vegetables. I sat and made up packets of seeds for tomatoes, cucumbers, pipian squash, giant papayas, watermelons, and other plants.

On his fourth voyage, Columbus landed at a river's mouth along Nicaragua's Caribbean coast. It was most likely Rio Punta Gorda, near present-day Monkey Point. While there, he kidnapped two indigenes, probably Rama, and forced them to serve as guides. Thus the Rama's initial contact with Europeans got off to a very bad start, which led to five centuries of bad relations.

The name Rama is of uncertain origin, though it may have come from the Spanish word for branch (rama) or possibly from the name of the Rama River, a tributary of the Rio Escondido. It seems that the Rama may have been part of the same tribe as the Voto and Melchora. Whatever their origin, it is certain that the Monkey Point area is one of the oldest archeological sites in all of Central America. A shell mound nearly thirty meters high possibly dates back over seven thousand years.

The Rama were some of the best boatmen along the Caribbean coast and were expert at making sea-going canoes. Over fifty men at a time could paddle in these huge dugouts. These were the boats that the Miskito tribe used to raid and terrorize the whole Western Caribbean coast, capturing slaves from as far north as Campeche, Mexico to as far south as the San Blas Islands of Panama. During those centuries dominated by the Miskito, the Rama were forced to pay tribute in the form of hammocks, canoes, and other goods.

The ethnographer Conzemius mentions how the influence of Moravian missionaries, starting in 1859, led to profound changes in the Rama, particularly in their language decline and a negative perception of their ethnic identity. Along with language loss came land loss, and loss of trust, as both the Nicaraguans of Spanish descent and the English claimed their land.

The small town of San Carlos is built on the southeastern edge of Lake Nicaragua, where the mouth of the San Juan River begins its 190-kilometer journey towards the Caribbean. The San Juan became the most important New World river, as it offered more hope for "a path between the seas" than any other. This was the river that Columbus was searching for but never found. Later it was proposed as a canal route, but was turned down by the US Congress in favor of Panama. They were swayed when lobbyists used a drawing of a Nicaraguan postage stamp with threatening volcanoes looming over Lake Nicaragua, and so decided on Panama.

In 1673, to protect Granada, the Spanish built a fort they called El Castillo de la Inmaculada Concepción on a hill on the right bank of the San Juan River. After many battles with pirates, Lord Nelson and 3,500 men took El Castillo in 1780. It appears that the next invasion will come from Chinese construction companies, which are poised to start building a new four-billion-dollar canal.

In 2013, on an overcrowded boat with over a hundred passengers, I headed down river with my load of books. The trip started in San Carlos, on the shore of Lake Nicaragua, and ended at San Juan del Norte. On that twelve-hour journey, I saw more alligators than I had on many journeys in the Amazon. They seemed to know they are protected and rested along the shore, unconcerned by our presence. Their days are numbered, though, as the river will soon be dredged and construction will begin on the new canal. Besides having gators, the San Juan is the only river in the world inhabited by sharks. Over time, these dangerous bull sharks have adapted to the fresh water and migrated up into Lake Nicaragua. As a result, people are reluctant to enter the water and seldom learn to swim.

San Juan del Norte, which is located near the estuary, is a quiet village without a single car. Although it is near the Caribbean, it is not a sea town—it is rather a river town. It is actually built along Rio Indio, which parallels the nearby Caribbean sea for miles. The population is mainly Black, but there is a small Rama barrio. The men fish the coastal waters as well as the rivers. At night the alligators trudge their way through San Juan del Norte, leaving trails of smashed plants as telltale signs of their presence. They love to eat dogs and many have disappeared as part of the food chain.

It was Charles Grey, Jamaica's British governor, who actually founded the town in 1848 and thoughtfully named it after himself, although no one calls it Greytown today. As was often the case, it was probably built on the site of an old indigenous community, probably Miskito.

Though it is now hard to believe, at one time there were 126 different embassies represented there. Because it was being proposed as a canal site, the British wanted to secure the mouth of the San Juan River and so insure their control of any future canal. This led to friction with the US, which took offense, as they had laid claims and considered it their "backyard" by right of the Monroe Doctrine.

In 1852, after friction led the British to burn the home of the US ambassador in Greytown, the US retaliated by having a naval ship, the Cyan, bombard the village. Greytown may hold the record for being the most-bombed town in North America. They say it was bombed three separate times. The shelling by the Cyan was the first. Then in 1894, Nicaragua's president Zalaya attacked it when the Miskito Coast officially became part of Nicaragua. About a hundred years later, in the 1980s, the Sandinista leader Commandante Cero strafed San Juan del Norte with helicopter gunships and burned it to the ground. This was because Eden

Pastora's Contra faction had made it their headquarters. A few years later, in 1990, the Sandinista government built the new San Juan at its present location. Then Hurricane Joan did more damage to the town in 1988 than any of the bombings and gunfire.

I arrived there with enough books for two schools, and soon located a Rama leader named Coyote to help me deliver them. He lived with his children in the Rama barrio, and I stayed in a hotel nearby. I enjoyed being in San Juan and getting to know its people. It was a pleasure to see thick gardens of dasheen (*Colocasia esculenta*), the well-loved tuber of the Caribbean, growing thickly beside some of the houses. For food, I would go out and buy a nice snook. Lolito, the proprietor of my hotel, would cook it for me Creole style.

After staying in San Juan for a few days, I journeyed upriver with Coyote and another man to deliver books. A small aluminum skiff with a fifteen-horsepower motor took the three of us up the Rio Indio as far as a Rama village of the same name. It was truly a picturesque river, full of fish, bird, and animal life. Coyote pointed out a school of large fish, called mojarras, swimming in a clear pool near the shadowy bank. A few minutes later, a pair of noisy blue macaws passed overhead. Howler monkeys regularly called out from the tree tops like noisy evangelicos. Red- and white-faced monkeys scurried like acrobats among the tree branches. A large green iguana fell from a low overhanging tree and landed right into the boat, surprising us all. It tried to avoid our pursuing hands as it scurried around the boat; finally it escaped by jumping into the river and swimming away.

In some places, especially further downriver, wide-leafed silico palms (*Raphia taedigera*) seemed to jealously line the banks, growing so thickly that nothing else could compete. This palm, Coyote told me, besides being used for thatch, also has properties that can alleviate malarial fever.

As we passed by a couple of riverside farms, I asked Coyote to tell me what he knew about them. Although the river is in an autonomous indigenous and protected bio-reserve area, the best properties have been taken by outsiders, mainly Ladinos. They had taken over some very beautiful property at the bends of the river. Not the law, but the lawless gun gave them the land, and the Rama can do nothing about it because of Nicaragua's dysfunctional government.

Not far before the small Rama community of Rio Indio, we stopped beside a typical Rama home that had been built on a hillside clearing above the river. It was Coyote's farm. An old Rama couple stayed there and the woman fed the three of us lunch. While the other boatman went to cut stalks of bananas to take back, Coyote proudly pointed out the Pejibaye palms (*Bactris gasipaes*), which he had planted some years before. Also known as the peach palm, black palm, chunga, or pono palm, these trees have a pincushion of needle-like spines covering their long narrow trunks. The Rama have cultivated them for many centuries. Besides using the small fruits, which grow in clusters, the very hard jet black wood is commonly used for bows, spears, and canes.

Although Rio Indio did not have a proper school like other communities, I decided to give the books to them anyway. I would use the method developed by the Nicaraguan publisher Libros para Niños and have some adults care for the books. Coyote also thought that it would be good, and that perhaps it would be an impetus for the community to get a proper school through the government. The fact that there is no school there is one of the reasons why the community is dying.

Somehow schools, despite the fact that they often lack pedagogical value, act as anchors for communities. Without a school, communities drift like boats with no direction. Rio Indio has lost about one hundred children because of the lack of a school, which does not signal a bright future for the community. Families with children move away, and most of the kids don't want to return once they have studied in San Juan. Ultimately this plays right into the hands of those who want to end their autonomy and take their land. The Nicaraguan government has known for years about Rio Indio's situation, but it purposely does nothing in order to lessen the Ramas' hopes for stronger autonomy and tribal cohesion.

Later the same day we returned to San Juan. I finished giving away all the books there and at one other school. Then I made arrangements with Coyote to visit the site of the original Greytown. The next day we paddled over in his dugout with his twelve-year-old son, Vladimir.

A hundred and fifty years ago, this was a bustling spot, but now it is only home to a new airport and the nearby Rio Indio Lodge, which is an ultra-expensive lodge for tarpon fishing. The first thing one sees there is a giant old dredger rusting in the lagoon; it had once been owned by Cornelius Vanderbilt. It is a massively clumsy collection of rusted iron looming six stories high and looking somewhat like an oil derrick. This dredger had once been used to carve out areas for ships in a protected part of the lagoon. Until the recent construction of cell towers, it had been the tallest man-made thing for miles in any direction.

Vanderbilt had run a transport service there beginning in 1851, which supplied passage across Nicaragua to those on their way to the California Gold Rush. The ferry used was once destroyed by William Walker, an enemy of Vanderbilt at the time. Mark Twain had also traveled these waters in 1867.

Coyote wanted me to see the old railroad landing, so we paddled over there across the quiet lagoon. The narrow gauge railway had once hauled various local forest products, such as sarsaparilla, chicle gum, and logs, to waiting ships for export.

As we paddled by the lodge, the owner called out to Coyote. Some dentists were there who wanted to talk with him about a free clinic they were offering the next day in San Juan. After landing at the dock of the posh fishing resort, I found myself talking with the owner, who Coyote had just been telling me about.

The owner is Costa Rican, but he has four or five American partners, and possibly an ex-president of Nicaragua as a silent partner. In 2007 or so he made an agreement to acquire the land through the Rama tribe for a fishing resort, which was to benefit the Rama as well. But as usual, as soon as the papers were signed, the contract was forgotten, having drowned in the ink. Though the lodge pays the San Juan mayor's office an annual tax, the Rama have never received a penny. On the contrary, they have been defrauded of their share in the lodge and lost their land in the bargain.

After the owner asked me what I was doing in the area, the conversation quickly turned to education. After I mentioned that we had just been in Rio Indio, he said, "Oh we paid for school uniforms." In his mind, I suppose that justified the theft of their valuable land. He went on to tell me how his lodge had once paid the American wife of a young Rama leader $150 a month to teach school in Rio Indio. It hadn't worked out, though, as she became pregnant and quit.

"What they need is their own school," I told him. "A village that continually loses its children to San Juan because they have no school is a village without a future. If this keeps up, in a few years Rio Indio will not exist and that would be a shame."

The owner agreed and then described how the lodge was helping the Rama community by hiring its men as fishing guides. His self-justification was spread so thick that it dripped like sickeningly sweet frosting off the sides of a cake. People usually have a way of doing things to cover up their flaws, or a guilty conscience. But this man certainly didn't see himself as a thief who got away with stealing a valuable piece of Rama land and defrauding the Rama community out of a lucrative tarpon fishing partnership. He is convinced that the lodge is helping the Rama.

When the lodge is full during the high season, it makes about $20,000 a day. Meanwhile the Rama workers receive two hundred córdobas (eight dollars) a day for ten hours of work and receive no benefits. They can barely feed their families with that, and the demanding work leaves them no time to farm.

Once we left I tried to convince Coyote that the Rama should sue the lodge for breach of contract.

"The Rama will win in any fair court," I said. "You should ask for five years of retroactive payments. That would be a minimum of half-a-million dollars! Don't you think the Rama community could use that money more than some rich foreign men who stole your land? You must do something for the children. This fishing lodge has stolen their future!" But these were easy words for a gringo to say.

Coyote could only sadly answer, "If we act, they will do something back. Maybe they will burn my house, or worse." It seems that the deck is stacked against them and there is little hope for the Rama community.

PART FOUR: PANAMA

Chapter 11

DARIÉN AND A GOAT TOWARDS THE GAP

"I have never let schooling interfere with my education."—Mark Twain

One of the first things I noticed when returning to the Caledonia section of Panama City in 2007 was that the Continental Book Store, where for years I had gotten nearly all the material for my work with Panama's indigenous schools, was going out of business. I was shocked to see a large sign reading "remate" (sale) hanging outside. Then I wanted to take advantage of it, for there is really nowhere else in Panama, or all of Central America, with affordable children's books. The three-story bookstore was being replaced with a parking lot for a Fiesta casino. How perfectly imperfect, I thought. For me, it seemed like a statement about Panama's values or lack thereof. But at ninety-one, the owner, a still elegant Cuban lady, had the right to shut down after forty years in business. If it was up to her she would have given me most of the books, but that did not happen because the owner of the building ran the sale. It was the last chance I had in Panama to get a lot of Spanish-language children's books at a very good price. Soon, with the help of a friend who paid for many of the books, we wheeled and dealed with the proprietor until he agreed to sell the books for $20 per box.

Meanwhile the old building adjacent had just been torn down by a crane with a wrecking ball. Part of a shared wall was demolished, which exposed some second- and third-floor rooms full of books to the busy street below. I spent three weeks there that December, searching through three floors of dusty shelves for books I could use. Nearly all of them had been bundled and wrapped in brown paper years before and were just sitting there, collecting dust. Every time I would lift a bundle off of the shelf and unwrap it, dust would cling to me like a mop. In the dark stifling heat with my dust mask, flashlight, and headscarf, I felt like a miner who had just found the mother lode. Besides the books, we purchased thousands of German- and Czech-made pencils. And we found notebooks, colored pencils, colored chalk, wooden rulers, triangles, compasses, maps, and more, all very cheap. We also found dozens of American-made crank-style pencil sharpeners that were still in their unopened boxes after thirty years. We bought them all for two dollars each. Finally, after days of searching, separating, and packing, I ended up with one-hundred and five bulging boxes, each containing about a hundred and thirty children's books. We had more than 13,000 books and more than a dozen boxes of supplies.

Later it took three of us a couple of days to separate and sort the books, so that each box contained a selection of about twenty books for each of the six primary grades. A dictionary, a children's version of *Don Quixote*, and Jose Marti's classic *El Edad de Oro* (*The Age of Gold*) graced each box. There were also lots of books about fauna, flora, and nature, which kids always like. Whether in a quixotic way or not, the boxes of pencils seemed like bullets, and the books and notebooks seemed like bombs, all ready to explode the demons of illiteracy and ignite the imaginative minds of bookless little kids. This was the ammunition dump for my little battles against illiteracy among Panama's indigenous.

Each indigenous primary school would receive a box of books and lots of school supplies, while each student would get a notebook, a pencil, and a pen. I would spend the next eighteen months traveling among Panama's seven indigenous tropical forest tribes: the Naso, Bri Bri, Ngabe-Bugle, Kuna, Embera, and Waounan. Some of the qualities that all of these indigenous primary schools shared in common were a material emptiness, a sense of abandonment, and an intense desire to learn.

For me, the hardest part of getting the books, besides the dust and the darkness, was dealing with the owner of the building. He was a Spanish man, Manolo, and he took charge of selling everything.

"The only thing you want to do is to count money. You should have been a bank teller," I told him once when paying, because he wouldn't lift a finger.

He was part of a very separate cabal, a quite disliked community of Spaniards, mostly from Galicia, who own most of the hotels in Panama City. Since I was doing all the work alone, from getting and assembling the boxes, to sorting through and packing everything, I literally stuffed the boxes with books until they bulged. I wanted to buy all of the children's books, pencils, paper, and supplies, but Manolo wanted to keep some for other customers. Fair enough, I thought, but he did so thinking that he could make more money selling individual books. But he hardly sold any and in the end he had a huge amount left over. His problem was that the building was being demolished faster than he could sell things. After buying all we could, I left for Darién.

People later told me that a big dumpster finally came and everything left was thrown inside and taken away the same day. "Manolo wouldn't give anything away, but he didn't mind throwing it away," they said. I also heard that he kept more than twenty boxes of children's books, the ones he wouldn't sell me before. Months later in Panama City, I saw him with his young sons in a restaurant. We spoke briefly and he told me that thieves stole the twenty boxes of books. What a pity for the school kids, I thought, but it served him right. Surely the thieves didn't know what they were stealing.

Rarely do any students in indigenous or marginalized schools hold a children's book, for books are virtually never found in either their schools or their homes. The government never purchases children's books and this is something the tribal organizations should invest in for themselves, although they don't. The Kunas, for instance, will hire the best lawyers of all the indigenous tribes in Central America to work for them, but they never help out their own schools. I find this very odd, because they appreciate books and surely could afford to do this.

Panama's MEDUCA, the Ministry of Education, didn't seem to have any problem shelling out money for gilded framed portraits of every Minister of Education from 1903 onward to line the walls of its lobby, or even to purchase colorful logo golf shirts for its workers. Yet it never spends a dime to buy children's books for remote schools, especially for indigenous comarcas (counties). As with so many other countries, it seems that the schools exist for the Ministry of Education and not the way around. Very few rural families can afford to spend a day's wage to buy their children a book, especially when they are lacking food and clothing. This is true for required textbooks as well, which amount to about sixty dollars a year for a fourth grader.

Unfortunately, basically the only printed materials available in Panama are lottery tickets, counterfeit dollars, a few rag newspapers, and some glossy-paper business magazines. The neediest places in terms of books are government primary schools in the semi-autonomous comarcas, Panama's indigenous homelands. The poverty index there can go off the charts. Juxtaposing dirt floor primary schools in the comarcas to marble-floored laundromat-like banks in Panama City's Mar Bella banking district is a sad commentary on greed. Panama ranks only behind South Africa and Brazil in economic disparity. According to the 2009 *Statistical Journal* from the Economic Commission for Latin America and the

Caribbean (CEPAL), cognitive functions are impaired among 25% of all indigenous children in Panama because of malnutrition—and it is not getting any better. This is something one doesn't expect in a place whose capital boasts of being home to some 250 banks, the very lucrative Panama Canal, and shopping malls filled with stores with all the expensive brand names.

Purposeful governmental neglect of indigenous schools seems to be the way things work. The Panamanian government seems to be penalizing the indigenous for wanting autonomy and control of their destiny and natural resources. In all of the five indigenous comarcas, a very high percentage of the people live without money. Kinship connections of shared reciprocity are still more valuable to many than money. "Money makes us poor!" a Kuna writer complained. While time once allowed kinship obligations of sharing and helping to sustain them, now relying on money has changed all that. Working for daily wages often leaves no extra time or resources for people to help their needy kin. The more that indigenous people rely on money, the more their ancient ways disappear. Only their gardens of yams and other root crops, plantains, bananas, rice, and wild fruits maintain them.

More than a quarter of the books I had were going to poor indigenous primary schools in Darién. For the first journey I decided to visit ten riverside Embera and Waounan communities up two rivers, the Chucunaque and the Tuira rivers near Yaviza. The Chucunaque is Panama's longest river. It empties into the Tuira, which was the first waterway to export gold on the continent.

I bought some topographic maps from Tommy Guardia, Panama's cartographical office, and then it was a matter of just getting there. Not only did my friend help buy some of the books, but he and another friend offered to drive me down as far as Santa Fe. This is actually the first town in Darién. We took more than twenty boxes for the schools in a long-body Ford van.

On the way to Santa Fe, we stopped at a dirt road school near the headwaters of the Sabana River. We had met the teacher in

Panama City and promised her some books and supplies for her one-room school. Because the school was so hard to find, we arrived late, just after most of the kids had left. Quickly realizing the situation, the teacher had one of the boys mount his horse and ride after the other children, who were already far down the road. Soon they all returned, most running on foot behind some others on horses. Most of these kids were from poor Ladino ranching families and several rode horses to school. But despite living better than nearby Kunas or Waounan Indians, their school was just as needy.

The next day we stopped at a Waounan Indian school in Puerto Lara and also at the Kuna village Ipeti. Though just off the paved road, Ipeti seemed a universe away. A couple of rows of small cane and thatch homes revealed a stark poverty. In the years before, Ipeti had been a flash point because the Kunas there were losing land to land-lusting Ladino ranchers. Though the perimeters of the comarcas are defined, enforcement is deficient, difficult, and left up to the tribe. Historically it is aggressive ranchers who are the better armed.

From Santa Fe I caught a chivo, a goat, which is a collective pickup truck, into which we loaded the boxes from the van. Though he already had several passengers, the driver crammed fifteen boxes into the back and onto the roof rack of the truck. So it was that I was riding in a goat towards the Gap.

Before continuing with my journey up the rivers, allow me to relate some of the twisted history of Darién. It is a place seldom written about or visited. Yet it was the first place Anglos settled on mainland America nearly five hundred years ago.

The Yaviza Road, though pitted with potholes in places, was better than a lot of others we had just left. Soon the whole road to Yaviza would be paved. The road was "finished" in 1985, but in the 1970s this end of the Pan-American Highway was stopped by a U.S. District Court order against the U.S. Department of Transportation. Panama failed to do an environmental impact study and analyze such problems as hoof-and-mouth disease and the impact of the highway on indigenous communities. It was found that the importance of fluvial-maritime commerce in the Darién declined with the building of the highway to Yaviza. Now several Embera villages up the Chucunaque River use an access road directly from the river to the Pan American highway just outside of Meteti. This saves them a two- or three-day float trip down the river to Yaviza. For centuries indigenous people used to tie together large thirty- or forty-pound yams and float on them for days down the Chucunaque to sell in Yavisa. From there, boats would take them downriver to La Palma on the Gulf of San Miguel and then by sea to Panama City.

The chivo first went to Meteti and then on to Yaviza. Much of the land down to Meteti, three hours from Yavisa, has been logged off long ago for ranch land. As in all of Latin America, many people want to be cowboys and raise their holy hamburger cattle. For those looking to launder money, beef cattle can be very tempting as they are easily traded at auctions. Brands are easy to change and cows are hard to trace. So just as some Kunas trade cocos for coca, some ranchers trade cows for coca.

It was the historian Bancroft who once described Panama as "that double flexion of isthmian land twisting like the Greek sigma." Always seeming to challenge one's sense of direction, magnetic north in Panama doesn't seem to be constant. The sun appears to rise where one would think it should set and set where it should rise. The Pacific Ocean is sometimes in the south and other times in the west, or east, or both.

Panama's isthmian geography determined its destiny and its people's mentality. If Panama were a little wider it would never have been the place of passage it became, but rather Nicaragua would have been the "path between the seas." Darién is still an enigma hidden inside a riparian wilderness of labyrinthine riddles. It is a difficult place to get to, but an easy place to get lost in. Not only individuals, but whole countries have gotten lost there, body, mind, and soul. In 1700, Scotland went bankrupt and lost its sovereignty and independence because of their disastrous colonial Caledonia adventure in Darién. It was then, after over-investing in their colonial failure, that Scotland became part of Great Britain and signed the Treaty of the Union.

The Spanish chronicler Peter Martyr, who coined the term "New World," was also the first to mention Darién. Originally Darién was the name of a village and river on the western shore of the Gulf of Uraba. It was the home of Cemaco, the "Lord of Darién." Here, in 1510, Balboa chose to build the mainland's first long-term Spanish settlement, Santa Maria de Antigua del Darién. But it was built on expropriated land, thus ensuring the lasting hatred of its cacique, (chief), Cemaco, and his people. Though many other indigenous leaders, such as Hatuey of Cuba, had already suffered similar losses, now the Spanish were no longer confined to islands, but had two whole continents to take.

What Infante Cabrera said about Fidel Castro holds true for Balboa: history may forgive Balboa, who was far nobler than any of the other conquistadors, but geography will not. For by founding the first mainland New World settlement on land stolen from Cemaco and his people, he set a precedent for the theft of indigenous land and gold for half a millennia. After building on stolen indigenous land, Balboa had Darién's name changed to Santa María la Antiqua del Darién, as if the mother of Christ legitimized this real estate theft. It was the original sin of the New World mainland.

Today the settlement would actually be found inside of Colombia, along a river flowing into the Gulf of Uraba. As soon as Pedrarias beheaded Balboa and abandoned Acla and Santa María la Antigua del Darién for the new capital of Panama City, Darién was quickly burned by Cemaco. Darién has remained forgotten ever since. How odd a fate for the continent's first colonial boot prints on the ground to have been covered over by the jungle of time. Today no one really knows where Santa Maria de la Antigua del Darién was located. Today much of Darién, in addition to the location of Santa María la Antigua del Darién, remains a mystery.

Funneled between two continents and sandwiched between two seas, Darién has always been a place of passage, a crossing for birds, merchandise, and people. Four gulfs and hundreds of islands grace its two forbidding shores. On the north the three hundred and sixty San Blas Islands are hinged between two gulfs, the Gulf of San Blas and the Gulf of Uraba. On the south coast the Pacific Ocean forms a gulf inside of a gulf, as the Gulf of San Miguel hemorrhages out of the Gulf of Panama. Where else in the world is there a gulf inside of a gulf? The Gulf of San Miguel is flanked behind by the Maje Range and the Toad Range along the Pacific. Embossed on the Pacific horizon are the Pearl Islands, and all around the gulf are the estuaries of the Tuira, Balsa, Sabana, Congo, and more than a dozen other rivers, all feeding into the gulf's mangrove-choked shoreline. Further down, the Pacific coast becomes a continual cliff with the Embera hamlet of Playa de Muerto being the only beach before the villages of Puerto Pina and Jaque, which are closer to Colombia.

As the first place the Spanish landed on the mainland, Darién is full of superlatives. For centuries the name Darién has conjured up a sense of the wild and dangerous. It was first a place where Balboa took the Spaniards to escape and seek refuge. From their first encampment of San Sebastian they were soon fleeing the curare-tipped arrows used by the Carib tribes east of the Gulf of Uraba. The deadly curare, made from a concoction of *Strychnos toxifera* plants, the blood of tiny colorful frogs (*Phyllobates terribilis* or *Dendrobates auratus*), and other poisons, only needs to enter the blood stream to be effective.

In 1501, Rodrigo de Bastidas was the first European to sail Darién's Caribbean coast. He was also the first to capture and transport slaves from mainland America. A boat full of captured indigenous Caribs, from what is now Colombia, were taken back to Hispanola, paraded, sold, and then all quickly died. A few years later Vasco Núñez de Balboa, a member of Bastidas' previous voyage, who later traveled as a bankrupted stowaway escaping agrarian debt, managed to smuggle himself into history. Soon after he led the Spaniards from their encampment of San Sebastian, he remembered that the indigenous across the Gulf of Uraba did not use curare. After founding the first settlements at Santa María and later Acla, he found the austral sea.

It was Darién in 1510 which inspired the auriferous dreams of Spanish royalty to boastfully name their newfound mainland territory "Castilla del Oro," Gold of Castilla. Then in 1513 King Ferdinand changed the name to Castilla Aurifica, Golden Castilla. Because of "the power of the name," this gold-fevered ostentatious name soon atrophied into the more humble name of Panama, meaning "the place of many fish." It seems that an advertisement for fisherman suited Spain better than an advertisement for piracy.

Gaspar de Espinosa first used the name Panama in 1517 in reference to a newly found south coast fishing settlement. From this area he is recorded to have taken his first 2,000 indigenous slaves. So the "place of many fish" could have been named the "place of many slaves," for Panama became a capital for slavery, just like it is a banking capital, or narco-laundromat, today.

In 1518, the Spanish crown issued the first license to import African slaves. The contract was mostly made with merchants from Genoa, whose slaving specialty soon formed the "House of Genoa" in Panama City. But the misleading name change to Panama came too late, for news of gold and pearls was out. Within sixty years every pirate, starting with John Oxeham in 1577, set their sextants and sails towards Castilla del Oro.

For the next two hundred and fifty years, Darién's shadowy history became associated with Indian slaughter, black slave revolts, pirates, and gold mines. Today it is known for nothing except tropical rainforest tribes, narco-traffickers, snakes, and Colombian FARC guerillas.

Though Darién has staged many a dark horror story it nonetheless was home to the New World's first two love stories, both involving Balboa. The first one saved his life, but the second one took it. In 1510, Cemaco gave his daughter Fulvia as a wife for Balboa. She was supposed to spy on him, but love saved the day. She disclosed her father's plans to attack. Cemaco then fled with Balboa in pursuit. That is when Balboa found him and his family taking refuge in a giant tree house of a neighboring tribe. When Balboa threatened to cut the tree down Cemaco soon descended, but then fooled Balboa by telling him he would return with his gold, only to disappear in the jungle.

Darién's spectacular round Carreto Bay was the stage of the second tragic love story. Before knowing of the Pacific and searching for another settlement site, Balboa traveled to what is now Careto Bay. It is a beautiful, perfectly round bay some miles west of where Santa María la Antiqua del Darién was. Soon he fell in love with Caretita, chief Careta's dazzling daughter, who became his wife. Caretita's beauty also drew the unwanted attention and jealousy of one Andes Garabito, a soldier under Balboa. He sexually assaulted her while Balboa was in Acla. But when Balboa found out he let it go with just a stern warning. Later Garabito was used as a false witness against Balboa for treason, which led to his beheading. Balboa's nemesis, the governor Pedrarias, then awarded Garabito a promotion to lieutenant and Caretita became his prize. We never hear of her again.

Careto Bay's beauty has not faded in five hundred years. Today the only block building is the school, surrounded by the bamboo and thatched-roof village. Large breaking waves make it very rough for sailboats to enter the perfect pearl-like bay. With the jungled mountains just in back, FARC has kept it free of tourism. On another book journey the old cacique, after inviting me to drink chicha, told me that I was the first foreigner to visit in ten years.

The 16th century Spanish chronicler, Andagoya, reported that while Balboa was kept in a cage in Acla, some seven hundred people died from starvation in one month in Santa María la Antiqua del Darién. "Young noble men in brocades and scarlet silk coats, who had pledged their estates in order to come to Darién, dropped dead from hunger while crying for bread in Cemaco's old capital," wrote Charles Anderson in his 1911 seminal work, *Panama, Castilla del Oro*. Las Casas adds that more people "died from hunger than disease," despite Pedrarias having over four-hundred and eighty barrels of flour. It was at that time that the storehouse was torched, making bread even rarer. This is how the mainland's first settlement degraded. Knowing Balboa's popularity, but also knowing the people's hunger and poverty, Pedrarias sought to buy their allegiance and silence criticism of his murder of Balboa. Pedrarias immediately had bacon and other sparse food sold at cost or credit. Thus the allegiance of the New World's first mainland settlement was bought off with bread. "What is that freedom worth if obedience is bought with bread?" Dostoevsky's Grand Inquisitor mockingly asked.

It was from Acla in 1514, while ignorantly cutting lumber for his ill-fated journey, that Balboa penned his famous letter to King Ferdinand, pleading with him not to allow any more lawyers into the land. Balboa wrote: "Most mighty Lord, one favor I want to entreat Your Highness to do me, for it conduces much to your service, and it is that Your Highness order to provide for no Bachelor of Law or any other thing, unless it should be medicine, may pass to these parts of the mainland under penalty that Your Highness order to provide for it, for no Bachiller comes here who is not a devil, and they lead the life of devils and not only are they bad, but they even contrive and possess methods how to bring about a thousand lawsuits villainies...." So when Pedrarias set sail from Sevilla in 1514, one of the conditions was to forbid any more lawyers from entering Castilla del Oro. After Ferdinand's death, the law was lifted and lawyers actually were accomplices to Balboa's beheading.

Now some five hundred years later, Panama has one of the highest percentages of lawyers in the world. And it is my advice not to trust a one...except Carlos George.

Eventually the name Darién came to refer to the whole eastern part of the isthmus. Today anything east of the Bayano reservoir is considered Darién. Though it was the first area settled on the Spanish Main, today there is very little there and it has virtually no coastal road access. Surely not many places in the world have stagnated like Darién. On the Caribbean side, the Llano-Carti track is the only road access. And Puerto Quimba, on the Sabana estuary near Meteti, has Darién's only Pacific coast access road. From there vans and taxis take people to or from buses in nearby Meteti. Most of the well-maintained indigenous trans-isthmian trails of the past returned to jungle centuries ago. To hike them today is much more difficult than it was five centuries ago.

Darién in general and especially the no-car-to-graphical Darién Gap has always had a bad reputation. Though historically Darién has been considered a lawless place, the lighted streets of the world's big cities are often more dangerous than most of the dark trails of Darién. But yes, parts of Darién are dangerous with venomous narco-traffickers and reptilian FARC, who the US allows inside Panama in order to create excuses for new military bases. The Kunas oppose any plans for a US military base along their shore. There are areas in Darién, of course, where one cannot go, but nonetheless Darién proves to be a welcoming place. It was the only place where a whole village, the Waounan village of Cemaco, came out to celebrate my gift of books with dances and then gave their own gifts to me. And Playa de Muerto is the only place where villagers wanted to give me a wife and accept me into tribal kinship. On the Caribbean side there are precious bamboo villages like Pine Island, Anachucuna, and Carreto Bay, which are nearly unchanged from hundred of years ago. There the only sounds are the birds, the waves, and the laughter of children.

The name Darién Gap, that elusive geographical link, is a breach or breaches between the mountain ranges along the jungle border of Panama and Colombia. It is not the missing link in the Pan-American highway as some believe. The fifty-four miles, in which no cars can pass, on the 28,800 miles of Pan-American Highway from Alaska to Patagonia, did not give the appellation Darién Gap. Early explorations were not looking for a road connection, as there was not yet even a road to Yaviza, when the search for the Gap began. Rather, they were looking for a hopeful low place, a gap between the mountains, which might become the "path between the seas." At that time the Atrato River, located just inside Colombia, was considered as a possible link for a canal site connecting the Gulf of Uraba to the Tuira River and the Gulf of San Miguel.

Though Balboa landed on the Darién isthmus and traversed it twice before 1515, the area remained basically unexplored for the next three centuries. In 1616, King Phillip III ordered explorations up the Tuira River to search for an interoceanic connection, but nothing was determined. During the next two-hundred and fifty years only occasional teams of explorers entered the area, and always with more people than they left. Though gold was found, no one sought for the missing "cartographical gap" between the seas. The entire upper Tuira drainage was not explored until 1875, when two Frenchmen, Reclus and Wyse, poled upriver and hiked in, seeking for a possible inter-coastal connection. They decided that an Atrato/Tuira sea level canal was best; but Lesseps spoke the last word for the Panama/Chagres route.

Almost one hundred years later, in the 1960s, a team from the US Atomic Energy Commission even went up the Tuira to search for a site to make another canal. This one, though, was not going to be dug by men and machines, but rather by a chain of small nuclear explosions. Protests by the Kunas, Emberas, and Waounan sparked world opposition and the plan was shelved.

Key to the Darién Gap is Cerro Pirre, the small 1200-meter-high central mountain range pushing up between the two coastal ranges. A gap-like valley on either side leads into Colombia. Just to the east of Cerro Pirre, the Tuira flows between the Darién Mountains. On the west, a headwater of the Balsa River, the Tuira's largest tributary, also leads into Colombia. The best known route, though, follows the upper Tuira and then its affluent, the Paya River. From Paya a track leads to the border where the Tree of Letters once was. It was on this tree that intrepid travelers recorded their names.

Behind Cerro Pirre is Santa Cruz de Cana, where the first Spanish gold mine on the American continent was located. Because of this, the Tuira was the first river to be used for commercial navigation in the conquest of the New World. For centuries, first indigenous and then African slaves would be transported up the Tuira River from its huge estuary near Chepigana; then the gold would be shipped back down to the Spanish fort there. But the mine's gold today is as rare as the bush dog, perro de monte, (*Speothos venaticus*) found only at Cerro Pirre. The world's largest rodent, the very shy capybara or poncho (*Hydrochoerus hydrochaeris*), is also found there.

No road has ever wound along the rugged border with Colombia. Today it is one of the few international borders without road access. Hopefully, it will remain like that. The Kunas are determined to never allow a road on their land. The paved road that runs east from Panama City and bisects the large Lake Bayano reservoir, known for its peacock bass, is the only road entrance into Darién.

The Bayano reservoir, the western entrance to Darién, is named after the little-remembered "king," Bayano. He became the most feared leader of Panama's African slave rebellions. Bayano, along with other freedom-loving Cimarron leaders such as Philipio, Mandinga, and Luis de Mozambique, started the first slave revolts in the early 1550s from their forest hideouts, palenques, in Darién. They raided the trans-isthmian mule trains, which trudged from Panama City to Porto Bello with precious metals, mostly from Peru.

Referring to Bayano, the Spanish chronicler Pedro de Ajuada wrote that, after finally working out a peace treaty in 1553, the Spanish authorities deceptively planned a banquet for him and other slave revolt leaders. After lacing their wine with a narcotic, the Spanish made toast after toast, until Bayano and the others passed out. When he awakened, Bayano allegedly found himself in chains and castrated.

Today the large black population, Dariénitas, comprise most of the Darién's small-time merchants. The indigenous tribes are typically reliant on them for supplies. Historically the indigenous, especially the Kunas, had a terrible relationship with Black people, for the Blacks were used by Panama as police to control the Kunas. Today the relationship of the Embera and Waounan with their black Dariénita neighbors is usually good, though they traditionally live on different sides of rivers from each other.

Finally, after five hours of riding in the back of the crowded "chivo" pick-up, we arrived in Yaviza. Originally I thought that, since it was the last town at the very end of the North American half of the Pan-American Highway, it would be a pristine place. On the contrary! Unfortunately, it seemed like all the debris and detritus along the Pan-Am Highway had funneled itself down to this end of the road. The opaque Chucunaque River, which bisects this nearly four-hundred year old village, has become the town dump. Somehow, Panama still doesn't know how to dispose of its trash.

Though Yaviza is at least fifty river miles away from the Tuira's estuary near La Palma, the inland tides flow and unroll upriver like a long tongue of an iguana. The massive river mouth works like a giant funnel through which the Pacific tides flux and flow; they can reach two meters at Yaviza, before gradually ending a mile or more upriver. During the dry season, when the Chucunaque River is low, it can actually have a reverse flow during high tides. After the dogs have gone through the piles of garbage and trash discarded along the river bank, then the incoming tides carry away anything they have left. All sorts of floatable refuse passes upriver through the town. With a life of its own, it will return with the ebb tide in a homecoming parade of floating plastic, polystyrofoam, rubber thongs, pampers, and whatever else floats. Some things float back and forth for days before finally sinking or getting trapped. One has to get beyond the turbid tide's reach to be free of the garbage.

Thus the fate of the lower Chucunaque River, which is the longest river in Panama, has morphed over the centuries from being a riparian highway, on which captured Indian and African slaves, and gold were transported, to being a dump for Yaviza's garbage.

Just beside the river, where the chivo stopped, was the Pension Reposo. It was truly the most horrible lodging I have ever been in. A room cost four dollars, but that was five dollars too much. I needed a place close to the river to store the boxes, though, so I thought it might do. It was built on rickety pilings above the muddy tidal banks of the Chucunaque. An inky black stream ran below the pilings, feeding into the coffee-colored river which is the drinking water for many. The room seemed more like an oversized rabbit hutch, with slats for flooring through which one could see all the filth and garbage collected along the river bank. I barely wanted to even enter the room, or set the boxes down on the grimy mattress, for fear of what may try to get inside. I soon decided to change to another location, after having been told that there was a good chance that my boxes would end up being stolen there. I used a wheelbarrow to move the boxes across the village, to the not-much-better Hotel America, a place of little pride but a lot of roaches.

The population of Yaviza is basically all Black Dariénita. Only a few Embera Indians live there, mostly near an office for their comarca. Though not a very pleasant place, Yaiza is quite gentle. Little stores and painted wooden houses, many on high stilts, line the few raised cement lanes. Like many Dariénita towns, there seems to be no one around all day. Only when the deafening cantinas open late in the afternoon does it seem to wake up.

While walking through the village one day, I heard the drone of a motor and the shouts and laughter of some little kids. Turning I saw a thick white cloud of mosquito spray trailing behind a government pick-up truck. They were spraying DDT, I was told. The kids, playing behind the truck, ran in and out of the noxious cloud, disappearing and then appearing, oblivious to any dangerous health affects. Dengue fever, as I can testify, is common there; and hemorrhagic dengue kills people every year.

That night I stayed in the ten-dollar Hotel America, which is directly beside one of Yaviza's noisiest cantinas. The amiable owner came from Ecuador fifty years ago. He married a local woman and never left. Returning one day I was shocked to see his wife outside the hotel barbecuing a piece of chicken on a modern grill. But instead of using charcoal, she was using a burning plastic bottle to cook it with. The burning chicken fat would drip onto the melting bottle and send a sizzling flame flashing upwards. Watching her adept culinary skills, it seemed that this was not the first time she had cooked this way. Chicken ala dioxins, an acquired taste, perhaps.

Three days after arriving in Yaviza I took a very overcrowded piragua, a flat bottomed dugout, about half an hour down the Chucunaque River to the Tuira confluence. Then we went up the Tuira for about an hour, to the little village of Pinogana. I went there in order to check on a base camp and a boat to take me to some schools further up the Tuira; I had the name of a boatman there. I also wanted to wait out the Easter holiday away from the deafening noise of Yaviza. Having no hotel or pension in Pinogana I stayed in a funky storage room of the boatman's house. I made arrangements with him as soon as I could to have him take me upriver to six villages on the Monday after Easter.

The next day, which was Good Friday and a terrible day to travel, I returned by boat to Yaviza. I wanted to retrieve the boxes of books and supplies as soon as I could. This time the Hotel America was filled with Easter guests, so I had a difficult time finding a place to stay. Finally I asked an old woman at the Mi Returno restaurant, where I ate, if she had any room upstairs. She was glad to accommodate me with a six-dollar, bare-bones room. Old Chela had as many wrinkles in her friendly flaccid face as the termite-eaten walls of my room had holes. Light from a lightbulb burst through the termite holes, piercing the Darién darkness like a jack-o-lantern. It glowed just like her wrinkled smile beamed with the light inside of her.

But even her coffee could not sooth my somnolence. The downstairs cantina's inescapable all-night blare, though now a bit softened by distance, totally challenged any attempt to sleep. For some reason which I have never discovered, Panamanian bars, cantinas, and homes all love to play music deafeningly loud. It is impossible to have a conversation anywhere near one. The Dariénita denizens watched Saturday's sun rise over the jungle and finally exhausted themselves around mid-morning.

After my sleepless night, I left Yaviza that afternoon and returned to Pinogana, again in a very long and overcrowded dugout piragua. This time there were nearly thirty people aboard. It was low tide and in places soft fluctuant mud flats had a greenish hue from the algae. There in the turbid tidal zone, the Tuira's banks were often densely lined with four-meter-high *Calophyllum* plants, which looked like giant green spears, prohibiting any entrance. Along the river, buttressed trunks of huge trees tapered upward. Towering espave trees (*Anacardium excelsum*) whose name is taken from the Sapnish "es- para- ver," i.e. "is for sight," were once climbed as lookouts. Bongo trees (*Ceiba pentandra*), whose trunks are smaller at the base than slightly farther up, and huge huipo trees (*Cavanillesia platanifolia*) form a canopy high over the shadowed jungle

My piragua to Pinogana was going to continue several more hours up the Tuira River, to the village of Boca de Cupe. I would get out in Pinogana, though, with my nine boxes. By chance a woman passenger, a primary school teacher in Boca de Cupe, turned out to be the daughter of old Chela, whose place I had stayed in. Before I knew that, though, she had already asked me for some books, since she had heard from her mother that I had many. She told me that her school had almost two hundred kids, but no books. Though I wanted to help, I told her that I preferred helping smaller schools with a few dozen or so children. Otherwise, my supplies would run out after helping just a few schools. What impressed me about her was that, after I explained this to her, she became an advocate for a small school in the tiny village of Cupe, which was near Boca de Cupe. "There are just twenty children and they have no books or notebooks or anything," she told me, "And the children sit on the floor." So before we left I quickly returned to the storeroom of the Hotel America and got a box of books and supplies for Cupe. She promised me that she would make sure they got them. A few weeks later I heard that FARC guerrillas had taken over Boca de Cupe for two days and no one could enter or leave.

Today the tiny community of Pinogana is basically just a collection of small houses along two wide, shady cement lanes bordering the Tuira River. It is a mix of Ladino and Dariénita. Cacao trees and yuca plants are found around the houses. The school that I gave books to sits at one end of a grassy football field, just back from the river. Most people rely on the river for drinking water and washing. A few dugouts are always tied to the bank. To relieve the heat, people often spend some time in the afternoons bathing in the sandy-bottom river. A couple of years before, though, an eleven-year-old boy was killed by a crocodile while swimming there. At about the same time, a woman was killed by a viper; she was bit on the neck when she walked beneath a cacao tree.

The Tuira riverside community Pinogana, along with Chepigana, and Yaviza, were all founded in 1638 with the help of a truly incredible Spanish youth named Julian Carrizolio de Alfaraz. In 1623, as a twelve-year-old crewmember, his coastal supply ship was surprise attacked by Kuna warriors. Young Julian was the only one not killed; he was kidnapped by the Kunas. After living with his Kuna captors for some time, he became one of "the other" and both impressed and influenced them. Some five years later, when he was seventeen, he convinced the Kuna leaders to make a peace treaty with the Spanish authorities. From somewhere in Darién, Julian Carrizolio then led a peace march all the way to Panama City. As an unknown chronicler wrote: "Barefoot and wearing a large straw hat in the manner of the Indians due to the long time he lived among them, I saw Julian Carrizolio when, at the head of a band of Indian friends, he went to visit don Enrique Enriquez de Sotomayo, President of the Royal Audience to make friendly overtures." He was, I believe, the first lay peace activist in the New World. This young peace activist in Darién in 1628 stands out as utterly unique, far ahead of his time and place. After being kidnapped as a boy by "the other," he eventually became "the other" while "the other" became like him. Julian Carrizolio should be remembered as an incredible peacemaker.

Many dark deeds of Darién are known and recorded, for it was a place with a "heart of darkness," dense and tangled like the shadowed jungle. But then suddenly a wise boy appeared, like a piercing ray of light. What the power of an empire could not do with its mighty men of battle, an unarmed youth did alone. In weakness he found strength, and in non-violence, he found power. Some years later Julian Carrizolio, along with a Dominican monk named Father Adrian, received government assistance and founded the three Darién villages of Yaviza, Pinogana, and Chepogana.

About fourteen-hundred Kunas and two hundred Spanish colonists moved there. We know that Julian was given a tract of land, but we never hear of him again. His few barefoot footnotes are enough for us to read volumes into the transcendent nature of this remarkable young man. After Father Adrian's retirement in 1651, a military fort was built nearby in Yaviza, which ended any hope for peace. It was built in such a position that it separated those Kunas who were considered pacified from all the rest. Soon the settlement became a center for Kuna opposition.

With the discovery of more gold at Cana and later the discovery of rubber and tagua nuts (*Phytelephas seemannii*), an invasion of colonists soon started the Chucunaque War. Armed rubber tappers were bleeding both trees and men. It was probably at this time that most of the Kunas left the river banks of the Pacific drainage for protection along the Caribbean shores and the San Blas Islands. Later the Embera, their enemies, filled the vacuum. Thus some decades of peace ended. As Bancroft wrote, "the verbal promises and contracts of oral cultures held far more weight and honor than a drowning 'signatory sea of legal ink.'"

The wild mountains which form the Darién Gap were never far in the distance and still support cloud forests. Sometimes large cut logs are tied together along the river banks. Both the indigenous and the Dariénita Blacks float them downriver to sell. Though seemingly healthy, these forests are in decline, not just from the voracious teeth of unforgiving chainsaws. It is also because of the increase in nocturnal temperatures, even though slight. Unlike forests in temperate zones, these tropical rainforests are not growing as fast as they were twenty years ago, scientists now claim. Because tropical forests are growing more slowly their consumption of carbon dioxide and other burned fossil fuel gases is decreasing. The question to be answered is: what determines the amount of carbon a tropical rainforest retains?

On the Monday following Easter, my Dariénita boatman prepared his dugout to go up the Tuira. Three people, several boxes, and some sacks of rice that he hoped to sell, all filled his small dugout.

Our first stop was Vista Alegre, the next village upriver after Pinogana. Along the Tuira River, the Waounan Indians live in villages on the right bank and the Dariénita Blacks live in villages on the left. Vista Allegre is entirely Waounan Indian, but has a small Panamanian National Police post just beside the river. After helping to tie the dugout to the small dock, I was asked to register. The National Police are very concerned about FARC and illegal Colombians coming downriver, so there are occasional posts and patrol boats that regularly travel the river. I walked from the dugout up the steep metal steps with a box containing about a hundred and thirty books and placed them on the ground in front to the sandbagged police post. A village man followed me with a box of notebooks, pencils, and other school supplies. It turned out that I mistakenly had left my passport in the boatman's house in Pinogana. That didn't seem to matter to the police, though, as long as I gave them any name and number.

Very rarely do any foreigners frequent those parts and I was a curiosity for both the soldiers and the villagers. While one young soldier scribbled my name on a single sheet of palimpsest paper, another one carved up a watermelon with a machete. He kindly handed me a piece. After asking me how far upriver I was going, a soldier radioed another military post to let them know.

While I was waiting there, a few of the Waounan villagers curiously gathered around. They saw it as a perfect opportunity to possibly sell some of their crafts. I disappointed them when I told them that I had no money with me—but I surprised them by saying that I had some carving tools to give away. The Waounan men are master carvers and the Waounan women make some of the finest baskets in the world. Nearly all the men and boys carve the ivory-like tagua nuts and rosewood, i.e. cocobolo, (*Dalbergia nigra*). One young man had an incredibly realistic carving of a harpy eagle with its wings spread wide and neck feathers ruffled, made from a very large tagua nut. It was excellent. Like everyone else there, he had carved it with a very crude little knife. I thought, "If he can do this with such a crude knife, what could he carve with some good tools? Then I watched his eyes widen as I handed him a set of carving tools that I had brought from Panama City.

The three-room school beside the Tuira River in Vista Allegre had about sixty children. It opened at seven in the morning, about half an hour before we arrived. On a pole in the front, the national flag lay limp in the still air of the tropical morning. Like all Panamanian grade schools, it was a cinderblock building painted blue and cream. It and the health center were the only concrete buildings in the village. And like all rural or remote Panamanian grade schools, it was completely empty of any children's books.

Immediately after we entered the school grounds, we were met by the impressive principal, the directora. She was an energetic thirty-some-year-old woman. More than anyone else, she knew the school's needs and the emptiness of the place. "No, we have no books!" she lamented, answering my inquiry. "There are sixth graders here who can barely read, because we have no books," she frankly added. Excitement is something hard to conceal when one is surprised. Her excitement leapt like a fish jumping from water when I told her that I had some books for the school. Her joy splashed over through the open classroom door, where wonderment turned every ear and eye. She called for all the classes to come outside. We were immediately surrounded by a crowd of lively Waounan kids, and the principal and I handed out notebooks, pens, and pencils to each of them.

More than half of these Waounan kids had no school supplies, even though each of them was dressed in a uniform, a white shirt with blue pants or skirt. They were like uniformed soldiers without guns, unable to fight the war against illiteracy. Uniforms have a way of covering over poverty, but sometimes they also expose extreme poverty. There is a stigma attached to the kids who don't have uniforms, and there are always some who do not.

While we were there, a village woman who was obviously very poor came over and approached me. She asked me to please give her some notebooks and pens for her children. I immediately asked her, "Well, where are your children?"

"At home," she answered shyly.

"Why aren't they in school?" I pursued.

"Because they have no uniforms! We have no money for the uniforms," she said with some shame.

Feeling the burden of her poverty I tenderly touched her shoulder and said, "Señora, uniforms don't matter! They aren't the important thing. Learning is the important thing!" Trying to influence her I asked, "Your children don't need uniforms to learn, do they?" While I was saying this, the principal nodded in agreement and tried to convince her that it was fine if her children didn't have uniforms.

"Alright, I will give you notebooks, pens, and pencils for your kids, but you have to have them go to school," I made her promise. Oh, how I wished that I had taken a few dollars to give her for those stupid uniforms. But she was delighted to leave with the school supplies and seemed to be encouraged by my words.

As I often do, I had all the kids gather in front of the school to take a photo. They all stretched their arms up, holding their new pens, pencils, and notebooks. Like a tight cluster of freshly rained on heliconias, they stood proud and happy. But I knew that Panama's scorching sun of unconcern would return. After awhile all the notebooks would be filled and the pens would be empty and the students would again have nothing.

Vista Allegre was not the "happy view" of its name, but rather a collection of stilted shacks scorched by the shadeless sun. Now in many Waounan and Embera villages, the people live quite close together. But until recently, homes of small kinship households were separated about one-hundred meters or so. They started congregating together because of the influence of the military, officials, and missionaries, who could control them more easily that way. Before it had been customary, but now only a few of their houses have small "huertos," gardens for herbs, pineapples, and some fruit trees, growing beside them. Old worn out dugout canoes are still sometimes used as planter boxes for herbs and flowers beside the houses.

On the Tuira River just before Vista Allegre, we passed fields of watermelons and lots of bananas, and yams called nahme and nampi. The larger nahme yams (*Dioscorea trifida*) can get huge, sometimes as large as sixty pounds. These are the ones that would be tied together and floated downriver to sell.

The World Bank's country study, the "Panama Poverty Assessment," soberly states that, "Education constitutes the single most important determinant of inequality. The failure and difficulty of many poor indigenous children in school too often recapitulates their social place." During Simon Bolivar's time, in 1825, literacy was a constitutional prerequisite for citizenship. Since most indigenous and Blacks have historically been illiterate, they were barred from citizenship. Today, almost two-hundred years later, the indigenous and Blacks are often deliberately neglected by government, even though they are now citizens. The direct costs of schooling in Panama are high and constitute a barrier to enrollment among the poor. "Lack of money" was the single most common reason for not enrolling in primary and secondary school (accounting for roughly half of absentees). This suggests that the direct costs (fees, materials, etc.) of attending school are prohibitively high for the poor and indigenous. This report says that, "Roughly double the share of indigenous primary school students report repeating their current grade than those in urban and rural areas. Dropout rates are also higher among indigenous primary school students. Of indigenous residents aged 13-17 who enrolled at some point, half did not complete primary school. This compares with only four percent and thirteen percent of urban and rural youths respectively. These disparities in internal efficiency could arise due to differences in the quality of education or demand-side constraints. They are less apparent at the secondary level, where very few poor students enroll." The report also states that "Lack of books among indigenous children" affects close to 60% of all primary and one fifth of secondary students in indigenous areas. "Lack of money" is the main reason (70%) for not having books.

It has only been some seventy years since most of the Waounan arrived in Panama from the Choco part of Colombia. Now there are about 3,000 Waounan living in Panama and 12,000 living across the border in Colombia. Social violence and a 1949 Colombian law prohibiting indigenous from buying firearms for hunting caused many Waounan and Embera to cross the border into Panama.

For most twenty-first-century indigenous people, it is the schools which are the central unifying factor and the anchors of their communities. But these anchors have no weight. These humble communities are abandoned to drift alone in the rough waters with no way to attach themselves to present realities.

Education, though endorsed as a government priority, is of course always poor at best. Missionaries, especially the Mennonites, have helped both the Waounan and Embera with "campaigns of alphabetization"in the past. Loewen, one of their linguists, transcribed the Waounan language, Woun-mea, into Spanish orthography in the 1950s. Their language has three dialects and is unrelated to any other languages. After teaching a certain Waounan man how to read, Loewen regrettably records that the man then told a group of illiterate people that they were ignorant, because they are products of "a mind not cleansed by the message of God." There always seems to be a snake in their Genesis grass,

Further up the Tuira River, it continues to narrow and we next stopped at the small school in Yape. It is a Black Dariénita village near a larger Embera village called Union Choco. By the time we finished there, the school was closing for the day. As I was talking to the teacher, many of the kids excitedly ran off to show their new notebooks and pens to their parents. Like nature, poverty is thankful for even little things.

Not far in the distance, the Gap revealed itself between the jungle-clad mountains. The Tuira continued on to it, but the Panamanian National Police would not permit foreigners to enter. It is just too dangerous, with the FARC lurking like jaguar for some fresh meat to kidnap. In Yape my boatman sold his rice. We were all out of books, so we returned to his home in Pinogana.

I still had several boxes of books in Yaviza, so I decided to take them to some Embera villages up the Chucunaque River. By that time, Yaviza had been emptied of its festive Easter visitors and I got a room again in the Hotel America. The Ecuadoran owner found a boatman for me, and we made plans to make the journey the next day in his six-meter dugout. The boxes were stacked in the middle and I sat in the front.

After passing through a mile or so of Chucunaque's riverine refuse, things started to become more natural. Howler monkeys called out and a small crocodile rippled the placid waters. Jesus lizards (*Basiliscus plumifrons*), so-called because they can walk, or rather run, on water occasionally scurried in front of us. Though it is the longest river in Panama, the Chucanaque is not very wide. Along its scarped river banks, a tangled web of vegetation creates a kind of hallway. At the confluence of smaller streams, large taro bamboo were planted to avoid erosion. They pointed skyward like bushy eyebrows, and lianas hung from the arboreal shadows like fallen telephone wires.

The Chucunaque is known for its varieties of deadly snakes, including the viviparous equis, the fer-de-lance (*Bothrops atrox*), and the mute bushmaster (*Lachesis muta*). Nearly all of the clay banks are pocked with small, deep holes made by large river shrimp. While slowly going upriver, we twice broke the shear pin on the fifteen-horsepower Yamaha motor within an hour. The first time, we stopped at a little sandy beach where the boatman quickly repaired it. Later, the prop hit submerged logs a few times, and the pin broke again. There wasn't another to replace it, so we had to resort to cutting and using a 16-penny nail instead.

Continuing upriver, we soon we saw the thatch roofs of the first village peeking out through some trees along a high-cut bank. At the riverside, some Embera women were rinsing freshly dyed fibers of the chunga or black palm (*Astrocaryum standleyanum*), from which they make their basketry. They were all naturally dyed from various plants, coloring them black, red, green, and yellow. As we walked through the village, I was impressed with some of the stilted, two-story round houses, with round thatched roofs. Everything here was clean, unlike Yaviza.

The Chucunaque River was once described "as one of the most tortuous known to geographers," and scholars now believe that Balboa used it in his mad plan of transporting sawn boards for brigantines overland to the Pacific. It is said that as many as two thousand indigenous porters died on that totally unnecessary journey. Many also perished in a Darién deluge, in which almost all of the boards and other material were swept away. Centuries later, in 1870-71, the US government's nightmarish Selfridge Darién expedition also found disaster on those twisted waters. And in 1924, Richard Marsh led a failed Smithsonian-backed expedition up the Chucunaque.

The tiny one-room school I visited had about twenty kids and was, of course, empty of any books. While I was there, a couple of little boys who had been playing hooky showed up to receive a notebook and pen. It seemed that they didn't have much reason to attend school without such things. The fine young Ladino teacher was elated beyond words, for they were out of everything and could only learn by rote. When I showed him a box of colored chalk, it was like blowing breath into a dying man. Then I handed him a large wooden compass designed to hold the chalk. No one there had ever seen a ruler, a pencil sharpener, or even an eraser. This had once been an area where rubber tappers used to ply their trade, but now it seemed that the school had been pedagogically erased.

The village cacique, or chief, a man of about seventy also came over to the school. He thanked me several times for the books. Later he wanted to show me some of his cocobolo wood carvings. As with the man in Vista Alegre, I asked to see what tools he carved them with. Just as I suspected, he showed me a little old pocket knife. I was sorry that I had forgotten the remaining set of carving tools and chisels back in Yaviza. But I told him about them and of course he was interested. I invited him to return with us, after we finished visiting two more schools up river.

When we returned later, he was there all dressed up and eagerly waiting beside the river. He heard the motor and knew we were returning. On the way to Yaviza, he told me that the kids had not left the school the entire day and were still there looking at the books.

Though I had wanted to go to more villages farther up the Chucunaque, I was now out of books. The Embera primary school at the village El Salto received the last of them. The school there was large, so the notebooks, pencils, and pens only went to the first and second graders. What could I do? I would have to wait for another journey to go further upriver. For as Balboa had once said, "A man goes as far as he can and not as far as he wishes."

Chapter 12

Houses without Walls

"Nothing enfranchises like education."—Voltaire

Flying in a small airplane from Panama City's Albrook Airport to places in Darién takes about an hour. I was going to Garachiné with some books and seeds for two indigenous communities, the Waounan and the Embera. From the air, Panama's ultra-modern metastasizing architecture is striking, especially juxtaposed to the adjacent jungle. We flew directly over the huge new American Embassy complex. I had been there applying for a new passport just a few days before. Within a minute, the low tide exposed the wide grey mudflats that border parts of the roadless Pacific shoreline like a dirty sleeve. The Pearl Islands appeared, with the Gulf of Panama on one side and the Gulf of San Miguel on the other.

The three weekly flights from Panama City to Garachiné's tiny airstrip are the village's biggest events of the week. While waiting for my boxes beside the small plane with the other passengers, I was amused to see the lanky young attendant struggle and curse as he moved my eighty-pound box of books.

"What's in here, rocks?" he questioned.

"No, books," I responded with a laugh.

"Well, you sure got some heavy words," he joked. Inquisitive, he then asked, "What are you going to do with so many books anyway, sell them?"

"No, they are for two primary schools. Some for Cémaco and the rest for Playa de Muerto."

Later that afternoon I made arrangements for a motorized dugout to take me the following morning to the first school at Cémaco. To get there we had to cross an arm of the Gulf of San Miguel to a village called Tiamati, or Puerto Nuevo as it is also known. From there we would walk to the nearby Waounan indigenous village of Cémaco.

In much of Darién still to this day, the rivers are the roads, the ways and means of life. Perhaps it is fitting that the Emberá have a creation myth in which "the world tree" was cut down and became a series of rivers. Looking at the Gulf of San Miguel on a map, the many rivers and the tributaries leading into them appear like a giant tree of rivers.

We had to leave no later than six in the morning for our trip to Cémaco, because of the extreme tides that regularly affect that part of the Pacific. Tides there can differ by over five meters. By the time we reached Tiamati, the ocean had already receded at least a hundred meters from the shore and still had another hundred to go. We anchored in knee deep water and proceeded to walk towards the small, mangrove-bordered beach.

The short walk from Tiamati to Cémaco follows along a wide, riverside trail bordered by thick jungle. Soon, a clearing and a couple of thatched roofs appeared in the distance. Two Waounan brothers from Tiamati and the boatman came with me to this seldom-visited village. Not far outside of Cémaco, we startled two women, who took off running along the other side of the narrow river towards the village. When we arrived, a crowd of about a hundred people curiously gathered around us beside the cacique's house.

One of the brothers explained in the Waounan language that we had a gift of Spanish-language children's books for the school, so together with all of the villagers, we walked to a nearby gathering house with the boxes. The whole area around the thirty or so stilted houses was graced with soft fine grass, creating a beautiful lawn like that of a golf course. I took off my sandals and enjoyed the softness of the place and the people.

On a couple of large tables, we placed the books for all to see. Every villager, young and old alike, wanted to look at them. Most had never paged through a book before. Though a high percentage of the villagers were illiterate, it didn't keep them away, since there was no shame in not being able to read. Within minutes, some of the children were reading aloud to themselves, and others to the old people. A cacophony of readings added a new sound to the jungle. The books about animals and birds proved to be the most popular.

The little school, still closed for summer holidays, was next to the open-sided gathering house. It was one of two buildings in the village with walls and a door. Ironically, the only place with a lock was the door of an abandoned Protestant church. In all indigenous villages in Panama, primary schools are the "centerpieces of village formation" and anchors of the community. Despite having so much importance in people's minds, they are too often neglected.

In a show of appreciation, the village cacique arranged to have three different women's dance groups perform. For the next hour, dozens of women and girls danced inside the gathering house. Most of the villagers stood with us in a circle, watching the dancers. The cacique was the only person I saw who was not barefoot. And the only man involved was a drummer, who improvised drumbeats on an overturned dugout canoe.

Each dance related a tribal story. One told of their former enslavement. Another, which evoked laughter, was a story about a stolen banana. The final one, which seemed to have the best dancers, was choreographed to imitate birds, herons or egrets, walking in unison while stalking fish. After nearly an hour of dancing, many people left. They returned moments later, and I was shocked to see that dozens of them had brought gifts. It was the only village I have ever worked in where so many people expressed their gratitude with gifts. Several men brought fine wood carvings of frogs, fish, and birds. Some of the women presented me with colorful, exquisitely made baskets. The Wounaan women are some of the finest basket makers in the world. They sew together the very fine, thread-like fibers of the chunga palm. Their visual acuity in making these is extraordinary. Some of the larger ones may take months to make, and incorporate images of birds, flowers, and animals—all colored with natural plant dyes. They can be made so tight that they can even hold water.

Knowing their extreme poverty and their reliance on handicrafts for their sporadic income, I found it hard to accept these gifts. I took only a couple of things and had to gently say, "No, gracias" to the rest.

Later my helpers and I began to divide up the seeds that we had brought with us. The Waounan, like all of Panama's indigenous people, are swidden farmers. They plant their crops in family plots some distance from the tiny village. They only plant a few things, since poverty limits their access to seeds. Root crops like yucca and a few types of yams, along with plantains and bananas, are their staples.

The word for food is t'ach in the Waounan language. This is also the same word they use for plantain, which suggests how reliant they are on it. The seeds we brought for watermelons, cantaloupes, squash, peppers, cucumbers, and tomatoes were especially appreciated. Those plants grow well there and the people like to grow them, but the seeds are in short supply. We passed out the seeds I had brought and hoped that they would bring a good harvest.

Though I had been reluctant to accept their gifts, I was happy to make the rounds to several houses where they fed me venison, iguana, and fish. As with most Waounan houses, we entered up a notched balsa (*Ochroma lagopus*) log to a raised bamboo floor some seven feet off the ground. Each had a low, thatched roof but there were no walls.

One common custom of both the Waounan and Emberá is body painting. They use a plant dye made from the inky juice extracted from a small, green fruit called jagua (*Genipa americana*). Before I left, some of the people wanted to paint my arms and face, so I let them. They applied the black liquid with a thin pointed stick, making a series of geometric designs. This is still a very common custom and some people are covered with it nearly from head to toe. They say that jagua helps to prevent insect bites and has dermatological benefits. After a couple of weeks, it wears off. "According to oral tradition, the Creator Himself, Hewandam, ordered the Waounan to paint their bodies with jagua; and told them that their sins would consequently be lessened" (M. Callaghan). So I was possibly not quite as reprobate as usual, for the next couple of weeks anyway.

By late afternoon, because of the tide, we had to leave and return to Garachiné. When passing the gathering house on our way out of Cémaco, I was surprised to see a group of people still looking at the books. Several kids and a couple of elderly people had been contentedly absorbed for several hours with their new gifts.

"What a refreshing culture!" I thought to myself. The people seemed so transparent; there were no walls to separate or doors to lock. They lived so peacefully without electricity. There was no stigma about the bare breasts of the women. Their art gave them pleasure and they delighted in sharing it with me.

Returning to Garachiné, I was surprised to find that the restaurant next to the only hotel had no food. For a small town with an airport, it was shocking to see how empty of commodities the place was. So I went to one of the nearby small stores and bought a few things for the restaurant to cook for me. The bar right next door had plenty of beer though, and people caroused all night to eardrum-breaking music. There is only one volume in Panama and that is loud.

The following day the same boatman took me and the rest of the books and seeds to an Emberá village called Playa de Muerto, the Beach of Death. Though the hamlet has a horrible name, it is a paradisiacal place. Bodies supposedly washed ashore there after some forgotten massacre, which is the source of the name.

Point Garachiné sticks out into the Gulf of San Miguel like a fishhook. Somewhere nearby is an old Spanish fort, long ago reclaimed by the jungle. Once past Point Garachiné at the southern point of the gulf, the Pacific coastline suddenly turns into towering cliffs. Huge huipo or bongo trees (*Cavanillesia platanifolia*), leafless till the rainy season, stood out like skeletal sentries above the cliffs. Yellow guayacan trees (*Tabebuia guayacan*) were aflame with color against the backdrop of the dark jungle. A white frangipani (*Plumeria alba*) hung suspended over the cliff in full bridal bloom, scattering its scented petals seaward.

I had wanted to buy a topographical map of the Playa de Muerto area before I left Panama City. Tommy Guardia, Panama's national cartographic office, sells maps of the whole country. But when I asked for a map of that area, I was told that they did not sell that one. I found that quite odd and asked, "Why not?"

"There are too many clouds in the area," they told me, which made things seem even shadier.

"It rains more in Bocas del Toro and you have those maps," I responded.

"Well, that is what I'm told, sir," the attendant replied.

Along that whole fifty miles of wild craggy coast between Garachiné Point and Jaqué, there are just a few places to land a boat. Since there are no roads inland, it makes this area perfect for operating drug kitchens and smuggling ventures. Fast Colombian drug boats sometimes hide out at Playa Escondido, one of the tiny inlets hidden among the jungle-lined cliffs. The government knows this and doesn't want people poking around there, so that is probably why there are no maps, except those for the narcos.

The palisading cliffs of the Toad Mountains only separate once before Playa de Muerto, forming a tiny beach at the mouth of a stream at Casa Vieja. We stopped there because the boatman had news of the death of a very old woman in Playa de Muerto. The news had been radioed to Garachiné and elsewhere, but Casa Vieja and its handful of people are very isolated. They knew the old woman and some said they would walk there the next day, although it's a five hour walk along a ridgeback trail.

Pushing off from beside the stream on the tiny beach, we waited for the right wave to break. The boatman made a dash to reach the next wave before it broke, since with our tiny ten-horsepower motor it could bring disaster if not timed exactly. Once beyond the breakers, the waters were black and calm. We rode for another hour along the cliffs. Schools of dolphins, like escorting emissaries, surfaced from the dark depths to play tag with our little boat. Then, placed between two bookend-like hills, Playa de Muerto appeared. Palm-lined sands stretched for a kilometer and I could see a few stilted houses scattered among the coconut palms. But the high waves pounding against the steep beach prevented us from landing. Instead, we had to go ashore further away at a small protected beach called Cocal.

Finally ashore, I was surprised to be greeted by a soldier from the Panamanian National Police. To put his disciplined body to use, I recruited him to carry the box of books over the hill to the village. I soon learned that there were a dozen more soldiers occupying two small military camps along the beach. Poking out from between sand bags, two fifty-caliber machine guns pointed out to sea. They had been there since 2003, to protect the two hundred and fifty Emberá inhabitants from Colombian FARC guerrillas. Colombia is just an hour away in a fast speed boat, and in the past, FARC would sometimes raid the village at night. They would loot the almost empty store, fire off their automatic weapons, and steal boat motors and other things. After the leaders of Playa de Muerto petitioned the Panamanian government for help, they posted the soldiers there.

The soldier I met wanted me to register my name in a log book at their makeshift headquarters. As soon as they found out that

I had brought several varieties of seeds with me, they earnestly asked me to give them some for their garden. I agreed. A couple of days later, their officer came by asking about the seeds. I never thought that I would be giving seeds away to the Panamanian National Police, but it humored me that they wanted them. "Why not?" I thought. Maybe it would help turn their weapons into plowshares.

Unlike most indigenous communities in Panama, the Emberá in Playa de Muerto get on quite well with the soldiers. I can't imagine the Nasos, Ngabes, or Kunas ever asking for the National Police to come to their villages, for they have burned too many of their houses. They have also fought the National Police during protests over illegal dams and mining concessions for years. But FARC hasn't threatened the other tribes, so there was another dynamic present.

The women of Playa de Muerto operate a small, stilted bamboo guest house just off the beach, where they also cook meals. When I arrived, a man was at the village gathering house, making a coffin for the dead woman. Her body was beside him, wrapped in a blanket, and some of her daughters and granddaughters were sitting there and weeping. This was in the early afternoon and it took until almost midnight, working by oil lamp, for the man to finish. The women sat vigil all night and their wails penetrated the darkness and my dreams. By mid-morning, many of the villagers had gathered and I noticed a couple of people from Casa Vieja. A funeral procession soon formed and followed the rough coffin, and I trailed along behind. We walked about one-hundred meters down the main trail and then turned a short distance into the jungle. There, a nondescript gravesite had already been dug in the sand. Amid tears, the coffin was lowered and covered with layers of fresh palm fronds and sand about a meter above ground level. The palm fronds reveal the close connection the Embera have with trees. After some months the grave would settle and the mound of earth would flatten out, and then all would return to forest.

The Emberá prefer to live a bit separated from their neighbors; their stilted houses without walls are normally bordered by small gardens of herbs, bananas, and pineapples. Just like the Waounan, they enter their two-meter high floors from a balsa wood log, called a "tume," which is notched with narrow steps. At night it is pulled up and placed inside; during the day it is placed underneath the house when one leaves.

Behind the beach a short distance, shaded by some large mango trees, was the small cinderblock school. As in Cémaco, it was closed for the summer vacation. After a couple of days, I talked to the village cacique and some other leaders about the books I had brought. As usual, the answer to my question, "Do you have any children's books?" was negative.

The following morning, the cacique sent word for all the children to gather at the school. Perhaps a dozen inquisitive children already knew that I had books and schools supplies, so in anticipation they came looking for me at the guest house. The cacique heard the commotion and came over, followed by more children and some of their parents. They were excited and anxious to see and hold the books, so I opened the box and handed one to each of them. Then we all walked together to the school, each child proudly carrying a book. It was a pity that the two teachers were on vacation, although they would be back in a month. A few of the kids didn't want to give the books back, until the cacique assured them that they could read them again when the school year started. Otherwise, they would have been ruined in no time.

The children in Playa de Muerto were some of the most innocent that I have ever been around. As in Cémaco, none of them had ever seen a car or a television. Those two defining features of modern culture never entered their minds, or altered their sense of time and space. The furthest away from the village most of them had ever gone was to their family gardens, a mile away along a jungle trail. Only by name did they know of Garachine, Jaque, Puerto Pina, and Panama City. When an occasional airplane or helicopter passed overhead, they would point skyward with considerable interest. Though becoming rarer every day, there are still scores of poor indigenous villages in Panama where life is like this.

As with the Embera, the children frequently tattoo their bodies with jagua. When I arrived with my face and arms already painted, their accepting smiles only widened further. As the only foreigner in the village, I immediately attracted a group of curious kids; the jagua tattoos and the seeds and books that I brought with me only increased my appeal.

After talking with the cacique one afternoon, I sat at a table to started my seed work. The next day I was going to give them away. He had already told the people, and so I wanted to be prepared. Within minutes I was spotted by some kids who watched as I started to write labels on some manila coin envelopes. After spooning in some seeds, I sealed the envelopes with a glue stick, something that none of them had ever seen before. This is a long process, especially when making up hundreds of packets, so I chose the oldest boy and showed him how to glue the packets. Then, of course, they all wanted to try it.

Like most remote indigenous villages, Playa de Muerto was as empty of seeds as they were of books. I had been unable to get organic, open-pollinated seeds and had to be satisfied with hybrids. Two American commercial seed companies, Bonanza and Emerald, have cornered most of the seed market in Latin America. But even these are difficult to find and expensive. As a result, people seldom have even the most basic fruits and vegetables.

In the gathering house the next day, I gave away the seeds. I was happy to see grandmothers and mothers coming for them with their children. Seeds are so rare that the kids don't know much about them, and it is impossible for the elders to pass on their knowledge of planting if they have none. They only plant a few traditional things such as bananas, plantains, rice, corn, yuca, otoy, name root, and a couple of other root crops. They also have coconut, avocado, mango, guava, sapote, and other fruits that grow wild. It is the fish and other seafood which makes the difference in their diet. These coastal people often live better than those in the mountains, where malnutrition is a reality. The Panama Poverty Assessment, published by the World Bank, stated that a third of the Emberá and Waounan children are malnourished. Data from the World Bank's Living Standards Measurement Survey, an index for measuring poverty, found that over eighty percent of the Emberá and Waounan live below the poverty line.

Knowing that many of the indigenous are excellent wood carvers I had brought along several sets of chisels, some with grooves. They can actually make money with these, unlike with the books or seeds. I did not have enough for everyone, so I had kept them for Playa de Muerto. One day, when my friend Clammer Grijalva showed me his beautiful cocobolo bowls with four legs that he polished with a deer antler, I surprised him with some Stanley chisels. He especially appreciated the grooved one, and told me that he now needed to get some more wood.

He invited me to go with him and some of his friends to gather wood. Clammer had found a perfectly dry fallen cocobolo tree about thirty inches thick, which had fallen down a hill. Its branches had kept the trunk from touching the ground, so it had not rotted. The root ball was unearthed and the exposed roots were beet red, having been washed clean by years of rain. The wood's specific gravity is like stone and it sinks in water. After cutting some large pieces with a chainsaw, they struggled to carry them back up the hill.

We returned along an overgrown old skid road made by a bulldozer many years before. I commented about the road to Clammer, and he told me that after World War II, a lone American had come and logged off all the mahogany around Playa de Muerto. With a sad look, he stretched out his arms to emphasize the size of the trees. Trees are the life and love of the Emberá. Nearly all men can identify several dozen varieties of trees. Their shamans cure disease with healing sticks of various woods, each for a different malady. They love the quiet of the forest; because of it, they live separate from each other. Clammer told me that the American had a bulldozer which he used to make the skid roads. He would skid the cut mahogany logs down to Cocal beach to a barge. During calm days in March, a tug boat would pull them to Panama City. Then he'd ship them back to the US. Thanks to him, there are no mahogany trees left in Playa de Muerto; they were all used to make furniture in the US.

Cémaco, "The Lord of Darién," once tried to escape Balboa's wrath and desire for gold by fleeing to a neighboring king's tree house, "whose trunk could not be surrounded by seven men." Balboa threatened to cut the tree down with steel axes and machetes, and Cémaco wisely descended. But though he cleverly escaped, the forests did not. Just as axes and machetes were the main means of acculturation at that time, today it is the cell phone. Cell towers have replaced the giant trees, rapidly changing the social and physical landscape. One of the tallest trees is the sentinel-like espavé (*Anacardium excelsum*). The espavé has morphed into the cell tower, and Panama now has a forest of them.

Slowly but surely, like all indigenous people, the Emberá and Waouaan are becoming acculturated. Perhaps only poverty slows down the process. More so than any of Panama's remaining seven or eight indigenous tribes, the Emberá intermarry with the Dariénita, the dominant Black population in Darién and move to their towns. Blowguns have long since been replaced by rifles. Once, like the Incas, they used quipus to record dates and quantities of things. But just as in Peru, this system of knotted strings was forgotten long ago. The common calculator now does the math.

Western medicine has almost completely replaced their shamans (jaibanas). Their finely carved wooden prayer sticks, which they once believed to be inhabited by disease-curing spirits, have been replaced with injections. The juice of certain plants that once instilled visions are now forgotten, replaced by bottles of rum. Their world-class basketry is never used by them; instead they are only sold to tourists and replaced with plastic. Polygamy and female puberty rites have disappeared because of the nation-state. The bare breasts of the women are now covered by bras, thanks to the shame taught by missionaries. When old papa Grijalva dies in Playa de Muerto, who will be left to walk the streambeds hunting river shrimp with a long spear, dressed only in a loin cloth?

One day I was reading in my hammock on the porch of the guest house, when I suddenly heard a group of children shouting on the beach. Getting up to look, I saw them pointing out to sea and excitedly yelling, "Crucero, crucero!" ("Cruise ship, cruise ship"). Looking far off to the ocean's horizon, I saw a white speck, which I took to be a passing ship. Unlike the kids, I had no idea what was going to happen. Some of them ran back to their houses, and I returned to my hammock and book. After a few minutes, I heard the ship's horn bellow over the pounding surf. Looking again, this time I saw that the ship was nearly in front of us. "Cruise ships come here?" I said to myself. I was shocked! Realizing that the tranquility of the tiny village would suddenly change made me feel a bit uneasy. But my curiosity led me to join the children watching from the shade of an almond tree. Within a few minutes tourists started descending down a stairway from the cruise ship and boarding a small boat. They were coming ashore.

Not wanting to be part of a welcoming party, I retreated again to my hammock. For nearly an hour, several boatloads of people were taken ashore. The relatively small cruise ship was making a beach-head invasion with its seventy-some passengers. It had come from Limón, Costa Rica, through the Panama Canal.

From my hammock I watched as a gaggle of tourists filed by and entered the round, open-sided gathering house. The contrast seemed surreal, like something out of a Fellini movie. Standing in their glitzy designer clothes and safari outfits, with hats too big and pants with too many pockets, they seemed like some strange species next to the drooping loin cloths of the local men and the bare-breasted women. Almost everyone, of course, toted a camera or movie camera, to capture till eternity their encounter with the nearly-naked natives.

As I lay in my hammock, taking it all in from the shadows of the porch, I noticed one of the tourists focusing her binoculars on me. I guess she was looking for the wildlife. When I scratched my armpits like an ape and showed my teeth, she quickly turned away. Then I saw her say something to a man standing beside her. Carrying his camera he walked over and stopped just ten feet in front of me. Without saying a word he raised his camera to his face to take my picture. Cameras, it seems, can give people the right to be rude. A bit put off, I interrupted him saying, "Sir, don't you think it's proper to ask my permission first?" Made somewhat nervous by my unexpected response, he told me, "Oh, I saw your face painted like an Indian and wanted to take your picture. I didn't think that you would mind." Perhaps if he hadn't been such a gawking garish tourist I wouldn't have told him, "Well, I do mind!" He never got his picture of the "white Indian" of Darién. After an hour, they all returned to their cruise ship, which soon disappeared into the distance like a phantom.

I was glad to see them leave, but for the Emberá villagers, it was their only real source of income. It is people from the ten cruise ships that come in a year who buy most of their fine baskets and wood carvings. Each guest is also charged three dollars by the village. So, all in all, the ten hours of cruise ship visits per year probably leaves the smallest footprint. Afterwards, the women are always eager to start their next basket and the men another wood-carving.

The day before I was going to leave, another vessel suddenly appeared. It was a small cargo boat returning to Panama City from Jaqué, near the Colombian border. It is on boats like this that many people and nearly all of the goods travel down the roadless Pacific coast. Realizing that I had an opportunity to travel back on it, I packed and was ready to leave within minutes. But by the time a skiff was arranged to take me out, it had left. "Never mind, we'll catch it," an Emberá boatman told me, and after chasing it for several minutes, we did. As the boat idled, I climbed aboard. Much to my surprise, the deck was completely packed with passengers, sprawled out every which way. The only space I could find to sit was in the bow, where no one else wanted to sit because of the spray. For the next fourteen hours, it moistened the tarp I covered myself with.

Once back in Panama City, we moored out in front of the public docks, in old San Filipe. The next day I called the US embassy to check on my passport. "Yes, it is ready," I was told. At the embassy, I waited my turn and approached the counter window when my name was called. When the older consulate worker looked up from her desk, I saw her eyes widen. My still-painted face shocked her. She glanced at my passport, trying to compare the person before her to my photo. "Have you been in Darién?" she asked with concern. "Don't you know that they are kidnapping people there? FARC just took a Spanish doctor and his son." Our eyes met and I answered, "Darién? What makes you think that I have been in Darién?"

Chapter 13

THE KING OF POVERTY

"Without a gentle contempt for education, no man's education is complete."—G.K.Chesterson

The story of the Naso people in Panama today is the story of a king without a kingdom and his poor people without a land. It is the story of a family and tribe in conflict. The Naso are the only remaining indigenous kingdom left in Central America; they are a small, troubled, tropical forest tribe of about 3,500 people. It is also a story of both written and spoken lies and continual deceit on the part of a nation-state, titan corporations, behemoth banks, and corrupt world powers. Because of all this, it is the story of a divided kingdom, with not one but two Naso kings. Therefore, the Naso are a "kingdom divided against itself," a kind of Judah and Israel in the sodden rainforest of present day Panama.

Tito Santana almost became the victim of regicide in 2004 after he sold his signature, thereby allowing three hydro-electric dams to jeopardize the future of the land and water of his small tribe. Soon after, his wise elderly uncle Valentín was chosen tribal king, leaving Tito with nothing to rule but the kingdom of poverty.

Having already helped the other Panamanian tribes and their schools with book and seed donations, I had purposely kept some of what I had in reserve for each of the Naso village schools. Of all of the seven tribes in Panama, none have suffered as much as the Naso.

The Naso (also called the Terraba) have record of a continuous line of kings and a queen dating back for over five hundred years. They sometimes refer to themselves as Tjer Di, the Water of Tjer, a wise mythical grandmother figure. This shows their profound connection to their waters: their rivers, which originate in mountain springs and flow to their sea islands. Their first encounter with Europeans was in 1502, when Colombus landed on the island of Colon during his fourth voyage. For ages their homeland had stretched from the offshore Caribbean islands of Bocas del Toro to the clear mountain rivers of the mainland.

It took another thirty years after Columbus's first footprint on Isla Colon for the area to be revisited by Spaniards. The first to explore the area was Hernandez de Badajoz during 1534-37. It was around this time that the Naso royal family took the name Santana. In 1564, Juan Vásquez de Coronado (brother of Francisco) was first to write about the Naso, describing them as rebels against the Spanish king. But from their perspective, they already had a king and saw no need to serve another. Today many of the Naso people still maintain their proud tradition of opposition.

At the time of the Spanish incursion, there was an Aztec trading post (most likely near the village of Silencio) at the confluence of the Teribe and Changuinola rivers. This may explain why the Naso have many loan words from the Nahuatl language. For perhaps centuries, the Naso were connected to an extensive circum-Caribbean trading network.

In 1611, the Naso revolted against the ever-increasing presence of Spanish settlers. Some eighty years later in 1692, Frey Nicolas, the bishop of Leon Nicaragua, mentioned how barbaric the Naso were because of their repeated attacks on regional churches. The Franciscans entered the context of this conflict in 1700, when they succeeded in founding the mission village of San Francisco de Terraba in what is now Costa Rica. When the Naso burned the mission in 1719, the Governor of Costa Rica, Diego Fernandez, called them "the most bellicose of all Indians in America."

Considering the fact that the Naso were the ones being invaded, the charge seems harsh.

The Nasos have historically had many enemies. Even today they are fighting battles on several fronts at once. From the end of the seventeenth century they suffered as a result of the slaving raids by ocean-going Moskito Indians. These slave raids, promoted by the founders of the new Moskito Kingdom, the British, led to many Naso slaves dying in Jamaica. The raids also led to the Naso paying an annual tribute to the Moskitos from the end of the seventeenth century until the 1840s. These tributes were usually in the form of cacao, sarsaparilla, turtle shells, silkgrass fishnets, and other goods, much of which was traded to the British. In addition to having to deal with Spanish attacks and slave raids from the Moskito, the nearby Bri Bri and Talamanca tribes (from along the mountainous Costa Rican border) both defeated the Naso in 1827. This drastically reduced their population from over twenty thousand in the seventeenth century to approximately twelve hundred by 1874.

According to an American explorer William Gabb, there were only seven Naso villages left in 1874. In recording the 1873-74 Naso/Bri-Bri wars, Gabb noted that, due to their reduced numbers, young Naso had problems finding mates from their own villages. By the 1900s, though, their numbers gradually started to increase. But now, after five hundred years of tribal decimation for defending their homeland, Panama uses their low population as an excuse not to set aside land for a Naso comarca, a district homeland. This has long been known as an thinly veiled justification for exploiting the natural resources of the Naso.

Today the Naso are one of the most endangered of all the indigenous cultures left in the Americas. One would think that they could garner some respect as the only indigenous monarchy left in Central America, but that is not the case. On the contrary, this tiny tribe is instead battling corporate, national, and global powers. Invasion of their land by multinational and local corporations is the modern equivalent of invasion by conquistadors. Like all indigenes, the Naso are still reacting to crimes perpetrated against them for centuries.

In the early 1900s, the United Fruit Company saw the flat, fertile, coastal land around Changuinola and determined to take ownership of it. What was once the Naso heartland has been, for most of a century, one of the largest banana-producing areas in the world. No doubt we have all eaten these fruits of deception. The Naso were never compensated for their land. On the contrary, they have been tossed aside like the proverbial banana peel, upon which the Panamanian and the international community's sense of justice slips and falls.

The difference is that today it is not just Naso land being taken, but their rivers as well—the defining locus of their way of life. The Naso people are inseparably connected to their whitewater rivers and the mountain refuges beside them. Three dams have already changed not only the rivers, but the Naso's very existence. The dams have also divided the tribe just as they have divided the rivers.

Historically, the Spanish crown retained ownership of all land on the isthmus. This was considered justified because the colonists there were merchants and adventures rather than farmers. It did, however, grant large tracts of land to favored subjects and continued the communal tradition of Panama's indigenous peoples by selling some lands to villages to be owned collectively. Most lands remained untitled and in the public domain. The Spanish crown recognized the right of small farmers to use, but not own, as much land as they needed.

When Panama separated from Colombia in 1903, all of its lands reverted to the state until owners revalidated their claims. Since the cost of doing so was prohibitive for the vast majority of indigenous and poor, the government continued to retain most of the country's land; as late as 1970, this amounted to close to ninety percent. Where guns had failed, the nation-state's inky "violence of the letter" did not, as people were defrauded of their land. Truly the pen is stronger than the sword. According to Andrew Zimbalist and John Weeks, "Wealthy Panamanian farmers appropriated almost a million hectares of government-held lands between 1950 and 1980, using them to graze cattle, plant commercial crops for export, or simply sit idle or underutilized."

On these lands where indigenous communities once planted yuca and collected wild fruits, many Ladinos started planting monoculture crops, such coffee, pineapples, and sugarcane. Teak plantations became forests without birdsongs. Some even used the land to facilitate the illegal drug trade in various ways. But the big players, like the state and its partners, prefer to bribe and defraud with the pen, as ink is cheaper and not as messy as blood.

For centuries, many of the Naso have lived in fear, even in their own homes. Just as the Moskito Indians once conducted slave raids and burned their villages, the National Police are burning them now for trespassing—even though they are on their own land.

In today's reality, the Naso and their neighbors, the tiny Bri Bri tribe, are the only indigenous people in Panama to be denied a comarca, an officially recognized indigenous district with political representation. The official government excuse for denying a comarca is their small population. The real reason is hydro-electric power.

The three hydro-electric dams in the area were first proposed long ago by the World Bank, the Inter-American Development Bank, and the Central American Investment Bank, all in partnership with the Panamanian government. In the 1980s, the government set up two giant parks as part of a high-powered environmental ploy. These were La Amistad International Park (a UNESCO World Heritage Site), and the huge Palo Seco Forest Reserve, bordering Panama and Costa Rica. Together, they amount to over one million acres of lowland and mountainous tropical jungle. This is part of the World Bank's Mesoamerican Biological Corridor (Corredor Biológico Mesoamericano), forty-seven percent of which is comprised of indigenous land. These are just three of scores of dams they have planned in the Corridor.

Setting up these parks was part of a devious strategy to build the dams. The powers knew that if the Naso had a comarca they would never allow the construction. So, they set up the parks knowing that the dams would follow. It took a lot of hubris and hypocrisy to give a name like La Amistad (Friendship) to a place where the rightful indigenous occupants are denied right to their land.

The largest of the three dams is on the Changuinola River. Another is on the Bonjic, a tributary of the Teribe River at Sieyik. The third will be near the headwaters of the Teribe in a very remote location called Palenque. This is where Valentín Santana, the Naso king, was born some seventy-five years ago. Palenque has long been abandoned due to its remoteness, but nonetheless it is part of Naso tribal land.

Work on the dam constructed on the Changuinola River by the Colombian-based Empresas Publica de Medillin has been completed. Though Panama has concerns about its need for more electric power, it is believed that the energy produced will be sold elsewhere, not used in Panama. Surely the Naso will never see a kilo-watt dollar or a light bulb. The "powers that be" value the hydro-electric power which the dams will produce far more than indigenous rights. Panama acts as if the Naso don't exist; if there are no lights in the dark forest that must mean that no one is there.

The first time I visited the Naso was in November 2008. It was the last of many trips I made that year with books and seeds throughout Panama. This time I traveled by bus from Panama City with a dozen boxes of books, school supplies, and seeds. I stopped in David for a couple of days to buy more vegetable and fruit seeds. From David I took a "coaster," a small Mercedes bus, over the isthmian pass to Bocas del Toro. It was raining hard, which is quite normal in the mountains. In Bocas it can rain any time of year and no one gives it a thought, for unlike the Pacific side, there is really no defined summer between January and March. Little did anyone know that this was the start of one of the worst rainstorms in thirty years.

When I arrived in Changuinola, I was the last to leave the bus. The beating rain chased a crowd and a curious cop onto a covered storefront porch, just next to the bus stop. As I began unloading my boxes and placing them on the dry porch, the ticket taker approached me and wanted me to pay. "No problem," I thought at first. But it was in that vulnerable rainy spot that the driver and ticket taker cheated me on the price of my fare. They wanted me to pay four times more than normal. Not only that, but a few of my boxes had gotten so wet during the journey that they were falling apart. Only the plastic garbage bags lining the inside kept the books from getting wet. The bus men showed no concern. Instead of the nine dollars they told me it would cost in David, they now wanted thirty-seven dollars.

"No way!" I said.

When I asked why they had changed the price, the driver didn't answer. They said that if I didn't pay I couldn't take the boxes. After some hard words in the hard rain, I paid them the money. What else could I do?

Disgusted, I told them, "I am going to report you to your office then. You also almost killed us all by talking on your cell phone in the rain on that dangerous road."

In the downpour, I flagged a taxi and the driver helped me load the dozen boxes, filling the back seat and trunk of his small car. He knew from the start that I had some problems with the bus driver. An acute attack of "Panamania isthmusia," as I came to call it, a nauseous feeling of contempt for the place, left me irritated.

"But señor, not all people here are like that," the driver replied when I told him what had happened.

I told him, "I don't think there is one trustworthy person in Panama! This is the second time in two months that busmen here either cheated me or stolen something. These guys must be stupid if they think people won't complain and do something."

In the next half an hour, though, he proved me somewhat wrong. We drove around Changuinola in the rain from one dive hotel to the next, but all were full. Arab-owned establishments like the Hotel Golden Sahara seemed out of place to me. The Golden Sahara in a rainforest? But the driver was determined to find me a room, and he finally did.

First, though, he had to pick up his seven-year-old daughter from school. First things first—I liked that! With her sitting between us we drove to more hotels until we finally found a room at the Changuinola Hotel, directly beside the airport. He never said a word as he helped me unload his taxi in the rain, but I could tell that he wanted a couple of books for his daughter. In Panama there are few bookstores, and children's books are something parents always want for their kids, but can never buy.

"How much for the fare?" I finally asked him, thankful for all the time and trouble he had just gone through.

"Whatever you like!" he responded humbly. I valued his help and wanted to show it, so he left smiling as his daughter proudly held her first books.

My start in Changuinola was far from ideal, but so be it, I remember thinking. I didn't want to accept being cheated or robbed by another bus worker as I had been a few weeks before. The memory resurfaced of the time when I had a box of notebooks worth fifty-six dollars stolen on another bus. We finally figured out that the theif was the baggage handler in Panama City. Surely he didn't even know what he was stealing.

At that time, the station manager in the David office had asked me, "How much were the contents of the box worth?"

I foolishly told him the truth, "Fifty-six dollars."

"Well, the company policy is to reimburse one-third of the value of the goods lost."

"So I lose a fifty-six dollar box of notebooks on your bus and you only want to give me eighteen dollars? In other words, you're only one third responsible for the loss then. You have to be joking!" I protested.

After deducting the $19.30 freight charges for the other twenty-four boxes, he wanted to hand me seventy cents. I told him with some bite, "Keep it, go buy yourself some breath mints."

I learned from that experience. I knew if I ever had anything else stolen from the storage compartment of a bus in Panama, I would tell them it cost three times more than I paid for it, so I could be properly reimbursed. They force one to lie to get justice, I thought. I kept that in mind when I later went to the bus office in the center of Changuinola. I asked the receptionist there if I could speak with the manager, who turned out to be a middle-aged Black man. He was in an adjacent room talking with a group of men, but when he realized I wanted to speak with him he kindly called out in English, "Come on in!"

Most Blacks in Bocas del Toro speak English, which gives them a rare advantage over the Ladinos. He asked me in English how he could help me, which gave the conversation a privacy which neither I nor his inquisitive associates wanted. I actually wanted the whole office to know what had happened, so I spoke in Spanish. Hearing me, every office worker turned and paused, listening intently to catch my every word.

"Besides cheating me on the price of my boxes, your reckless driver also almost killed us while talking on his cell phone! It was in a bad rainstorm and on a curve," I told them. Just after I had denounced the driver as being unfit to work there, in he walked! No doubt he had seen me enter and knew I was going to complain.

Almost immediately the manager asked him, "Why do we have a problem with a passenger?"

Without waiting for an answer, the manager asked him how much money I had paid. The driver answered correctly and was then firmly told to give me back all of the thirty-seven dollars. I told them, however, that I just wanted to be reimbursed for what the man had overcharged me. Thanking the manager, I left feeling somewhat vindicated. A few days later I chanced to pass by the same driver walking along the main street in Changuinola, and silently laughed when he gave me a dirty look.

Before visiting the Naso village schools, I needed to go to the Ministry of Education offices in Changuinola and get their enrollment figures. As soon as I entered the administrator's office the lights went out, leaving us in complete darkness. She suggested that I return in the afternoon, when she would have a copy of the schools' enrollments ready. The eleven schools on the list had enrollments ranging from seventeen to eighty-seven students. That information helped me know how to divide up the notebooks, pencils, and other supplies.

Bocas del Toro is a rainy area, but three weeks of constant rain is rare. It rained so much during those three weeks that the rivers rose nearly seven meters. The swollen waters finally crested just a few inches below the old one-lane wooden bridge over the Changuinola River, at the entrance to the gritty town. Now a new two-lane cement bridge spans the river beside it. Levees broke on the far side of the flooded Sixola River in the nearby town of Guabito on the Costa Rican border. The place was inundated for days. People in Changuinola were worried that the two swollen rivers on either side of them might flood over and merge.

For more than two weeks the whole region was cut off. Food and supplies had to be airlifted by helicopter to dozens of nearby flooded villages. The Changuinola Airport must never have seen so much traffic before! Many relief agencies provided assistance and Colombia sent planeloads of supplies. Huge front-end loaders, usually used for mining, with tires higher than I could reach, were filled daily and used to deliver supplies.

The road over the pass to David was a disaster thanks to the many large landslides caused by the rain. The Panamanian government offered stranded people, even tourists, free air tickets back to Panama City or David. I chose not to go because I would have to return again anyway. I stayed in my dingy hotel, paying full price despite having no water or electricity. Changuinola was filling up with many destitute homeless people, mostly barefoot Naso, Bugle, and Bokota Indians, who calmly congregated in and around a couple of evangelical churches, some of the few places offering any hospitality.

I spent the next couple of weeks waiting for the rains to stop, but they refused. I couldn't even get out of Changuinola, much less up the Teribe River whitewater. I would walk into Changuinola under an umbrella to get food. There are many Arab-owned shops lining its cluttered main road and several times in passing I met a Lebanese man from Sidon. Simply saying "As-Salaam-Alaikum" caught his eager ear. He told me he was working in a relative's shop and constantly thought about returning to Sidon. He just couldn't adjust. Like the Chinese, who operate many mini-markets across Panama, the Arabs have clothing and variety shops. Unlike the Chinese, their workers are not indentured. Most seem to dislike being in Panama and want to return home.

One day I went to a restaurant in Changuinola. Sitting down in the large room, I noticed there were with just a few customers. After awhile, the waitress brought me a menu and waited for me to order. I decided on the broiled fish, but she quickly told me, "We have no fish." Ok, I thought, and started to page through the sizeable menu for something else. Unsure, I asked her to give me a couple of minutes to decide. When she returned, I ordered spaghetti, only to be told me in the same flat manner that "We have no spaghetti."

"Well, what do you have?"

"We have chicken, pork, and beef."

"Well, why didn't you just tell me that to begin with and save us both the trouble?" I asked her, a bit put off. She didn't understand my point, so I left. But of all the luck, the exact same thing happened at the next restaurant. I left there as well, before I had another attack of Panamania isthmusia.

Since there was no way I could go up the Teribe River as I had planned, I decided to go and check things out at the riverside village of Silencio. A local bus from Changuinola drove the few flat miles past continual banana plantations.

Beginning in the early 1900s, all the banana farms belonged to United Fruit (now Chiquita Brands), until they pulled out some years ago. They sold their vast land holdings to smaller local growers. Farms in the area are impersonally numbered instead of named, and there are dozens and dozens of them in no apparent order. Over the years they have contaminated the soil and water table, and cancer rates are very high. For generations, they have offered the only work available to local families and now nearly all are affected. The main concern for the company, though, was the Panama disease (*Fusarium oxysporum*) that wilted the bananas, not the cancer of the workers.

The village of Silencio was no longer silent. Its silence had been invaded by the noisy machinery used for the dam and bridge construction. A deafening dirge signaled the end for the wild rivers and the Naso way of life. The bus from Changuinola left me off next to a little riverside cafe. Directly across the swift Teribe River was Zegla, a tiny Naso village. A new bridge project was just being started. Some days before in Zegla, a five-thousand-gallon gasoline tank, belonging to the contractor for one of the dams, had been washed down river by the flooding. Opponents of the dams saw it as divine justice, but it was too little and too late. It seemed the river, knowing it was going to be harnessed by the dams, was taking its revenge.

Some men were shouting beside the river and it caught my attention. I walked down some steps beside the cafe and immediately noticed a large road grader entering the river. I watched with curiosity as it went deeper and deeper, slowly approaching an abandoned half-submerged tractor. Somebody from the company had foolishly tried to drive across the flooded river. The waters were too deep for the grader as well, and its rescue effort failed. Not only that, it also went too deep and got stuck. Now both vehicles needed to be rescued. I sat and watched the situation unfold with a group of amused onlookers. Finally, a crane came and saved both of them. Cables were attached between it and the grader, and between the grader and the tractor. The waves splashing against the sides of the vehicles seemed to mock them with liquid laughter.

In addition to checking out the river, I also wanted to talk to Tito Santana, the forty-year-old ex-king of the Naso, who I knew lived nearby. I found him living with his family in a new, rapidly-built Naso community. It was located in a muddy clearing in the jungle, just a few hundred meters behind the National Police post and the gated headquarters of the construction company. Perhaps two hundred Naso were living in this new barrio. Obviously, they had chosen the location for protection from their irate Naso opponents. They had quickly constructed the shabby barrio soon after Tito's violent eviction from his village of Seiyik in 2004. Nearly all of the families living in the barrio are Tito's friends and followers. They joined him after he was forced to flee for his life from his "forest palace," to which he can never return. Nor can he ever again wear the King's crown, made from green parrot feathers.

Tito's followers are all in favor of the dams, as nearly all have family members working for the construction companies. Several were working on the new bridge across the Teribe River to Zegla. It was being constructed in order to take large earth-moving equipment across the river. A new road was also being made to the other dam site at Bonjic.

In the previous few years a major shift had occurred in the lives of the people who now lived there. They were forced to relocate after Tito's near regicide. For the majority of them, it was the first time they had ever had jobs. Before that, they had eked out livings as subsistence farmers, raising small plots of bananas, oranges, and root crops. Now they rarely return to their villages upriver, where most have family and former friends who adamantly opposed the dams. Instead they devote themselves to their work and seldom leave, other than for occasional visits to Changuinola.

Besides Tito, Panama, the banks, UNESCO, and the Colombian power company, the other major player in this drama was a famously crooked and powerful Panamanian politician who served as a congressman in the National Assembly for over twenty years. He had a very cozy, convenient, and lucrative private business contract for leasing the earth-movers and other big equipment to the construction companies. In permissive Panama, this was not considered a conflict of interest.

I had to be careful to stay out of his sight, because he was the one who had paid Tito the bribe and I had already been warned by one of his family members not to stick my nose in the congressman's business. In addition to making lots of money off of the dam construction, he was also doing the bidding of the Panamanian government. There was a lot of corruption in high places at the time, including a minister who was prosecuted for embezzling funds earmarked for asbestos removal from grade schools.

Knowing most of the Naso story, I had wanted to meet Tito for some time and it seemed that children's books were the best bait. I could not reveal my true intent, though, or the meeting would never have happened. Before meeting Tito, I had first run into his teenage son. The boy carried with him a cell phone worth several hundred dollars, and with that came an attitude. No doubt Tito's signature for the dams was the currency that had paid for it. Not only had Tito gotten himself dethroned, but now very few Naso would ever accept his son as a future Naso king.

The son used his fancy phone to call Tito, who asked us to come over to the company office. I followed the son through a funky, heavily guarded entrance gate that separated the end of the riverside road in Silencio from the National Police post and the adjoining construction company office. They all must have known Tito's son, because we walked right through the guarded gate. The National Police were there primarily to stop any monkey-wrenching against the construction equipment.

Tito still considers himself the King of the Naso, as does the Panamanian government, though for different reasons. When we arrived, he was on the porch of the company office talking on his cell phone, similar to the one his son used. As soon as he finished he came over and told me that he was interested in the books and hoped that I would give him all, or at least many, of them to distribute. He wanted to see the books and told me that he would come over to my hotel the next afternoon at two. I left without promising him anything, and did not reveal my intention to never give him a single book. I was interested in interviewing him, however, so I guess I set him up. Tito had no idea that I was baiting him with the books. I knew that he wanted the books for bait as well—maybe he thought they could retrieve a feather from his fallen crown. But at the same time, he also had kids and knew how empty of books the schools were.

Tito arrived he next day on time. Though I had my own agenda, he came there for one reason and one reason only—the books. I got him a cold bottle of water and had him sit on the terrace while I brought out a box of books to show him. He liked them immediately and briskly paged through a couple of them. Clearly, he expected me to give him some, since he had made the effort to come and see me. But I told him that I thought it was better if I brought the books to the schools myself. I didn't have to explain why when I told him that I was going to Sieyik.

I could soon tell that Tito realized he was wasting his time and that I had never intended to give him any books. He knew he wasn't going to get his bait and he was right. When I tried to change the focus of the conversation from the books, he seemed put off and suspicious. Just mentioning the word "dam" was enough to alert his delicate senses. I wanted to ask him about the dams and the tribal situation, but losing out on the books meant that he was no longer in a mood to talk. With the bait gone, he had seen the hook and like a fish diving out of water, he spit it out. Putting down the book he was looking at, he suddenly got up to leave.

I kept my silence, although I wanted to tell him that he should maybe buy some children's books with money the corrupt politician had paid him for his sign off on the dam. The last time I saw Tito was on one of my later trips up the Teribe River. He was with some other men along the rocky bank, cutting storm-downed trees with a chain saw. Though we both recognized each other, neither of us waved.

The dams have radically divided the cohesion and life of the Naso community, sapping its vitality, just as they will do to the rivers. Most of the Naso identify with the rivers, but not with the dams, because they were something imposed on them against their will. Most would rather see their clean, clear rivers and their lives flowing freely again.

It was Tito's choice of money over justice that ultimately divided his tribe. None of the Naso know how much he was paid, but he was probably bought off for very little. He surely didn't spend it on his house, because it's as poor as those of his neighbors. And he didn't spread the money around—that's not his style. It's no doubt stashed away in some Panamanian bank. Through this act, Tito has done more to hurt his tribe than any Naso king in half a millennium of their history. His pen has brought the gun, and his signature has brought the soldiers.

After waiting more than two weeks for the weather to clear and the rivers to recede, I returned once again to Silencio. This time, I brought seven boxes of books and several other boxes of supplies for the seven Naso primary schools up the Teribe River. I decided to store them there as I prepared for the journey.

First, I visited the small Naso community of Zegla, located directly across from Silencio on the Teribe River. It is situated precariously on the triangular point of land between the confluence of the Teribe and Changuinola rivers. In the Naso language, Zegla means "tree fern," and dozens of storm-torn tree ferns were strewn all along the rocky river bank like collapsed umbrellas.

Zegla was the site of a new bridge over the Teribe, where a dirt road follows the river up to another dam site at Bonjic. The bridge was obviously not built for the Naso community of Zegla, and despite their protests they received no compensation. The road was being cut through the middle of Naso family farms and orchards, as if butchering meat.

Just a week or so before my arrival, the primary school in Zegla had been inundated with four feet of muddy water from both rivers. Like other schools upriver, it was still full of mud, and like the other schools, there had barely been any materials inside to begin with. Though they had little to lose, it did not make the situation any easier.

The most obvious casualties from the new bridge at Zegla were a couple of ferrymen with dugouts. For hundreds of years, boatmen had eked out a living poling cargo and passengers in their dugouts across the river's swift currents. When people needed to cross they would just stand beside the river. For twenty-five cents a man would stand and pole his dugout across the granite-lined river bed. The bridge will change all that. I had to use the ferry to carry the books to the Zegla school since the bridge had not yet been completed. Given the rapids that existed at the time, I doubted the old ferryman's ability to keep the books and other things dry, but he did.

One passenger left his dog along the river bank, but then called it once we were on our way. They seem to have used this technique before, as the dog lunged in when its owner beckoned. As soon as it reached the main current, the river carried it down for a couple of hundred meters, before it could finally swim to the other shore.

The best I could do at the mud-caked school was to leave the books and supplies with the school principal, so I shortly crossed the river again to Silencio. Traveling upriver proved to be even more difficult, not only because of the unruly river, but also because there was a gasoline shortage in the area due to the flooding. I finally located eight gallons of gas and I was obliged to use Ricardo, a Naso man from Tito's barrio, to take me upriver in his motorized dugout. Few people have motors and because of the recent weather, there was little river traffic. Ricardo was glad to go and despite his pro-dam position, I found that he had misgivings about Tito. It seems he thought that the dam would give him a chance to help his village, which he left the year before. On this trip, he brought along his two teenage sons, as well a Naso man from Sieykin named Moises, who worked as a government health worker in his village.

As we traveled upriver, the strong current of the Teribe cast a high and wide wake as it beat against the bow of the twenty-foot dugout. Looking down at the fast current gave the impression that we were traveling faster than we actually were. By looking at the river bank, it was clear that we were just inching our way along. Pieces of wood and whole trees that had been carried downriver by the flood littered the granite-studded banks. The recent high-water line was revealed by the debris and brush clinging to overhanging tree branches several meters high. A river otter searching for something on shore paid us no attention. In some of the steeper places, landslides had left large earthen scars in the thick forest. A few times we passed men floating downriver in makeshift rafts of banana stalks bound together with vines. They were floating and poling their way down to Silencio, as people have done for centuries—an ancient but appropriate technology. These types of disposable rafts are still used because there are few dugouts, due to the need for both a motor and gas.

About halfway up to the community of Bonjic, the site of the second dam, we encountered some strong whirlpools churning against a granite wall. Because of rapids, the boatman's two sons and I went ashore to lighten the load. This was at a place called

Wekso, also known as Panajungle. During Noriega's time it had been a military training camp for jungle warfare. Though now rarely used, the Naso have it available as an eco-lodge for tourists.

When we arrived in Bonjic, we found the river bank strewn with hundreds of banana trees, all toppled by the flooding. Typically the Naso farm along river and stream banks; because of that, the flooding had devastated their gardens, practically wiping out their main source of food and thus survival.

It seemed surreal to see huge Caterpillar earth-movers parked along the riverbank in the middle of nowhere at the Teribe's confluence with the tiny Bonjic River. They seemed out-of-place, like dinosaurs from another world. The name Bonshik or Bonjik in the Naso language refers to the mouth of the bon fish. Bon is a common river fish and jik or shik means mouth. The Naso have always used these fish for food, but the construction of the dam will change that.

In Panama's remote villages, the primary schools are usually built directly next to a health center. Despite being anchors for indigenous communities, both are normally empty of supplies. Thus they are anchors with no weight. Government health workers using western medicine, like Moises, have replaced traditional village healers. But unlike the herbal medicine chest of the jungle, the clinics are often closed and poverty prevents purchases. And since there are few pedagogical materials made available, teachers are there mostly just to instill acculturation and a spirit of nationalism. In the schools the football and the flag, the two f-words of acculturation, always take precedence over books.

When we arrived in Bonjic, a group of people were cleaning out the school. Like the school in Zegla, it had taken on four feet of water just a few days before. Dozens of chairs were piled haphazardly outside, along with stacks of textbooks covered in mud which were beyond salvaging. Arriving when we did brought some smiles of hope, though. It seems that I couldn't have come at a better time, as the teachers told me they were wondering how they could go on. Like most indigenous schools, they have good reason to feel abandoned by the government.

While we were talking, a teacher received a call on her cell phone. The caller warned her to not let people go further upriver, because a landslide had toppled trees which were floating down dangerously. Once again, we had to postpone the trip for another day. We decided to return to Silencio and I retreated to my dive hotel in Changuinola.

After a couple more days of rain we returned, and this time we made it further upriver, stopping at the village schools in Solong and Sieyik. Both of these schools had escaped the flooding since they were built on higher ground. Some sizable rapids just below Sieyik required us to unload the struggling dugout to reduce some of the weight. A few local boys helped carry the boxes into the village. A series of small stilted wooden houses, separated for privacy amongst the forest and fruit trees, stretched along one bank of the river for a couple of hundred meters. I followed the boys to the village center, which was carpeted with an expanse of short grass.

Beside a thatch-roofed shelter, several children were playing games, while inside some elders were sitting and conversing. One of the boys who had carried a box of books addressed a couple of the men in the Naso language. Knowing that the school was closed, the boys took us to a teacher who lived nearby. Soon a key was found and we stored the boxes inside the school.

Sieyik could be considered the capital of the Naso nation, even though the king, Valentín Santana, lives across the mountains in San San Druy, several miles away. It was in Sieyik in 1939, that the Seventh Day Adventists established the first Naso school. And it was in Sieyik where Tito had been banished from the now empty "forest palace." I wanted to see it, so a dozen or more laughing Naso children walked me over to the plain block house. It was one of the village's only concrete structures and they were quite proud of it. Though I didn't want to mention his name, I thought of Tito several times while I was in this village now forbidden to him.

I consider Tito an example of indigenous miseducation and the ills of acculturation. For a few greasy coins, he signed his name on the dotted line, sacrificing the future of his tribe, his family's royal succession, and their rivers and land, and torn the tribe apart. How ironic, I thought, that I was helping his alma mater, the "forming mother," where he learned how to write his name. Oh, that he would have never learned how to write his name, or rather, too bad that he had only learned how to write his name, but not when or where to write it.

Though Tito's failings had opened the door for hydroelectric dams, we can't blame the letter or the pen. On the contrary! For even if Tito Santana had never learned how to write his name, his X would have been considered sufficient by the crafty Panamanian officials. No matter how clumsy or illegible his signature might have been, it would still have been used as a way to conquer, as it is an even slicker thief than the illiterate gun.

Half an hour by boat above Sieyic is the village Sieykin, the last Naso village up the Teribe River. It is tucked out of sight in a forest clearing about a kilometer inside the jungled mountains. At one point, the Teribe narrows between some rock cliffs pressed tightly against both sides. Topped with clinging jungle like a bad haircut, the cliffs soon lower and the river widens, which opens up to a panoramic view. A couple of thatched roofs of houses peeked out in the distance amongst the forested hillsides. The gaping river valley had a very haggard and disheveled look about it. Driftwood littered the banks and more toppled banana trees stretched for several hundred meters. All hopes of a harvest lay in ruin.

Once at the riverside, we called to some nearby young men who agreed to lend a couple of their horses to help carry the boxes to the village. Despite the mud, it felt good to walk instead of sitting. Crossing a stream bed lined with towering bamboo, we followed up a steep, well-worn trail to the village.

Moises, the government health worker, had a house in Sieykin and invited me to stay there, so I hung my hammock for a few nights on his stilted porch. It was a pleasure to listen to the jungle and breathe in the fresh scents emanating from it after weeks of rain. His neighbor had a very beautiful plot of pineapples, which seemed to embroider the hillside near his house. They were planted so thickly that there was no room for weeds!

While walking with Moises through the tiny impoverished community, I immediately noticed a satellite dish surrounded by a cyclone fence that also enclosed a two-story house. It was distinctly different from the normal stilted shacks and drew my attention.

"Who lives there?" I asked.

"Oh, this is the home of Simon and his family. He's an American working with a missionary group and is a Bible translator. But he is in Panama City right now."

Moises told me that Simon had been in Sieykin for eight years and spoke perfect Naso. But I was also told that he and his family live very separately from the impoverished community.

"His four children are home-schooled and they never play with the village children," Moises said.

"What does the missionary group do for the village?" I pressed.

Slowly shaking his head Moises answered, "Nothing!"

It was clear that Moises was not overly fond of Simon or his group. Perhaps he resented Simon's generator, computer, radio phone, fax machine, large screened-in house, and other amenities in a place where most of the villagers can't even afford candles. Later, after a glass of wine, Moises talked more.

"When helicopters came and delivered food and supplies during the flood two weeks ago, Simon demanded that he should distribute it, because he told us the food came from America." Apparently, it was Tito who gave them permission to come there.

"We don't want them here, but there is nothing we can do," Moises complained.

"Did the missionary group pay Tito like the dam companies did?" I asked.

"I don't know," Moises answered. "I do know that Simon pays a village man five dollars a day to help him translate the Bible."

"Five dollars a day?" I questioned.

"Yes, five dollars a day and the man works from eight in the morning till four o'clock in the afternoon. He has four children and a wife to support and they really can't live on five dollars a day," said Moises.

"I guess that they don't value Bible translation very much," I answered sarcastically. "If they don't value the translator, how can they value the translation?"

Moises answered, "If my people want one of the Bibles, they must pay a dollar. No one here has an extra dollar for a Bible when their kids need shoes."

After I finished my work up the Teribe River, I returned to Changuinola. Although I still wanted to visit the three other Naso villages along the San San River near the Costa Rican border, I had run out of books. Nonetheless, having already met the dethroned Tito, I now wanted to meet the new king, Valentín Santana.

I needed to ask some questions and the king's permission before I could return with books and seeds, so I caught a ride to Guabito on the border with Costa Rica. From there, a covered pick-up truck with several Naso in the back was ready to leave for San San.

After turning off the pavement, the driver followed for some miles along a flat dirt road bordered by lush pastureland. Patches of heliconias occasionally pushed their way up through encroaching barbed-wire fences, seemingly protesting, not unlike the Naso themselves. This expansive pastureland belonged to the Bocas Cattle Company, whose owners were accused of instigating the police to burn dozens of Naso homes. Here the Naso had been fighting for their survival more than anywhere.

San San, along with San San Druy and San San Tigra, are three small Naso villages built along the narrow meandering San San River, which eventually drains directly into the Caribbean. These three San San villages are as unobtrusive as the slow San San River, but when provoked they can also spill over with rage. Their sense of justice has increased even as that of the government has foundered.

I was going first to San San Druy to meet Valentín Santana. The long straight dirt road ended at a turn-around just in front of a metal swing foot-bridge. Here the truck stopped and a dozen of us got out. Beside an old tamarind tree was a two-story wooden house, whose ground floor served as a five-item store. The whole area, having been flooded for almost a month, was still caked in thick shoe-sucking mud. I found a nearby pile of cut lumber to sit where I could ready myself and get my bearings.

On the other side of the swing bridge there was a wide soupy trail which led straight back towards the dark mountains rising abruptly from the coastal plain. I soon found out that without high rubber boots, the best way to go was barefoot. Like most of the eleven Naso villages, San San Druy is not linked by road and it has no electricity. To get there, one must cross a couple of cable swing bridges over the San San River.

Though it was only a few kilometers to San San Druy, walking alone for the first time in the cloying mud made it seem much longer. Finally, at the base of the mountains some stilted Naso houses poked out of the trees like clinging bromeliads.

I was told that "El Rey," as King Valentín is referred to, was in the village. Continuing down the muddy trail, I passed a dozen or more humble homes scattered alongside the river. Soon I found the dismal primary school. By the looks of things, it was not a place conducive to learning, but rather appeared to support a "pedagogy of oppression." Perhaps that's the point, for it seems that Panama prefers uneducated indigenes who cannot articulate their desires, their oppression, or their desire for rights.

A couple of kids led me to the king, who was at the abandoned National Police station along with his wife, his daughter, and a bunch of his grandkids. Since the recent flood it had become his daughter's new home. Just in front of and beside the river lay the ruins of the house of the king's only child, his daughter Adelina. The house had been a casualty of the flood, and soon after its destruction Adelina and most of her eleven children took refuge in the empty police post. They lived in the two upper rooms, where they slept with just blankets on the cement floor. The police had evacuated a year before in the chaotic situation during which many Naso homes were burnt to the ground.

Unlike his nefarious nephew Tito, King Valentín was very humble. Because of his vehement opposition to the dams, the Panamanian government did not recognize him as king. But then Panama had never recognized the Naso right to self-determination, nor any of the ancient tribal boundaries. During my visit, I asked them about their school and what kind of seeds they wanted. The school was a place in dire need, with little lighting inside and even fewer educational materials. Like other Naso villages, they had no seeds nor any money to buy them. The fact that virtually all of their banana trees were destroyed in the flooding meant that tough times would be even tougher. It would take at least eight months for them to even get a salvage crop. Only their root crops were saved, so seeds were badly needed.

When I asked what seeds they wanted, the king mentioned rice. Others wanted beans, corn, squash, and peppers, so the only thing to do was to return to David, for more seeds, and to San Felix, where I had more books. By that time it was getting late and the rain had started again, so I was invited to spend the night.

One of the king's grandson's took me upstairs to the second story porch of the abandoned National Police post where I hung my hammock. The block building was built about thirty meters back from the narrow river on a little rise to keep it from flooding.

I looked down in horror at the destroyed hovel where Adelina and her family had once lived.

It didn't take long before my hammock was noticed and soon Adelina wanted to try it out. Of course, I said "Please, help yourself," and soon she was in it, swinging back and forth. Then her septuagenarian mother, the king's spicy, humorous, diminutive wife, had to have a go. Soon her tiny body and her long black hair were wrapped in my hammock like a wriggling larva ready to hatch into a floating butterfly.

Suddenly it dawned on me that I was visiting royalty, but had failed to bring a gift. It wasn't hard to tell that they would love to have my hammock, but they were too reserved and too sensitive to ask for it. The image of the king's tiny wife, swinging with a smile as big as my hammock, was tied to my memory like a wet knot.

Wondering what I could do to make up for not bringing the king and his wife a gift, I decided to make some popcorn. They had all heard of popcorn, but I found out that no one had ever eaten any, much less made it. I asked for a pot and a little cooking oil. Some of Adelina's kids and their friends took me down to the ground floor kitchen, where a small fire was burning. I poured a little oil into the pot, heated it, and then poured in part of the bag of popcorn. Once the popping started, they all were curious and gathered around to watch. Once I heard a frenzy of popping, I quickly slid off the lid to shouts and laughter, as the exploding popcorn escaped in flight. I brought a bowl up to the queen resting in my hammock, and thus began her love affair with popcorn. It struck me that she was very much like popcorn herself: tiny, airy, weighing almost nothing, but having an expansive personality. Soon, the others were making the rest of it.

Adelina and some of her sons were going to Changuinola early in the morning, so we decided to walk together through the cloying mud. In order to catch old Solano's taxi-truck next to the store at seven o'clock we had to leave by five-thirty. Weeks of rain seemed to have caused a proliferation of frogs; they croaked all night and sounded as if they were as numerous as the mosquitos.

Before five o'clock, the king came over to make sure we were awake. In the glow of my flickering candle I turned to see his smiling face wishing me a good morning. His daughter was below in the kitchen making some of the coffee I had brought: a rare treat! After thanking me for coming and encouraging me to return soon with the books and seeds, the king asked me for a favor. "Please, my wife would really like you to bring her some more popcorn," he humbly asked.

In David, a rice growers' co-op called the Association of Rice Producers in Chiriqui (APACH) sold me two-hundred pounds of seed. I later wished I had bought five or ten times that much. They figured that about a hundred pounds of seed will plant a hectare, and each family likes to plant at least a half a hectare of rice and more of corn if they can. All of the rice seed is planted by hand, with five or six grains of rice placed in shallow holes made by a planting stick. In addition to the rice, I took fifty pounds of Pioneer corn. Even though they all prefer their traditional strains, I bought this hybrid variety because it is so productive and can generate cash faster. I also brought seeds for over a dozen varieties of vegetables and fruits, such as melons, New Zealand spinach, tomatoes, onions, peppers, zucchini, and cucumbers.

Within a week I was on my way back with the promised books and seeds, as well as the popcorn that the king asked me to bring for his wife. I had also gotten her a royal red cotton hammock. Once I arrived at the end of the road beside the five-item store and the swing bridge over the San San River, some Naso men helped me unload. I needed to contact the king's grandson, so the owner of the store let me use his cell phone. Just as the machete was once the most acculturating item of colonization, so the ubiquitous cell phone is now for globalization. I called San San Druy and asked the grandson to come with at least six horses. In the meantime,

I sat with a book on top of a pile of milled lumber, as it proved to be one of the few places not covered in thick mud.

After an hour or so, a few men and some children arrived with several horses. Soon we had loaded up and were walking back to the village through half a foot of liquid mud. I knew from previous trips on horseback that the best way to carry the boxes was inside large plastic sacks, like the white ones used for flour and grain. So we tied the open ends of two filled sacks together and placed them on back of the blanketed horses. Two of the horses carried a hundred-pound sack of rice each. Another one was loaded with a fifty-pound sack of Pioneer hybrid corn and thirty pounds of beans. Three others carried the boxes of books, notebooks, and other school supplies. One horse carried a little girl, along with my bag and some supplies.

I was wearing rubber boots and the mud tried to suck them off my feet. A series of shack-like homes appeared, which meant we were approaching San San Druy. Under one house a crested guan and a great curassow, wild fowls kept as pets, took shelter with several chickens from a sudden shower. A drying jaguar skin was nailed to the outside wall of another house. Two jaguars stalking the area had been shot in recent days. They were hard up for food because of the recent flooding. A large fang from one of them was later given to me before I left. Once the six horses reached Adelina's house at the old National Police post, we carried everything upstairs to a dry area.

I was surprised to find a lone Peace Corp worker there, a very gentle young woman named Jannel. She had lived in San San Druy for several months in a newly constructed cabin in a forest meadow. She told me that teaching weekly English classes and providing agricultural assistance wasn't enough to keep her from being bored. Her superiors, following Peace Corp rules, did not allow her to take any role in the Naso's political activism. Although she had gone through the flood and felt the Naso's plight when the National Police burned down many houses in nearby San San, she was restricted from participating in any protests or direct action. She felt torn between acting as a human being in support of the Naso, the people she had come to help, or just being a US Peace Corp worker. I didn't want to speak my mind and tell her that Peace Corp workers, though often well intentioned and pure of heart, are unknowingly information gatherers for the CIA and its cousin, USAID. This is the reason some people refer to the organization not as the Peace Corps, but as the "Pig's Corpse." Within the next few months she was relocated elsewhere.

I was back in my hammock again on the second floor porch of Adelina's liberated National Police post. Knowing that I would be eating with Adelina's large family and knowing how little they had, I had also brought a bunch of extra food along. Popcorn had been underlined on my list, as well as candles, which were scarce.

This time I observed proper protocol; as soon as I was settled, I walked over to the king's house with a few pounds of popcorn, a large slab of beef, candles, and the royal red hammock for the queen. In typical Panamanian fashion, I let out a little high-pitched hoot to announce my arrival. The king and his wife had adopted an abandoned Naso boy named Adonis, who invited me in. Within minutes, the king's wife was happily swinging in her new hammock while eating popcorn.

When Valentín Santana dies, the exuberant fifty-some year old Adelina will probably be queen. The traditional royal succession passing from the king to his brother's eldest son or daughter and back again had been interrupted by Tito's treachery. In the 1980s, the Naso started voting for kings from the royal family and Tito had virtually eliminated any chance that anyone on his side of the family would become king.

Adelina happily helped organize the seed distribution, since seed safety is women's work. She first sent word out to the neediest outlying families and then to anyone who wanted some. For two days I separated the different seeds and carefully spooned them into small manilla coin envelopes, which I labeled in Spanish.

Though not all Naso speak Spanish or can read, there is usually someone around who can. I enlisted a couple of Adelina's kids to help me and we sat for hours working on the second story porch. The word "palomita," popcorn, came up often. What better use could be made of this former police post, I thought. Where provocative soldiers had once put bullet clips into their guns, little kids were now putting seeds into envelopes. Soon people started showing up, often times older women with grandchildren. This was ideal because they take the best care of the seeds and pass on knowledge about them to their children. Most of the kids had never seen such a variety of vegetable and fruit seeds before; but now they were taking notice and commenting, such as observing how tiny the onion seeds were. One thing was certain: just as no one can read without books, no one can plant without seeds.

In Panama, although all GMO seeds are forbidden, there are few open-pollinated seeds available. Nearly all of the fruit and vegetable seeds for sale are from commercial American seed companies, the largest ones being Emerald and Bonanza. The variety is limited and most are hybrid, not open-pollinated, so farmers cannot recover seeds from their harvest. Instead they must buy new seed every year, which most cannot afford. They do keep their favorite strains of heirloom corn, and sometimes squash and peppers, but there is very little of it. Thus, kids are unfamiliar with many seeds except for a few staples like corn, rice, squash, and peppers. Even though the land is good and people have a desire to plant more, poverty prohibits it.

Adelina told me the story of events that occurred one night, a couple of weeks earlier, during the three-week storm. A landslide had suddenly covered her new home. She told me how two families had appeared at her house in a downpour at two in the morning, "completely dazed and muddy and walking like soaking wet chickens with their naked children in their arms." They had heard it coming and just managed to escape with their lives. Their belongings, pigs, dog, and chickens were left behind and buried.

Adelina wanted me to visit the site and see what had happened. When I walked over, men were pulling lumber and other things out of the mud, salvaging whatever they could. A couple of their sons were pulling nails from a pile of muddy boards. The river hadn't destroyed these people's homes—the mountain had. And if the mountain hadn't done it, their lives would still be in a precarious position from the police and the corporations. They must have felt that life had not only abandoned them, it had evicted them.

The Naso have no titles to their land, only right of possession, or ROP as it is called. Though they want their comarca and titled land, they still believe their land was entitled to them by God. Having lived there for hundreds of years was title enough. The title to their lands was not written with ink on paper, but with their sweat and blood and knowledge of the natural surroundings. They know their boundaries, or what's left of them. All they want is to be left alone to live their lives on their land.

A few weeks after my visits, the Bocas Cattle Company influenced the governor to send the National Police to San San. They burned six more Naso dwellings—some might call them shacks, but they were family homes nonetheless. These were tucked inside a contested fringe of forest near the San San River. The Company claimed they were evicting trespassers, but the Naso said that they had always been there.

The incident was sparked when several water buffalo, recently purchased by the company, threatened people and trampled some of the remaining crops not claimed by the flood. The Naso women were especially terrified of the unruly beasts, which they claimed were released in that area as a provocation against them. When the Naso complained, nothing was done; when they protested, it was used as a pretext by the police to burn the homes. It seemed that the imported water buffalo had more rights than the indigenous Naso.

Eliseo Vargas, a Naso leader, accused the Panamanian government of abandoning them and turning a blind eye. But the Bocas

Cattle Company and the National Police were acting under the umbrella of the authorities, because they claimed to have had an eviction notice. The notice came right from the governor, a friend of the company's owners.

Though they have already lost most of their ancestral lands, the Naso are still fighting battles on at least two fronts. At San San they are being squeezed between the Bocas Cattle Company fencing in the fertile plains in front, and the energy companies damming the rivers in the mountains in the back.

The large Bocas ranch was "acquired" from the Chiquita Banana Company, which had sold it to them many years before. For years there has been friction, but the house burnings sparked a mass Naso protest, which was covered by Panamanian TV and newspapers on January 20, 2009. The governor of Bocas del Toro ordered more than one hundred riot police to the San San area. Again, they burned more homes. Since I had just been there a few weeks before, I keenly watched the news report on a restaurant TV in Panama City. It caught everyone's attention.

"Look at the fires! And the Indians have nothing but bows and arrows!" a waitress said loudly, taken aback with disbelief.

In early December of 2009, I visited the Naso again. During that year, at least thirty more of their humble homes had been burned by the National Police. This time I brought no books, but I took a thousand pounds of planting rice from APACH and lots of other vegetable and fruit seeds for the three San San villages.

One of my objectives was to help start a papaya nursery. I brought seven hundred black plastic grow bags for Caribbean Red Lady papaya seeds, a good hybrid Hawaiian type from Taiwan. They are the ones now used throughout Panama in commercial ventures. After about six weeks, the tiny trees can be transplanted permanently.

Back in Changuinola, I waited for my pickup taxi at the roadside cafe. A sign in English caught my attention on the side of a building just across the road. In large letters it read "Caribbean Naked

Construction Company. Nothing to Hide." Definitely gringo humor, I thought. Next door, at the storage room of the trucking company, we loaded ten one-hundred-pound sacks of rice into the back of the pickup taxi. It is about an hour's drive from Changuinola to the end of the road at the swing bridge over the San San River.

I noticed that the gravel turnoff road towards San San was in better condition than the year before. It was graded and the giant puddles had been filled in. I soon found out why when a man at the side of the road warned us that the National Police were at the end.

When we arrived, I at first didn't recognize the place. The two-story rough plank house with its five-item store was gone. It had been burned down by the National Police. New bright green grass sprouting up defined where it had once been. The large tamarind tree where I had rested in the shade had been cut down.

The place had a bad feeling. There were no Naso around, but there were several young policemen. A bored-looking one stood propped against the concrete pillar of the swing bridge, brandishing a sawed-off twelve-gauge shotgun. Three other police congregated around their four-door pickup truck. Two more stood guard nearby with M16s. They were all young Blacks, decent guys, but they had been ordered to do indecent things. Though they all wore camouflage uniforms, their actions stood out plainly. From its inception Panama has always played the "race card," using young Blacks in the national police force to do the state's dirty work against the indigenous.

The young officer in charge asked to see my passport. Taking it, he immediately walked over to the truck and sat down with his cell phone. With the door open, he called police headquarters in Changuinola. After a few minutes, he came over and told me that I could not enter any of the three San San villages. Using the taxi driver's cell phone, I immediately called a Naso friend in San San Druy. I told him what was going on and asked him to bring several horses as soon as possible.

I subsequently learned that Eliseo Vargas, one of the leading Naso activists, had recently been jailed again in Changuinola. The National Police did it to try to intimidate him. Just the week before, he led a protest after they had burned ten more Naso homes.

At first, the police would not allow me to even unload the sacks of rice and other things. Fortunately, my driver knew one of them, so they allowed us to put the sacks under a newly-built shelter with a cement floor. This was especially helpful since it was raining. The only things inside were three large plastic barrels, each containing dozens of canisters of tear gas. I asked a soldier if I could see one. They were unable to read the English language on the canister labels, so they were curious about what they said. While he held one, I read it aloud telling them that it said they were all lovingly manufactured by Defense Technology Laboratories in Casper, Wyoming.

I felt lucky to have unloaded the ten sacks of rice, knowing that the National Police could have caused me real problems. I stood under the open-sided shelter with a couple of them, to keep out of the rain. After about an hour, another police pickup truck arrived with five more cops. Four were plain clothes detectives who came specifically to check me out. For awhile I thought I was going to be deported, especially after chiding them for being on the side of injustice rather than justice. I told them they misrepresented service to both Dios y Patria, God and Country, which is the motto written on the doors of their vehicles. But as it turned out, they did nothing except ask me more questions.

For over an hour it continued to rain. A Naso woman and her young daughter came by and wanted to join us under the small shelter, but the police would not allow it. So, the woman and her daughter had to stand out in the rain for over an hour; like me, they were waiting for old Solano's pickup taxi coming from Guabito. I was so glad when it finally stopped raining!

While I was waiting, the officer told me that someone was coming from the Peace Corps. I was a bit confused because the only Peace Corps worker I was aware of in the area was Jannel, the woman who had left months ago.

But when a Spaniard named Paco showed up, I realized that he was the supposed Peace Corps man. "That is like calling an eagle a duck," I told him later. Paco worked as a journalist and also a human rights worker with the NGO Human Rights Everywhere. He was there investigating the recent house burnings and helped move forward the legal case that the Naso filed in the Inter-American Court of Justice.

After a while, several Naso arrived on foot. One was from San San Druy and the others were on their way to San San and San San Tigra. I asked the one to tell King Valentín that I said "Hello." I asked the others to tell their village leaders that there were three hundred pounds of rice and other seeds waiting for each village. That was the best I could do. A couple of the Naso men convinced me not to worry. They assured me that they would wait there until the horses came, and would make sure that all the seeds would be evenly divided and planted.

Then Solano's pickup truck was spotted in the distance. I had only a few more minutes to finish arranging things before it would be there. Solano doesn't wait long and that was his last run. Soon the back of the truck was filled with Naso families, their feet inside their black rubber boots the only dry thing about them. They were just glad to get inside. Paco got in the front seat next to Solano and I squeezed into the back.

Chapter 14

THE NGÄBE-BUGLÉ INDIANS

"Education is a progressive discovery of our own ignorance."—Will Durant

On the fourth voyage of Columbus in 1502, we find the first case of censorship of the written word in the New World. It was of the journal of a sailor. Though never published and most certainly destroyed, it sowed the seeds of soon-to-be-banned books in the New World.

All of this directly relates to the Ngäbe-Buglé tribe, the largest indigenous group in Panama. Queban, a north coast chief at the time, was one of the first to make contact with Columbus on the mainland. His territory along the Caribbean coast had some of the richest goldmines ever found, and his people were master goldsmiths and potters. Their extremely fine gold work was far more valuable to them than the metal itself.

When Columbus realized the content of the items he saw, he wanted to know the location of Queban's gold mines. Though he never found out, he wanted the story of their existence to remain secret. When he discovered a journal kept by a sailor, he was worried that it might reveal the general location of the mines, so he confiscated it and either expurgated the text or threw it into the sea.

Some years later, Queban was taken prisoner by the Spanish and another attempt was made to discover the location of his gold mines. But like the more famous Ngäbe chief Urracá, he escaped and then went on to make war against the new Spanish settlement of Belén. Such was the introduction of the Ngäbe-Buglé tribes to over five hundred years of imperial-colonialism, yet it seems like the story could have happened yesterday.

I had just spent six days hiking into the Ngäbe-Buglé comarca (i.e. district or reservation) with Oli, my multilingual Ngäbe friend and guide. With us were five horses loaded down with books, notebooks, and other supplies for five remote communities.

More than an hour before, we had departed from the two Ngäbe horsemen traveling with us. We had given them most of the remaining food, but we had forgotten our water and were thirsty. Luckily, we saw smoke rising from a traditional Ngäbe house along the trail, so we stopped to ask for some water. We noticed that some women there were cooking, so Oli had the idea to trade a couple of tins of sardines for some lunch. Delighted with the offer, the old Ngäbe ladies invited us in.

We had to bend way over in order to enter the conical house through the four-foot-high door. The structure was designed for protection, so entering was uncomfortable. The seven-meter-wide circular wall was made of wooden poles a meter-and-a half high, stuck in the ground and placed tightly together side by side. Its steep roof was made from thick layers of grass draped down so low that it brushed against my back as I entered. Our eyes had to adjust to the darkness. There were no windows and the only natural light was what entered through the little door and the cracks between the vertical poles.

On the dirt floor was a hearth made of three stones, in which a small fire was kept slowly burning from the end of a log. A huge, charred pot full of unripe bananas was their food for the day. Suspended above was a cane barrier to stop whatever rain might enter in a storm. It was completely covered with a nest-like matting of soot-blackened cobwebs. Hanging from the rafters were several baskets containing what few possessions they had. Off to one side was a bed with thin sticks for a mattress. A few round logs served as chairs.

The two women were sisters in their seventies who lived together with two grandchildren and their shared husband. We all ate the boiled green bananas along with the sardines. It was a treat for them, for in their poverty and remoteness they rarely had access to any fish or meat. Margarita, the younger sister, was surprised that a foreigner would even enter their house, much less eat their food, or so she told Oli.

During our lunch Margarita spoke a lot to Oli in their Ngäbare language. Later he told me what she had said.

"Times are different now," Margarita lamented. "The Panama government doesn't want Ngäbe women to have the same husband anymore. We have been happy for fifty years, but they want to change our people. Why? My daughters and my sister's daughters will not be able to marry the same man, like my sister and I have," she complained.

Oli smiled, with a tinge of sadness, as he interpreted her words to me.

"But, how refreshing," I said, "to see an old Ngäbe woman voicing her support for their traditional family values, polygamy. This puts a whole new slant on women's liberation. Usually a woman fights to get rid of a man, not to keep him," I jested.

Many Ngäbe-Buglé Indians in the mountains of Panama still practice polygamy, both sororal, where two or more sisters marry the same man, and non-sororal, which often gives access to additional agricultural resources. The Panamanian government, though, is trying to encourage a new tradition of monogamy through the village schools and health clinics, which is what Margarita was complaining about.

Oli had told her that we had just finished visiting some schools. Neither she nor her sister had ever been to one, so like most women there they were illiterate. She questioned the government schools, although her grandkids walked over an hour by trail everyday to the one in tiny Ratan.

For almost fifty years Margarita lived in this house with her older sister, who was the first wife. Now some of their children have houses nearby. This is a typical Ngäbe kinship group, which may have five or six homes spanning a few generations. Several of these family compounds, which are separate from each other in a certain area, make up a casaria, or hamlet.

Like the majority of the Ngäbe and Buglé Indians in their comarca, this family lives almost completely outside of the monetary system. Rarely do they buy anything, for they seldom have money. Perhaps when one of the women sells a sisal bag or a hat, they will purchase something. It is their dozens of banana trees, yams, corn, rice, chickens, wild fruit, and sometimes wild meat that sustains them. They are content with very little.

The Ngäbe and Buglé tribes have their comarca, a semi-autonomous district, in three parts of the central Panamanian highlands: in Chiriquí, Veraguas, and Bocas del Toro. Along with several sub-tribes they are also known collectively as the Guaymi, which is pronounced like the question, "Why me?" They are the largest and perhaps the poorest indigenous group in Panama with about 220,000 people, comprising about fifty percent of the total indigenous population. They are also one of the fastest growing indigenous cultures in Central America.

Those in the comarca live mostly from traditional subsistence swidden agriculture. At that time of the year, in early May, they had just finished their burning. Many steep hillsides were still charred and their rice was just coming up, giving a soft chartreuse tint to the blackened ground.

Nearly all of the coffee, fruits, and vegetables grown and harvested in Panama's Chiriquí highlands are from Ngäbe labor. Just as there would basically be no harvests in the US without Mexican laborers, so in Panama there would be no harvests without the Ngäbe. Although this seasonal labor is one of their only ways to make money, it has led to various problems and abuses. Often it means that their children never go to school, since many families go back and forth to eke out a "living" on farms in both Panama and Costa Rica. Their kids are never registered in school, so they are condemned to a life of illiteracy and the continuing cycle of perpetual poverty. The rich farm owners normally do nothing to help—some of the world's finest coffee is sold at the expense of Ngäbe children's future. This helps make the coffee growers wealthy and insures that a cheap labor pool will always be available. The government also turn a blind eye.

The Ngäbe are traditionally looked down upon and considered wild and dirty. Because of traditional fighting games and a propensity to drink, many Sunday mornings after pay day will find Ngäbe men bloody and "dead-drunk"—passed out in nearby cantinas. The few dollars a day they have made will all be gone. Sometimes their wives will angrily come looking for them before they piss all the family's money away.

Unfortunately, over half of their comarca land does not have productive soil. Add to that the lack of roads, transportation, and horses and it's easy to see why transporting any agricultural goods is impractical. Having lost all of the good bottom land to Ladino ranchers, poverty pushes whole families to spend months living and working on large commercial farms, often in extremely stark conditions. I asked some of the men about their work and pay, only to be told that they can barely survive on the six to eight dollars they make in a day. But they have no other options and know that their wages are kept purposely low; the farm owners know that in the comarca they can make nothing. As a result, they live with their families in virtual indentured servitude, housed in horrendous hovels provided by the farms.

Unlike the Indians living on reservations in the US, indigenes in Panama's comarcas have direct political representation, with elected tribal representatives serving in the National Assembly. In all of Panama's comarcas, however, it seems that once they are formed, the government simply abandons them. In fact, the standard of living drops precipitously and the poverty index rises as soon as one enters. Infant mortality and child malnutrition rates are many times higher than the national average. While the national illiteracy rate in Panama is about four percent, among the Ngäbe it soars to at least forty-five percent. Electricity, roads, and basic infrastructure don't exist. The government has constructed a paved road above the town of San Felix, but it was put in because of the Cerro Colorado copper mine, not to transport poor Ngäbe up and down the mountain.

If a person in the comarca has to travel somewhere, a lot of walking is required. They think nothing of walking for a few hours, or even for days to visit someone or do something. One thing is certain—from my experience, it is hard to keep up with them walking!

Oli and I had previously gone into the comarca with horses the September before, in 2006. This time we wanted to return and go even further in, so in May 2007 I rented five horses for five dollars a day each. The horsemen were supposed to meet us at a casería called Hato Pilon, an hour by truck above San Felix.

In San Felix we had to wait for the truck to be filled with gas before we could leave for Hato Pilon. I bought something to eat from one of the ubiquitous Chinese mini-markets and fed the chicken bone to a petitioning dog. A few Ngäbe families were also waiting. The women and girls were dressed in their colorful, ankle-length traditional cotton dresses. Some were braiding hair and others picking out lice. Beside them, a small boy was holding a tiny puppy tightly against his body. One woman's front teeth were all filed—twelve of her upper and lower front teeth were all pointed. Though not very common anymore, some people living in remote areas still practice tooth pointing. It is considered beautifying and is usually done to young girls or boys by a grandmother. The filing takes many months and is said to be very painful.

Private 4x4s are the only transportation into the comarca and, like ours, often carry more than twenty people, along with animals and luggage. After we finally left, we rode for an hour almost continually uphill to the end of the road at Hato Pilon. A few times there were rough spots and everyone had to get out and walk while the truck struggled to make the ascent.

Near San Felix, the mountains rise quickly from the coastal plain that stretches out like a green blanket to the Pacific, just a few miles away. Within minutes, the convoluted coast of the Gulf of Chiriqui appears with its mangrove estuaries and islands dancing down the coast, like the lacy trim on a Panamanian pollera dress.

When we finally arrived at the end of the road, the young attendant climbed up and handed down to us the eleven boxes of books and materials he had previously packed onto the roof. Oli went off to buy some plastic grain sacks that we had forgotten to bring. We would place the boxes inside of them and then tie two sacks together and place them over a pack frame on a horse. By the time Oli returned, the horses had arrived. I thought, "Wow, that's pretty good timing, considering we'd come from seven hours away."

Three young Ngäbe men had started out at five in the morning so they could meet us at noon. And they did! Before leaving we also placed tarps over the five loaded horses, for rain was on the way. Within minutes it had arrived and we were facing a six-hour walk to the village we planned to visit. The trail was wide at first, but soon narrowed. On hills, it was often worn to a knee-deep rut. In some places the trail became a slippery trench, two meters deep, created by centuries of erosion and wear. During heavy rains, which we periodically found ourselves in for the next three days, the steep parts of the trails turned into small, fast-flowing streams.

After walking in the rain for a couple of hours we came to a tiny hamlet. Several round houses were scattered just off the trail in the thick sodden forest. They stared out like hooded people, somber in the rain. We heard talking before we saw anyone, then found two very drunk Ngäbe men having a friendly fist fight. Both had their shirts off, and a few other people stood around watching them. It seemed to have just stopped; one of the men was slightly bleeding, which is the decisive factor. Fighting for them is a common male sporting ritual, which traditionally stops when blood appears. Later they will walk off as friends, or at least not as enemies.

Unless under the influence of liquor, the Ngäbe-Buglé are usually quite meek and mild, despite suffering from continual racism anywhere outside of their comarca. Many, though, enjoy fighting and they also play an traditional stick-fighting game called *balsaria*. The name is taken from the long balsa wood sticks that contestants throw at each other.

In autumn, the Ngäbe have large gatherings, at which men from one casaria challenge men from another in this rather violent game. As a prerequisite, large amounts of corn beer, chicha, are prepared by the women. After masticating corn (or sometimes yucca), they will spit the pulp into calabashes or pots and add water. The ptyalin enzymes in saliva act upon the starch and cause fermentation This game is accompanied by fires, and music from drums, bone whistles, conch shell horns, and stringed sea turtle shells. Players compete wearing feathers and animal skins, and with painted faces. They are circled by drunken spectators, often numbering in the hundreds.

One man will throw one of his dozen four-foot long balsa wood sticks, from a distance of seven or eight meters, aiming at the lower legs of the competing player. The object is to knock him over. Then the other man takes his turn. The first to fall is the loser. As with polygamy, the Panamanian government has also tried to outlaw the *balsarias*.

Continuing on the embowered and rain-soaked trail, we circled around Cerro Otoi, which means Otoi Hill. An otoi is the name of a large manioc type of white yam. The 200-meter-high rock hill sticking out of the earth here resembles one. The sky suddenly brightened up and the continental divide appeared in grey silhouettes.

At that point the elevation was about 1,600 meters and the vegetation had drastically changed from the lowland tropics below. I recognized a few varieties of mushrooms, such as oysters, boletus, and russulas. Large-leafed *Gunnera* plants thrive there, as do several species of both blackberries and blueberries. Finally, well after dark, we arrived soaking wet in a little hamlet called Carrazal. We went right to the school and unloaded the horses.

We were lucky because there was still food left over from the teachers' dinner, which they happily served us. Unluckily for me though, my bedding and the clothes in my pack got totally wet on top of the horse. The tarp had shifted and we never noticed, because the two horsemen following us were out of sight. This radically challenged my attempt to sleep on the cold cement floor of the school classroom.

At remote schools, teachers usually live in a little dwelling nearby or even in the schools themselves, because the commute home is impractical. One might have to walk on trails for hours, or sometimes for over a day. Some teachers only go home on the weekends and others might not leave their school for months.

The following day, after giving out the books and supplies we'd brought to the Carrazal school, we went on to a very small community called Viroli. Because the trail between Carrazal and Viroli is so steep, we could not use the horses. They needed a rest anyway, after having walked over twelve hours the day before, and the grassy area around the school suited them well. The four of us set off walking. The three Ngäbe men took turns carrying a heavy box of books and supplies for Viroli.

The narrow trail wound its way through a thick forest of highland hardwoods. At overlooks, we could see the nearby walled peaks topped with flat, treeless grasslands called savannahs. Clouds often brushed against their palisades, sponge-bathing the rock faces and foliar feeding the bromeliads, which clung to it like stowaways.

From a mirador, an overlook, Oli pointed out where Viroli was in relation to some distant peaks. Far below, a few conical grass roofs faintly stood out in a clearing beside a stream. As at Margarita's, some elderly sisters lived there with their children, grandchildren, and the husband they shared. The only level ground for miles was along a narrow shiny stream, disappearing in and out of a forested canopy some three hundred meters below.

I remember being doubtful when Oli told me that Viroli was only three hours away. I told him that distance is not as far for the Ngäbe as it is for other people, because they walk so fast. All throughout the Ngäbe-Buglé comarca, people measure distance by the hours it takes to walk.

When we reached the casaria, the few people there were surprised to see us. The children never attended school, because of the distance and because the Viroli school has no boarding. As we continued through the forest, the trail kept crisscrossing the clear stream. At one point we found some old avocado trees, a telltale sign that a house had once been there. We rested there, washed in the stream, and ate avocados.

Finally, we saw the welcoming sight of Viroli. My sleepless legs still felt like rubber from the day before. I decided that it was the end of the line for me that day. The others would be returning later to Carrazal and it would be even more uphill than our hike to Viroli. Later they told me it rained most of the way back and they returned well after dark, cold and soaking wet. They slept again on the same cold bare cement floor, without a complaint.

It would be a challenge to find a tougher, fitter, more stoic, and enduring culture. For centuries the Ngäbe-Buglé have suffered slavery, loss of land, and all types of colonial mistreatments. They will eat bad food every day and just be thankful for a full stomach. Meek as Moses, they have a deep sense of justice and will stand up against tyranny. No wonder the Spanish conquerors always avoided fighting the warriors of Urracá.

I was the last to arrive at the one-room school. The three others, walking like Olympic athletes with the heavy box, were there well before me. The school was closed, but even so about twenty kids were there waiting for me. They had been told what was in the unopened box and were eager to see the books and get a notebook and pen.

The Viroli school was built beside the most tremendous overlook in the area. Sheer cliffs across a huge chasm formed a backdrop to the silence. The group of Ngäbe students had spotted me from the large cliff-side in front of the school long before I saw them. The final two-hundred meters of the steep twisting trail leading up to the school had me pausing at the bottom, where I found a very sweet orange tree.

Hearing voices, I looked up and realized that I had been spotted by a group of Ngäbe kids. They were all peering over the cliff beside some fruit-bearing nance trees (*Byrsonima crassifolia*). The tiny yellow fruit are an age-old favorite, often made into preserves and drinks. Soon the kids would be consuming the books and notebooks, just as they were now devouring the nances.

The Viroli school had twenty-six students and had been described to me by a teacher as being "the most forgotten school in the comarca." The one-room school was built from concrete blocks, though the nearest road was over twelve hours' walk away. I knew how the materials had gotten there, but I still had to ask. "A few horses and many hands," was the answer given. I nodded my head in respect.

Like the cover of a book, the six-year-old building presented an acceptable image, but the pages inside were blank. A partition of bed sheets on one side divided the classroom into two small bedrooms and a kitchen. It was the only one-room school I can remember visiting where the teachers were actually living inside. The married woman lived on one side and the man on the other. A part of the back wall served as storage for sacks of rice and lentils, the usual lunch served in remote schools. A couple of years before, powdered milk had been taken off the menu by the Ministry because of problems with the dairy lobby. The teachers later told me that the kids were not being adequately fed.

When I arrived, I was covered in mud from two days of hard hiking. Nonetheless, twenty kids gathered around, all anxiously waiting for me to open the box. It was getting late and some had miles to walk back home on small trails. After displaying the books for them to look through, Oli and I handed out pens and notebooks.

Not one notebook was to be found in the Viroli school, so you can imagine the kids' joy when they received something so small yet so vital. It is the notebooks, those books with no words that are waiting to be inscribed and sprout their germinating seeds of growth, which the kids always love. And the pens, those inky facilitators of the inner text, are always held proudly like the great Ngäbe chief Urracá once clutched his spear. Perhaps they will be inspired by these simple supplies to use them both as tools to heal and weapons to destroy their afflictions. Just to have a small gift is so meaningful when poverty and the "politics of recognition" have disregarded them.

As it was late, they soon took off like birds, freed from the cage of educational prejudice and political corruption. We sat and watched as the group ran to the edge of the school grounds and disappeared down the trail, as happy as spring lambs.

By that time Oli and the two other Ngäbe had to leave, too. They had a four-hour walk back to Carrazal and it was already late afternoon, so I gave them my flashlight and we said "Adiós." I would stay and sleep at the Viroli school, so we made plans to meet the next day. They would take the packhorses with the supplies for the three remaining schools and meet me at Cascabel, another small village. I would travel there on another trail accompanied by a boy from the Viroli school.

Once everyone had left, the female teacher offered to wash my clothes. I gratefully accepted, or else they would have remained in the same unclean state for several more days. With two hours of the tropical sunlight left, she hung them out to dry and then finished the job with the nearby stove.

She cooked dinner for the three of us by candlelight. When I offered to buy a few things from a little nearby "store," she told me that the only things they had there were sugar, rice, beans, and sardines. So, I bought some sardines. During dinner she told me that she had a husband and children, including a year-old baby, in Santiago. Since it is too far to commute for just a weekend, she only gets home once a month at most.

I asked her if Viroli ever had visitors.

"Once, five or six years ago, the police came here to look for someone, but not since then," I was told. "No one comes here. It's like we don't exist," the male teacher added.

Later I pushed aside a few desks and they put down a mattress and clean sheets for me. If nothing else, the tiny school at Viroli surely had a big heart and a great view. But in the comarca, only twenty percent of the kids go beyond the sixth grade and the average academic attainment is grade four.

I left the next morning after the woman teacher cooked me breakfast (and even packed me a lunch!). The teachers arranged for one of their students to take me by horse to the village of Cascabel, a four-hour walk away. There I would meet up with Oli and the horseman.

I was glad I had stayed at Viroli instead of returning with the others. I had a mattress that night, a horse to ride the next day, and I had learned a great deal. Not long after breakfast, my eleven-year-old guide showed up at the Viroli school with two horses. He gave me the larger one and we started our journey. The forested trail led past more expansive views and down into narrow shaded ravines, where ferns clung like thick soft beards around waterfalls.

The village of Cascabel took its name from the rattlesnake, one of a few venomous snakes at higher elevations on the isthmus. It is one of the largest Ngäbe villages and also one of the highest.

Perhaps five hundred people live nearby in kinship households scattered amongst the pines.

As is the case in many remote schools in Panama, a health center had been built nearby. I noticed that several women with children sat beside it most of the day. One very sick woman was taken out by helicopter the next day. Luckily for her, it had come to pick up some government workers issuing identification cards. Otherwise, she would have had to be carried out in a hammock, like a boy we had passed whose leg had been cut with a machete.

I was pleased to find that the school had a very fine young principal. He was Ladino, but was very aware of and sensitive to tribal issues. He was extremely grateful for the books and supplies I had brought. The next day, all the kids gathered to look at the books and to receive a pen and notebook. The girls looked like a flock of parrots in their multi-colored dresses.

Later that day, the principal wanted to show me something. We walked a short distance to a panoramic viewpoint overlooking a mountainous area. Barely visible on a far distant ridge was a cluster of whitish dots, which he told me were the abandoned housing at the Cerro Colorado copper mine site. This area has up to four billion metric tons of medium grade copper, making it perhaps the largest concentration in the world. It was supposed to become one of the most extensive copper mines ever.

Since the copper deposit was discovered in 1957, Cerro Colorado has changed hands from one multi-national mining company to another. Control of mineral rights passed from Canadian to Texan to Panamanian companies, but never to the Ngäbe-Buglé. These orporate conquistadors only offered the Ngäbe-Buglé tribe a mere two percent. It was a token, just like the image of their chief Urracá on Panama's copper penny.

Not only would the tribes get very little out of the deal, but they would also lose very much. The proposed open pit mine would have created an ecological disaster by using and polluting much of the land, as well as the Tabasara River watershed. For the companies and the government, problems like this and the relocation of Ngäbe villages were just "technical" issues.

In the 1970s, Panamanian president Omar Torrijos pressured Ngäbe-Buglé opposition by hinging their comarca status to the development of Cerro Colorado. When a cacique (chief) voiced continued opposition, Omar Torrijos labeled him a communist. Today, the area remains closed and any activity would spark massive Ngäbe-Buglé opposition as well as the closure of the Pan-American Highway.

That night we again slept on the floor of the school. I was surprised to find that one teacher had his small tent set up inside, too. He had been camping there for a year and a half. Teachers in remote places usually have a two-year contract.

Talking that night, Oli told us how he used to be punished as a child when he spoke his native Ngäbere language in school. He stressed that many Ladino teachers call it a dialect, rather than a language. Though quite different, both the Ngäbe and the Buglé languages, as well as their four dialects, are Chibchan based, just like the Kuna, Naso, and Bri Bri languages. But as with other indigenous language speakers in Latin America, their languages have been usurped by Spanish and are considered uncivilized to speak. Unfortunately, very little has been transliterated into print, Ladino teachers never learn it, and the government does not provide them with any cross-cultural training.

After two days in Cascabel, we left. The horses were happy, having rested and grazed for two days in the highland grasslands. Getting rid of more boxes also lightened their loads. We were going next to the new Ngäbe capital tucked away in the pine forest. It is called Buabti in Ngäbere, or Llano Tugri in Spanish, and is a road-less and car-less capital.

It was drizzling, which is more normal than not along the continental divide of the isthmus. We arrived at the school in Buabti after a couple hours, and I was stunned. Though I had been to dozens of dirt-floored schools, this was not a school building, but rather a long, opened-sided shed.

Tiny Viroli had no books, but at least it had a school. Buabti's "school" was nothing more than a long, open pole barn, where one would expect to find cattle or horses. Without a doubt it was the worst school I had ever visited. In addition to the wind blowing in through the twenty-five-meter long open front, the roof leaked onto the dirt floor. Kids moved their chairs around to avoid the puddles pooling on the hard clay floor.

The school had been there for four years. Just across a field was the original school, which had lost its roof four years before. In the interval, the interior had deteriorated drastically. After so many years, there was no excuse for MEDUCA to have eighty kids schooled in an open-sided shed— especially in the comarca's new capital.

This was a purposeful punishment and payback for recent protests against proposed plans to construct three new dams on their comarca. The Ngäbe were never consulted and no one was compensated for the loss of their subsistence farms. Adding this to the Ngäbe's long history of standing up for justice, the government took out their frustration on the kids.

After exhibiting the books, I took photos of all the kids and teachers standing in front of the school, holding high their new notebooks and pens. Then a couple of teachers wanted to show me their living quarters. Again, I was shocked. Three men were crammed inside a very small dirt-floor hovel. It was windowless and dank and a very unhealthy place to live. Two women teachers lived in another equally bad room nearby. The teachers asked me to take a letter to MEDUCA describing their conditions. I took photos and a signed letter with the school's stamp, and later brought them to MEDUCA. But because of government corruption and indifference, the letter did little good.

That night in Buabti we slept in the old roofless school, hoping that it would not rain. The horses grazed out in front on the level field. In the morning the teachers managed to get some eggs and cooked us breakfast. They thanked us again as we left, heading for the village of Ratan.

"Civilizing the uncivilized" was a euphemism used by the Panamanian government to describe Ngäbe-Buglé primary and secondary school education, and was meant to cover over centuries of obloquies and lies about what was done to them. The Panama Poverty Assessment Study conducted by the World Bank revealed that home economics and the principles of electricity, as well as other subjects they would never use, were taught. Acculturation, not education seems to be the objective.

Nowadays, most of the Ngäbe-Buglé families want their kids to go to school and are in favor of "voluntary school." Sometimes schools provide a way and an opportunity for their communities to organize beyond traditional kinship groups. The kids also get a free lunch, despite how inadequate it can be. And it gives the parents some time away from their kids, to work and earn more money.

Compared to the Kuna tribe, the Ngäbe-Buglé are not nearly as organized. They have been manipulated and exploited by the government for a long time. Though politically acephalous, they now have three deputados, or congressmen, who represent the comarca in Panama's National Assembly. Often the manipulation is done in the National Assembly. The Ngäbe-Buglé have little organization beyond their traditional kinship-based social system. They have regional caciques and public councils, which people will sometimes walk for days to attend, but culturally they are decentralized.

Today, there are still many undefined aspects of their comarca. Many parts of the legal borders are kept purposely unclear by the nation-state. Panama does this in order to allow access to "insider" outsiders, especially mining companies and ranchers. Most of the contested area comes from encroachment by Ladino cattle ranchers, who are still winked at by the government. This adds to the ever-worsening land shortage.

But when Panama gained independence from Colombia in 1903 (courtesy of the USA), it required re-titling of all lands. Because of poverty and illiteracy, that was a time when large amounts of indigenous land changed hands. The Chiriquí Land Company took a huge area of Ngäbe-Buglé land, as did the United Fruit Company, for planting bananas along the Cricamola River near Bocas del Toro. Only a banana blight caused United Fruit to pull out of the region some years later.

In the early 1960s, unresolvable land problems led to a political/religious crusade for Ngäbe-Buglé separation from Ladino culture led by a visionary known as Mama Chi. The principles of the movement were based on her apocalyptic visions of the Virgin Mary and possibly of Jesus. She called for a return to the old ways—reduced reliance on cash and increased trading of farm goods. The gatherings she drew were closed to outsiders, which generated fear among the local Ladino ranchers.

After the death of Mama Chi in 1964, the group became more political. That resulted in hundreds of ranchers organizing and arming themselves near the Ngäbe town of Tole, to protect their ill-gotten gains. Today, the Ngäbe-Buglé comarca boundaries usually start where the steep slopes of the isthmian spine rise from the Pacific coastal plain.

On our way to Ratan, we stopped at another school along the way. Doing our usual routine, we left within an hour. As with other times, we met a group of kids along the way. Many walk for over an hour to get to school and often end up soaking wet and sitting cold all day. The two boys we met were probably nine and eleven and were wearing typical black rubber books. But the two girls, one no older than six, were both barefoot. They were surprised to see us, so Oli said something to them in Ngäbere to make them laugh and not be afraid of me. Few foreigners ever set foot in that part of Panama, and the sight of any white man will always conjure up old horror stories.

They answered Oli's questions and I watched as they nodded their heads in agreement. Yes, of course they wanted a notebook, pen, pencil, and sharpener. So, we unpacked one of the horses and found those simple things that none of them had ever had before. Within a few seconds after receiving the supplies, they went running off happily down the trail in a collage of colors and sounds towards their school.

Maybe these kids will finish primary school—just maybe. Perhaps like many they will be taken out of school by their families during the coffee harvest on farms in Chiriquí. For many of these kids, primary school is the only chance they will have to develop any reading or writing skills. If they don't learn how to read and write by the age of eight or nine, the chances are that they never will.

Sometimes talented kids like Oli get "farmed out" to Ladino families in a city to finish secondary school. Sometimes they suffer abuse in these homes and have little recourse. But in the comarca they have little reinforcement for getting an education, because many of the adults are illiterate and there is virtually nothing to read there. That is why having some books in their school is so important. How could they ever learn to read and write without books and supplies? Panama has always been ready to invest in the commercial development of the Ngäbe's rich natural resources, but has almost never been willing to invest in the development of their children's future.

Ratan was our last school. We arrived while the kids were eating their usual lunch of white rice and lentils, so the four of us ate with them. We didn't want to open the few cans of sardines we had left, because there wasn't enough. The principal there was thrilled to suddenly have some pedagogical materials. Soon after lunch we displayed the books and handed out the supplies. The principal gladly wrote me a stamped receipt as proof of our visit. After we took some photos of all the kids in front of the little school, we left, disappearing along the forested trail just like we arrived.

An hour or so later, Oli and I parted company with the two horsemen. I paid and tipped them, and they left happy. Soon after that, we met Margarita again and shared our last tins of sardines with her. The rice and lentils hadn't filled us up at the Ratan school and Oli was still hungry.

After Margarita's buffet of cooked green bananas, we continued on the trail. Not long after, we came to a high overlook and took a needed a rest. This is one of the few places in the world where one can see both the Pacific and Atlantic oceans at the same time. Unfortunately, everything was enveloped in clouds and we couldn't see either one. We sat and rested, picking some nearby blackberries, and looked out over the patchy clouds at the area we had walked through during the past six days.

As we sat, Oli talked about his people's problems and their historic heroes.

"No one compares to Uraccá," Oli told me. "Montezuma and Atahualpa were also captured, but only Urracá escaped. He made the Spanish leader Gaspar Espinosa afraid to fight the Ngäbe. Urracá died old and free. When the slaver Espinosa came hunting for him and the coalition of Ngäbe kings, he only found Parita, King of Azuero. Urracá had already died.

"As was once our tradition, he was mummified with smoke and was found sitting upright in his house. He wore his finest gold ornaments and stared from the other side of life, as if mocking his hateful pursuers.

"And now, five centuries later, not only do international companies, our new conquistadors, dam our rivers and mine our gold, but others even want to rob our genomes. In the mid-1990s, we were confronted with the problem of genome theft from a US pharmaceutical company. Being robbed was nothing new to us. What was new was that some Ngäbe are carriers of the HLV2 virus, which is similar to the HIV virus, but does not develop into AIDS. Blood tests were taken from several Ngäbe women. The company tried to get a US patent for the genome as a scientific discovery. Protests from our communities opposed the taking of our genomes for profit. Eventually this created what became known as the Kupseni Declaration. After pressure was put on the US government, the patent application was refused and the situation quieted.

"But problems like this just continue to add to the mistrust my people harbor against Western companies. Our healers guard their herbal medicine secrets more carefully than gold. Some of our sukias (shamans) are especially knowledgeable about herbal remedies for snake bites. But there is little chance that this knowledge will be shared, though there is a great need that it be documented."

Then I asked Oli about his family. He told me that his grandfather had had four wives.

"What was that like?" I asked him.

"Everyone always got along and no one was jealous of the others. They liked having the same husband. Life was easier for them together," he said. "But now the government wants us to stop this, like Margarita said. The government schools teach the children that people should only have one wife."

"And you, what do you feel?" I questioned.

"Oh, if I took another wife, my wife would leave me. That's what she told me. I can have a girlfriend, though, but she doesn't want to hear about it."

PART FIVE: PERU

Chapter 15

FROM THE DEVIL'S CURVE TO THE LAND OF LAUGHTER

"Human history becomes more and more a race between education and catastrophe."—H.G. Wells

"Nine tenths of education is encouragement."—Anatole France

Flying from a sunny, tropical place to Peru on June 1, 2010 was a shock to the system. Lima can be a cold, clammy, and drab place during their winter. The garúa, a cold, moist fog peculiar to coastal Peru and northern Chile, makes Lima one of the dampest cities on earth. That is unusual, since the area is a coastal desert. I took a taxi from Jorge Chávez Airport to the Plaza San Martín in central Lima. Luckily, I was able to get my favorite room at the Hotel Inti. I had to share a bathroom down the hall, but I had known the kind owners for years and didn't care about that. The best part of being there was that it was near to where I got all the books: Plaza San Martín was just half a block away. Prominent there is a monument to José de San Martín, the great liberator, on his charging steed with his sword in hand.

I bought a cheap sweatshirt there and proceeded to get the books and seed I needed as quickly as possible. Between the Amazonas Book Market and some bookstores on Quilca Street, I managed to accumulate thirty-two boxes of books in the next two weeks, in addition to boxes of notebooks and pens. I used two five-gallon plastic buckets to hold dozens of sealed cans of US seeds, from the Bonanza and Esmeralda seed companies. A nearby printer sold me two thousand tiny envelopes to put the seeds in.

I was going to take everything to the wild Condor Mountains on the border of Peru and Ecuador, home to the indigenous Awajún, also called the Aguarunas. They are the largest tribe in Peru's Amazon region, numbering about 45,000 and comprising about 20% of the indigenous population in that region.

The Awajún, together with the Huambisa, Shuar, and Auchar tribes comprise the Jivaro culture. Jivaro is a derogatory term meaning "savage," so it was not their name of choice. Though the name Aguaruna has been translated as "men of the water," a more likely meaning is "weaver men," since it is the men's tradition to weave bags and baskets from tamshi vines (*Carludovica divergens*) and the Chambira palm (*Astrocaryum chambira*).

This tribe of the tropical rain forest mostly inhabits the river banks of the Condor Mountain area. Their territory stretches along the Maranon River and its tributaries, from the Pongo de Rentema outside of Bagua Chica to the Pongo de Manserriche, just below the confluence with the Santiago River. But their territory traditionally extended up to Bagua Chica. It was there where inter-tribal trading took place with the Chachapoyas culture, and with those on the coast.

In 2008, the attention of Peruvians was focused on the June 5th Bagua massacre that took place outside Bagua Chica at a place called Devil's Curve. Forty-one of the Awajún and thirty-two state police officers were killed at a protest against the encroachment of oil and mining companies. It was the worst political violence since the 1983 Lucanamarca massacre perpetrated by Sendero Luminoso (Shining Path) guerillas.

The massacre dominated the news in Peru and even spawned a new word: "baguazacion," i.e. a corrupt and blundering government illegally selling concessions to foreign companies on indigenous land and then precipitating violence against indigenous protestors.

That year, I was there just days after the massacre. Knowing the needs of the Awajún, I had decided to go back and work there. To do so, however, I needed special permission, since the area is off limits to tourists. Twice while in Lima, I met with Alberto Pizango, the impressive Shawi Indian apu (elder), leader of Peru's largest indigenous organization, AIDESEP (Asociación Interétnica de Desarrollo de la Selva Peruana, i.e. Interethnic Association for the Development of the Peruvian Rainforest). It is the organization of organizations of Peru's native peoples.

Pizango had returned just a few days before from a year of political asylum in Nicaragua, after the Peruvian government had tried to place him under arrest and blame him for the deaths of National Police officers. They wanted to charge him with fomenting unrest and sedition.

When I visited Pizango's office in the first week of June 2010, I told him that I had more than a ton of children's books as well as a lot of seeds, and that I hoped to work with the Awajún. I told him my history of working in the Amazon and that I wanted to take the books and seeds to some Awajún schools up the Cenepa and Comaina rivers. Alberto Pizango was very accommodating and pleased that I wanted to help, but said that I needed permission to work there since it was aa restricted area. He provided me with a signed letter and some contacts in ORPIAN-P (Organizacion Regional de los Pueblos Indigenous de la Amazonia Norte del Peru) in Bagua Chica. This is an Awajún and Huambisa Indian organization which assists their combined population of about 60,000 people.

The Bagua massacre, as it became known, was precipitated because of an illegal concession on Awajún land granted to Canadian gold mining company, Afrodita, by Peru's president, Alan García. For six days, a large gathering of some 3,000 Awajún, Huambisa, and other indigenous peoples had blocked the road at a bend in the National Highway called Devil's Curve.

Many people came from afar to protest the recent exploitation of their land by foreign-owned mining companies, such as the Afrodita, Gold Sac, Lowel Mineral Exploration, Petrol Peru, and others. But it was the Canadian-owned Afrodita Mining Company that became the focus.

The Peruvian government had been helping Afrodita move heavy equipment into the inaccessible Condor Mountains with military helicopters. This was a direct violation of the rights of the Awajún and so they protested. "During times of universal deceit, telling the truth becomes a revolutionary act," George Orwell once wrote.

Soon heavily armed National Police were called in, civil liberties were suspended, and a state of emergency was called by President García. On one side of Devil's Curve were hundreds of heavily armed Peruvian military in fatigues; on the other side were a couple of thousand war-painted indigenous men and women holding wooden spears. At Devil's Curve the Marañon River flows by swiftly on one side of the road, past a papaya plantation and some scrub brush. On the other side a steep, unfriendly scarp rises, consisting mainly of rocks and cactus.

The protesters claim that after six days the military conducted a surprise attack, breaking their promise to negotiate. At dawn, helicopter gunships flew overhead and indiscriminately opened fired on the protestors. Soon blood was flowing. In response, a group of indigenous men ambushed and charged the National Police compound, killing eleven of them with their spears and confiscated police guns.

Twenty-three Awajún and Huambisa people were killed that day and 160 were wounded. The Army entered hospitals and took some of the wounded away. There were reports that they burned the corpses of several dead demonstrators and dumped others in the Marañon River. Several indigenous, especially Huambisa, were convicted of murder and sentenced to twenty years of jail time at Chachapoyas. Two of them are brothers of Bernadino, a Huambisa man who later traveled with me.

Bagua suddenly had international political implications. The Minister of Interior, Simon Yuhuda, fell on his political sword and quit, in order to distance himself from the scandal surrounding the Peruvian president. Then, some months after igniting Peru's worst indigenous uprising in decades, the government was forced by international pressure to indefinitely suspend Afrodita's concession. Nonetheless, Awajún people in the Condor Mountains claim there is still illegal activity occurring there.

While the Peruvian government was accusing indigenous leaders, especially Alberto Pizango, of sedition and fomenting unrest, President García was trying to keep stories about mining payoffs from leaking out. Most Peruvians blamed the Bagua massacre on the president, since he was responsible for the concession to Afrodita Mining along the Cenepa River headwaters and had given the order to unleash the gunships and heavily armed police on the civilian protesters.

Only the National Police, the Army, and many members of Peru's white ruling class blamed the indigenous. It seems that many people prefer to believe a comfortable lie rather than an uncomfortable truth. A large, two-sided billboard with pictures of Jesus has since been put up at Devil's Curve by the Seventh Day Adventists. It reads: "The Curve of Hope," but to everyone else it is still the Devil's Curve.

I shipped the books and seeds to Bagua Chica by truck and departed myself one night by bus. Peru has thousands of double-decker Volvo and Marco Polo buses that show movies and provide snacks. They make the Greyhound buses in the US look like some sickly street dog. I woke up in the morning on the north coast, just outside Chiclayo, famous for its ceviche. Within minutes we were in the bus station and shortly thereafter I was in a collectivo station wagon with three other passengers on my way to Bagua Chica.

After spending time in cold and clammy Lima, the sunny countryside felt good and I soon started peeling off layers of clothing. I gave my sweatshirt to the bus driver, not wanting to carry it into the heat of the Amazon. He was illiterate and I realized he could not read the road signs. One of the other passengers cuttingly joked, "Green means go and red means stop," referring to the signs reading "pase" and "pare," held up by highway workers at several places.

We traveled east towards Bagua Chica from the deserts of coastal Chiclayo, passing through a forest of algorrobo trees (*Prosopis pallida*), which are disappearing for charcoal. It was their carob beans that once helped sustain the ancient Mochica culture, and even today they still provide a popular molasses-like syrup called algorrobina. These were soon replaced by small huarango trees (*Acacia macracantha*) and a dry tropical forest. A newly paved highway wound up the arid mountains along the Olmos River to the Porcuya Pass. The Porcuya Peak at 2,700 meters is the highest point in the area. The National Highway from Chiclayo leads to Tarapoto and Yurimaguas on the Huallaga River. This pass was the original gateway into the roadless Amazon.

Unfriendly underbrush and various cacti cling to the rocky slopes along the road. Despite the fact that the Pacific Ocean is just 250 kilometers to the west, all waters flow towards the Amazon and eventually to the far-off Atlantic Ocean once the relatively low pass is crossed. As we drove upwards, small checkered fields of barley and wheat were etched out amongst the tangled brush in the distance. The higher up the mountain we went, the greener the landscape became.

After the Porcuya Pass, the descent starts along a dry arroyo whose seasonal waters feed into the Huancabamba River. It flows down from the Huancabamba heights, known for vision-seeking shamans who still gather the tall San Pedro cactus (*Trichocereus pachonoi* or *Echinopsis pachonoi*). The Huancabamba is a river from whose headwaters one can almost see the Pacific, but like its shamans is destined to flow another way, to another shore. The Atlantic-bound Huancabamba flows into the Rio Chamayo, and the Chamayo into the Marañon River along the sunburned hills before Bagua Chica.

Without changing names like the Ucayali River does, the Marañon is the Amazon's main tributary, with its source high in the Andes in Ancash. At one time it may have even been the name of the Amazon River. Some say the name Marañon comes from the Spanish, Mar-o-Non, Sea or Not, referring to the size of the Amazon. Another etymological explanation finds its origin in the Spanish word maraña, meaning a snare or tangle. But the Marañon's quick, cold, splashing waters seem to be in a hurry, like eager tourists fleeing the cold and wanting to get to the tropics. The slow, muddy flow of the Amazon Basin is close by. Over fifteen-hundred kilometers away, the Marañon becomes the mother of all rivers, the Amazon, when it joins the twisted Ucayali near Nauta, Peru.

The highway on the eastern slope was being repaved. In places, groups of donkeys stood beside huge idle earth movers, waiting with empty packs to carry rocks for retaining walls. Along the Chamayo River, the first rice paddies stood out in striking contrast beside the brown hillsides and crumbling cliffs. Rows of coconut trees lined some of the paddies. The brilliant green color satisfied the soul and soothed the eyes from the harsh, barren terrain. Just a short distance away, in the selva, the verdant jungle, they would not even be noticed. But there in the desert dryness they called out in glory, like a colorful cubist painting on a bare wall. Just as dazzling as the chartreuse rice paddies was a stunning Huancabamba Indian woman in a long bright pink and yellow dress. She was standing in the shade of a tree, like a giant blossoming flower, seeming to be waiting for a ride.

Not far away, some Brazilians were building a large dam on the upper Chamayo, the kilowatts to be sold abroad, even though most local homes remain without power. Another Brazilian company built a toll road near Bagua, but since the massacre only commercial trucks are checked and charged. Occasional riverside road signs tell the locals, "Don't fish with explosives." Other government signs call for protecting the environment, but silently seem to say: "Never mind the new dam and all the illegal mining concessions!"

Once in Bagua Chica I headed to the humble office of ORPIAN on Sargente Lores Street. I was surprised to find their large front room had a dusty dirt floor and some computers living under plastic. I would store thirty-two large boxes of children's books there.

Bagua is a place of rapid and dramatic transition, both culturally and geographically. It always marked the edge of Awajún territory, since they don't like the desert; the land is dry and gets progressively more arid as one goes toward the coast, and gets progressively wetter in the other direction, as one descends into the Amazon. The jungled mountains in the distance divide the sky like a dark curtain that is suddenly pulled back by the cord-like Marañon River, revealing the largest forest on earth.

Pressed to its limits, the jungle is kept at bay by the inexorable advance of the desert's dry breath from the cold of the Humboldt Current along the Pacific coast. An endless expanse of Amazonian greenery on one side is juxtaposed against coastal desert on the other, where other forces and laws of nature govern. In the jungle, time slows down, space expands, and vision shortens. The rivers become roads, dugouts become cars, and hanging lianas become snakes. The long clear vistas of the desert are exchanged for the jungle's inner horizons and biodiversity.

Within fifteen kilometers the land goes through drastic changes, some of the most radical on earth. Just beyond Bagua Chica is a rare confluence of three fast flowing rivers: the Chinchipe, which flows from Ecuador in the north, the Utcabamba from Chachapoyas, and the mighty Marañon.

The Pongo de Rentema are some rapids that mark the decisive point of transition. Above it is the desert with long views, many cacti, and scrub trees; below is the sodden, opaque jungle. Once below the Pongo de Rentema, both the Marañon and the road descend into verdant Amazon jungle. The cactus-clad hills are no more but are rapidly replaced by the rubbery-leafed rainforest. The nearest cacti to the east are found along Brazil's Atlantic coast, thousands of roadless kilometers away.

The thirty-two large boxes of children's books had arrived safely, thanks to the trucking company, and I stacked them on the dirt floor in in ORPIAN's office. I still had to rent a 4x4 to take them to Santa María de Nieva, an old Jesuit town founded in 1549 along the Marañon. It is about an eight-hour drive from Bagua Chica, but one should expect it to take longer. My new friend from ORPIAN, an Awajún man named Idelfonso "Chinchi" Espejo Tiwi, managed to arrange a truck for us. The road to get to Santa María de Nieva is one of the few in Peru where there is no bus service. If I had known about the condition of the truck ahead of time, I would have said something to the driver like, "Don't you think it would make sense to replace the two missing lug bolts on that back wheel before we leave?" But since I was picked up in the dark at four in the morning, there was no way of knowing. He, Chinchi, and the Huambisa man, Bernadino, had loaded all thirty-two boxes an hour earlier, while I slept in.

A few hours later I heard a grinding sound piercing through the loud music of the truck's radio. When we stopped, I was shocked to see just one lug nut on the driver's side back wheel. The sheer weight of the books had literally snapped off two of the remaining three lug bolts. To be sure, the fast driving and heavy breaking on the rocky road hadn't helped any. Within an hour we were back on the road, after switching out two of the lug bolts from the other back wheel.

Less than an hour later another alarming sound caused us to stop again. This time, the leaf spring on the same side of the truck had broken loose on one end. The truck was overloaded, that was all there was to it. The driver had bit off more than he could chew. Originally, he had wanted to use two trucks, but in order to make more money had decided that one was enough. We jacked up the truck and placed stones under the axle so that we could block the spring in place with a small piece of carved wood. Later, just at dark, we finally limped into Santa María de Nieva and quickly found a place to unload.

The Amazon has a history of its forest people not being seen, because of their trees or because of their gold. When people think of the Amazon it is usually the trees, or perhaps the snakes or the piranhas, which first come to mind, not the people. After all, it was the gold and the plants that first brought outsiders to the Amazon. The cinnamon tree (*Cinnamomum verum*) and the myth of El Dorado drew the attention of the first Europeans to come. Cinnamon (sin-of-men) was the first agricultural product sought, but it proved as elusive and unprofitable as El Dorado. Gonzalo Pizarro led a disastrous expedition into the Amazon in search of cinnamon and gold in 1541. It cost the lives of 4,250 people, most of them indigenous porters. Later, it was the cinchona tree (*Cinchona officinalis*) which could be used to produce quinine and treat malaria that drew attention. The exploitation of rubber trees in the period between 1870 and 1912 saw some 40,000 indigenous Amazonians die as slave laborers. Then, as today, gangster bankers sought to squeeze maximum profit from the land and its people

For nearly two hundred years, beginning in the sixteenth century, the Awajún dealt with attempted encroachment on their territory by the Spanish. But their remoteness, fierce opposition, and tradition of shrinking heads usually left the Spanish looking elsewhere. The genocide that happened around Iquitos (the largest city in the Peruvian Amazon) connected to the rubber trade had less effect on them.

Today the Peruvian government treats the indigenous Amazonians like historians consider the myth of Amazon viragos: they simply don't exist. For the government, the Condor Mountains are part of Peru first, and Awajún land second. For the indigenous, of course, it is the other way around. Perhaps that is why the schools are bare and there is no medicine, infrastructure, or means of communication. It would be psychologically harder to justify plundering a place if the people were actually considered. In a place where the people are all but forgotten, the decision to grant concessions to foreign companies can be reduced to cost/benefit analysis. It is easier to abuse forgotten and ignored people and rob them of their minerals, oil, forests, and waters. It is easier on the conscience and better for the pocketbook.

Chinchi and I were heading for Haumpami, his village and the capital of the Awajún world. First, though, we had to coordinate some things in Santa María de Nieva. Haumpami, home to some 2,000 people, is about an eight-hour journey in a motorized dugout from Santa María de Nieva. Located along a high bank of the Cenepa River at the confluence of the Huampami River, it commands an impressive view of the steep Condor Mountains. Grid-like earthen lanes center around the village plaza, where Chinchi's family lives in a large, two-story barn-like house with a dirt floor. Because her husband had abandoned her for a younger wife, his mother was forced to rent out rooms on the second floor to make ends meet. The other wife lives in a very small dwelling next door, with her baby. Chinchi's father visits occasionally from Santa María de Nieva, where he is a teacher and lives with yet another woman. His selfish, dysfunctional polygamy leaves his children hungry and ill-clothed. Chinchi's grandfather was once the village cacique, so Chinchi is respected around the village.

A swing bridge crosses the Huampami River to the primary and secondary schools, built on a large flat area beside the Cenepa River. Over an acre of rice and a couple of other crops are planted there. The schools board about 170 students, who come from villages too far away to commute. The kids work the fields to supplement their meals. My bringing them various types of vegetable and fruit seeds was very much appreciated. Now they could plant onions, tomatoes, peppers, and other things which they did not have.

Some Awajún, such as Chinchi's father, still practice polygamy. This is not the polygamy of old times, for now things have become modernized into the simple abandonment of one wife for another, as with Chinchi's mother. Before, marriage was often between cross-cousins, but today's customs have left a swirling wake of social and health problems such as poverty, hepatitis B, and orphans crying out for attention. Around Huampami, there are supposedly over two hundred orphans, and in the Santiago River area amongst the Huambisa communities, things are even worse. If the grandmothers are alive, they usually end up caring for abandoned and orphaned kids, but sometimes there is no relative to look after young children. Chinchi, to his credit, adopted little Beto, who was abandoned. They share their poverty and laughter is free. "He will be your apu (leader) someday!" I told him. Orphans are not unfamiliar to the Awajún, and they even have a myth in which the Pleiades are a group of orphaned children, watched over by the star Aldebaran.

But Chinchi himself, reverting to old polygamous customs, got his sister-in-law pregnant. Because levirate polygamy is seldom practiced today, however, he would not take her for his second wife. His enraged young wife would not allow. When his wife found out, she then got pregnant herself by some village man, which created even more problems. Not wanting to keep the baby, she drank a bottle of shampoo, causing a miscarriage and almost her death. Doctors had to remove her uterus. Sometime later little Beto was adopted.

The nearest neighboring tribe to the Awajún are their ancient enemies, the Huambisa. Numbering about 6,000, they live mostly along the Santiago and Morona rivers. The historic antagonism between the tribes still exists. When we reached Santa María de Nieva, Bernadino, the Huambisa man, did not want to sleep in the same room with Chinchi and wanted me to buy him his own room.

When I refused he was incensed, but finally relented because he did not want to sleep on the street. Both of these tribes prefer to stay within the confines of the jungle, feeling uncomfortable in the barren lands beyond Bagua. The tribes have forged alliances on occasion, resisting invasions by the Mochica, the Incas under Tupac Yupangui and Huayna Capac, the early Spanish expeditions, the rubber barons, and now the global mining companies.

The fierce cousins of the Awajún, the Shuar and Achuar, live mostly on the western slopes of the Condor Mountains in Ecuador and around the Pataza River. They are the fiercest of the Jivaro tribes and mostly responsible for the fear associated with the term Jivaro. At one time, the killing of rival tribal members was considered a duty, and even a sport for them. In 1599, in a rampage of terror, the Shuar murdered upwards of 20,000 Spanish settlers in two days around the village of Logroño, on the western side of the Cordillera del Condor. In the collective memories of the indigenous are stories of frenzied, blood-covered Jivaro warriors, dancing ecstatically with foreign, fair-haired heads—heads that would be made into tsantsas, shrunken heads. There were fewer real estate problems after that and the Condor Mountains stayed off limits to settlers for a long time.

The famous taxidermy custom of making shrunken heads, tsantsas, was once practiced by all the Jivaro tribes. Basically, a tsantsa was made by carefully peeling away the facial skin and then filling it with hot sand and curing it with herbs. This unique custom of all four Jivaro tribes has stigmatized them for centuries to outsiders. A shrunken head was not valued as a war trophy, but rather as an empowering container of a captured soul.

Imagine a bearded conquistador killed by Jivaros, whose decapitated shrunken head hangs in a Jivaro hut, lips everted and sewn shut, and no facial hair remaining other than his eye brows. In the early twentieth century, some Ecuadorian taxidermists would buy unclaimed indigenous bodies from morgues and make their own tsantsas to sell to foreigners and museums, though they usually lacked certain defining characteristics of authentic tsantsas.

While the Shuar and Achuar once found pleasure in reciprocal violence and murder, and the Huambisa in deceit, the Awajún, though known for some xenophobia, love to laugh. It is they who live in the Land of Laughter. Laughter is their life and flows from them like swift waters: sometimes as tiny clear streams to drink from, and other times with roaring rapids and whirlpools that can carry you helplessly along in its current. Drink a little masato (yuca, pineapple, corn, or banana beer) and it no doubt will.

The Awajún cultivate laughter like they cultivate their yuca fields, and like the yuca, it helps to sustain them. They are a quiet, good-natured people, and words for them are just foreplay for laughter. One thing is certain—the Awajún would rather be laughing like the clear rapids of their headwaters than having to come out of their beloved forest to protest the illegal invasion of greedy foreign mining companies. As the caretakers of their ancestral lands, they will have the last laugh.

In spite of recent mining activity, it is only because of the Jivaro's violent hostility to outside exploitation that the Condor Mountains have remained wild. This differentiates them from the more passive Huitoto, Yagua, and other tribes that live further to the east. These people once faced extinction, suffering industrial genocide through enslavement to the owners of the rubber plantations. A man like the rubber baron Julio Arana could never have built his "Devil's Paradise" empire amongst the resistant Jivaro, as he did with the more tractable tribes further down river. The Condor Mountains remain wild because of the "No Trespassing" policy enforced by the Jivaro.

The Condor Mountains are one of the few places where the indigenous have been successful in keeping outsiders out. The fear of death was the only thing that stopped the colonists. Had they not been stopped, the rivers flowing out of the Cordillera del Condor—the Cenepa, Comaina, Nunpatkay, and many others, would be tainted with arsenic and mercury from placer mines. It is now one of the last undocumented tropical mountain ranges on the planet.

After two days in Santa María de Nieva, Chinchi and I, along with the others, found two large dugout canoes, each with a fifteen-horsepower peque-peque motor, to take us to Huampami. The peque-peque motors, which are also used in shallow waters in Southeast Asia, have an eight-foot shaft that extends beyond the rear of the boat, with a small propeller at the end. The thirty-two large boxes filled both of the boats. The boxes were placed on pallets and wrapped in a tarp, but I was still concerned that they would get wet. But even though the water-line was just three inches below the top of the boats, they stayed dry, just as the boatmen had promised.

Traveling up the swift Marañon from Santa María de Nieva, we occasionally passed sloping beaches raising up about two meters high, some made from smooth stones and others of white sand. During the rainy season they would be under water. Passing by, I noticed a sound I had never heard before, caused by the noise generated by peque-peque motor bouncing off small stones on the riverbed. It was a high-pitched, two-toned sound—like thousands of stones rubbing against each other. Passing the sandy banks, the thudding of the motor ricocheted a completely different sound. "What an odd phenomena the physics of sound can produce," I thought.

When we reached Huampami, we landed the two dugouts at a wide stairway of perhaps twenty cement steps, which rose up from below the waterline to the main dirt street. Within minutes, some local men had carried all the boxes to a storeroom. Walking up, I noticed a price list of local foods and other items at the top of the steps. The extensive list named several types of wild meat, including three species of monkeys. Two, kushi and kuji, are the most expensive and sell for fifteen soles (five dollars) a kilo. Not cheap for monkey eaters. The third, a smaller type called waiway, goes for five soles a kilo.

Other wild animals, including deer and three types of wild pigs (saijino, majas, and huangana), all go for eight soles a kilo. Some birds sell for five soles a kilo. Frogs and two types of toads each cost one sole apiece. Suri, the finger-sized white grub found in the rotting trunks of fallen aguaje trees (*Mauritia flexuosa*), are priced at ten for one sole. Cocona (*Solanum sessiliflorum*) are a small, round, orange fruit with a tangy flavor, used for making juices. They grow like eggplant, and sell for one sole a kilo. Both peanuts and the toxic plant barbasco (used for fishing) go for three soles a kilo.

Several types of fish from the rivers sell for five soles a kilo. They range from boca chicas to seventy-five kilo tsungaro catfish. The carachama, an ugly but very edible spiny catfish, is the most common. The etymology of this unpleasant name means "face of the Chama," referring to another tribe I have worked with, the Chama of the Ucayali River.

The list also included cacao (*Theobroma cacao*), which sold for three soles a kilo. Nearly every Awajún family has some cacao trees, and use them to make chocolate drinks and sometimes solid chocolate. The Condor Mountain area is where chocolate originally came from and there are some old and unique varieties. Cacao and bananas are virtually the only products that most people can make any money from. The three cacao harvests a year reward people with a little bit of cash from the buyers, who pick it up in boats. Though the Awajún growers who do all the work make just three or four soles a kilo, in Lima it sells for fifteen soles a kilo.

Along the few clay streets of Haumpami, nearly every home is made of either split bamboo or roughhewn boards. They all have a hard, earthen floor, which often has a narrow border of green moss. At sunset, young men play spirited football on the cement slab in the village square. At dark, the generator starts and runs for about three hours, though very few houses have electricity. Often, sitting together on cement benches beside the sports field, women pick lice from each other's heads and eat them when found. Just beside the cement court, a small group of young gay men regularly play volleyball. Sometimes they play with the women, but they never play football. There is no macho-sexist tension, though; everyone gets along with respect for each other. The Awajún have an accepting nobility about them. Theft is rare; there is nothing really worth stealing.

The Awajún, like most of the indigenous, only have their land and nothing more. Most people seldom touch money, except for the few coins they might get from the sale of some cacao beans. Their vocation is taking care of their land and they take that job seriously. They are the caretakers of their selva, while the politicians are the caretakers of concessions.

More so than most indigenous populations, the Awajún, Huambisa, and other Jivaro tribes are known for fiercely opposing exploitation by foreigners, especially mining companies, as proved at Devil's Curve. They are well aware of toxic rivers and mine tailings dumped and leaking into rivers all over Peru. Fear of the contamination of their pure waters and land is what brought them to blockade the road at Devil's Curve. Stealing their gold contrary to all international conventions was one thing, but to pollute while doing so was another offense, an irreversible crime.

Though the Incas and the Spanish conquistadors never made it back to the Condor Mountains, the Afrodita Mining Company did. Next to this company's gold mine are some Awajún villages, largely forgotten, with bookless schools and no health clinics. Rabies has become rampant in the area and there is no snake-bite medicine within a day's journey. It is obvious that Peru's leaders care more about appeasing the gold lust of foreign corporations and lining their pockets than they do about the education and health of their country's own original inhabitants.

Afrodita is no different from any other foreign-owned mining and oil companies that have invaded the Amazon. Since the implementation of the Canada-Peru Free Trade Agreement, almost fifty million hectares, some 72% of Peru's Amazon, has been opened up to mineral, logging, petroleum, and ranching concessions. All of this was agreed to without any input from Peru's indigenous population. The president said that the indigenous were just "confused savages, in the way of progress." The Free Trade Agreement was their excuse to exploit the resources of the native inhabitants, in complete disregard to their acceptance of the United Nation's Declaration on the Rights of Indigenous Peoples and the International Labor Organization's Convention 169. Though Peru had signed its name to these agreements, its whispers for concessions reveal their lack of conscience.

Though toothless, Convention 169 is the best recourse the indigenous have for legal action. Ironically, it was Peru that introduced the UN Declaration on the Rights of Indigenous Peoples in 2007. But by violating both the letter and the spirit of Convention 169 and the 2007 UN Declaration, Peru left the indigenous no choice other than to protest this abuse.

The earliest incursions into the Amazon from the area that is now Peru came on foot—from Cajamarca, Chachapoyas, and Jaen. They all passed through Awajún and Huambisa territory. One of the first was the expedition of Alonso Alvarado, which left from Chachapoyas in 1532. The expedition of Juan Porcel, the first to enter the Marañon River, began ten years later. And then Hernando de Benavente, Alonso de Mercadillo, and Juan de Salinas, who named the Santiago River, all encountered Awajún territory.

Juan de Salinas, a soldier for both Cortez in Mexico and Pizarro in Peru, explored both the Marañon and Ucayali rivers around 1550, in search of El Dorado. The upper Marañon became famously unfriendly due to the curare-tipped arrows of both the Awajún and the Huambisa. Salinas was the first European to visit the Pongo Manserriche rapids, the traditional boundary separating these tribes from the lowland Amazon tribes below.

It took centuries for the Spanish to control this area, however. In 1618, Diego Vaca de Vega became the first to obtain permission from the Viceroy of Peru to colonize the lowlands east of the Andes.

For three centuries, missionary activities among the Awajún and other Jivaro were usually just subterfuge for exploitation. The Jesuits disrupted and usurped the intertribal trade networks, replacing them with their own. Salt, curare, and turtle eggs used for oil were traded for steel tools or cheap European trinkets.

After a riverside Jesuit outpost was founded in Santa María de Nieva in 1549, and in Borja soon after, some twenty-four encomiendas were granted to settlers around Borja. These encomiendas were the 16th century version of corporate concessions, except that machines do most of the work now, rather than the slave labor of the indigenous. Neither then nor now have the indigenous been consulted. In the thirty years between 1561 and 1591, the Awajún and Huambisa population dropped from over thirty thousand to about three thousand, due to slavery and disease.

"The wilder the Indian the wickeder the slavery," Roger Casement wrote. Both Santa María de Nieva and Borja were burned several times by tribes other than the Jivaro, including the Maynas and Cocoma. In 1866, more than three hundred years later, there was still indigenous opposition; the Huambisa burned both mission villages once again.

During the rubber years, a few brave barons like Amadeo Burga and Artemeo Izquierdo were allowed to do business by the Awajún and Huambisa because they traded guns and machetes in compensation. Burga later died by the guns he traded to the Huambisa. Roger Casement, the British officer who led an investigation into the genocide that accompanied Peru's rubber boom, wrote about Burga's demise: "The Huambisas when they attacked Burga at Santiago had been armed by him against an old priest who had a settlement higher up. The old priest had also armed the

Huambisas against Burga. The two 'opposing parties' came down one day and were wiped out, Burga and the old priest simultaneously; and so 'civilization' was extinguished for half a century on the gorge of the Upper Marañon."

Roger Casement, the incredible Irishman later hung for treason by the British, also had little good to say about "civilizing" the indigenous. "Where he becomes 'civilized' and can read and write and study 'cuenta' (accounts) with his 'patron,' then he ceases to be an Indian and becomes a 'Peruvian' and himself an enslaver," Casement wrote. For me, Casement's words cut deep, for I have brought books for the children in hundreds of remote indigenous schools. Today most indigenous do want their children to be educated. Ironically, their schools are so bad that they don't have to worry about Casement's words. The difficult part for them is not to lose their indigenous identity.

In many places outside of Condorcanqui, the district around the Condor Mountains, the laughter-filled language of the Awajún is not considered worthy of being anything more than a dialect, their food is seen as unfit to eat, and their lives are not worthy of notice. The Awajún and other Jivaro tribes have always existed outside the reach of the Quechua language, and so it remains today. The difference now is that they are all part of the nation-state of Peru, but the reality is that indigenous of the Amazon region are often discriminated against. Quechua dominates Peru's indigenous languages and non-Quechua speaking native peoples sometimes suffer for it. Awajún family names like Unkumshakai, Autukai, Wampankit, Ugkuch, Chuinta, Washikat, Achuag, Kunchikui, struggle for validity between the dual languages of Quechua and Spanish. Nonetheless, commercial powers in the outside world never consider the mineral rich lands of the Awajún to be separate, forgotten, or unworthy of notice.

In the Cordillera del Condor area there is no summer, no dry season like there is further east on the endlessly flat expanse of the Amazon. It can rain any day of the year and it usually does, whether for just a minute or an all-day downpour. While I was in Huampami, there was one twenty-hour period of torrential rain during which the Cenepa River rose four meters by the next morning. It was full of debris—whole trees were washed downriver and it was dangerous to travel. I spotted a lost dugout floating with the current that was full of water, then saw another one. At some bends in the river, sticks and debris collected in whirlpools and the surface waters reversed themselves in gyres of confusion. It is only in late July and August, when there is the least rain, that the rivers become clear—"celeste" as they say—the Comaina and Conga, both tributaries of the Cenepa, being famous for their beauty.

One afternoon Chinchi's father took us in his dugout to the first pongo of the Cenepa, the roaring rapids just above where he has a piece of land. We landed beside some huge moss-covered rocks, behind which velvety cliffs with clutching tree ferns towered as a backdrop. Heliconia, liana, and a waxy array of trees reached out to the light along the vertical river banks. A lively mist danced and dissipated above a stretch of white water. No boats go above the rapids; to go further up the Cenepa to some Awajún communities there requires a seven-hour hike over a very steep mountain. After that obstacle, dugouts can continue further up the wild river and very nearly reach the border with Ecuador. That is where I wanted to go, but my books had already been promised to other communities. It would have to wait for another journey.

Having gotten all the books and seeds safely to Huampami, we soon began visiting schools. Many had dirt floors, like most Awajún houses. Having a dirt floor in a school is one thing, but having no books or supplies is far worse. Chinchi and I made some day trips to village schools in surrounding places like Tseasim and Achu. Meaning "aguaje palm" in the Awajún language, Achu is a very old village on the banks of the Huampami River. Nearby, a large cliff rises directly out of the river with a huge, buttressed tree gripping the ground in front. Few outsiders have ever come there and the people were surprised to see me. To show their thanks for the books and school supplies, the teacher had the children sing a song in their language. Besides being happy to have books, notebooks, paper, pens, and paint, they were grateful that someone had just given them a little attention. Like most remote indigenous schools, they felt abandoned by the government.

As we were returning downriver to Huampami, a group of young boys clothed only in mud greeted us from below the swing bridge near the school. They were sliding into the river down a slippery groove which they had fashioned in the steep, muddy river bank.

On some days we took day trips to other villages. At one, we found a group of men mining for gold along the riverside, using a makeshift wooden sluice box. But gold mining by individuals is illegal in Peru, despite the fact that the wild rivers in front of their villages are often full of it and poverty is endemic. The fact remains that mining companies own the rights to the mineral wealth.

One of the better schools we visited was in the village of San Antonio. The teachers had the kids line up to receive their notebooks and pens, which only a few already had. The government had once provided notebooks, but this ended after the protests. The children were punished because their parents had protested an illegal abuse. Such is Peru. When I looked at the row of fifty or sixty raggedy little kids, I could not help but notice that nearly every one of them was barefoot. It occurred to me that, given the choice, most would choose notebooks and pens over a pair of shoes.

While we were at the school, we were invited to drink some masato, the thick, lightly-fermented alcohol made from various fruits or vegetables. We followed a couple of people to an area behind someone's house, where there was an outdoor kitchen. I was surprised to be greeted in good English by a twenty-one-year-old man named Oliver, who was in his third year of studying business administration at a university in Piura. This was his mother's house and he was home on vacation. The kitchen was very neat, clean, and pleasant to sit in. Unlike most Awajún homes it was screened in, but it did have the typical hard clay floor and a fire burning. A small dog lay calmly, tied with a short chain in a corner. Oliver's large pet turtle had walked the floor for years, he told me. With the masato we ate mocombo (*Theobroma bicolor*), a large oval fruit in the cacao family with delicious seeds that are highly valued and eaten toasted. Oliver told me that it was difficult for him to live in Piura. Besides the fact that it was so barren and cool, his identity as an Amazonian Indian made him feel unwelcome there. He loved his jungle, he told me. I wondered how he would fare in the concrete jungles of business administration.

Several of us were waiting for about a week to hike to two remote Awajún villages, Pantam Entsa and Tsawantus. To get there, we had to take a dugout to the village of Kusa Kubaim, which is not far up the Comainas River, just past its confluence with the Cenepa. Several of those who came along were returning to their homes there. All of them got out of the dugouts at the bank, but Chinchi and I continued with the boatman a little farther upriver. We needed the permission of the village apu before I could enter the area. Meanwhile, a group of vigilant young men from Kusa Kubaim stood sternly along the riverbank. As we passed by in the dugout they called out to us, insisting that we come over. They must have wondered what I was doing there, since it is so rare to have foreign visitors. Chinchi ignored them, though, and we continued on. Soon enough we trumped their demands with the apu's welcome. Because I was with Chinchi, a leader in ORPIAN, and because I had a letter of introduction from Alberto Pizango of AIDESEP, I was allowed to enter. The letter which Pizango had given me was read and passed around by various village elders. The young men's initial xenophobia was just an understandable defense mechanism; it wasn't long before I was referred to as "hermano" (brother).

From Kusa Kubaim several of us started an arduous hike into the virgin forest of the land of laughter. It was a grueling eight-hour hike on a narrow and sometimes dangerous trail to Pantam Entsa ("Banana Water" in Awajún). We passed trees along the trail with trunks that measured seven feet across—each home to thousands of living species. It is rarely dry in the lush embowered forest, which is always dripping like a greenhouse. The air is thick, resinous, and sometimes infused with scent from aromatic flowers. The sound of a large waterfall could be heard long before we reached it. About every half hour we would pause briefly at designated clearings. The men cut Heliconia and other leaves to sit on, for protection from ant bites. The inch-long black bullet ant is venomous and much feared; its bite can cause a reaction similar to that of a scorpion. Before descending the narrow trail to the Conga River, a man cut a walking stick for me that saved me from falling a few times. More than once in low spots, the thick mud sucked the high rubber boots right off of my feet.

Two of the men with us were teachers and one of them was Chinchi's brother-in-law. They lived and taught school in Tsawantus, a couple of hours' walk beyond Pantam Entsa. The day before, we had arranged to have some Tsawantus men come to Kusa Kubaim to help carry the boxes of books, which weighed two hundred pounds or more. We met the men on the trail about an hour outside of Kusa Kubaim, where we had left the books for them. Despite the time difference and the weight they carried, they arrived in Pantam Entsa just after we did and then continued on to Tsawantus.

Walking beside me for most of that day was a nine-year-old Awajún girl, a neighbor of Chinchi's sister and brother-in-law. The girl had come with them to Huampami for a week and we all walked back together. She had never been outside of her village before, much less been around any foreigners. Having heard oral history about "the white man," she was very afraid of me; I could see the fear in her dark eyes. But spending some days in the same house together (and the investment of a few sweet treats) helped me to gain her trust, though not much. She walked that day with a pack as well as a bag, but I still had to hustle to keep up with her. Especially on steep, rocky parts of the trail and in the cloying mud, her bare feet put me to shame. She walked all the way to Tsawantus with us, arriving after dark. When we visited her school a couple of days later, I was amused that she wanted to walk beside me and show everyone that she was good friends with "the gringo."

Before we arrived in Pantam Entsa, a man on the trail had offered us bowls of masato. Soon after, I had to slow down for Chinchi, who had wrenched his knee. At a rest point, someone gathered some nettle, hortiga (*Urtica urens*), and swatted at the sore area with it. Immediately, a rash of bumps appeared and Chinchi's knee was slightly anesthetized.

It was getting late by the time we finally reached Pantam Entsa. On a stick fence in front of the first solitary house were two kunkus, the shells of a large land snail (*Achantina*), which, like conchs, are used as horns. After speaking briefly in Awajún with Chinchi, the man from the house blew one of the shells, a signal for everyone to gather at the village's bamboo community center.

Waiting to greet us at the village entrance were several people who had anticipated our arrival. A growing crowd of curious, wide-eyed Aguaruna kids followed at a distance. After Chinchi and I told the villagers of our purpose in coming, we hurried to the river to wash while there was still light. We could hear whispers and laughter from a crowd of kids perched atop the stream bank, as we dove from a pebble beach into the pellucid waters of the cold Conga River. We then went to the school, where we would spend the night.

I was told that I was the first foreigner these kids had ever seen. Surely, they were not going to lose the opportunity to watch me! When we returned to the school about twenty kids gathered in small groups, but at a distance. They seemed to enjoy watching me, but none dared to venture any closer than ten or fifteen meters. Their body language showed that they were not going to take any chances. Even though they knew I came to help, they were still unsure and reticent to get too close. After all, I was the boogie-man.

Inside the school, Chinchi and another man were relaxing and placing makeshift desks together to sleep on later. I started hanging my hammock outside along the covered porch. The barefoot kids watched from a distance, still too shy and fearful to approach. Then I noticed a couple of young boys trying to sneak up behind a low bamboo wall bordering the porch. They were stalking me as if I were some exotic animal they wanted to check out. Realizing this, I took one long step, silently leaned over the top of the bamboo wall, and surprised them. Quickly turning, the two little boys looked up into my eyes, transfixed in fear. Fleeing like startled birds, one emitted a shrill-whine that pierced the sunset. I heard Chinchi laugh and say something to them in Awajún; they all knew that we had books, notebooks, pens, paper, and paints to give to them the next day.

After a few minutes, a couple of other brave children dared to approach. By then I was careful not to make any fast moves or even eye contact, knowing it would send them fleeing. Nervously, a couple more approached and then some more. I continued to read a book, purposely not looking up. Finally, several dared to enter the porch of their school. After a bit, as I lay reading, a hand reached out from amongst the small group gathered behind me and touched the blonde hairs on my arm. Then a second did the same. I slowly turned and again my eye contact caused five or six of them to scurry away, but this time with giggles.

I expressed an interest in seeing an oom, an Awajún blowgun, (called a pucuna in most of the Amazon), so a young man left and returned with one, all eight feet of it. Black, shiny and tapered slightly on one end, it looked like an extra-long pool cue. These weapons are made in different ways depending on the tribe, but normally they are formed from the very hard, jet-black wood of the pucuna caspi tree (*Iryanthera tricornis*), of the nutmeg family, or from the iron-like pona palm (*Socratea exorrhiza*). The long blowgun is usually made by carefully slicing lengthwise down the middle of a piece of wood; a narrow groove is then carefully cut into each half. The two halves are fitted together and wrapped with the strong roots of the philodendron vine and then covered with a tar-like resin.

The narrow, six-inch-long bamboo darts have a stabilizing swab of cotton on one end. They can be shot accurately up to forty meters. During Peru's 1995 border war with Ecuador in the Condor Mountains, Awajún men silently fought with their blowguns for Peru while their cousins, the Shuar, did the same for Ecuador.

While we were in Pantam Entsa, a very energetic older Awajún woman named Rosa cooked for us. She was pleased with the tins of tuna and sardines we had brought. If not for those we would have been eating yuca and boiled green bananas for breakfast, lunch, and dinner. Wild meat, fish, and chicken occasionally make their way into a meal, but most are bland. Sometimes they will gather the dark green leaves of the unkuch plant (*Piperaceae longipilosum*), which tastes like cabbage. They also gather the Chontaduro palm (*Bactris gasipaes*), eating the fibrous layers of the tender trunk raw in salad or cooked.

During one special meal at Rosa's, after I had finished a chicken leg, I laid the drumstick bone on my plate. A man sitting across the table from me asked if he could have the bone. When I passed it to him, he ate it like a starving dog.

A well-known indigenous delicacy is suri (*Rhynchophorus palmarum*), a finger-sized white grub that is the larvae of a palm beetle, which is gathered from the rotting wood of fallen aguaje palms. One day in Huampami, Chinchi's wife Rita gathered many of them and cooked them for dinner. I had already talked about suri with Chinchi and I think they wanted to see my response. She placed several that had been fried on my plate, along with some boiled yuca and some mashed raw unkuch. I surprised her a while later when I asked for seconds. Suri are sometimes eaten raw and are certainly an acquired taste. Normally they are fried and the small black head turns crispy, like chicharrón, while the thick white body is a gooey pâté. Suri are often the subject of jokes; its corpulent rubbery wiggles challenge all but aficionados. Whenever I mention to Peruvians that I have eaten suri, they always smile or laugh outright. Though the name suri is well known throughout the gastronomic world of Peru, most people will never eat them.

In Pantam Entsa, in the middle of nowhere, I was surprised to find an ultra-modern telephone system with a microwave dish and some solar panels. These were next to the totally empty health center. Knowing about the phone, Chinchi decided to call his cantankerous wife in Huampami from the bamboo phone booth.

I was even more surprised to find fifty-eight green Chinese laptops in the school storeroom. Later in Tsawantus I found another pile in their school's storeroom. They were all stacked high in boxes and had never been opened. I opened one of the boxes and took out the computer to check it out.

Amazed, I asked how they had gotten there. The teacher told me that they had been brought in by government helicopter a few months before, at the same time as the telephone. Peru's Minister of Education had given them as a peace offering because of the Bagua massacre the year before.

The health center and the primary school were both empty of any useful materials. The only school supplies were those that I had brought. The only access to medicine, including aspirin and snake-bite antidote, was many hours' walk away, in Huampami.

The students of the one-room school were waiting for people from the Ministry of Education to present a workshop on the laptops, so Chinchi and I decided to let things be. But for the people there, it seemed that the books, pens, notebooks, paints, and paper that I had brought were more necessary and more user-friendly than the laptops.

I'm sure the Peruvian Ministry of Education meant well, but they didn't understand the reality of the school's situation. Computers are great, but without having even one pen or notebook in the whole school, the writing ability of many kids has been challenged. Since they don't know how to properly write their names, pushing the buttons of computers may only further hamper their writing skills. When they have never had any pedagogical materials, how can the government expect them to suddenly join the computer age?

Using a keyboard to write does not mean that one can write legibly. In fact, there is much evidence to the contrary. Without also teaching basic reading and writing skills, the laptops seem like a waste of money. Why don't they also supply children's books, and pencils and notebooks, I wondered? These people are poor but they want their children to be educated, or at least to be able to read and write. Because of misguided policies, true education is not occurring there.

Weeks later, when I returned to Lima, I went to the very disorderly Ministry of Education to tell them about the computers. But I was only a "gringo" and I was just wasting my words.

Like all Amazonian tribes, the Awajún eat yuca for every meal of the year and never complain. Yuca is one of the most important staples in the world after rice, wheat, and corn. It is high in carbohydrates, but has no protein. Since this is their main staple, and often the only thing they eat, it helps explain why so many Awajún kids are small for their age. I asked a couple of kids how old they were and they told me fourteen, although they looked to be nine or ten. But without yuca they would not survive. Other than bananas, it is the only thing they plant. They keep the harvested stalks of the yuca plant and simply pushed them back into the earth, and tubers form again.

Though it requires little work to plant and care for, yuca takes eight to ten months to harvest, similar to bananas. I wanted to show Rosa and her daughters that I was not ignorant about their beloved yuca, so I decided to show them something new. I knew they had never seen it grated, mixed with some olive oil (or any oil), and then made into a patty and fried. They usually eat it boiled, which is very bland. I was curious to see their response so I cooked up a bunch. It was a hit! Knowing they had no grater, I gave mine to Rosa when I left.

"Why do they only plant yuca?" I asked Chinchi.

"Because they have no seeds," he answered.

"Of course!" I thought. "Well, they do now!" I responded, referring to the seeds I had also brought with me.

The Awajún rely almost totally on swidden (slash and burn) agriculture on their chacras, their forest farms. One constant problem, as Chinchi told me, is that virtually no one has any seeds to plant anything. Because of this their diet is very limited. Seeds are expensive and nearly impossible to find, except in agro-vet stores in cities. These stores can be like toxic waste dumps. Normally there are several of them close together, always with open doors; everything inside is permeated with an invisible cloud of noxious chemical smells.

The remote poor rarely have access to any seeds except for what they keep from their own few crops. As a result, they value seeds as much as they value books. They want more for their children than to be condemned to the cycle of poverty and illiteracy. It is the older women who are often most interested in the seeds. In Pantam Entsa, I spent hours at a large table in the community center labeling and spooning seeds into coin envelopes. Afterwards, with the help of a village leader who knew a lot about agriculture, we presented a workshop and explained various things about planting and taking care of the vegetables and fruits that the people hoped to grow from the seeds.

Most of the vegetables grown in Peru (and in all of Latin America for that matter) come from commercial American seed companies like Bonanza, Emerald, and Calseed. The Known-You Seed Company from Taiwan, Kaneko from Japan, and SAIS and

Raci from Italy also provide a few choices. Brazil and Colombia have access to seeds, but for some reason they are harder to find in other countries. There are only a couple of Peruvian seed companies, and they only sell a few seeds varieties, such as cilantro, squash, and chili peppers. The reality is that there are few choices in much of Latin America, and few are suited to tropical conditions, though they will produce. Open-pollinated, organic seeds are difficult if not impossible to find. Most are hybrids, treated with fungicides, and will not produce viable seed. The American companies do have some "standard" seeds, which will reproduce, but choices are limited.

Imported seeds from American organic companies like Johnny's Select Seeds, who will do all the paper work for the USDA's phytosanitary permitting process, can be very expensive. Johnny's is great and very helpful, but unfortunately SINASA, Peru's equivalent to the USDA, is very difficult. People at Johnny's once told me that Peru is the country where they have the most difficulties sending seeds. For some reason, they do not recognize the USDA permit and insist on doing their own inspection. While the USDA permits costs roughly fifty dollars, Peru charges about twenty-five dollars for inspecting each variety of seed. Their permitting process costs can easily equal about half of the price of the seeds!

The reality, though, is that without US seed companies such as Bonanza and Emerald, Peru would have very few seeds. Most of the common vegetables and fruits come from the US. For SINASA to charge so much is counterproductive for Peru and limits them, yet they do it. In Peru, where so many people are subsistence farmers and where child malnutrition is so high, this is a food safety issue.

I no longer import seeds to Peru anymore. Instead, I buy commercially grown US seeds in Lima or other cities. This is not what I would prefer, but unfortunately it is how things have to be done. The problem for poor farmers is that commercial hybrid seeds, unlike open-pollinated seeds, do not offer farmers the freedom to save seeds from their crops for the next planting. Instead, these seeds chain them into continually buying more seeds, which is good for the company, but bad for the farmer. At least they are not transgenic (genetically modified) seeds, which are prohibited in Peru.

The Peruvian anthropologist Enrique Espinosa-Benavides wrote that, "The natives set great score by education and consider it useful for the future: the problem at the moment is how to conciliate education with their own identity and natural wisdom…In the old days, by telling stories and chanting songs, parents would tell their children about the origin of plants, the behavior of animals, the origin of concoctions they drink. Today the concept of the school has banished this knowledge." Unfortunately, he is right.

"They need to foster an education adapted to the needs and aspirations of indigenous pupils, which will permit them to correctly incorporate concepts needed to live in today's world without renouncing the contributions of indigenous cultures," wrote Alexandre Surrallés, another Peruvian anthropologist. Everyone wants schools, though, and primary schools are often the anchor of the community.

Virtually every remote indigenous school suffers from an educational cachexia and a palimpsestic pedagogy. In many Awajún and other native schools, many children have never held a book. There simply are none! Is a school a school if it has no books? The kids are bright and have a real desire to learn, yet they can't. Our hope is that some of them, at some point, will take up the pen (or computer keyboard) in defense of their culture. They have a wealth of natural knowledge and wisdom from their "old ones," which needs to be recorded before it is forgotten.

Before we left Pantam Entsa and Tsawantus, the apus asked me if I could get them some medicine. I already knew they didn't have so much as an aspirin. Knowing their burden, but also knowing my limitations, I had to tell them that I was sorry, but that is not my work. None of them was satisfied with my answer and neither was I.

After giving it some more thought, I invited them to write a letter to the Minister of Health in Lima and promised to deliver it personally when I got there. They did that, filling four pages with official looking stamps, national ID numbers, and dozens of signatures of community leaders and members of different associations. Several provided inked thumb prints, which revealed the telltale tracks of illiteracy.

When I returned to Lima some weeks later, I put on a white shirt and took a taxi to the large, gated complex of the Ministry of Health, in the Jesus Maria section of Lima. The receptionist called someone after I explained that I had some documents for the Minister from apus of the Awajún. Mentioning the name Awajún in Peru immediately conjures up memories of the Bagua massacre. Soon a young man came over and examined the papers. The letters impressed him, especially the stamps.

"These stamps are important," he commented, then he told me to wait for a minute while he made a phone call. Within two minutes he was escorting me up a staircase to the fourth-floor office of the Minister. There I spoke to his secretary, who told me that the Minister was in a meeting. She kept the letter and some photos, and I was given a receipt and told to return the following day at noon. When I came the next day, she gave me a stamped paper indicating that they had started the process of obtaining some medicine for Pantam Entsa and Tsawantus. Some months later, however, there were elections, Ministers was changed, and everything was forgotten. Again, such is Peru! Months later, I took care of it myself on another journey.

While waiting to get past the heavily guarded gate at the Ministry of Health, I noticed a medicinal plant garden that occupied a good-sized area on one side of the Ministry building. As soon as I finished my appointment, I went over to have a look. Paths lined with rocks led past hundreds of plants with botanical labels. I was impressed, but noticed that I was the only visitor. Spotting a couple of gardeners, I asked them where the ayahuasca (*Banisteriopsis caapi*) plant was. They pointed it out nearby. I made some joke about them being ayahuascaros (ayahuasca takers), which made them laugh. Impressed by the size of the massive vine, I asked them how old it was. Seventeen years, one of them told me. The head gardener noticed my interest and walked over as I looked at the giant vine. Seizing the opportunity to tap his knowledge, I asked about some other plants.

"Do you have a chacruna plant?" I inquired.

"Yes, but our *Psychotria viridis* is suffering from the cold," he said, pointing to a very large-leafed bush. I tasted a piece of its bitter leaf.

When I expressed curiosity about snakebite medicine, he took me to see two plants. One, a type of piri piri called Yawar piri piri (*Eleutherine bulbosa*), is like a short, hollow-stemmed reed. The useful part is its small, reddish roots that resemble shallots. Another plant useful for treating snakebite, jergon sacha (*Dracontium loretense*), was in a pot in a greenhouse. It had two scaly, snakeskin-like brown stems. I mentioned how good it would be to have a farm of these plants and not just one in a garden. "Does anyone do that?" I asked.

"Not that I know of," lamented the gardener.

Then I asked him about barbasco. He took me over to see a four-meter high, sapling-like bush labeled *Lonchocarpus utilis*. He told me that there are other varieties of barbasco, one of which is called culi, a *Phyllanthus*. He nodded when I mentioned that almost all Awajún families have such a bush in their chacaras.

"It's the root which is poisonous," he said. "It has rotenone."

Barbasco is still sometimes used as a piscicide—a pulverized preparation will asphyxiate fish far downstream. Most communities prohibit it, but it is still used in certain remote waters. If ingested by humans, barbasco can kill a within an hour, accompanied by gut-wrenching pain. It is a well-known tool for suicide. When I was in Huampami, we heard that Chinchi's brother-in-law drank barbasco one night in Santa Maria Nieva, killing himself after a domestic fight. Barbasco and other toxic plants, like catahua (*Hura crepitans*) and la huaca (*Clibadium remotoflorum*), have been used as piscicides in rivers and streams for thousands of years, normally very cautiously. Nonetheless, abuse of these toxins by fishermen has long been an environmental problem within indigenous communities. In the rivers, though, unlike arsenic, mercury, and other mining contaminants which have killed rivers all over Peru, barbasco dissipates.

"Now I will show you the prize of the garden!" said the gardener. He brought me to a very leafy, seven-foot-high moonseed plant (*Chondrodendron curarina*), one of a variety of plants used for making the curare poison. Its impressive large, round leaves were so profuse that they gave the impression that they were purposely hiding something, keeping a secret. Curare is made from many things depending on the area, usually a combination of poisonous plants like the moonseed plant, skins of poison-dart frogs, venom of the bullet ant, juice of a liana, and who knows what else. Each tribe has their own recipes and ways of preparing it. Along with salt and turtle eggs, curare was once one of the Jesuits' most lucrative Amazonian products. To this day curare is prepared and traded on a small scale, mostly by the Ticuna people.

Medicinal plants for the Awajún and other indigenous peoples of the Amazon are very important. As in Pantam Entsa and Tsawantus, very few have access to any allopathic medicine. Unfortunately, tribes are forgetting their knowledge of medicinal plants. Like the foreign mining companies, who came into the Cordillera del Condor to take the Awajún gold, Monsanto, the high priests of agro-science, have "chemically prospected" this herbal knowledge. Some years ago, Monsanto wanted a patent for synthesizing a medicinal plant called uruchnumi (*Euphorbiaceae*), a type of cotton tree native to the Condor Mountains. The plant showed promise as a blood coagulant and treatment for fever. It has been known by Awajún healers forever. Monsanto's quest involved a US university and a bio-prospecting ethno-botanist who, instead of protecting the intellectual property rights of the Awajún tribe, sold out to Monsanto. Monsanto says it considers genetic resources to be "the common heritage of humankind" on the one hand, but their private property on the other. When Monsanto started testing uruchnumi, the Awajún never received a penny. In a rare case of poetic justice, the US government surprisingly refused Monsanto the patent. In the Land of Laughter, this is another Devil's Curve.

Chapter 16

HUANCAVELICA AND A LACUNA OF LITERACY

> Education is the point at which we decide whether we love the world enough to assume responsibility for it."—Hannah Arendt

When the old Andean town of Huancavelica is mentioned to Peruvians, they immediately associate it with poverty. Famously poor, it is located between Huancayo and Ayacucho, high amongst the mountain moors at nearly 3,800 meters. In November of 2006, I traveled there by bus from Lima with books for fourteen impoverished primary schools. Because of the need and that there were so many small villages or casarias scattered nearby on the treeless páramo, it was a good place for my work. In two weeks I visited fourteen schools, mostly by taxi. The rains had arrived and people were planting potatoes in the freshly-tilled earth along the roads and on distant slopes.

People there also plant the lupin tarwi (*lupinus mutabilis*). Like barley, it grows well at high elevations where corn does not. Tarwi has a remarkably high percentage of protein for a plant—a forty-six to fifty percent. This one- to two-meter high plant has pods of small white beans that form from bright blue flowers at the end large stems. The beans have to be soaked in water for several days to get rid of poisonous alkaloids. They are usually eaten raw after being rehydrated. The bean is twenty percent oil and is rich in the amino acids lysine and tryptophan. Tarwi is very adaptable and tolerates frost. It is also a great composting crop, fixing nitrogen in the soil.

Another plant called kiwicha (*Amaranthus caudatus*) has tiny white seed that also rival meat in protein and are very high in lysine. They are similar to casein, the protein found in milk, and thus are good for infants. Kañiwa (*Chenopodium pallidicaule*), a tiny morphological cousin of quinoa, is another seed grown at extremely high altitudes. This cereal-like grain is toasted, ground into flour, and added to soups or hot beverages. Many of these uncommon grains are purchased by the Dutch Army and used as a breakfast cereal. Ulluco (*Ullucus tuberosus*) and oca (*Oxalis tuberosa*) are root crops grown in the region that flourish at high altitude. The tuber is the part of these plants eaten most often, although the leaves can be eaten as well. Maca (*Lepidium meyenii*) is another highly-valued plant that growns there, which has a brown, radish-like medicinal root.

In 1563 the Spanish found gold in Huancavelica and named the town Pesa de Oro, meaning Weight of Gold. They also found cinnabar, an ore from which mercury is mined. Even in pre-Inca times Huancavelica was known for its cinnabar; it was traded throughout the Wari culture, even up to the time of the Chavin culture. When the Spanish arrived, they found the mine and immediately began to export the cinnabar to Potosi, Bolivia and other places. Mercury from the cinnabar was used to extract silver from ore. It is estimated that 50,000 tons of mercury were produced from the Huancavelica mines between 1560 and 1813. The mine is still in production, but it has severely polluted the fast flowing Ichu River and adversely affected both humans and animals.

When I arrived, I found a cheap hotel beside the plaza and used a storeroom there for my boxes. One morning, I took a taxi to a primary school on the outskirts of Huancavelica with approximately forty students. They were as friendly as they were needy. I then left to visit another school in a nearby casaria.

An hour later, I doubled back, passing the same school again. The kids were outside for recess and spotted the taxi from a distance. All forty of them ran off the school grounds and blocked the rocky road as we approached. With a din of excited laughter, they purposely made us stop. Like bees around a honey jar they flocked around the car, not wanting us to leave.

This was their way of expressing gratitude. Just an hour before few of them had a pen or notebook, and none had any books to read. As we drove away from the riotous crowd of waving kids, I looked back at a turn in the road and saw one little girl, still standing there alone and waving.

The parents of these children, and others like them, had been prime ideological targets for the Sendero Luminoso, the Shining Path, during their twenty-year campaigns of terror in the late twentieth century. While a few were recruited, many more were maimed and murdered in Peru.

The poverty and suffering in Huancavelica and similar villages provided fertile recruiting grounds for the revolutionary ideas of the Sendero Luminoso leader, Abimael Guzmán. Guzmán was commonly known as "Gonzalo," a name perhaps inspired by Shakespeare's character, the advisor to Prospero in *The Tempest*. He was also sometimes referred to as Dr. Shampoo, because of his ability to brainwash. He alienated rural peasants and the indigenous population with his brutal methods, however.

In addition to ordering massacres, he prohibited buying and selling in open markets, which proved to become a catalyst for resentment against the Shining Path. Peru's peasant population proved that the path from hunger to revolution is never a straight line, as Guzmán had hoped.

Guzmán had been an educator, a professor of philosophy at the university in Ayacucho, a heavily indigenous area. Perhaps he brainwashed himself, but for whatever reason, he seemed to have a pronounced disinterest in Peru's indigenous peoples. He eschewed any appeal to their Andean social roots for his political ideology. For example, he could have related his Maoist ideas to the ancient Incan social system called mit'a, where all able-bodied people provided compulsory communal labor for some days every year.

He never called for "diversity in unity," as did Luis Valcárcel, Peru's pro-Quechua Minister of Education in the 1940s. For Valcárcel, "The new school is the nursery where the seedlings of the resurrected race can grow." But for Guzmán, the school became the locus for a bloody class struggle that lacked any initiatives in favor of solidarity.

It was not in the lineage of indigenous Peruvians such as Tupac Amaru, Atahualpa, or Manco Inca that Guzmán found his political ideology; rather it was in Marx, Lenin, and Mao, figures the common people never heard of and could not relate to. In the end, the Shining Path failed, as the neo-liberalism they opposed had failed, condemning the rural people to more years of poverty and solitude.

In the 1950s, an adult literacy book called "Pedro" was introduced into some of the indigenous schools by the Peruvian government. Pedro "was not the simple literacy book that its title announced," wrote Marisol de la Cadena, but one which promoted the "conversion" of Peruvian indigenous kids into the dominant culture. Though "Pedro" was published long ago, very little has changed.

According to Marisol de la Cadena: "The surprise comes at the end: Pedro's children have undergone cultural changes that effect visible bodily transformations. Neatly combed, Julia has got rid of her braids, and Pancho does not wear his chullo anymore, and wearing industrial cotton clothes they make their way to school. Pedro's children are not Indians any more—they are Peruvians. This promise has not been channelled through some programme of matrimonial/reproductive eugenics but through 'programa de desarrollo integral' with education as its crucial component.

on as its crucial component. With this evolutionary tale ending happily, Pancho and his sister Julia have been transformed into mestizos, the category that awaited improved Indians." Though the story doesn't mention it, the children's next step will be to leave the family farm. They will move to a poor barrio in Lima and eke out a living in some factory.

Thus, literacy became a nation-building tool aimed at the amalgamation of its diverse non-white population through the hegemonic use of the Spanish language. According to Marisol de la Cadena, "Pedro" "represents the defeat of purist indigenismo," as the little Quechua-speaking Indian boy is transformed into a Spanish-speaking campesino (country person).

"Schooled literacy has been a hegemonic practice," writes James Collins, "involving the displacement of nonstandard varieties of language and shunting aside or discrediting of alternative literacies." On the one hand it is a question of social authority and on the other, the politics of linguistic identity or, as linguist Charles Taylor calls it, "the politics of recognition."

While driving to various villages around Hauncavelica, I came across one called Pumacoya, just across the cold white waters of the Ichu River. Ichu is the name of the tall stiff grass that grows on the western slopes of the Andes. It is still typically used as roofing material by poor families.

One day we stopped the car along the road side and looked down at the river and across to a tiny village. We could clearly see a little school there, built beside a copse of eucalyptus. It was surrounded by a couple of dozen adobe dwellings and a small church, all with ichu grass roofs.

The problem was that there was no bridge. Pumacoya was totally cut off from the blacktop road. To get to it, people had to cross the river a couple of miles downstream and then walk back on a trail along the riverbank. That was the only way to get there we were told. I wanted to visit the school, but it was very impractical because of the long walk with boxes. I was so close, and yet so far away.

I didn't want to give up so easily, so I asked the taxi driver if he thought we could ford the river. From above, it looked like it would be easy. I asked him to drive down a rocky old service road that stopped beside the river bank. Once we got to the bottom, however, things appeared very different. The current was strong—in most places it could easily make you lose your footing and wash you away. And the rocky bottom of the river seemed very unstable. For nearly an hour we walked up and down the bank, searching for a shallow place to cross. We finally decided on a diagonal route, which stretched between a few tiny rock islands.

After stripping down to our underwear and placing our clothes in a day pack, we edged our way into the freezing water. Cautiously, I led the way with a box of books on my shoulder. I thought that it would be better if I carried the books, for I didn't want the taxi driver to feel responsible if they fell. We had searched for walking sticks, but there was no wood to be found anywhere. Almost immediately, just a few steps into the frigid whitewater, I stepped into a hole and nearly lost both my balance and the books. Without a walking stick, the current of the waist-deep water made the going slow and difficult. Just looking at the current was almost enough to make one lose one's balance and be carried away with it, so we focused ahead. After making it to the first island, I put the box down and returned to the river bank for another one. Then from one little island to the next, and finally to the opposite bank, I carried three boxes.

From there, it was only a couple of minutes' walk to the school. The surrounding area was green with sprouting shoots of barley, freshened by recent rains. I was tired from making the crossing and carrying the books, so I was relieved when a man walking his bicycle offered to help lighten our load. He helped take the boxes to the open gate of the school, where we were immediately spotted by the surprised students, who were eating lunch in the large grassy courtyard. No sooner did I introduce myself than a teacher invited us to eat. The cooks, two older indigenous women with long braids, served us barley and fava beans. Afterwards, while I was handing out the pens and notebooks, one of the cooks asked me if she could have one, too. "Of course you can!" I told her, "But what grade are you in?" "Second grade," she said, at which everyone joined her in laughter.

Chapter 17

OLLEROS TO CHAVIN

High in the Ancash region of the Peruvian Andes, a rocky trail some thirty-seven kilometers long winds through the Cordillera Blanca mountain range between the villages of Olleros and Chavin de Huantar. The trail is an ancient one, made over 3,000 years ago in the time of the Chavin culture, or perhaps even earlier, when the Kotosh civilization ruled. Chavin is nearly as high in meters as it is old in years. The village was built at the confluence of the Huanchecsa and Mosna rivers on the eastern slopes of the Andes. It flourished for a few hundred years starting in the 9th century BCE, as a nexus point between Pacific coast cultures—such as the Pachacamac—and those of the Amazon. According to the Peruvian archeologist Julio Tello, Chavin was a temple-based culture, with rituals based on various animals from the Amazon jungle (jaguars, anacondas, and crocodiles) as well as the conch-shell trumpets of the Pacific desert coast.

In Quechua, the name Chavin was most likely taken from the word chaupin, which means the center of the center. Finding no evidence that Chavin had an army, some scholars believe that their culture spread through their art, rather than their arms. For over three hundred years, Chavin culture influenced an area that ran from Ecuador in the north to Ica in the south, along the central Peruvian coast. Pablo Picasso wrote, "Of all the ancient cultures I admire, that of Chavin amazes me most. Actually, it has been the inspiration behind most of my art." Archeologist Alfred Kroeber praised Chavin artwork as "the pinnacle of prehistoric South American art." Richard Burger, a Chavin scholar, stresses that their religious art style was meant "to convey or evoke religious awe," or feelings of the "wholly other."

In addition to revolutionary technological advances in textile weaving, the Chavin are also well known for their stonework art, which is full of motifs inspired by the hallucinogenic San Pedro cactus (*Trichocereus pachanoi* or *Echinopsis pachanoi*). The degree to which the cactus influenced Chavin's growth is debatable. Nonetheless, the use of DMT (Di-methyltriptamine) from the cactus, as well as concentrated snuffs made from powdered seeds of vilca (*Anadenanthera colubrina*) and epena (*Virola calophylla*) were an integral part of Chavin shamanic rituals.

Today, people visit Chavin for the same reason they did three millennia ago: because of its massive temple. At one time it was an impressive truncated pyramid nearly five stories tall with an extensive hydraulic system, but now it is reduced to a hill covering a subterranean labyrinth of stone passageways ending in small ceremonial chambers. Occasionally, tenoned stone heads still protrude, staring out from the temple's high exterior walls. Here, amongst its very refined acoustics, hierarchical keepers of the cult partook of Dionysian rites.

Nowadays most people travel to Chavin by bus, which takes more than a couple of hours from the town of Huaraz. I had traveled that way once before, but this time I was going to hike the mountain trail for three days to get there. In October of 2006, prior to the rainy season in the Andes, I brought books to the primary school in Olleros. Olleros is an adobe village located up a steep-sided valley, just off the main Callejon de Huaylas, about half an hour's drive south of Huaraz. While I was there, one of the village leaders came into the school, introduced himself as Calixto, and told me that he worked as a guide. He said that he had horses and a donkey, which he sometimes took into the mountains. We were soon planning a trip to several remote village schools to deliver books.

Three days later, after returning to Huaraz to make arrangements, I was back in Olleros with several boxes of books, notebooks, and other supplies. Then, along a solitary cobblestone street, we spent the next hour or so packing everything onto Calixto's three horses and donkey. The cracking walls of adobe houses and the strong smell of eucalyptus were soon left behind, replaced by vast expanses of golden grasslands and páramo of Peruvian feathergrass (*Jarava ichu*) sloping below glacial snows. Groups of giant bromeliads called puya de Raimondi could be seen far in the distance. These amazing plants, known as queen of the Andes, can live for twenty-eight years, grow to a height of twenty-five feet, and spend three months in bloom each year with thousands of tiny flowers. Towering snowcapped peaks, hidden behind closer ridges, came into view as the trail climbed. Soon, the only trees were occasional clumps of scrubby Queñoa (*Polylepis*), the world's highest growing species of trees. The only sign of humans was the narrow trail, which had been trodden for thousands of years.

After ten hours of walking and taking turns on horseback, we came to an old shepherd's hut at the base of the 4,700-meter-high Yanashallash Pass. It was a round rock structure with a sunken floor and a roof of ichu grass. We spent a frozen night there, waiting for the sun to rise and thaw the frost which had coated the ground with white crystals. While Calixto made us breakfast, I rounded up the animals which were grazing in a distant sunny spot. The blankets Calixto had placed on their backs the night before were frozen stiff. Within a couple of hours though, the sun again ruled and was mercilessly burning my exposed skin.

In single file we walked carefully upwards. Looking behind and below, we could see a herd of alpacas grazing beside one of the many fens. At one point where the trail narrowed and steepened, a horse nearly fell over a cliff. Its hoof sent a rock tumbling and its back leg started to follow it. At the pass, we sat and looked in both directions at views unchanged for thousands of years. Not far beyond the pass, the trail led us past the ruins of an old Inca fortress. It had probably been destroyed in 1548 by Spanish troops under Pedro Cieza de León, the first foreigner to visit Chavin.

When Cieza de León found Chavin, he found a people already subservient to the Incan empire who told him that the ruins had been built by giants. Chavin had been in decline for nearly 2,000 years prior to his arrival. It was eventually replaced by the Wari culture, which was in turn replaced by the Incas. Spanish chronicler Antonio Vasquez de Espinosa recorded that, "Nearby the town of Chavin lies a great building of carved stones of notable grandeur; it was a temple, a sanctuary for the most famous gentiles, such as Rome or Jerusalem were for us."

Switch-backing down and down, we rounded a mountain and finally saw far below us a shepherd and some animals, the first sign of human presence. After a while, we passed recently harvested fields of barley, the straw neatly stacked in piles. In that area the people also grow kiwicha (*Amaranthus caudatus*), a whitish grain similar to amaranth and quinoa, and tarwi (*Lupinus mutabilis*), a large lupine-like plant with a small white bean.

It wasn't long until the eucalyptus-shaded banks of a stream and the grass roofs of small adobe houses came into view. Chichucancha was the first and largest of several villages we came upon. In their poverty, the adobe houses hugged to the side of a dry hill tightly, like a hungry flock. A couple of dogs trailed behind us, relentlessly barking to let everyone know that some strangers had arrived; they followed us all the way to the gate of the school. Calixto knocked on the steel gate and soon it was opened. Everyone inside knew that something was going on, but they didn't know what. The school gate was a double gate and a man swung back both sides so that we could enter with the horses. I entered the compound without dismounting, followed by the other horses and the donkey.

The open doors of the classrooms were like picture frames, full of the surprised faces of students and teachers. Within seconds the classrooms spontaneously emptied and we were surrounded by seventy or eighty curious schoolchildren. Like millions of highland Andino children their cheeks, like their lives, were very rosy but often chapped from the harsh elements. The equally curious principal and three teachers welcomed us. They were taken aback by the books. To control the excitement, they had the students stand in rows and placed a table in front of them, upon which I displayed the books. I asked the children, "Who likes books?" In unison, they answered with an ear-shattering "Me, meeeee..." that the whole village could hear.

After showing them the dictionary and encyclopedias, I explained that the books were a gift to their school, and should remain in the school so they wouldn't get lost. I then asked, "Who needs a notebook and pen?" Knowing that my words would be like a spark lighting a fuse, I covered my ears with my hands as I prepared for another explosion of joy. Sure enough, they discharged another salvo of shouts and screams. Their spoken words called out for the written. They wanted desperately to give voice to the silent letters, those funny marks they were told we base our world upon. Their answer expressed a thirst for learning. Then, amidst more shouts, Calixto and some of the teachers handed each exuberant kid a pen and notebook.

How can schools be so empty when Peru has enough money to maintain fighter jets in their air force? Illiteracy and the poverty it engenders is their enemy—not Ecuador or Chile. Illiteracy continues to conquer, to challenge the lives of millions. Is this planned, or are the powers that be so inept that they overlook the primary educational needs of thousands of schools? Does the white ruling class in Lima want to keep the campesino and indigene uneducated to maintain access to cheap labor? The Conquest continues by neglect, it seems. Even more insidious than that, the school system is also a factor in child malnutrition. Children are required to go to school and many walk for miles to get there, but they are not supplied with an adequate meal while there. The food, usually a bland gruel-like drink, is so unsatisfactory that the kids' health and learning suffer because of it. But nothing is done and things continue on the same course. Peru seems more concerned with erecting bronze monuments to generals defeated long ago than it is with caring for its children.

We left the school in Chichucancha abuzz with energy. It was as if we had brought food to people who were starving. Calixto knew a man in the village, so we looked him up in hope of spending the night at his house. After finding him and making arrangements, we left our gear there, taking enough books and supplies for the school in the neighboring village of Jato. We wanted to get there before the school closed after lunch, so we loaded everything onto one horse and we each rode another toward Jato. This village was not far away, but it is on top of a ridge. The trail proved too steep to ride up on the way there, or down on the way back, so we walked with the struggling horses.

Compared to Chichucancha, Jato is pleasant, with an excellent view of the 6,400-meter-high snowcapped Huanstan mountain on one side and the narrow valley leading to Chavin on the other. As we entered the gated school grounds on horseback, we were surprised to see a large, grassy playground. Once again, wide-eyed faces peered from the open classroom doors. Though the school in Jato had fewer than thirty kids, it was just as empty of materials as Chichucancha, and just as thankful to receive some.

There are a few more small villages near Chavin. One is Lachan, at 3,650 meters, and Nunupata, which is a bit lower. The shabby old school at Lachan did not have even one pen to share among its dozen students. All of these villages perhaps date back to the Chavin horizon, but lost in time, they have no horizon.

I ran out of books in Lachan and said good-bye there to my guide and friend, Calixto. He returned the same way we'd come, alone with the horses and the donkey to his home in Olleros and I continued on to nearby Chavin. The experience of bringing books to such old, empty, and poor villages had been humbling. It amazed me to realize that people are probably as poor there today as they were three thousand years ago. I also know that the smiles I had seen were for more than just the books. The people also smiled because they were being remembered. As I have heard at so many schools, the teacher in Lachan told me, "We are forgotten!"

Chapter 18

PISCO SOUR

"Whoever neglects [or is prevented from] learning while young, loses the past and is dead to the future."—Euripides

It was a book of all things, a Catholic breviary, which Pizarro used in 1532 as pretext to conquer the immense Inca Empire. Because he came from a culture with an oral tradition, the Incan Emperor Atahualpa had even less use for the book than the illiterate Pizarro. Thus it was that a religious book became the first example of the "violence of the letter" in South America. It set the stage for slaughter in Cajamarca, and later, throughout the entire Empire.

Cieza de Leon's account of the first known book in South America reads, "After Pizarro seemed to get nowhere (through his interpreter) with Atahualpa about making a pact of friendship; then the Friar, Vincente de Valverde, with a crucifix in hand handed the book up to him, and he began to eye it carefully and listen to it page by page. At last he asked, 'Why doesn't the book say anything to me?' And still sitting on his throne, he threw it on to the ground with a haughty and disdainful petulant gesture..."

According to Wamán Poma, chronicler of the Inca, "...then Friar Vincente shouted something like the Indians were against the Christian faith and ordered the Spanish soldiers to attack." Cieza de Leon also says that the priest gave the order to attack. Though Atahualpa came from a bookless culture and could not have been expected to understand, it seems that the book also had nothing to say to either the illiterate Pizarro or the literate priest Valverde.

The various cultures of the area all practiced an oral tradition, centered around oracles. Lima, for example, was built in a place called the Valley of Rimac, which means "he who talks" in Quechua. It was so named because of the oracle associated with the place.

Though various mnemonic devices were utilized, none of the cultures there had any form of writing. Frank Salomon writes, "The apparent exception that the Inca state and its predecessors present to V. Gordon Childe's famous judgment of writing as fundamental to civilization (1936) is usually treated as a curious loose end." The Inca Empire stretched over thirty-two degrees latitude, and had 25,000 miles of stone roads. It was an empire with no money, no hunger, no wheels, and no writing.

Garcilaso de la Vega, the Inca historian, tells us that the magnanimous Inca Roca was the first Inca to start yachaywasi, state schools. The Amantas, or philosopher advisors, did the teaching. Their purpose was to train the sons of the nobility and also to acculturate the sons of nobles from client states in the Tawantinsuyu, the four parts of the Inca Empire. This was in Cusco, sometime around 1350, after Roca had conquered the Chanchas (a small tribe from Ayacucho), near Pisco.

The Inca Pachacutec erected palaces in the immediate vicinity of schools to show the esteem he held for learning. Among the many things students learned were the identification of up to a thousand medicinal herbs, as well as the intricate language of the quipu. This ingenious system, using colored knotted cords, dates back at least to the sixth century AD. As a form of writing without words, the quipu are independent of any language, and therefore international. They became a "visible precipitate of social action."

In addition to the quipu, the Inca also used pebbles, decorated beans and seeds, and carved staffs (called varayug in Quechua and varayo in Spanish) with different colored bands as mnemonic aids. Noted Inca scholar Larco Hoyle hypothesized that the decorated beans, carried by runners in small bags, were an ideographic writing system. The trained runners, called chasquis, carried quipus and wore special costumes made from bird feathers—a feathered express.

The "engraved staffs of authority rank among the deepest-rooted of Andean symbols. The coded staff makes its bearer an executor of folk legality...." With these mnemonic aids, people enthusiastically alphabetized their internal processes. Salomon asks, "do staffs and books form an integrated legible whole as, for example, prose and numerical tables do in monographs?"

With the advance of the Spanish Conquest, however, these mnemonic devices were also conquered. Even more than the illiteracy of the populace today when it comes to books, most people then were illiterate to the meaning of quipus. Lacking a history based on a system of writing, it is little wonder that Peru has always had a high percentage of analfabetos—illiterates.

In 1551, Lima was the location of the first university in the New World. In 2007, I was again in Lima buying books. I would go to my old haunts on Quilca Street, but mostly to the Amazonas Book Market. I planned to take the books to villages in remote areas of the Ancash Department, high in the Andes.

About eight at night on August 15th, I was in bed reading on the fourth floor of a cheap hotel in Lima when the region was struck by a magnitude eight earthquake. Shoeless, I fled down the staircase into a dark, foggy street full of screaming people. Lima was lucky and sustained little damage, but areas to the south, including Pisco and Ica, were devastated. Upon learning that seven hundred schools had collapsed, or were rendered unfit for use, I decided to work in the Pisco area instead. Though I had to wait a few weeks, I went and purchased books for thirty more schools.

During the recovery period, hundreds of unusable schools were replaced by makeshift structures. Most common were woven cane mats, estreas, that were tied together to create small classrooms with sand floors. Other schools held classes inside black plastic netting, plywood panels, corrugated metal, or whatever else could be found. They all shared one thing in common—a lack of books and school supplies.

Historically, Pisco had been home to the Paracas Culture around 300 BCE. In 1925, the famous Peruvian archeologist, Julio César Tello found mummies in his excavations there. Pisco today is best known for giving its name to the local white grape brandy, and the drink called Pisco Sour: just blend crushed ice, lemon, Pisco, a little sugar, and top with a whipped egg white.

Not far to the south is the desolate Paracas Peninsula, a desert hook-like point in the Pacific that forms the Paracas Bay. It was here that José de San Martín landed in 1820, to liberate Peru from Spain. It is now part of the Paracas National Park, famous for its abundance of birds.

When I was ready, I loaded a few dozen boxes of books and supplies into the storage compartment of a bus. Just twenty kilometers south of Lima, along the busy divided highway, I saw Pachacamac, a twenty-five-hundred-year-old religious site, far atop a hill overlooking the Pacific Ocean. In Quechua, Pachacamac means "World Shaker." For over two millennia, it was the most important religious site in all of the Americas.

It was here that the main oracle resided, to whom all Inca paid homage. Members of the Chavin Culture paid tribute to Pachcamac as well. Because of its significance, the conquistador and chronicler of Peru, Pedro Cieza de León, mentions that Pachacamac was the only coastal site where high-prestige goods were collected, rather than being transported to Cuzco. Pachacamac's reputation led it to be the first place the Spanish visited after they captured Atahualpa in Cajamarca. It took Hernando Pizarro twenty days to arrive there by horse. They were hoping to loot its temple site and tambos (store houses), which collected tribute for the oracular cult, but they found little gold. Now Petrol Peru has built a tank farm below but the barren islands just off the coast, the place where departed spirits resided, remains the same.

The bus I was on did not go into Pisco because of the quake, but stopped along the highway instead before continuing on to Ica. So, with a mountain of boxes I found myself standing on the side of the dreary road. Within a short time, though, I managed to get a pick-up truck to take me to one of the few open hotels.

Large areas of the old adobe town were completely wrecked. Pisco had always had some rough edges, but after the quake that's all it had. I was shocked to see four-story concrete buildings standing askew, looking like disheveled drunks ready to fall over. Tent camps, casarios de carpas, had been set up for displaced people, the damnificados. They popped up everywhere, like fruiting mushrooms on the barren coastal landscape. Groups of men with sledge hammers beat the rebar out of broken concrete at numerous demolition sites, to sell it by weight to scrappers. On the Plaza de Armas, the once massive San Clemente Church had only its two bell towers left standing. They looked awkward and clumsy, like two bookends with no books, or two gravestones marking a collective grave. A large blue tent covered the nave like a burial shroud, but in front, undisturbed, was a bronze statue of José de San Martín on horseback with sword in hand. He seemed to be charging out of the ruins of the church, like Pizarro at Cajamarca.

Nearby, one-room prefabricated wooden buildings lined some of the streets, a donation from a Turkish NGO called Kimse Yok Mu. They seemed to be the most popular of the many different types of temporary housing.

Though I had a few thousand books for thirty-some schools, I still had to divide them. Once again, my hotel room became like a book market. Fortunately, I was able to soon find the taxi driver I needed. He was an Afro-Peruvian and knew the area well. We spent the next two plus weeks driving to thirty schools on the sandy roads and tracts that connect the communities. Because the rural and remote schools are always the last to receive help, I went to a farming belt east of Pisco. The area is composed of dozens of hamlets where nearly every poor family is part of an agricultural cooperative. Historically, the best of Peru's cotton has been grown here. It still is, along with corn, artichokes, yams, and other vegetables. The earthquake, though, had caused the concrete around many irrigation sluice gates to crack and drain, which made farming impossible.

Before the earthquake, the schools there had nothing. Afterwards, it seemed that their only function was to feed the kids some thin gruel for lunch. The books and school supplies I brought were the only pedagogical materials available for most of the thirty schools.

I wanted to go to Tambo Colorado, an ancient archeological ruin on the Ayacucho Road, so I decided to take a bus there because of the distance. I took along enough books and supplies for two small schools. As always in Peru, the bus was crowded, so I placed the two boxes and a sack beneath the seat.

Unlike some of Peru's first-class double-decker buses, this one was old and well-used. It stopped like a milk truck to drop off or pick up people. After a while, a woman and her young daughter entered. By chance, the seat next to me and one behind were empty, so the two of them sat there.

The little girl, who was nine or ten years old, sat beside me. I must have been the first foreigner she ever sat next to, and I could tell she was not too comfortable. Her mother sat behind, to keep an eye on her. The sack with books and supplies was open between my feet. Soon, I noticed her crane her head to look at a children's book that was visible, so I asked her if she liked books. Naturally, she said yes. So reaching down, I pulled out a book called *Tales of the Andes* and handed it to her. "This is for you," I told her.

The first thing she did was turn in her seat to proudly show her mother with a full blossomed smile. Her mother, seemingly illiterate, took it and they paged through it together. Within a couple of minutes, another passenger asked to see it and the mother handed it to her. Then, for the next fifteen minutes, the book was passed all around the bus. Finally, someone handed it back to the little girl. At that point, I reached in the sack and found a pen and notebook. "This is for you too," I told her.

Within minutes the bus stopped again at some trailhead. It was their stop, so the woman and her daughter got off. As the bus drove off, the two were standing a few feet up the escarpment. The little girl was beaming as she held the book and waved good-bye.

That girl had most likely never had a book in her life, and because the government had stopped supplying notebooks to school kids, chances are that she never had one of those either. She had been disenfranchised from learning and condemned to paraliteracy.

It only took a moment before another woman approach me to say that she had two daughters who needed books. I told her that the books were for two schools, but nevertheless she persisted. After a few more pleas, I melted like a spent candle and said, "Okay."

That, of course, started a landslide of requests. I told them I wouldn't have enough for the destroyed schools. Luckily, my stop at Tambo Colorado was coming up and I made my escape.

At Tambo Colorado there is a tiny school of just twenty kids. I had a watchman at the ruins place one box in a small shed and I walked to the school with the other box and my pack. I was shocked to see a tiny corrugated structure was being used for the school. It was like a big tin can sitting in the sun like an oven. Beside it were the ruins of the old adobe school. To me, it symbolized the failure of the education system. When the kids saw me crossing the field carrying a box and sack, they came running over. Though they had salvaged some desks from their old school, there hd been no books to salvage.

Chapter 19

THE AMAZING AMAZON AGAIN AND AGAIN...

> "If you are thinking one year ahead, plant seeds. If you are thinking ten years ahead, plant trees. If you are thinking one hundred years ahead, educate the people."—Chinese Emperor Kuan Tsu, 5th century BCE

At the time of European contact there were at least a thousand different indigenous tribes living within the Amazon basin. Today there are only a fraction of that. Of the remaining tribes in Peru's Amazon, I brought books and seeds to at least eleven: the Shipibo, Chama, Cocama, Ashaninka, Bora, Huitoto, Ocaina, Ticuna, Awajun, Matsés, and Yagua.

It is the Yagua Indians who are probably the reason that the name Amazon was given to the largest river and jungle on earth. Most likely it was their warriors, with grass skirts made from the huge leaves of the aguaje palm (*Mauritia flexuosa*), who convinced Francisco Orellana's sixty-man party that they were the mythic A-mazos (i.e. "women without breasts"). The Greek myth says that the Amazons cut one breast off in order to better shoot their bows.

Both the skin of the Yagua as well as their fibrous skirts were dyed red from achiote seeds, which now has the scientific name *Bixa orellana*. This taxonomic honor was given to Orellana, and the name Amazon is credited to him as well. Orellana, who was blinded in one eye by an arrow, saw the Amazons with the other.

Francisco Orellana and his lost troop of men were the first Europeans (and probably the first of any people) to travel the length of the Amazon River. They began their journey on the Rio Coca in Ecuador to look for food for Gonzalo Pizarro's expedition. He was called a deserter, but in reality he was unable to return because of the current. With nowhere to go but with the flow, their raft entered the Rio Napo, which enters the Amazon at the place where there is now a town named after Francisco Orellana. Several months later, they found themselves at the mouth of the Amazon.

According to the Amazon scholar Georges Landau, "The history of the Amazon has always been one of greed." This has been true from the days of Gonzalo Pizarro's disastrous Cinnamon Expedition in 1541, which Orellana was part of, to the 19th century rubber barons, to the multi-national mining and oil companies of today.

Diego de Lepe explored the mouth of the Amazon in 1499, and may have first called it the Marañón (i.e. Mar-o-Non, that is, Sea-or-Not). It is not known what the different Amazon tribes called it before it became the Amazon, but the Marañón is most likely its first Spanish name. Over time, the name simply migrated upriver.

Popular Spanish "pulp" fiction (mostly chivalric in nature) from the sixteenth century probably led to the naming of the Amazon River. Many conquistadors had such reading material with them on their expeditions. Books like Montalvo's *Amadis de Gaul* and its sequel *Sergas de Esplandian* were steeped in Amazonian and other legends of old. Other early books such as Sabbastin Munster's *Cosmographia* just added to the mystique of the times.

With the advent of mass production, books and literature of the late 15th century played a direct role in forming the world's zeitgeist. As Erasmus of Rotterdam remarked, during this era "readers began to feel themselves transformed by the mere act of holding these almost divine instruments."

In his *Books of the Brave*, Irving Leonard writes, "Like motion pictures of the latter day, these romantic novels exerted a proud influence on contemporary culture, conduct, morality, and thought patterns." Many of these books recited the fabulous deeds of

Spanish soldiers fighting the Moors. They were also steeped in mythical lore and miracles. Leonard writes that, "the more interesting they found a book the more inclined they were to believe in its veracity."

The fabulous stories of war-like Amazons, the fountain of youth, the seven cities of gold, and other fantasies all had their origin in the chivalric literature of the age. Leonard demonstrates that the printed page had such an "aura of authority and mystery, that the spell cast by reading of the adventures of the knight-errant was hypnotic."

Like many of his time, Gonzalo Pizarro was greatly influenced by stories of El Dorado and was searching for "the lands of gold and cinnamon." His search for the "spice of life" in the Cinnamon Expedition of 1541 cost over 4,250 lives in eight months. The Spanish lost more men on that expedition than in the initial conquering of the Inca Empire. Gonzalo Pizarro left Quito with 350 Spanish men and 4000 Indian porters, but not a single Indian porter returned. They also took along 200 horses, 2000 dogs, 2000 llamas, and had 2000 pigs following behind. After eight months, only eighty of Pizarro's 350 men remained alive. Much to the horror of the inhabitants, they turned up in Quito starving and in rags.

My work in Peru's Amazon usually begins in central Lima, in the huge Amazonas Book Market, with its hundreds of crowded book stalls. I get my books from there, and from some other book stores along Quilca Street near Plaza San Martin in central Lima.

To get almost a ton of children's books to the Iquito in the Amazon, my only choice was to go overland, first by bus and then by riverboat (or a launch as they are called). The journey by land and river takes five days minimum. The only other way is by plane, which takes only an hour and a half, but is too expensive.

I shipped three dozen boxes of books with a trucking company while I took a bus to Pucallpa, where I picked up the books. Peru has many bus lines, but the system is decentralized and each company has its own station. The finest Volvo and Mercedes buses are available for service to most major cities in Peru and they all show movies to keep the passengers occupied. But to cross the Andes to Pucallpa, which is on the edge of the Amazon, they normally use older buses without amenities. The roads are too bad for companies to use their best buses and the ride can be grueling. This time my bus trip to Pucallpa took sixteen hours; the year before, the trip had taken almost twenty-four hours. On that occasion, we had to wait for hours in the freezing darkness on the heights of Cerro de Pasco when the bus had broken down.

Countless hairpin corners cause occasional screams from frightened women and the smell of vomit from small children. But after a couple of hours in the white-water heights, people start to peel off clothes by the layer as the bus descends into the thick heat toward the opaque waters of the Amazon.

Pucallpa means "red earth" in Quechua. It was founded by Franciscan missionaries in the 1840s and it is still Peru's gateway to the Amazon. Built on the bank of the Ucayali River, it is a gritty frontier town centered around a large commercial port. It has become a base of operations for oil and natural gas explorations in the surrounding jungle. It is also a place where cocaine is produced. More than anything else, though, Pucallpa is a wood port, an arboreal Auschwitz of the Amazon. It is where the river meets the road, the main road out of the Peruvian Amazon. Because of this, there are numerous lumber mills stretched along the filthy riverfront, each vomiting a mountain of sawdust into the brown waters of the Ucayali River.

The port has places where hundreds of giant logs are all tied together and float next to the clay bank. Later, the tropical hardwood logs or processed lumber will be shipped to Callao, Lima's port. From there they will be shipped abroad. Like most cities and towns in the Amazon region, Pucallpa has its share of chain saw shops: Stihl, Husqvarna, Wood Mizer, and other enemies of the forest are all too common. There is nothing so unforgiving as a chain saw, except perhaps the gun or the clock. Just as the six-shooter "won the West," the chain saw has nearly "won" the Amazon.

Most lumber passes through an unbroken chain of complicity reaching to the highest levels of authority in Peru. Paying off community leaders allows illegal logging mafias to obtain documents for forestry permits on behalf of the communities. This has caused various intra-tribal problems. The logging companies have so much power that no one can oppose them. They are a law unto themselves. Like the old-time rubber barons, logging companies will buy food and goods for a village as an up-front payment with no money trail. Although Peru is signatory to the Convention on International Trade in Endangered Species of Wild Flora and Fauna (CITES), there is no way to enforce the law, just like there is no way to curb rich people's appetite for mahogany.

Around Pucallpa there are several indigenous Shipibo Conibo villages. On one journey I brought kid's books in Spanish to a few of their primary schools. The Shipibo are one of the main tribes along the lower and middle Ucayali and have a population of about 35,000. They have villages up and down the river from Pucallpa, built out of sight along oxbow lagoons and natural levees. Spanish soldiers and missionaries carried out bloody campaigns against the Shipibo as far back as 1657. In 1680 a small pox epidemic killed most of them. Until 1698 they were under Jesuit influence, although like many indigenous tribes they resisted.

Late in the 19th century the Shipibo dominated the Upper Amazon. Using rifles supplied by Peruvian and Portuguese rubber barons, they captured other indigenes and sold them into slavery. Like the Moskito of Central America, they used the gun ruthlessly to dominate the region.

Many Shipibo now belong to Catholic and Protestant churches, although shamanism still plays a big role amongst their tribe. Despite acculturation, however, they manage to maintain an ethnic identity and have a radio station and newspaper in their own language. Shipibo shamans are especially famous for their use of the hallucinogenic vine ayahuasca (*Banisteriopsis caapi*). Their art, especially the designs used in pottery and clothing, is influenced by phosphene-derived design motifs caused by harmaline and DMT found in the "soul vine," ayahuasca

Until the 1940s, these sometimes still polygamous, Panoan-speaking Shipibo were known for flattening the heads of their babies with small boards. It was considered a beautification practice, but somehow it gained them the moniker "monkey people." Today many Shipibo women travel to Iquitos, where they eke out a living selling their crafts to tourists. More than poverty, and perhaps more than the forest devil Chullachaqui, the Shipibo fear dysentery and tuberculosis. Rain for days on end causes worry.

In Pucallpa I had to go to the Ministry of Education offices to get the needed matriculas of the Shipibo schools I wanted to visit. As I was leaving the offices, a very proper man beside the gate chided me because I was wearing shorts. To get to the Shipibo schools, I usually took a taxi on a day trip. Most schools were less than an hour away on muddy back roads that eventually lead to some lake or river. Once, rounding a curve too fast, the driver slid sideways off the slippery clay road and into the weeds.

The four Shipibo schools were unimpressive to say the least. Like most indigenous schools they existed more to acculturate the kids than to educate them—they were more for propaganda than for pedagogy. As always, the government provided a flag and a football but little else.

In one bilingual school I was surprised to find that UNESCO and Finland had provided copies of two different children's books in the Shipibo language. When I saw a copy of one, I asked about it and the principal took me to a store room, where hundreds of copies of the books were all neatly stacked. I found it odd that there was only one copy for the kids to use while hundreds sat gathering dust, so I told the principal that I would not give them my books if they remained unused like those from UNESCO. He promised me that the books would be used. This is a problem I sometimes face, but there is little I can do to change the ineptness of teachers. Somewhat disgusted I told him, "Books do children no good sitting in your storeroom; and I don't think UNESCO intended for them to remain there. It would be better if you would give each of the children one of the books. Why not? It is better that they are worn out from use than never used." Even though I knew that he wouldn't do it, I surely had to tell him.

Other Shipibo schools I chose to visit were a few hours upriver. I arranged passage on a forty-foot wooden boat and took four boxes of books for another four schools and some seeds for the communities. The sky was overcast and the boat was crowded with people and cargo, so I decided to sit on the flat roof. Along with several other men, including the owner of the boat, we sat up there for a couple hours as the boat made its way upriver. While the others lay resting, I suddenly noticed the boat veering off its course. Instead of following the bank it headed diagonally, directly towards some rapids in the middle of the river. Within a few seconds the boat was struggling sideways in the rapids and began to list from side to side. Lying flat on the roof, I grabbed the edge and hung on. Shouts and screams from panicked passengers burst out below as we almost took on water. I watched a bicycle and some boxes tumble off the tilting roof and into the opaque Ucayali. Then, amid more screams, the boat was tossed by the waves and listed back the other way. To keep from falling off, I had to scramble and change sides. While I lay on my stomach and grabbed the side of the tilting roof, I saw the owner lose hold and fall into the river. After rocking back and forth some more, the boat started to level off as we passed the rapids. Regaining control, the young pilot circled around to pick up the owner, who was waving his arm and floating in the current.

I later found out that the bicycle belonged to a teacher from one of the schools I was visiting. Despite losing his bike, he was still asked to pay his passage. Being a Shipibo, the teacher knew that he could gain nothing except more problems by complaining.

Everyone knew that the young boat pilot had fallen asleep, but no one said a word and we all continued on our way as if nothing happened. But everyone realized that we were very lucky, as we were just a few inches from capsizing, and few of the passengers could swim. There is a saying that "corpses don't exist in the Amazon."

Disembarking with the boxes at the Shipibo village of Betania, I was given a nice welcome and some food. Then I found a place to hang my hammock and mosquito net between some trees beside the river. The next day, I brought books to one tiny school and then to another upriver. Though the teacher in Betania was sad that he had lost his bicycle, the books and school supplies gave him reason to smile.

Later I spent some hours dividing various seeds into coin envelopes to be given away. Indigenous women often do the planting and soon several curious Shipibo women came over with their children or grandchildren to see what I had for them. Peppers, tomatoes, and onions were the favorites.

One morning after returning to Pucallpa, I went down to the river and found a 900-ton, three-story barge named *Men del Norte*, which was leaving for Iquitos in two days. The captain was there, so I booked a cabin through him. He gave me the best of the ten small rooms on the third deck. Instead of the usual steel bunk beds, I was surprised to find a decent wooden bed. The room's two long louver windows helped, but it still became oppressively hot during the day because the sun baked the flat steel ceiling, which was also the roof. It could burn one's hand within a few seconds if touched. The boat was carrying bags of cement, thousands of them, which had been loaded one at a time by dozens of stevedores. There were also tons of toilet paper, endless sacks of salt, crates of very sweet oranges, four milk cows, a pickup truck, and a horde of other things, in addition to two hundred passengers.

The second floor was soon filled with hammocks, hanging thick as cobwebs. Dozens of cocooned voyagers, occasionally wiggling like ready-to-hatch larvae, relaxed in their hammocks.

Other than myself, the only other foreign passengers were a young German couple, very much in love. They were on their way to Belem (Bethlehem), Brazil, at the mouth of the Amazon. They had a couple of inadequate hammocks that were more like throw nets for fishing, and they tied them so close together that they seemed like one. Strumming a tiny churango, the young man laughingly sang out in English, "Going down the Uca-ya-li with a Uku-laaaaa-leee. Laying in my hammock with my l---a---d---y. For there's more to life than making baaaa---bies."

Roger Casement once wrote that the Ucayali River is "the true Mother of waters of the Amazon system." As the Amazon River begins at the confluence of the Ucayali and the Marañón, the Ucayali River begins at the confluence of the Urubamba and the Apurimac. The Urubamba River eventually leads up to Machu Picchu, but like the much longer upper Apurimac, it has no river traffic. These 2,700-kilometer-long branches of the Amazon River family tree read like the names of Biblical patriarchs, where so-and-so begat so-and-so, who begat so-and-so.... The Amazon begins from springs that form a tiny cold pond, which then drains into a stream called the Carhuasanta, which is some 5,000 meters above sea level near Nevada Mismi peak. For the Carhuasanta joins the Apacheta to become the Lloqueta, which becomes the Challamaya, which becomes the Hornillos, which becomes the Apurimac, which becomes the Ucayali, which joins the Marañón to become the Amazon River. Like notes of the musical scale, an octave of rivers crescendo as they join and become one on their way to the sea.

The Ucayali River was not used as a colonial inroad into the Amazon rainforest until the 19th century, and really not until Pucallpa was built. Until then, any travel into the Peruvian Amazon used the Marañón River (first called the Bracameros) or its affluent, the Huallaga (once called the Motilones). Most river traffic then went to or from Yurimaguas, the spotless Huallaga River town built by the Austrian, Father Fritz. The Huallaga was the river that the inimical "Wrath of God" Lope de Aguirre descended on the hellish second Spanish journey into the Amazon.

My *Men del Norte* launch was over a day late to leave, which is normal in the Amazon. Waiting aboard, I watched from outside my third-floor room as more than thirty men unloaded a barge next to us. Hundreds of heavy hardwood boards were being carried one at a time to a waiting truck. The whole front of the barge was over a meter deep in large-dimension milled lumber. I couldn't believe these small, slight Peruvian men could carry so much weight. Visitors have said the same thing for centuries. Every board, many of which were 4x16 inches and 12-foot-long, was carried on the back of a single man. It was all a mahogany-like wood called tornio (*Cedrelinga catenefirmis Ducke*). It seemed as if the men never stopped or rested during their ten-hour days, except for one lunch break. Twice I heard other passengers refer to the stevedores as "ants." Though Peruvians paid them little attention, I did, and they liked joking with a foreigner. Finally, one board was too big for any of the men to carry. I called down from the third-floor deck and questioned if any of them could carry it. This brought a lot of laughs, and it finally took six of them just to lift it up. Then, one man got under it to try and raise it with his back. He nearly buckled under the weight. Later, eight men carried it some seventy-five meters and loaded it onto the truck.

For me, the worst part of traveling in the Amazon basin, unlike in the mountains, is that one seldom walks very much. Any journey over a few kilometers is usually made on water. There are some trails, of course, but these usually lead to chácaras, farmed clearings. Most people who live in villages along rivers travel by boat. Traveling on a large four- or five-floor launch is one thing, but being restricted to a narrow seat in a dugout, for hours everyday and for days on end, can be very taxing. It is said that Richard

Spruce, the eminent British botanist, paddled some 40,000 miles on rivers in the Amazon basin in the 1850s. That equates to about 10,000 hours, or nearly 400 days of just sitting. Perhaps this is what led Spruce to write in 1851: "It may be true as Humboldt says that perils elevate the poetry of life, but I can bear witness that they have a woeful tendency to depress its prose."

Traveling by river during the dry season restricts one's view to the flat, forested river bank, but even during the rainy season one can seldom get a glimpse beyond the tangled forest of the river's edge. During this low-water trip in September 2007, the captain had two teams of men take soundings as we left Pucallpa. One group went ahead in a small motorboat. They used a long, calibrated pole, and would signal back to someone watching with binoculars. Other men dropped a weighted line from the starboard side of our launch and would call out the depth in feet to the captain. With all of the large boats passing near Pucallpa, one would think that the river would be marked with buoys, but no, there are none. Every boat has to do its own soundings or follow another.

When we left Pucallpa, another boat did just that, following us for most of that day and part of another. Unfortunately, they were not paying enough attention, took a very tight bend too close to the shore, and bottomed out on a sandy shoal. I was sitting on the third-floor roof at the time and could hear our captain and his mates laughing as they watched with binoculars. After a couple of hours, though, the boat had freed itself and caught back up to us as we were unloading ice.

Along the high bank of the Ucayali, a continuous escarpment drops down seven or eight meters to the muddy waters below. It's not uncommon to see sections of the sandy bank break loose and tumble into the river, leaving debris floating in the current. Often the riverbank is thickly lined by a very tall curtain of cane grass amongst patches of heliconias, and trees matted with vines descend from an opaque green backdrop. Occasionally large-leafed aguaje palms (*Mauritia flexuosa*) stand out against the jungle, usually revealing an old home site.

At nearly every bend during the dry season, the river forms crescent-shaped beaches of white sand. Rice, peanuts, melons, and chiclayo beans are planted in these seasonal flood plains when the river is low. Though these beaches are inundated for most of the year, the upper reaches, often an acre or more, get hand-planted by people from the nearest village, as soon as they become exposed. Often there is nothing around for miles, except for a thatched seasonal hut. People come from distant villages in dugouts and live there for days to tend their gardens. September brings the rice harvest and the riverside farms are either golden with ripening heads, or lime green after being hand cut.

Most of Peru's Amazon basin is a flat arboreal plain. The only hills that lie along the Ucayali River below Pucallpa, and for hundreds of miles or more downriver, are the Canchauaya Hills. They are perhaps 400 meters high and thickly forested, with sizable old-growth trees sticking out of steep slopes. Though there are logged off in areas near the river, further back these hills are seldom penetrated by humans. Everyone in the area believes there are uncontacted tribes dwelling in the interior.

Because the Ucayali is so convoluted, we spent hours seeming to approach and then seeming to leave behind those mysterious Canchauaya Hills, although in reality we were always working our way closer. In testament to the river's twists and turns, in one stretch the hills would face us and in the next they would be at our backs, as if they were playing some game of hide and seek.

At one point our launch followed a long loop that returned to the very spot we had just passed awhile before. Here, the river bank was so narrow that it was just three or four yards wide between the waters. Before long the river would eat its way through the narrow sandy bank and form an opening joining the waters. In the future, this will eventually become an oxbow and the long loop we followed will become detached from the river.

There are scores of oxbow lagoons along the Ucayali that testify to its many changes of courses. Only from the air can one see the old river pathways. Different colored plant growth and sometimes a chain of lagoons point to old riverbeds that often flow into themselves during time of high water. And only from the air can one see the extent of the deforestation taking place.

We passed a hamlet named Canchauaya on the narrow plain between the river and the Canchauaya Hills. It is inhabited by the Chama indigenous tribe and is part of a group of five riverside communities that are trying to get entitlement and official status. Looking at my map, I noticed that these hills border a very wild area about seventy miles from the Brazilian border. I chuckled at the twisted Peruvian humor that led to naming a distant village Liquidacion. Not far beyond it is Monopolia, followed by the sinisterly named Desprecio, i.e. Contempt. Nearby is Desengano, or Disappointment. These were all across the Canchauaya Hills and pathless places to get to.

A famously ugly armored fish, called carachama (face of Chama), is found throughout the Amazon. It burrows its way into river banks to lay eggs. Though it is disgusting to look at, it is delicious and highly sought after. Like their relatives the Shipibo, the Chama formerly practiced flattening the skulls of infants by binding their heads with thin wooden blocks for a year. The Chama also used a type of pepper (*Piper pseudohurumayo*) to blacken their teeth. These are the origins of the name Chama Face, but even though these practices have stopped the association carries on in the derogatory name of the fish.

The Chama also practiced female circumcision and genital mutilation by removing the clitoris. Young girls were tied to trees during the ordeal. This was followed by wild orgies in which people would ingest the plant *Brunfelsia grandiflora* as an aphrodisiac.

Due to the amount of my cargo, I could not stop there that time, but I did on subsequent voyages. During those visits, I brought books and seeds for three very challenged schools. Because of the terrible condition of these schools, the teachers would sometimes have the kids carry their chairs to an open place beside the river. Months later, after traveling three days upriver from Iquitos, I brought several hundred kilos of corn and rice seed. Another time I brought one thousand fruit trees, five-hundred of which had king mangoes grafted onto them. These were divided so that every family received some. These grafted mangoes were brought to hopefully provide some cash to the village, since there were so few sources of income.

The Canchauaya village president, Guillermo Eduardo, always invited me to stay at his house. I stayed on his porch for some days, but later moved to an empty room in the school because his place had so many scorpions.

I had heard that the area had a ninety-eight-degree Celsius river with a massive four-story-high steaming hot waterfall. Other hot waterfalls and pools nearby were cool enough to enter. We talked about how good it would be for Canchauaya to get financial backing for a small water bottling factory, since the water is sweet and pure. Just in front, large boats travel up and down the Ucayali to Pucallpa and Iquitos.

Almost everywhere in the Amazon basin, the riverside villages are unattractively plain and poor. The only exception on the Lower Ucayali is Contamana, just a few hours upriver from Canchauaya. It has a nice riverside boardwalk, a charming central park, decent accommodations, and some old colonial buildings which give it a touch of class. In the hills behind the village there are some other hot springs, and a rare macaw calpa, where the colorful birds flock each morning to pick at the mineral-rich clay.

There are always crowds of people waiting above the steep banks when the launches stop there, because these boats are their lifeline. We stopped to drop off some ice at one hamlet downriver from the village of Orellana. Each village has some large wooden crates with sawdust lined up along the riverbank, which are ice-boxes for their fish. The launch edges its square bow right into the soft sandy bank, and for the next half an hour, young men unloaded blocks of ice. At the same time, other villagers packed it into the wooden crates.

For some reason the whole time we were there a continuous school of fish called boca chica, i.e., small mouth, dove out of the water and against the side of the three-story *Men del Norte*. It was as if they were attacking it. Some dove higher than ten feet. The crowd of amazed passengers laughed as we watched the cook grab a foot-long fish out of the air from a second-story window. If there had been openings or windows below, then hundreds would have jumped through and landed inside. This does occasionally happen, I was told, but no one could explain why.

Peru's Amazon produces an abundance of fish; 1,300 species comprise over 80,000 tons of consumable protein in Iquitos annually, compared to 10,000 tons of beef. Every shape and size of fish can be found, from the tiny, dangerous canero to the two-meter long paiche, and two types of dolphins. The canero is feared because it is known to enter any bodily orifice. After it becomes lodged, hemorrhaging occurs and death comes within a few days.

For two days we followed the riverside border of the huge, triangular 20,000-square-kilometer Pacaya-Samiria Reserve, the largest and one of the wildest in Peru. The Ucayali River is on one side and the slightly larger Marañón is on the other. Especially in the early morning and at sunset, the riverbanks become filled with continuous birdsong. Unfortunately, the roar of diesel motors often smothers the sound of anything else.

Vast numbers of jabiru storks were ever-present during the journey. As white as tablecloths, they gathered for dinner along the beaches formally dressed in their tuxedo plumage and red scarves. With stiff, long steps they walked like aristocratic fishermen. Sometimes they would gather in the air by the hundreds, soaring in circles so high that they were almost out of sight.

Animals are seldom seen along the Ucayali, unless they are wandering along a beach, like a tigrillo I once spotted, or a swimming peccary. The wall-like jungle, though too thick to see into, cannot contain the sounds, like the shrill call of a sloth. The sounds emitted by cell phones, beepers, buzzers, and doorbells are like nothing compared to the Amazon. When darkness arrives, the insects take over and their electronic sound system and messenger service becomes a cacophonous choir of the unseen.

In the Pacaya-Samiria Reserve, selective logging is limited to a few isolated Cocama communities which still exist there. In a few places we passed some large logs waiting to be pushed over the sandy cliff into the river. They were so large that they seemed like a pod of beached whales. They would be floated down to a mill in Requena and then taken back upriver to Pucallpa, to be cut into boards.

At sunset on the fourth day, we finally reached the Ucayali's confluence with the Marañón, near Nauta. Here the riverine bloodlines mix into one and form the giant Amazon. The Ucayali is basically the Asháninka bloodline, while the Marañón is the Jivaro.

It took several more hours to reach Iquitos, about one hundred kilometers downriver. Once there, we saw the lights of Massui, the port of Iquitos, where three rivers come together, almost making an island of the town. For a couple of kilometers along the riverfront, hundreds of large barges and launches rested side by side with their bows pressed into the muddy, trash-covered bank.

Everyone on board was waiting with their belongings, happy to have finally reached Iquitos. Dozens of three-wheeled mototaxis waited in the darkness on shore amongst all the commotion. I left my thirty-some boxes of books to come back for the next day. Like everyone else, I just wanted to get off the launch and out of the port. The *Men Del Norte* had been no luxury liner, with the hellishly hot cabin, bad food, and overcrowding. After weeks spent gathering and transporting materials, now I just wanted a cheap, quiet room at the Dos Mundos Hotel in central Iquitos.

I had enough books with me to supply more than thirty indigenous schools, and it would take some time to organize everything and then find boats and launches to get me to them. Though the first journey would just take a few days to get to some Cocama schools, I had also planned a much longer trip to visit schools of five tribes: the Yagua, Bora, Huitoto, Ocaina, and Ticuna. All of these tribes had suffered for centuries at the hands of slavers, soldiers, priests, and rubber barons. Today they are considered endangered tribes, so to know some of their background is vital to understanding them.

In 1561, the first European explorers visited the area of Iquitos. Orellana encountered the Amazon River a little further down at the Rio Napo confluence. But whereas Orellana's odyssey seemed to be watched over by angels, the expedition hijacked by Lope de Aguirre may have disgusted even the worst of devils. It is worthy of note since it set the standard for crimes committed in the Amazon. The mind of Aguirre was even more twisted than the convoluted Ucayali.

His blood-soaked journey, which finally ended in the Caribbean, was called "the most appalling in the annals of Spanish enterprise." Though Gonzalo Pizarro was wrong to say in 1541 that Orellana "went off and become a rebel," the journey of Lope de Aguirre in 1561 was just that. Aguirre, like Gonzalo Pizarro, was looking for El Dorado, but found the Amazon to be only an "ill-fated river" with "nothing but despair." Though Werner Herzog made the movie *Aguirre, The Wrath of God*, not even his talent could capture Aguirre's depravity. It is even said that he killed his own daughter.

Flying a black flag dotted with red daggers and supposedly claiming, "I am the wrath of God," Aguirre, along with about two hundred men who called themselves "the Marañónes," went on a mutinous nine-month journey of murder down the Huallaga, Marañón, and Amazon rivers. If the Marañón River was the first Spanish name for the Amazon, then Aguirre's rebels may have named themselves after the mighty river.

Despite his criminal insanity, Aguirre's treachery is considered "the first act of American independence" against the Spanish crown. In his treasonous letter to King Philip II, Aguirre defiantly stated, "Beware, King and lord, that you cannot take, under the title of legitimate king, any benefit from this land where you risked nothing..." Then, before signing his name, Aguirre calls himself "the traitor."

Iquitos was founded by the Jesuits in 1757. Ten years later, in 1767, they were expelled from over forty missions, and Spanish traders took over their monopolies. The Jesuits were "accused of carrying out independent businesses, which was strictly forbidden," according to Reeve. Following the Franciscans, the Jesuits had been in the western Amazon since 1638, establishing missions along major waterways. But the Jesuit, Franciscan, Augustinian, and Dominican ventures were embedded in a militarily enforced missionization.

The Jesuits, though under the Peruvian Viceroy's orders, were often in conflict; this did not prevent them from establishing their "reducciones," i.e., geographically restricted tribal areas. Though these reducciones found success as havens for the indigenous from Spanish and Portuguese slave raiding, the abuses of Spanish soldiers, and the encomienda system, they also became graveyards as small pox, malaria, measles, and other imported diseases decimated the native population.

"As missions became established throughout the region in the period between 1670 and 1767, missionary activity shifted the focus of indigenous exchange networks and undermined former long-distance exchange patterns" (Reeve). By using indigenous trading patterns, the Jesuits upset the dynamics of the area's traditional trade and alliance networks. Although the Jesuit missions gained a trading monopoly in the western Amazon, this led to a breakdown in the traditional trading networks of the indigenes.

This was accomplished by monopolizing salt, turtle eggs for oil, curare, resins, wax, and local handicrafts, which were exchanged for European goods at the missions. Salt was the major item traded. "Jesuit control of the salt trade was a critical strategy in gaining hegemony in the region" (Reeve). Some old red salt mines can still be seen along the cliff sides of the Huallaga River, outside of Tarapoto. Just downriver is the Pongo Aguirre, the rapids where "the Wrath of God" started his blood-soaked journey.

Salt from the Huallaga mines was followed in importance for Jesuit business by curare, the blowgun dart poison acquired in Pevas from the Ticuna. They traded the Ticuna's curare to many tribes for their salt, iron tools, glass beads, trinkets, and cloth. This "established the priest as a nexus for distribution of such goods" (Reeve). It was also the Jesuits who caused the near extinction of the charapa turtles by selling some two million of their eggs a year. Pity the poor turtle, the first to cross the extinction line on man's race to deplete the planet of wildlife.

It was not until 1864, when Peru broke a Brazilian blockade against its ships traveling the Amazon, that Iquitos was used as a port. It had only 2,000 inhabitants during its heyday, around the beginning of the twentieth century, which all revolved around the new demand for rubber.

From the 1880s to 1910, the dark shadows of the "green hell" were colored red with blood because of the white gold latex found in its forests. It was during this period that several tribes nearly became extinct at the brutal hands of greedy rubber barons. The larger-than-life rubber kings like Carlos Fitzcarraldo and Julio Arana helped Iquitos thrive as a port, but it was all based on their greedy exploitation of innocent tribes. Like *Aguirre, the Wrath of God*, Fitzcarraldo was popularized by a Werner Herzog film, although the issue of debt slavery as the source of the rubber baron's wealth was overlooked.

In that land without stones, where the native people are as soft as rubber, they were easily drawn into debt slavery. Debt was an important thing then, just as it is with today's bankster gangsters. Keep the people in debt, for with debt comes control. In their arboreal Auschwitz, it was not written, "Work will set you free," but like the bandito banks of today, "Debt will set you free." Thus it was that the Huitoto, Bora, Andoke, and dozens of other tribes became impoverished so that rubber tires could roll.

Fitzcarraldo was the son of an Irish-American immigrant and he more than anyone first caused Iquitos to prosper. He had fled to Iquitos as a youth from Lima after being accused of being a spy for the English during the War of the Pacific. In 1879, in his mid-twenties, he entered the Ucayali area and within ten years was the wealthiest cauchero, i.e. rubber tapper, on the Ucayali River. He literally had thousands of Ashaninka and Piro natives gathering rubber from different types of wild rubber trees, mostly the Panama rubber tree (*Castilla elastica*).

These trees were not tapped like the better quality Pará rubber tree (*Hevea brasiliensis*) grown in plantations, but had to be cut down and processed. The more they were cut down, the further the native tappers had to go to find more. As Roger Casement wrote, "The caucho was a great source of wealth, but the caucheros have destroyed in ten years, the Captain says, every milk-bearing Castilloa within reach of the banks of the Ucayali. How many Indians of the riverine tribes have also been destroyed, God alone knows, which an entire industry ruthlessly killed in a decade."

In 1891 Fitzcarraldo discovered a river route, now named the Fitzcarraldo Isthmus, linking Bolivia to the Atlantic. This may have been the most important geographic discovery of nineteenth century Peru, for it connected the waters of the Ucayali with the opposite-flowing Madre de Dios River. After his discovery the Bolivian rubber tappers had a way to get their product out, as well as a way to receive supplies up the Amazon from Europe. His new route led to a partnership with Bolivian rubber baron Antonio Vaca Diez. In 1897, they left Iquitos on an ill-fated boat journey; they were both drowned when their boat wrecked on the Pachitea River.

After Fitzcarraldo's premature death at age thirty-five, Julio César Arana del Águila became the greatest rubber baron of them all. It was said that nothing of importance was done in Iquitos without his blessing. Arana and others were so powerful that for two years they even printed their own money. Casa de Fierro, an iron building designed by Gustav Eiffel, and many other buildings of Moorish style, all beautifully sided with Portuguese tiles, still gracefully testify to the wealth Iquitos once had. During its heyday from 1900 to 1910, when rubber traders were lighting cigars with large denomination notes, eighty percent of the indigenous people in that part of the Amazon died or were killed as the result of debt slavery.

The incredibly diverse plant life has always been one of the main interests in the Amazon for outsiders. The first was the futile search for cinnamon during Gonzalo Pizarro's "Cinnamon Expedition," then cinchona (a valuable source of quinine), and then rubber. Though medicinal plants have always been sought, the exploitative commercialization of ayahuasca by outsiders is the most recent.

Today, thousands of mostly young foreign travelers come to Iquitos to drink ayahuasca (*Banisteriopsis caapi*). This mind-altering brew, made from the bark of the entheogenic liana called "the soul vine" in Quechua, contains the hallucinogenic beta-carboline alkaloids harmaline, harmine, tryptamine, and dimethyltryptamine (DMT). It is prepared over hours as a concentrated infusion usually along with a synergistic plant called chacruna (*Psychotria viridis*). A small cup, ingested in the dark, will soon stir the sound of the wind, which brings an intense fear of death. Brief nausea is followed by three hours of visual photic sensations, phosphene designs, and sometimes visions.

In the 1850s, the British botanist Richard Spruce saw fit to include the word "banister" when he first catalogued it taxonomically as *Banisteriopsis caapi*. This is because its effects extend like a railing along the borders of consciousness.

Allen Ginsberg drank ayahuasca, also called yage or caapi, in Pucallpa in the 1960s. His book, *The Yage Letters*, co-authored with William S. Burroughs, drew attention to its psychotropic powers. The difference is that Ginsberg did not seek a commercial venue. Today there are dozens of foreign-owned ayahuasca lodges in the Iquitos area. These places steal the soul of native people's intellectual property rights, just as the caucheros, the rubber men, stole their bodies, the oil and mining companies stole their minerals, and the timber companies stole their forest. These outsiders commercialize and sell the plant for personal gain, paying tribal shamans to sing prayer-like ikaros during their money-making ceremonies. Online bookings have made some foreign ayahuasca lodges rich, unfortunately at the cost of abusing tribal intellectual property rights and commercializing autochthonous ceremonies. As Iquitos was built from the blood of Huitoto, Bora, Andoke, and other indigenes during the genocidal rubber years, so too are gringo "aya" lodges built from sacred native traditions today. They are like strip miners and grave robbers, taking sacred ceremonies and prayers and selling them commercially for enormous private gain. According to the United Nations Declaration on the Rights of Indigenous Peoples, of which Peru is a signatory, these foreign lodges are an abuse. In Brazil, ayahuasca lodges are illegal, although ayahuasca churches there have gained the status of a state-recognized religion. "Why do we need Jesus Christ? We have ayahuasca!" some say.

The situation is not unlike peyote and the Native American Church. Any private business use of their sacrament would be considered profane, but in permissive Peru everything is for sale. Having taken ayahuasca on several occasions I am not against its use, but rather its misuse and abuse through foreign commercialization. Like opportunistic TV preachers, these foreign "shamans" put on robes and use prayers and sacred ceremonies to make money.

After being in Iquitos just a few days, I decided to bring some of the books and supplies to schools up the Río Momón, a tributary of the Nanay, which enters the Amazon at Iquitos. The Ministry of Education provided me with computer print-outs of the matriculas of all twenty-seven primary schools along the Río Momón. This included the number of students and the names of the principals. I planned to visit the upper six communities.

At Momóna Concha, the dirty port on the Nanay River in Iquitos, I found an old wooden forty-foot thatched-roof boat. It was leaving the next morning and the amiable captain, Segundo, said he would stop wherever I wanted. He was a wiry little middle-aged man with a set of epiphytic eyebrows that seemed to cling to his face like bromeliads. He had been transporting people and cargo up and down the Momón for years and was a fount of information about the area.

In the morning I needed two moto-taxis to carry the boxes of books and materials for the six schools. I spent most of the next three days on the boat, hanging my hammock above the cargo at night. Passage cost five soles ($1.80) for the eight-hour ride up to a village called Maynas. During high-water season the lower part of the meandering Momón is crisscrossed by many interfluvial plains—narrow, shady shortcuts which dry up in the dry season.

Overhead, monkeys would sometimes scurry across branches, keeping a watchful eye on "big brother." Some five hundred species of tropical fish can be found in these flooded forests. They are caught as they enter the area to feed on fallen seasonal fruits. Iquitos is second only to Manaus for its trade in freshwater tropical fish. Many common varieties of aquarium fish, such as neon tetras, angelfish, and painted guppies, are netted here. The deforestation of flood-plain forests, however, is constantly reducing the number of fish available.

Out of the twenty-seven hamlets on the Rio Momón, only the last two are indigenous, mostly Tupian Cocama. The last one is called Nueve York, which boasts 140 souls. Its humble leaders joked with me about the village's proud appellative. The only thing the two New Yorks have in common, though, is an over-crowded apartment complex of sorts: a tree sprawling over the river, full of the pendulous nests of noisy oropendulas (*Cacicus cela*).

Because the river became too narrow for Segundo's cargo boat, I had to take a small motorized dugout (called a peque-peque) to get to Nueve York from the community of Maynas. Even at Maynas, Segundo's boat could not turn around, but had to float backwards to a wider spot downriver, since his boat was longer than the river was wide.

The viridescent jungle along the river was so thick that the sound of the thirteen-horse-power motor bounced off of the trees like a sound board. Lianas dangled like downed telephone lines from overhanging branches into the river. Patches of heliconias, erect from daily rains, and umbrella-like tree ferns burst from the opaque green banks. Tangarana trees (*Triplaris peruviana* or *Triplaris surinamensis*) were in blossom and huge prolific white or rose-colored flower clusters dusted the quiet waters with pollen. Sometimes the tree is used in ayahuasca mixes; I was warned never to touch the tree because of voracious ants that live in them.

Suddenly, the intoxicated flight of a large, brilliant blue butterfly, the *Morpho menelaus* species, brought it within an arm's length of our small boat, and then, like a flirting fashion model on a runway, it turned and disappeared into a dark fold of the forest. They like to follow the banks of rivers, perhaps to see their reflection, which can make even the sapphire sky envious. This particular species of *Morpho* is said to be attracted by blood; to catch these marvelous butterflies, they are sometimes lured with a bloodied animal skin into a trap.

Today, the Cocama number some 15,000 people. They are part of a Tupi-Guarani language group and originally lived mostly on the islands of the lower Ucayali, where they raided and traded with their neighbors. Unlike their Ashaninka cousins, farther up the Ucayali, they wear western clothes and are quite acculturated. Those who live along the larger rivers still practice floodplain farming by planting rice, chiclayo beans, peanuts, melons, and a few other crops on the seasonal beaches. First European contact may have been the Juan de Salinas expedition up the Ucayali in 1549, but little followed. Not until 1640 did the Jesuit priest Father Lucas de la Cueva make permanent contact. In 1650, they accepted a Jesuit mission on the Ucayali.

By 1660, Father Cueva and his Jesuits established sixty missions, mostly up the Marañón and Huallaga rivers, with about 60,000 Indians gathered around them in reducciones. With the coming of the Jesuits, the Cocama had a direct line to Western goods and tools and no longer needed to rely on intermediary Jivaro and Mainas Indians traders.

In 1666, while the Black plague was ravaging Europe, opposing Cocama raided some missions, including Borja on the Marañón River. They returned up the Ucayali with the prized head of a certain Father Figueroa. In a reprisal raid, Spanish soldiers found and returned Father Figueroa's head to his acephalous grave. Unlike the Jivaro, the Cocama did not shrink heads, but it seemed to have had some totemic value. The Jesuit historian Jounen wrote that the Spanish punishment for these revolts "were carried out over several years with inhuman rage and cruelty."

Unfortunately, the school in Nueve York was closed the day I came, because the teacher was in Iquitos. Teacher absenteeism is quite common and it seems that some schools are closed more often than they are open. That did not stop the grateful village leaders from calling the kids together to look at the books I had brought. There was no way that those books would sit unused, as I had feared would be the case in a couple of the Shipibo schools. The school was just beside the river and after a few minutes some kids started running across a large grassy field. Once several of the kids had arrived, the village president opened the boxes, surprising everyone with books, notebooks, and pens, and paints.

We took the hamlet's president with us on our way back to Maynas. All of a sudden, a fish called a zorro jumped into the dugout. Though it was only ten inches long, I was amazed at the size of its teeth. That night a friend of Segundo brought some armadillo meat over to the boat for dinner. It was as tasty as it was illegal. Then, as a light rain began to fall, I strung my hammock beneath the low thatched roof of the moored boat. Regrettably, I had left my mosquito net behind, so I slept in my clothes and took my chances. At least the malarial mosquitos (*Aedes aegypti*) feed mostly in the daylight.

We spent the second night downriver at Punta Allegre, where we again ate wild meat. This time it was mahaus, a small peccary-like wild pig. The cook ruined it, though, with too much salt. Because they lead a subsistence lifestyle, these people have no qualms about killing protected animals. They often supplement their diet with wild game ranging from deer to anteaters, and everything that walks, swims, flies, slithers, or crawls. Even in the market in Iquitos, several kinds of wild meat can be purchased, including venison. Their favorite is suri (*Rhynchophorus palmarum*), a large white grub of the palm weevil, which can be purchased to eat live or grilled. Though their gastronomic virtues can perhaps be learned, their gooey cheese-like flesh can be challenging to the uninitiated.

The next morning people came by from the tiny hamlet of Agrario de Shambillo, which is up a shallow slough and is very poor, even by local standards. Somehow, they had heard about the books and came to ask me to help their little school. I told them, "Of course I will come, but later in the day."

Unfortunately, it was impossible to reach the village by boat because the small shallow river beside it was too low. The only way to get there was to walk and it was a two-hour hike through the jungle from Punta Allegre. A local man agreed to take me. The school had only a dozen students, so I made up a smaller box of books and school supplies to bring for them.

The two of us started off on a trail that soon passed by a swampy morass and a pond with giant water lilies (*Victoria regia*) floating like round green rafts. Walking into dark shadows, we soon entered the impressive three-canopied primary forest. Though my guide carried the box of books, I still had trouble keeping up with his brisk pace.

For quite a while I had been wondering if we were going the right way, for I saw no footprints and the trail was getting narrower and narrower. Finally, the meandering trail narrowed to nothing. The high-canopy old-growth forest cast a dark shadow of doubt. Suddenly, my guide stopped and mumbled something about going the wrong way. Just as I thought, we must have missed the cutoff trail. Obviously embarrassed, he suddenly turned and quickly disappeared, retracing his steps while still carrying the box of books. Having broken my sandals, I followed him barefoot; but even with a pair of Nike Airs, I could never have caught up with him. The forty pounds of books didn't seem to slow him down at all. Finally, I found him waiting for me beside the trail, but by that time it was too late in the day to correct our mistake. We could never make it to Agrario de Shambilo and then back to Punta Allegre before dark. Plus, a threatening cloud bank was building up in the distance, promising rain in about an hour.

The only thing to do was to return to Punta Allegre and leave the box of books in the care of the village president. No sooner did my lost guide put the box of books down outside the president's house than he disappeared, too embarrassed to face his friends. I was told that people from Agrario de Shambillo would come in a day or so and take the box to the school. That was the best I could do. I was only sorry I couldn't visit their community, for it is often the out-of-the-way little places that I enjoy the most.

On our way downriver in Segundo's boat, we had almost passed by a hidden hamlet when I suddenly noticed a sign with its name, Almirante Guisse. I called out to Segundo to stop and he swung his peque-peque motor to the other side, edging his boat towards the muddy riverbank. Going ashore required leaving our footprints deep in its cloying mud before reaching spongy grass.

  Of all the schools I have visited in the Amazon, this tiny place stands out not only as one of the poorest and neediest, but also as one of the most receptive. With the help of Segundo's worker, we walked to the village with a box of 135 children's books, another box of twenty children's encyclopedias, and a box of school supplies. Their incredible teacher, Carlos Mario Paredes Guillen, and his fourteen students were all taken aback at our arrival. No one had ever visited their school before, I was told. The dirt-floor school was constructed from an assortment of bamboo, broken pieces of lumber, and thatch. The children shared a few tattered textbooks, and had only some stubs of pencils, and a few scraps of paper to write on.

  Within a few minutes, almost all of the villagers had shown up, happily surprised that someone had thought enough of their kids to pay some attention. I could tell their poverty brought them shame, because a man apologized that they had nothing cold to offer us to drink. Like all of the villages there, Almirante Guisse had no electricity and everyone drinks from the river. They wanted to give me a bag of sacha inchi nuts (*Plukenetia volubilis*). I told them that I wanted to see the plants, so they showed me some rows of low vines on which this oily nut grew. Once they are dried, the nuts are pressed for an oil that is rich in omega fatty acids. It brings a high price and is their most valued crop.

  Before we left, the teacher Carlos asked me to take some photos of the makeshift school. Realizing both their extreme poverty and their desire to learn, I asked him to visit me in Iquitos, so that I could give him some art supplies. He stays in the village five days a week, and returns to Iquitos on the weekends, which requires a seven-hour boat trip. He showed up the next Sunday afternoon with his wife and young granddaughter. In addition to the art supplies, what he wanted was copies of the photos I had taken, to show to Peru's Ministry of Education as proof of just how bad the conditions at his school really were.

Further downriver at another Momón River community called San Luis, Segundo's boat again slowly eased into the intractable mud at the base of the escarpment. The school there stood out, as usual, as the village's only block structure. It appeared as uninviting as the river bank. Together with the boat attendant, we each again carried a box. As usual, there were more books and school supplies in the boxes we had brought than were available in the whole school.

When we returned to Iquitos, our boat was jammed full of people and cargo, and there was hardly a place to sit. Inside were stacks of palm thatching, bags of aguaje nuts, bundles of tamishi sticks (*Heteropsis flexuosa*) for wicker and broom fibers, more bundles of chonta palm stalks (*Euterpe catinga*) for dinner salads, some lumber, a couple of noisy pigs, and one large river turtle. I retreated to a solitary part of the roof until a sudden tropical shower brought me back inside.

To relieve my thirst, I reached for my bottle of San Luis "purified" water, produced by a company owned by Coca Cola. As I did so, another passenger dipped an old paint can into the river and handed it to his small son to drink. Water-borne diseases are common there, due to practices like this. When we had almost reached the confluence with the Nanay River, we passed by the two foreign-owned jungle resort lodges. One is owned by a wealthy British citizen, who also runs South America's largest radio station, based in Lima. The lodge was designed for jet-setting tourists who want to "experience" the Amazon jungle.

As we passed by in Segundo's leaky old boat full of cargo and very poor local people, the lodge seemed very much out of place. Seven or eight colorful macaws sat on the front railing above the river, while several garishly dressed guests sipped drinks in the shade. Those birds are better fed than most of Segundo's passengers, I thought. A resident shaman will serve guests ayahuasca if they want. There are swimming pools and a water slide for those unwilling to enter the muddy waters of the Momón. But seeing this elite luxury lodge juxtaposed to the deplorable poverty around it disgusted me. I wondered how anyone could really enjoy themselves in such a situation. As Thomas Gray wrote, "Where ignorance is bliss, 'tis folly to be wise."

Sitting next to me in the beat-up boat was a woman with a severely infected finger. It was so swollen that the skin had peeled back. All I had to give her was some aspirin. She had no medicine, nor was there any in her village, Agrario de Shambillo, the place I had tried to walk to. In two of the six communities I visited on the Rio Momón, people pleaded with me to bring their village some basic medical supplies, especially for the children. There was not an aspirin, not a band-aid. "Give them to Segundo to take to us," they begged.

I still had the majority of the books I had brought with me in Iquitos. I wanted to take them to fifteen indigenous villages near the town of Pevas, further down the Amazon and halfway to Leticia, Colombia. To get to Pevas, I took a large launch, the *Carlos Antonio*. It was overcrowded, like all the launches, with some 250 people onboard, sleeping in hammocks on the two top floors. It was so crowded that it made it difficult to walk to the kitchen to get food.

There were dozens of Israelitas, a Peruvian religious sect, on board. Most were going to the village of Alto Monte, their capital. The men had beards and wore their hair in long ponytails, while the women and girls all wore long dresses and a nun-like head-covering that draped down their backs. One Israelita man had a few cows on board, that were all tied to one side of the launch. One morning, at one of our cargo stops, we unknowingly left without him while he was off cutting grass for his animals. We returned to pick him up, amidst a roar of laughter. In many ways they are like the Amish, although there are rumors of their involvement in narco-trafficking.

In the night, we passed the confluence of the Napo River and the town of Francisco de Orellana. Orellana had passed by here on his epic journey in 1541, when the river left him and his men no choice but to continue on. At that time, the Omagua Indians controlled most of the area until small pox, measles, slavery, and warfare decimated them, altering the region's tribal balance.

When traveling downriver, the large flat-bottomed launches normally navigate in the middle, where there tends to be more current. Going upriver, though, they usually follow close to the shore, sometimes just a few meters away. By mid-morning, after several stops to drop off cargo, we arrived in Pevas, Peru's first port on the Amazon River.

Somewhere near the confluence of the Ampiyacu and the Amazon rivers, a Jesuit and then an Augustinian mission were built, around 1686. No traces of them exists now, as either the river or the jungle have consumed them. These were early contact points and trading centers, which ended up being raided by Portuguese slavers.

The three-story, barge-like launch was only going to be in Pevas for forty-five minutes before it would continue on to Peru's last Amazon River town, La Isla, across from Leticia, Colombia. I had to unload my boxes quickly. With the help of four men, I took them directly to Francisco Grippa's Casa de Arte, where I was given a room. Francisco Grippa is a well-known Amazonian artist who sells his paintings worldwide. In the 1970s, he was the first trained artist to help the Shipibo by teaching them to sculpt. Twenty years ago, Grippa had built the Casa de Arte, his funky, wooden, ninety-five-meter-long monstrosity, on the hillside. Visually, it completely dominates poor Pevas. From his six-story high look-out tower, one can see far down the Amazon River and out across the jungle. Besides living there and painting in his large studio, he also rents rooms, though the first three nights are graciously free. Knowing of my work, Grippa gave me a room for free as long as I needed. He once had a Peruvian restaurant in Los Angeles, but left America's cement jungle for the Amazon's leafy one.

My destination was up the Ampiyacu River, and its tributary the Yarhuareacu, where there are twelve indigenous villages belonging to five distinct tribes: Bora, Ticuna, Yagua, Huitoto, and Ocaina. The people there are relatives of some of those who once worked in Julio Arana's "Devil's Paradise," not far away across the Putumayo River. This Putumayo area, more than anywhere in the Amazon, deserved the appellation, "the green hell." To the outsider, this referred mostly to the oppressiveness of the Amazon's seemingly endless arboreal labyrinth; for the indigenous, it referred to the crimes against humanity perpetrated under its embowered branches.

Before the 1927 Salomon-Lazano Treaty, a huge area north of the Putumayo River was part of Peru. Colombia wanted a port on the Amazon River, so they took Leticia and all Peruvian territory north of the Putumayo. The US encouraged this, having taken Panama from Colombia some years before to build the canal. A little more than a decade later, Peru annexed a huge part of Ecuador's Amazon territory. The border change of 1927 forced the remnants of Julio Arana's Devil's Paradise to move on. The many remaining indebted rubber slaves belonging to Arana's network were taken to lands up the Ampiyacu River, and it was to these dozen or so impoverished villages that I was taking the books and school supplies.

Out of respect for these tribes, it is vital to understand some of their horrendous history that the demand for rubber subjected them to. According to historians, the indigenous population of the Putamayo region was reduced from 50,000 to 8,000 between 1900 and 1911. This was mostly done to keep running civilization's newly developed motorized wheel, the automobile, and for other latex products. The "Heart of Darkness" conditions in the Putumayo region were even darker at that time than in Conrad's Congo. As Roger Casement wrote in his *Amazon Journal*, "there are today worse forms of slavery and its attendant barbarities among the Indians of the American continent than, I believe, ever prevailed in Africa." Only the downturn in the rubber market would stop the holocaust. "Finance takes little account of the methods whereby its golden counters are produced," observed Casement.

Julio César Arana and his Peruvian Amazon Company had the custom of keeping every rubber tapper in debt, usually indentured for life. They would start by supplying them with food, gear, and sometimes a rifle—this was enough to keep them in debt forever. Arana also had six hundred captive native women, who he used for breeding future workers.

Walter Hardenburg wrote that a Huitoto Indian informed him "that the Peruvians treated his countrymen very badly, and he gave me to understand that in case the Indians did not bring in a sufficient amount of rubber to satisfy the Peruvians they were flogged, shot, or mutilated at the will of the man in charge."

In the first decade of the twentieth century, Arana's saurian suzerainty left tens of thousands dead and many thousands more with "the marks of Arana"—the scars of floggings, burning, maimings, deformities, and every imaginable mutilation.

"It is too atrocious and yet one has only to look at these men and the dumb, terrified faces of the Indians when they speak to them to read it all," Casement lamented. The tractable Huitoto, shy and soft as rubber, numbered some 40,000 in 1900, but within a few years their numbers were reduced by eighty percent. Casement records that "there are plenty of Huitoto women and boys who have been sold in Iquitos, there is always a market for them. Men were known to give forty pounds for a boy or girl.... Everyone nearly talks of 'his Indians' just as if they were sheep or cattle—or rubber trees."

In 1907, a twenty-year-old American named Walter Hardenburg and his friend Perkins were on their way to do railroad work in Brazil but were abducted by Arana's Barbadian guards while floating down the Putumayo River. After he was released,

Hardenburg became a tenacious opponent of the ongoing indigenous genocide. Eventually, he became key to Arana's downfall. It would be difficult to find more unevenly matched opponents. Casement called Arana the head of a "syndicate of crime" and young Hardenburg had to watch his back around Iquitos as he investigated him. After his release, he secretly came back and documented his claims through interviews and photographs of "the marks of Arana." His photo of four naked Huitoto men chained together at the neck is shockingly revealing. In reference to the Amazonian genocide Sir Edward Grey, Britain's Foreign Secretary from 1906 to 1916 wrote, "It is not hard to tell the truth; the difficulty is to get it believed."

Both the slavery and industrial genocide against the indigenous Amazonian rubber tappers must be seen as "the by-products and ineluctable consequences of expansionary concessionary capitalism." It was not systematic extermination, but rather institutionalized violence that resulted in this industrial genocide.

"Men stumble over truth from time to time, but most pick themselves up and walk off as if nothing happened," Winston Churchill once wrote. Walter Hardenburg was not like most men, however, and he risked his life for these oppressed people. He relentlessly petitioned the British government at his own expense, and almost single-handedly exposed Arana's serpentine grip on thousands of Amazonian indigenes.

No British newspaper wanted to publish his story, but a magazine called *Truth* finally did, causing a public uproar in Britain. The British government then responded, along with support from the Anti-Slavery Society and the Aborigines Protection Society. It is certain that if Hardenburg had not spoken out, nothing would have been done about the genocide for a very long time. Without Hardenburg, there would never have been Casement, and without Casement, the crimes of Arana and the rubber barons would have gone unchecked and chances are those crimes would never have been known.

When the acting US consul in Iquitos refused to bring forth information against Arana, Hardenburg appealed to London. The situation was complicated because David Cazes, the British consul in Iquitos, where most of the Peruvian rubber was gathered, also sold rubber. He claimed that he knew nothing of the atrocities, yet during those years most of Peru's rubber was shipped to Great Britain. The British had such a monopoly on the market that the Peruvian name for rubber, jebe, is thought to have come from the Spanish pronunciation of the initials GB.

From 1900 to 1911, while some 4,000 tons of rubber was exported to Britain, approximately 40,000 indigenous people were murdered. Ironically, and hypocritically, this was happening in 1903 when Roger Casement was in charge of Britain's investigation of King Leopold's crimes in the Belgian Congo Free State. It was said that Britain was doing this not out of humanitarian convictions, but rather out of envy of the vast wealth coming from Leopold's private "Free" State. It was at that time, long before the Amazon investigation, that Joseph Conrad respectfully commented on Casement, saying, "I have always thought some part of Las Casas' soul had found refuge in his indomitable body."

In his book, *The Putumayo: The Devils Paradise*, Hardenburg wrote that "the 21 constables whom the Peruvian Government kept in the Putumayo in those days had all been bribed by the English traders and shut their eyes to what was happening in the jungles." But from Peru's Amazon, Casement soon rocked the British aristocracy by revealing the stockholders in Arana's London-based company.

After Hardenburg's revelations were made, he was quietly forgotten and settled in Canada. Arana cleverly liquidated his assets and escaped trial. He soon re-invented himself as a "protector of the Indians" and was rewarded by being made a senator in Peru. Only later, after continuous denials, did Peru do its own begrudging investigation. It then issued over 270 warrants, though none were ever enforced. As a result, the world's wheels went smoothly rolling along with vulcanized Amazon rubber, while whole indigenous tribes were "thrown under the bus," one could say.

After this, Casement, like Orellana, had "gone off and become a rebel" and was executed for treason, just as Pizarro had wanted to do to Orellana centuries before. Casement, having exposed the colonial horrors in Africa and the corporate genocide in Peru's Amazon, was hanged for treason in 1916, after seeking German support for Irish independence from Great Britain. He wrote, "The white Indians of Ireland are heavier on my heart than all the Indians of the rest of the earth." Like Orellana hundreds of years earlier, who also had an affinity for the indigenes, Casement was on a river of no return. He had gone too far in his human rights work in Africa and the Amazon to turn away from the fight for liberty of his own conquered people. Like the black and white waters of the Amazon, Casement's White Diary relates his admirable human rights work and the seemingly forged Black Diary fuels allegations of his predatory behavior with adolescent Indian boys.

In regard to the cause of the Amazon's indigenous genocide, Casement wrote in his *Amazon Journal* that "I think the Monroe Doctrine is at the root of these horrors on the Amazon," due to enforcing its hegemony over the hemisphere and preventing foreign influence, especially European. Referring to the genocide Casement wrote, "This blight in the forests of Peru and Bolivia would end tomorrow were it not for the Monroe Doctrine. Commercial civilization and its mouthpiece the Monroe Doctrine assume full immunity to the criminal."

Comparing the aftermath of the Amazon to the Congo he noted that "None of these guarantees of change can be found in the Amazon. The evil there is deeper and far older; and the remedy so remote as to have no bearing on the fate of the enslaved and disappearing Indian....Title deeds on the Amazon are drawn up in blood. If the Congo rubber was red rubber, Amazon rubber is crimson rubber....What I have seen before on the Putumayo exceeds in horror, in downright ghastliness anything I dreamed of before, and the state of things on the Putumayo was merely somewhat more acute form of what goes on over an extended area of he Upper Amazon forest. How it was produced, out of what a hell of human suffering no one knew, no one asked, no one suspected. Can it be no one cared?"

Casement attributed the lack of development in the Amazon to "400 years of the Spanish at its source and 300 years of the Portuguese at its mouth...first hell, then, a desert." Peru has always ceded the riches of the Amazon to foreign capital investments at the expense of the indigenous. Mineral rights have always taken precedence over human rights and foreign multi-nationals over local indigenous. Obfuscation, deliberate inattention, and "ethno-geographical blindness" to Peru's Amazonian indigenous has always relegated them to an invisible status, despite the fact that today they are the most active among Peru's diverse ethnicities, even after almost five hundred years of genocide, war, and oppression.

Only two of the communities I visited around Pevas were Yagua. There are many more further downriver near Leticia. They themselves do not use the name Yagua; rather, like many indigenes, they use the appellation "the People," which in their language is Nihamwo. Casement said it was the Augustinians who saved the Yagua from total extermination, especially at the hands of the Portuguese. At one time they were famous for blowguns and picunas, and those living far back still use them. The art of making them is not lost and they are far more cost effective than rifles. Casement calls the Yagua "a noble, graceful tribe" and wrote, "I never saw gentler faces, or more agreeable expressions... The strange thing is how they have survived and preserved their native customs, and dress, when all elsewhere along these 2000 miles of river the Indian has merged in garb and external show into the ranks of his so-called civilizers."

The Yagua primary school in San José de Piri, which is actually a barrio of Pevas, was bilingual and had thirty-six students. The more interesting place, though, was Mangual, a small Yagua village just a short distance down the Amazon from Pevas. The day we went there, dozens of men were out in dugouts checking their fishnets near the confluence of the Ampiyacu and the Amazon. Almost every boat was pulling in a good catch. On top of a high grassy flat on the left bank, the primary school at Mangual commands a view far up and down the Amazon River. Mangual must be an ancient site because of its strategic value; for years there has been a Peruvian military camp nearby.

In what was a common occurrence, the school was closed because the teacher was gone. When we asked for the cacique (chief), someone ran to find him. After a few minutes, he came with the key for the school, followed by about a dozen excited children. The school's matricula, which I had received from Peru's Ministry of Education in Pevas, said there were twenty-five students.

"Do you like books?" I asked the group of kids.

"Yes!" they responded in unison.

"Ok, this box of books is for your school so you can all read and enjoy them. Also, each of you will get a pen and notebook today. The other kids will have to wait," I told them. After they looked through the books for a while, I asked them to follow me to the riverside escarpment for a photo. Running ahead, they proudly waved their first books and notebooks as though they were prizes. So little can mean so much sometimes. Just the fact of being recognized and remembered caused them joy.

The next day I moved on to another nearby school for another tribe. The Bora, who originally lived north of the Putumayo, had their population reduced from over 15,000 in the year 1900 to below 500 a decade later. Now there are some 2,500 in Peru and about a thousand living in Colombia. From the matriculas, I realized that the two largest schools I would visit were both Bora. The nearby Bora/Huitoto Indian village of Pucaurquillo had sixty-five students and in Brillo Nuevo, a day's journey up river, there were seventy-two.

In Pevas, one of Francisco Grippa's employees, a local Ticuna man named José, had a dugout and agreed to take me up the slow Ampiyacu River. He also had an old nine-horsepower peque-peque motor, but both soon proved to be inadequate. As in places in South East Asia, this peque-peque motor had an eight-foot-long tubular shaft with a small propeller at the end. Usually the prop rests just below the water line, where it is easier to avoid floating debris because it can be maneuvered from side to side. But his motor kept stalling and his boat leaked. I didn't realize how shallow his dugout was until we were ready to leave. From the start, I was leery about taking on water and getting the books and notebooks wet, even though the boxes had been wrapped in plastic and covered with a tarp. We placed them on some thick branches to keep them above any puddles at the bottom, but his very shallow dugout needed constant bailing from the start. When the waves of a passing motorboat lapped over the side, I insisted that we find a better boat for our longer journey on the following day.

Traditionally, the Bora were enemies of the Huitoto, but because they had both suffered decades of genocide, some now live in the same villages, like Pucaurquillo. Though all the indigenes value education for their children, I have found the Bora especially responsive. Still, the emptiness of the school in Pucaurquillo left a "mark of Arana" on my mind. The effects of past direct debt slavery on these tribes was still directly indebting their children.

Afterwards, I entered the large thatched-roof community center and was impressed to see a very large, barrow-like, ceremonial manguaré drum. It was a hollowed-out tree trunk with both ends closed and resonating holes on top. I beat it with a mallet that had a fist-sized rubber ball on one end. They refer to the different sides of the drum as male and female, since one side has a deeper bass sound. Signal drums like this were once used for much more than music; quite a sophisticated messenger service existed until cheap cell phones took over.

The Bora are famous for their group dancing, in which long balsa wood sticks are thumped in unison on the ground. Today, tourist groups come to certain Bora villages near Iquitos to watch the topless women perform their dances. Their language, called Wikotan, is endangered, but most of this small tribe still speak it. Like the Ticuna language, the Bora language uses five distinct pitches and the same word has different meanings depending on the pitch.

Though once composed of semi-nomadic clans named after totem animals, the remnants of this now tiny exogamous tribe live in a few scattered villages and have been able to maintain much of their cultural identity. In some of the villages, Bora women still make traditional cloth called llanchama from the bark of a tree of the same name. Despite having been converted to Christianity from their animist roots, the spirit world for them is still very real. It is not separate from the physical world, but rather is seen as one of the two sides of life.

A day later, after finding a better boat and motor, we started off again, stopping about half an hour upriver at a Bora community called Santa Lucia de Prefecto. Like most Amazonian communities, there was a dilapidated school that stood alone in a grassy clearing not far from the high, red-clay riverbank. A wide cement lane separated the school from the impoverished village. Inside, an old chalkboard hung askew on the front wall and was the only thing to write on.

"Not one of my twenty-four students has a pencil or notebook," the thirty-five-year-old teacher told me. "Thank-you so much for giving these."

The endless problem with my work is that as soon as the pencils, pens, paints, and paper are used, the kids go back to having nothing again. Only the books would last for a while. As with all the other schools I visit, I asked for a receipt and permission to take a few photos. When I tried to photograph a couple of camera-shy kids, they hid behind the new books they were looking at. So, I waited. Then, wondering if I was still there, one little girl peeked over the top of a book to the sudden flash of my camera. Holding up my camera and showing her the photo brought a sudden downpour of laughter.

Several parents, most para-literate at best, and even a couple of curious old illiterate men came in to see the school's first books. Two mothers sat down, each holding books, and started reading slowly to their children. It was, as Barry Sanders wrote in his book *A is for Ox,* as if they were breast-feeding them with written words. The only sad thing was that the books were not in their native Bora language, so they could not breast-feed their children with their own milk, so to speak.

Although almost everyone now speaks Spanish, these kids rarely get a chance to read. These were the first children's books they had ever held, the teacher told me. After getting her permission, I took a group picture of all of the kids and several parents in front of the shabby, termite-eaten little school. Bunched tightly together, they proudly raised their new books, notebooks, and pens. They seemed like a patch of heliconias, happily refreshed from rain.

In 1770, Joseph Priestly invented the rubber eraser; how ironic to think that, even though the Amazon was once the greatest source of rubber, a rubber eraser can rarely be found in most rural or remote schools. And how ironic that the indigenous tribes that collected the raw latex were almost erased from existence in doing so. But no erasure can ever delete that memory—for while the world was being vulcanized, Peru's indigenes were being terrorized.

Like this one, most of the schools I visited were in deplorable shape, part and parcel of Peru's educational system and its near total social disregard for the Amazon. Several times, just like in other countries, I heard teachers call their schools "the forgotten."

Having completed a couple of day trips, we returned up the Ampiyacu for a three-day journey, bringing books to several schools. This time the dugout was full of boxes. As we passed the school in Santa Lucia de Prefecto, the teacher and class were at the riverside, all cupping their hands to get a drink. They saw us and waved. Their bodies must be riddled with parasites, I thought. We spent the next three days visiting eight more indigenous primary schools.

Several hours up the Ampiyacu River is the confluence of the Yaguasyacu, whose headwaters start just south of the Putumayo, on the border with Colombia. Like nearly all rivers in the Amazon Basin, both are brown and slow—one can barely detect a current. Only far up, where the rivers narrow, is there a noticeable current. Often, the only movement breaking the placid water is from the wake of surfacing pink or grey dolphin.

Except where there are steep banks, the rivers have no well-defined shore because their waters are constantly rising or receding. Along the low side of these turgid tributaries, tree trunks had turned dark grey on the bottom six or seven meters because of past flooding. By the low-water time in September, the waters will have receded by eight to twelve meters.

Further upriver at the Ocaina village, Puerto Izango, there was a school with only twelve students. The birdcage-like school burst into an indigenous song when the teacher asked the kids to show their appreciation. At the hamlet of Santa Lucia there was not a single pencil or notebook. Though the teacher there was very dedicated, he was limited by the lack of teaching materials.

In each of these communities, our arrival drew everyone's attention, since no one usually comes there unless they got lost. To show their appreciation, villagers would often invite us to eat and drink. At one, a woman called out for her friend to bring us some fresh banana masato. In the village of Estiron, a Huitoto man invited us to eat some freshly killed anteater he was cooking in a large pot. And at another village, we were given a small basket of aguaje fruit. This egg-shaped reddish fruit grows in large clusters that hang from the heart of the huge-leafed aguaje palm (*Mauritia flexuosa*).

As we continued upriver, we passed occasional chácaras, where families farm bananas, yuca, maize, coca, and other crops. Every now and then we would pass silent men in small dugouts, fishing among the inundated trees with simple stick fishing poles. The ubiquitous partially-inundated spiny trunks of chunga or black palm trees (*Astrocaryum standleyanum*) seemed like part of the Amazon's arboreal armory. Their fierce spines protect a very fine jet-black wood.

When we neared the steep, reddish-clay bank at Estiron de Cusco, a group of inquisitive Ticuna children ran along the top of a fallen trunk of a giant, dead catahua tree (*Hura crepitans*), to get a better view of their gringo visitor. José called out something in Ticuna which drew laughs and was no doubt a joke on me. He was happy to come there, as it was the only Ticuna village we visited. Soon, a large part of the small village followed us to the school, pleased to receive the village's first books.

The Ticuna population in Peru is about 4,000, but more are living in Brazil and Colombia. Like the Yagua, they were once expert at making curare, dart poison, and some still do. One type is made from *Strychnos toxifera*, whose name is almost as unpleasant as its effect. But these days, especially for those living near Colombia, they are masters at preparing cocaine for the drug cartels. Like the Yagua, they also make hammocks and bags from the chambira palm (*Astrocaryum chambira*).

About an hour upriver from there was the large Bora village, Brillo Nuevo, the New Shine. I checked my matricula paper and saw that there were seventy-two students in the primary school. It was already four in the afternoon and the school was closed. We decided to go anyway, though, since we were planning on sleeping further upriver at Colonia Ancon. We called out to some kids who were playing beside the river, and asked them where the school was. They pointed and told us to follow the narrow slough. From the boat we yelled to the curious kids that they should come to the school, because we had notebooks and pens for them.

Within a minute or two the news had spread, and dozens of kids were suddenly running noisily along the swampy bank, trying to beat us to the school. When we landed, a few came to the boat to help carry boxes. Soon several of the teachers showed up and within twenty minutes almost every kid in the village was there to claim a notebook and pen.

Though the school building was decent, very few kids had any school supplies. They knew how disabling it is to be without. After we presented the books, the teachers had the excited kids file up in a line while we handed the supplies out. Like nature itself, poverty is satisfied with very little. At each neglected place, it was the acknowledgment and care that they most appreciated.

In Brillo Nuevo, I was pleased to learn that the Bora there have quite an innovative and sustainable agro-forestry project underway. It is run by the women, who play an important role in the conservation of bio-diversity and the development of medicinal plants for sale. Some 1,500 plant species are known in the area.

In 2011, there was talk of a Hong Kong company signing illegal "carbon cowboy" agreements with certain people from the Peruvian government and members of Ampiyacu communities for carbon credits, forest clearing, and rights to natural resources. In exchange they would provide some social benefits, such as health care. But the Federation of Native Communities of the Ampiyacu (FECONA) and other entities would not allow this abuse and exposed the culprits.

Since it was already late in the afternoon, we needed to leave in order to make it up to Colonia Ancon before dark. This tiny place is the Ampiyacu's last community, and is just a few hours' walk through the jungle to the Putumayo. We would stay there in a Bora maloca (ancestral long house) with old friends of the boatman.

The river was narrowing; in places it became a hallway of lianas, hanging thick from the towering riverside trees. Suddenly there was a clearing, and the roof of a large maloca peeked out amongst the trees. When our motor stopped, some surprised villagers approached. After a warm greeting, they helped carry our boxes to the maloca. It was as large as a barn, with a well-made thatch roof that angled steeply down to about head high along the open sides.

While I was putting up my hammock, a couple of men returned from their chácara with a basket of coca leaves. One began to toast them in a large, open pot, carefully stirring them so they wouldn't burn. After about half an hour, they were placed inside a long wooden mortar and beaten into a fine, lime-green powder. They prefer to use the powder rather than chew the whole leaf. The man gathered a spoonful and put it in his mouth to test it. Using saliva, they form the powder into a lump, which is left to slowly dissolve against the teeth and gums.

The maloca was home to a whole extended family. Most of the inside was open, but a couple of short walls made from plaited palm fronds separated some raised wooden sleeping areas. A fire was slowly burning in a pit near the center.

Most places along the Ampiyacu have individual family houses—usually dark and dank little hovels built side by side. Though malocas still exist, they are in no way as fine as they once were. The Huitoto once had perhaps the most beautiful ones, elegantly decorated and huge, up to forty meters long with plaited palm roofs over fifteen meters high. Sometimes two hundred people would live together, almost swallow-like inside the airy building.

The story-telling ceremonies of this oral culture and the most solemn oaths taken by the Huitoto were performed in these huge malocas. These were often preceded by each person dipping a finger into a bowl of concentrated tobacco extract, which was then applied to the tongue. They only drank their tobacco.

It was the malocas that Christian missionaries ignorantly and wrongly condemned as being "a hive of promiscuity." But as research from the famed anthropologist Gerald Reichel-Dolmatoff indicated, the malocas were never used for sexual activity—that always takes place discretely in the forest. By "obliging the Indians to build miserable one-family huts... they are destroying a symbolic system that gives security to its inhabitants, an artificial memory in which every part, even the smallest, was charged with meanings. Inside is a sacred space, one where harmony and discretion reign. Rallying against the maloca upset the bonds and cohesion of the extended family. They have destroyed the cohesion of families' reciprocity, spontaneous cooperation. They have destroyed a work of art," said Reichel-Dolmatoff.

After helping fifteen schools in the Ampiyacu River area, I had finally run out of books. We finished just in time, though, because Peru's grade schools closed the next day, and stayed closed for two weeks because of a swine flu scare. We returned to Francisco Grippa's place, where I learned that a launch to Iquitos, the *Manuel* was coming the next morning from the Colombian border. I decided to take it and was waiting in a large crowd when it arrived. When I was finally able to get onboard, I found that the second and third floors were already completely full of hammocks. A spot at the very back of the crowded third floor was one of the last available spaces. No one wanted to stay there, because it was just in front of a long, open back deck and it was going to rain.

Some people in front of me were admiring a Colombian hammock—they are much better made than those from Peru. I strung mine up and staked out my unwanted territory. It's usually not a problem, but one has to be careful of thieves—often it is a crew-member. While I was sitting on the open back deck, I noticed a kitchen helper walk beside my hammock and run his hand through it, as if fishing for something. It was empty, but just a few minutes before he had seen me sitting there with my binoculars.

The *Manuel* arrived in Iquitos the next morning at four. Most people were up waiting, perhaps guarding their things. A few stragglers were still sleeping as the room emptied of passengers. As we entered the filthy riverfront of Iquitos in the pre-dawn darkness, I asked someone why there were so many police around. "For the thieves," the man answered.

Having completed my work, I needed to return to Lima. To finish this Amazon journey, I soon caught another launch, the large, four-floor, 1,200-ton *Gilmer*. It was going up the Marañón and Huallaga rivers for three days, to where the road begins at the old river port of Yurimaguas. This place is the oldest Spanish access point between coastal roads and Amazon rivers. The traffic there is dwarfed by that at Pucallpa, but the Marañón was the original "path" into the Amazon, almost connecting sea to sea. Into it drain the Huallaga, Santiago, Morona, Pastaza, and Tigre, most of which have traffic to Ecuador. A host of other branches, like the Utcabamba, Cenepa, and Chinchipe, join to form the immense Marañón branch of the fluvial tree called the Amazon.

I decided to wait for the *Gilmer* in quiet Nauta, sixty miles away, rather than stay longer in bustling Iquitos. The noise of 50,000 stentorian moto-taxis in Iquitos can be overwhelming. By contrast, Nauta is a mellow, clean village built on the right bank of the Marañón River about two kilometers up from the confluence of the Ucayali. There, at the very end of the mighty Marañón, it is only a kilometer wide—but what a river! It is normally deeper than the Ucayali and not as convoluted, although one can travel further up the Ucayali.

During those days of waiting I spent some time fishing for piranhas in one of the seasonally-connected black water lagoons. First the boatman spotted a boil of sardines and maneuvered to cast his throw-net into the river. With a single toss, he quickly had a few pounds of fat sardines for bait as well as food. Using them later, we readily caught several hand-sized red piranhas. Though interesting to see, they offer no challenge to the angler. The red piranhas are the most aggressive of the many species, but the white and the black are larger. Piranhas live in what is called black water: dark colored rivers and lagoon, which have high contents of tannic acid. Just before the confluence of the Ucayali, we followed a narrow interfluvial passage which led into a large, calm lagoon. We tied the boat to an overhanging branch of a giant renaco tree (*Ficus* spp.), just a few meters from the shore of the flooded lagoon. This tree, a type of strangler fig, had hanging root-like branches so thick that it blocked one's vision of what lay beyond. Its bark is supposedly one of the best bone healers and it was also a source of paper for the Aztecs of Mexico. Here, we fished.

The next day the launch arrived, and I was extremely lucky to get the last camarote (cabin). The *Gilmer* was by far the nicest riverboat I have ever been on. My spartan cabin with metal bunk beds was spotlessly clean and had fresh white sheets. It was on the third deck, where I could sit and watch the river go by. Including meals for three days, it cost 160 soles, about fifty-three dollars. The four-day journey between Nauta and Yurimaguas follows the Marañón River first, and then the Huallaga. Farther up the Huallaga is the rapids, the Pongo Aguirre, where Lope de Aguirre started his blood-thirsty journey. Beyond that are the old salt mines, which once enriched the enterprising Jesuits. Very close by are some salty hot springs. Today the Huallaga River Valley is the world's largest coca-producing area. This Amazon River journey ended in the very clean city of Yurimaguas, on the Huallaga River. A good road connects it to close-by Tarapoto and to Chiclayo on the distant Pacific coast.

In Yurimaguas I was told that a group of armed pirates had raided a sister boat of the *Gilmer* along the Huallaga, just a few nights before. They came in a speedboat, robbing and raping passengers at gunpoint before fleeing into the dark wilds. But I was now off the rivers, and travelling light, so I went to look for the salty hot spring in the cooler foothills, not far away.

Chapter 20

"Ya Vari Nice, Mista"

> "To be conscious of another is to be conscious of what one is not"—Sartre

In the spring of 2013, a Matsés Indian student group emailed me and asked me to help some of their villages schools with books, seeds, and medical supplies. A couple of months later, I spent a month in Lima, Peru gathering materials for ten schools—six for the Matsés and four for the Ticuna. These materials were for both primary and secondary schools. Then I began an eighteen-day journey, spending one day on a bus and seventeen more on river launches. I traveled to Puerto Alegre, a Matsés village in the remote eastern corner of Peru, far up the Yavari and Yaquerana rivers on the border with Brazil. If ever there was a place in the middle of nowhere, this is surely it.

    This isolated tribe of about 2,700 people are best known for three main things: kidnapping women and children from other tribes and settler villages, facial decorations using cat whisker-like palm splinters, and their tradition of using sapo, an extract from a poisonous toad. Though the outside world has known of them since the seventeenth century, they have purposely stayed out of contact for generations, choosing to live precariously along isolated affluents of the Yaquerana and Galvez rivers. Since 1969, though, they have stopped raiding villages and abducting people and have slowly accepted certain forms of acculturation. All of their villages now have schools, though mostly in name only. So, when some of their college students in Iquitos wrote and asked me to help their villages, I readily agreed.

Normally, I don't distribute medicine, but because of the need and because I was asked and because I had a good contact in Lima, I made an exception in this case. I went to the Promotorea Solidaridad in Callao to place an order. They are an affiliate of Caritas and sell medicines at a reasonable price. In a few days, I had a five-gallon plastic bucket stuffed with various types of medicine for each of the six communities—everything from aspirin to antibiotics, and from gauze to syringes.

Over the next few weeks, I counted at least sixteen times that I had to move the ton or so of books and supplies. As I had many times before, I bought the books in the huge Amazonas Book Market in central Lima. A truck took everything to Pucallpa while I took a bus. From Pucallpa, I booked passage on a large nine-hundred-ton launch, *Henry V*, to take me to Iquitos.

In Iquitos, I met with the Matsés students who had contacted me. They lived with about sixty other indigenous college students at a place called Red Ambiente Loereto (Loreto Environmental Network). This is a community established by a Christian Brother priest. After hearing about the villages' need for both fruit trees and more seeds, I purchased 220 saplings and a few hundred pounds of seed corn and rice. While I was in Iquitos, I returned to the fine Amazonica Library, where I was allowed to photocopy some hard-to-find literature about the Matsés.

After five false starts during my three weeks in Iquitos, the small ninety-ton launch, *Luis Antenor*, finally left Puerto Pesquero. In the hull were all the books, notebooks, seeds, 400 pounds of seed corn and rice, shovels, machetes, and medicine. On the deck and the roof were 60 gallons of gasoline and 220 fruit trees of various types: avocados, oranges, mandarins, lemons, grapefruit, caimitos, mangoes, guanabanas, rose apples, and more.

I had been waiting for almost three weeks to get going. The five false starts meant that the food I had bought for the long journey was going bad, like my feelings for the launch owners, who kept telling me, "Mañana, mañana!" Though time has little value in the Amazon, supplies do. On the plus side, the delay gave me more time to spend in the Amazonica Library, which I devoted to exploring Roger Casement's *Amazon Journal* and Steven Romanoff's Ph.D. dissertation about the Matsés.

The owners of the *Luis Antenor* were a Peruvian military officer and his wealthy wife. On their unreliable word, I kept leaving and then returning to my hotel room. They didn't care about my taxi bills or other inconveniences that their false starts caused me. When I found out that it was their first journey, I had even less confidence in them. They knew as little about the rivers as they did about buying sufficient supplies for the journey.

The last false start happened when they were stopped by the port authorities for transporting an illegal amount of gasoline. They had brought along 1500 spare gallons, but they had no permit. It seems that they cared as little about maritime laws as they did about their passengers.

At ten o'clock on the night of the final delay, the handful of passengers were told to go wait at another landing downriver because the launch was not permitted to take passengers. But then the launch never left, because of the unauthorized gasoline on board. After more than two hours spent in a soaking rain, I returned again to my hotel, only to find out that it was full. Unfortunately, this was the only launch to leave for the remote Yavari River for over two months, so I had no choice but to wait.

Besides my problems with the launch owners, other things also started to unravel. Twenty of the fruit trees suddenly started dying on the roof of the launch during the long wait in Iquitos. The nurseryman, whom I purchased the trees from, had used too much manure when he re-bagged a couple dozen of the trees. On the very next day, the leaves started looking burnt and curled up, and within three days they were dead. A Peruvian agronomist friend of mine confirmed my fears and went with me to speak with the nurseryman. Of course, the man denied any culpability and we left disappointed and disgusted.

Going on the flat-bottomed launch down the Amazon, first to Pevas and then on to Santa Rosa near Leticia, was painstakingly slow, as the owners wanted to conserve gasoline. Long journeys down slow rivers where the flat jungle rarely changes can become monotonous. and we were being passed by nearly everything that floats— sometimes it seemed that even the current was passing us. Instead of taking two days to get to the border with Colombia and Brazil, it took three.

At Santa Rosa, Peru, across the river from Leticia, Colombia and Tabatingua, Brazil, we stopped at Peruvian Customs for a few hours. The cell towers in Leticia were as numerous as the mosquitos and bristled like spiked hair above the horizon. It seemed that every drug lord had his own.

Leticia was part of Peru until 1931, when the United States gave Colombia the green light to annex it for a port on the Amazon. At that time, Sergeant Fernando Lores and a group of men from Iquitos tried to retake it. They succeeded, but they were forsaken and given no help from the Peruvian government. Lacking reinforcements, they were all captured and killed. Sargento Lores became one of those manipulated heroes, sacrificed by those who knew that they would end up same way if they acted in his defense. Peru was told to do nothing by the US and so Colombia took over the port of Leticia. This occurred three decades after Panama was removed from Colombia to build the canal, using the Monroe Doctrine as a pretext. From the time of Lores, no one from Loreto can be an officer in Peru's army. Perhaps they are worried that the huge department of Loreto might rebel and become a country itself, since it is about half the size of all Peru.

The launch stopped at Islandia, a Peruvian village near the mouth of the Yavari River, so that the owners could buy more barrels of gasoline to sell upriver. The village consisted of a few rickety boardwalks lined with small stores and houses, all raised on stilts. The shore, just three meters below, was mucky and trash-ridden, revealing the lack of concern of the inhabitants. While the owners bought more barrels of gasoline, everyone got off the launch to walk for a while and buy food. The nearest place to buy anything upriver was in Angamos, three days away.

Islandia is where the Yavari River joins the Amazon. During his travels in 1911 while investigating the genocidal crimes of rubber barons, Roger Casement wrote that there, "A great conflict of rivers occurs." The Yavari's large mouth opens like that of a big fish, but it is then suddenly swallowed by a much larger one, the ever-growing Amazon. The Yavari is just one branch on the Amazon's tree of rivers. It starts some 1,180 sinuous kilometers away, where its main tributary, the Yaquerana, joins the black waters of Rio Galvez, not far above Angamos on Peru's border with Brazil.

The Yavari is a very different river from its larger western neighbor, the Ucayali. For one thing, the Yavari's riverbanks have no cane grass, which often lines the Ucayali like a six-meter-high closed curtain. Also, there are very few aguaje palms (*Mauritia flexuosa*), which often reveal old homesites. Instead, the low shore is often lined with a mustache of willow-like iporuru trees (*Alchornea castaneifolia*), which is used as an aphrodisiac. This is only one of the almost 2000 medicinal herbs which the Matsés know. The narrow Yavari, unlike the Ucayali, has no islands. There are only a couple of communities on either side of the Yavari (tiny Angamos is the largest), while the Ucayli is more heavily populated. The Yavari is also not a river for commercial traffic like the Ucayali is, where huge 1200-ton launches pass up and down to Pucallpa. We only saw a few canoes and no other launches the whole way. The Yavari is a wilder river, and one has more of a chance to see animals and far more macaws than people.

In 1910, Algot Lange, the author of *In the Amazon Jungle*, visited the Yavari area and wrote about the village of Islandia, which later had a name change. "One of the reasons for the flattering name of the town Remate de Malas i.e. Culmination of Evils (or Auction of Evils), is the great mortality of the community, which it has as part of the great Yavari district." The armed hand of man was amongst these evils, as were the dreaded diseases and epidemics that convulsed the area soon after the time of first outside contact.

About the same time, Roger Casement noted in his *Amazon Journal* that "The Yavari was an important wild rubber river and the fact that each bank belonged to a different nation meant that it became the refuge for a dispossessed criminal element wanted by authorities within Peru or Brazil." Casement made two voyages up the Yavari in 1911 in pursuit of Putumayo criminals, especially his nemesis Julio Arana, who once traded on the Yavari. An associate of Arana named Encarnación Rojas worked the upper Yavari and added much to its ill fame.

In 1910, the Yavari River produced 1,451 tons of rubber, but by 1922 production had plummeted to just 386 tons. In 1876 an Englishman named Wickham had smuggled Brazilian *Hevea* seeds into the British Empire. By the 1920s, the trees had been well established in Singapore, India, and Sri Lanka. The Amazon rubber estates soon started closing because of the cheaper sources controlled by the British in Asia.

The Yavari area also had some *Castilla elastica* trees that were used to harvest the inferior caucho rubber. This was when the superior *Hevea brasiliensis* variety of rubber, which extended eastward towards the Madiera River, was discovered. The area became known for its rubber "estates," where thousands of indigenes were enslaved, either bought outright, or forced into labor through debt. Between the mouths of the Yavari and Angamos, seventeen of these estates supposedly existed during the heydays of the early 1900s. Some had seven-room houses for the bosses. Now they have all been reclaimed by the jungle, as if it is trying to cover over the memories of its horrible past.

The Hevea estates along the Yavari River were mostly worked by indigenes held in direct-debt servitude. But many of the rubber bosses were in direct debt as well—to trading/finance houses.

The difference, though, was that the rubber barons were not being killed. Still, the true value was in the debt, for when you control people's debt, you control everything, and the debt was controlled by a wide variety of inhuman punishments. It was the debt that was important, because it was through debt that the caucheros manipulated matters, just like the banks do today. These estates, like the mission reducciones, were centers of disease and death, and labor conditions were terrible at best.

One day, after six slow days traveling up the Yavari from Iquitos, the owner of the *Luis Antenor* got dressed up in his Peruvian army uniform. As I soon realized, this was because we would be passing a Brazilian army outpost, one of two on the Yavari River below Angamos. He wanted to impress the Brazilian soldiers, but the hardened, though very genial, Brazilian officer in camouflage fatigues waved us on without a search. Why the Brazilian military stops Peruvian boats going up the Yavari River was a question no one could answer.

Even before I started, this journey was already the worst of the many I had made on over twenty Amazonian rivers. In addition to the waiting and the poor food, which I often fed to the fish, the owners had their room adjacent to mine. That would have been alright were it not for the fact that every morning the man would bathe himself in a river of cologne, the scent of which would drift through the walls and almost asphyxiate me. "You smell like a perfume factory," I once reproached him. "Now no one needs mosquito repellent." Because of this, I spent most of my time on the roof, sitting among the fruit trees with a photocopy of Ramanoff's dissertation and some good green bud.

On the third day of the journey, the starter motor on our launch suddenly broke down. The owner, in a display of machismo, wanted to collect Taricaya turtle eggs from a beach, so he had the pilot turn towards the beach and cut the motor just before we touched the white sandy shore. Once stopped, though, the motor wouldn't start back up again. Instead of staying put on the lovely but shadeless beach, he decided to float down to a nearby shady spot. He had his workers pull out the long steel stake that secured the launch to the beach, and push the launch into the slow but gripping current. Little did he realize that the willow-like Ipururu trees that lined the bank were full of blood-sucking black gnats during the day and disease-carrying mosquitos during the night. The current pushed the launch into the tree branches, which blocked the aisle in front of my door. Then the launch, like a poorly tethered donkey, started toppling and breaking stacks of cinderblocks, tiles, and plastic pipe on the deck.

During the first of the three days we spent broken down along the bug-infested bank, a raggedy Brazilian fisherman and his young son came by asking for a cigarette. He asked a couple of times, but no one answered, not even the owner who was a smoker. Finally, the owner's wife told him that they sell cigarettes for eight soles ($2.75) a pack. The poor fisherman complained that the price was too high, so the woman lowered the price to six soles. His poverty caused him to still decline. What struck me was that the owners would not give the Brazilian man a cigarette, even under such circumstances in the middle of nowhere. He was the only person to come by our launch in three days, and we could have used his help. What kind of people are these, I wondered, to be so tight and unkind that they would not even give the guy a cigarette? He left with a frown on his face and some bad thoughts about Peruvians, no doubt. I can just imagine how frustrating it must have been, to be turned down for such a small thing as a cigarette, when they had boxes of them.

A few hours later, the man and his son returned from fishing, but did not come over. They had a camp somewhere in the area. I called out to him from the roof of the launch, "Hey, brasileño, venga aca. Quiero compro usted uno paquete de cigarrillos." ("Hey, Brazilian, come here. I want to buy you a pack of cigarettes.") Instantly his paddle entered the water and I heard the sound of positive responses from some passengers below. They had all witnessed the way the man had been treated by the cauchero-like owners. I went down and bought him a pack, paying the money-grubbing woman seven soles for a pack, not the six she had offered him. Along with the cigarettes, I handed the man a cup of red wine and watched him light up a smile and a cigarette.

"Do you like the Argentine wine?" I asked the Brazilian in Spanish.

"Ya, vari nice, Mista," he replied in broken English, to my surprise. Soon he began conversing with some of the other passengers, while he sat in his dugout smoking and drinking his wine. Later, we discussed among ourselves how terribly cheap and inhospitable the launch owners were. "They only think to make a profit," one passenger said of them. The Brazilian returned the next day. Knowing of our dire lack of food, he offered us a good-sized fish—a delicious doncella no less. Well, guess who ate the fish? I didn't even get a bite, though he supposedly brought it for me.

The frustrated owner had radioed Angamos, and on the second night a speed boat came down to help us. The owner left with them and returned a day and a half later with a rebuilt starter. By that time our drinking water was gone and our meals had been reduced to a bare minimum of rice and cooked green bananas. We were all relieved when the mechanics from Angamos replaced the starter.

Both the Yavari and Yaquerana rivers exude a feeling of emptiness; the riverside forests seem full of ancient dark secrets. It would be hard to find a border river with less boat and canoe traffic, and fewer people living along its banks, than the Yavari. And while places normally increase in population with time, the Yavari River area has been in reverse for the last century. This is not only true for the indigenes, but for other settlers as well.

We arrived in Angamos three days later, just after dark. It was the tenth night of our journey from Iquitos. Lights from the village generator revealed a silhouetted crowd of people lining the rim of the high river bank. My two Matsés helpers were among the crowd and came down to meet me. As it turned out, the *Luis Antenor* was the first launch to arrive in some months, so it was the only show in town. My anticipation of a confrontation with the launch owners materialized once we were in Angamos. Because I was a foreigner, I was charged almost double what Peruvians paid for one of the tiny, five-by-seven-foot dirty cabins. This was more money than the price of an airplane ticket from Iquitos. They also changed the price they had set to transport the trees. I refused to pay what they wanted and they refused to give me my cargo. We finally agreed on a price later the next day, but only after some people from Angamos intervened on my behalf.

Eventually, everything I had was carried off the launch and up the steep bank. About two dozen men who worked for the village carried the 200 trees off the boat and placed them in a large building beside the river. They were paid to do so by the Angamos municipality, which I appreciated. Five Matsés struggled with the heavy boxes and rolled my sixty-gallon barrel of gasoline up the steep bank. Instead of putting things in the nearby village storehouse with the fruit trees, they took them about three-hundred meters away to a villager's house. Not until three days later, just before leaving for Puerto Alegre, did I realize that a twenty-five-pound bag of seed corn they had stored there was missing. I realized I was being "played."

We needed either a good-sized boat or a few large dugouts to take everything on the final two-day journey up to Puerto Alegre. Though I was told that a large enough dugout with two Matsés was available, it turned out that their canoe was way too small; the boxes couldn't even fit into it. However, I saw a perfect-sized boat, about forty feet, tied to the riverbank the day before and I arranged to rent it for fifty soles, less than twenty dollars.

Before we left Angamos, I met a Matsés teacher from Buenas Loma Antigua, one of the villages for which I had books, seeds, and medicine, so I gave him the items for his village schools. He was ready to leave in his large dugout and head for the Chiriacu ravine. This would save us a long walk with the heavy boxes from Puerto Alegre and then down the ravine. For the third village, Buenas Lomas Nuevas, several young men later had to hike over five hours to carry everything back.

It took us forty-eight hours to travel up the meandering Yaquerana from Angamos to Puerto Alegre. The Yaquerana is a wild river with only three tiny communities in between, two of which are on the Brazilian side. The Matsés never stop there, because the Marabu tribe are their long-time enemies.

Not long after the journey upriver began, just before dark a downpour of rain and strong wind made us hustle to cover all the boxes of books and sacks of seeds with tarps. The Matsés boatmen hadn't used any of the tarps I had brought for the roof. The heavy rain leaked rapidly through the cracks in the plank roofing, that the tarps should have covered. Suddenly, everything was getting soaked.

"It does no good to cover the boxes when this rain is filling the boat through the cracks on the roof," I told the young Matsés. "We have to use the tarps to cover the roof."

We scrambled to cover the cargo in the downpour. I realized that if we didn't do something fast, everything would be ruined by the rain. In the downpour and darkness, two of us climbed to the roof with more tarps. Because of the number of fruit trees in plastic crates and the dark unstable conditions, however, we had to beach the boat and redo everything. Luckily, there was a white sand beach at the next bend, so we landed, shuffled all the crates of trees around, and tarped the roof. I could only blame myself, I thought, because I trusted untrustworthy people to do a simple job.

Soon we started off again, with just my flashlight to guide us through the night up the dark and winding river. We spent almost an hour bailing rain water from the incredible downpour. The boat was like a floating nursery with a few dozen crates of young fruit trees on top and larger ones poking wildly out the sides below.

After rearranging things, I placed my air mattress on top of the boxes, where I would spend the next two nights.

Though home to few people, these rivers support many dolphins—both the gray and pink varieties gracefully broke its calm waters. The red eyes of crocodiles glowed periodically at night, and pairs or flocks of noisy macaws regularly flew overhead during the day, always landing in the tops of the tallest trees. Red-faced Uakari monkeys seemed to blush at our presence and bright blue *Morpho menelaus* butterflies checked out our boat, as if Menelaus himself was searching for his fickle Helen.

A few times along the way, we stopped at bends in the river to gather Teracaya turtle eggs. Fresh tracks ascending the steep white sand beaches from the river were a telltale sign. Digging down a foot by hand into the soft sand exposed nests of thirty or more golf ball-sized eggs. Knowing that the eggs are decreasing by the year, the Matsés men took out about half and then covered the others back up. They always leave some eggs behind, but even so, the eggs are being depleted by each passing dugout. Considered a delicacy, demand for the eggs has hastened the decline of the endangered turtle.

In the Amazon, the Teracaya and the larger charapa turtles were perhaps the first animal species in the New World to face near extinction by the wayward hand of man. Pity the poor turtle, the first to cross the finish line in man's mad race to deplete the planet. It was the seventeenth century Jesuits who first imperiled the charapa and Teracayas turtles. Their enterprising egg oil market was perhaps the first New World industry to deplete a species. Though now considered a protected species, the Teracaya turtle meat and eggs are nonetheless openly sold in markets in Iquitos.

Famous as hunters, the Matsés make group decisions about hunting, the anthropologist Steven Romanoff learned back in the early 1970s. Their hunting parties have roles for all the participants, including women and older men. Husband and wife hunting teams are also common. The animals killed are controlled by certain sharing rights. For instance, a woman will usually get the liver of the animal, as it is generally prohibited for men. Hunting takes place around a plot of land far into the jungle, which has been purposely cleared to attract game. Ever since the Matsés began using rifles, they also made rubberized hunting bags used to carry bullets and shotgun shells.

Though the two days on the river were long and full of black flies, the nights were longer and full of mosquitos. The boatmen did well, though, and guided our way upriver all night just by the light of my dim flashlight. The best thing about the rough boat was that the hull did not leak. The only water that came inside was from the first night of rain, through the leaky roof. Though there was no floor, the boat had a very old and ornate brass captain's wheel. A chain from it ran along both sides, and was connected to the motor and rudder in the back.

Finally, one of the Matsés boatmen told me, "Four more turns and then Puerto Alegre." We were all happy to get to Happy Port, after two hard days and nights moving slowly up the Yaquerana in very cramped and challenging conditions.

When we arrived in Puerto Alegre, which is the last village in that part of Peru, a crowd of inquisitive Matsés kids were waiting on the beach. More watched from the top of the cliff. They had all heard the motor and knew we were coming. Very rarely does anyone visit the place, and even fewer come with something for the people. All of the kids were waiting for the promised notebooks and pens which they had already heard news about.

Within a few minutes dozens of villagers, both young and old, showed up to help unload the fruit trees and all the sacks and boxes. One by one, they carried the sapling trees up the steep riverbank trail and placed them together in the shade. But a low cloud bank had moved in, creating an eerie feeling and a day later, the temperature began to plummet. For three nights it became uncomfortably cold. Sleeping on my air mattress, I was freezing even with my sheet and all my clothes on. In the morning, I could see my breath, which is very unusual in the Amazon. At dawn I joined a bunch of little kids who had started a fire to warm themselves in the clearing in front of their houses.

The Matsés built Puerto Alegre in 2002 when about fifty families came from villages on the Chiriyacu ravine. It was built to stop illegal logging further upriver. As with all indigenous lands, unless tribes monitor things, the nationals will come and take what they can. Now there are about sixty homes all made from pona palm (*Iriartea exorrhiza*) and bamboo, with thatched roofs of finely plaited leaves of the llarina palm (*Phytelephas* sp.).

I was impressed with how neat and tidy most things were in the village, unlike those of many other Amazonian tribes. The white chalky soil around the houses was cleared of all plants, which gives a clean appearance, and even gives off light during full moons. There is no trash, because their remote poverty leaves them with nothing to throw away. Basically, there is nothing to buy, since there is no store. If there was a store, there would be very few customers, since most of the people have little or no money. Money interests them, for sure, but if someone has something to sell, they have to take it fourteen hours downriver to Angamos. The people live mainly from hunting, gathering, and fishing, but they are also known as good horticulturalists.

Their longhouses are often quite large, with several clean rooms but no furniture except perhaps some stools. A raised earthen hearth is always in one corner. At one time, the Matsés, like many Amazonian tribes, had much larger longhouses (malocas), where up to one-hundred people lived. In each stilted house, a few banana stalks hang by ropes from rafters. They will be used to make chapu, a thick banana beverage served at every meal. Some jaw bones of animals may adorn a corner to ensure future hunting success.

Like most remote places in the Amazon, the children have never seen a car or held a book, but they all know airplanes. And like in most places, the young boys play with toy guns, although theirs are hand-carved from balsa wood.

Three days after arriving, I met with the whole community in their long assembly house. We brought the books, school supplies, medicine, and seeds to display and distribute. After some of the village leaders spoke, all of the kids filed through and received a notebook and a pen. Though seemingly appreciative, I was surprised by the lack of parental response. Maybe I should have brought them toy guns instead, I joked to myself. Other tribes living in worse conditions had shown much more interest in the books for their schools.

Though it lacked books and supplies, the concrete block school was only a few years old. It was far better than the mud-floor schools of other tribes. Perhaps it was partly because they lacked a history of pedagogy that they seemed so disinterested. Somehow, though, it was more than just that.

The next day, which was July 28th 2013, the village celebrated Peru's Independence Day. It was quite shocking to see the Matsés teachers, who had just thanked me for books the day before, now armed with rifles and leading the whole school in a goose-stepping military march. It seemed that parading around the football field with guns satisfied them more than the encyclopedias and other materials I had brought them all the way from Lima.

When they reached one end of their sacred football field, they shot off their rifles and twenty young boys pretended to do the same with their balsa wood AK47s. Perhaps without a flag or a football, the two f-words of acculturation, there would be no reason to go to school. As in most indigenous schools, these are basically the only things that the government supplies. In comparison, the Awajun, one of the Matsés ancient enemies, would never mimic Peru's irascible army. It seemed that perhaps the books I had brought would help them to become better soldiers, which seems to be the Matsés pedagogical paradigm.

The percentage of Matsés in the Peruvian army is high. No doubt some of these school kids will later join Peru's army, too, because armies are often an escape route from the harshness of poverty. Seeing that the Matsés have a very aggressive history, perhaps that is understandable. After all, one often becomes like one's conqueror. I also believed that the lead teacher was a government plant, sent to militarize and subtly recruit young Matsés boys and girls into Peru's armed forces. He was gung-ho about the military, which I found quite disgusting. On that day he was brainwashing his students by punishing anyone who was out of step. "Why not whip the teacher when the pupil misbehaves?" Diogenes once asked.

But such is Peru, which seems to live for military parades. Iquitos and many other large cities waste thousands of dollars to have a military march every Sunday around their Plaza de Armas, but never buy books or notebooks for their schools. Some boulevards in Iquitos are lined for blocks with gold-painted statues of defeated generals that promote a malignant militarism, and yet the schools are utterly forgotten.

In his 1984 doctoral thesis entitled "Matsés Adaptation in the Peruvian Amazon," anthropologist Steven Romanoff wrote: "Literacy training has been exclusively for men." He was referring to the Summer Institute of Linguistics (SIL) basic literacy program which was set up in the early 1970s at Choba Creek, a tributary of the Yaquerana. "The classes have resulted in a substantial number of Matsés young men who can read and write texts in their own language. First elderly men learned to copy individual letters, but not to read. But the uses of literacy were largely limited to religion, that being the nature of the written materials that I have seen distributed," states Romanoff.

In the forty years that have elapsed since then, virtually all Matsés children go to primary and secondary school. Nearly all young people can read and write, but even though many students have studied to become educators, nurses, administrators, and other professionals, many adults, especially women, are still illiterate. Although the kids can read and write, there is virtually nothing to read and nothing to write with. By 1993, there was about a forty-two percent literacy rate overall, although for those over thirty years of age, the rate was only twenty-three percent. Now the literacy rate is about sixty-two percent overall. That is why I was asked to bring books, to provide an educational impetus for the youth. Without books to instill the desire for learning, nothing will change. The military will still remain attractive and even more Matsés will enter their ranks.

Historically the Matsés were one of several interfluvial, clan-based border tribes of Panoan descent who lived in the frontier areas of Peru and Brazil. In Peru, the Matsés territory extends over the Yavari, Yaquerana, Galvez, Blanco, and Tapiche rivers area. There are about 1,700 Matsés in Peru and another thousand in Brazil. At one time, this tribe was thought to have lived in the Huallaga River area and around Moyabamba, but none live there today. Nor do they live along the Yavari River as they once did. Though they are sometimes referred to as the Mayoruna, the name has no significance for the Matsés today. Instead, it is a non-specific Quechua appellative denoting "River People," as "Mayo" means river and "Runa" means people.

A Matsés man told Romanoff a story that described their territorial withdrawal from the Yavari River area. "Before the Matsés knew about rubber, my grandfather and other Matsés were gathering turtle eggs on the Yavari River when some nationals came upon them. The Matsés accompanied them back to their camp. After the nationals had gone out to hunt, the Matsés ate some of the meat left in camp. When the hunters returned they asked who ate the meat, but the Matsés said that they did not know. Then a national hit a Matsés in the mouth with a machete. The Matsés left and then returned to kill the three nationals. After that time the Matsés very rarely made houses near the Yavari."

The upper Yavari and Yaquerana rivers were once famous for slaving attacks, as well as reprisals from different Panoan tribes against the few nationals who dared to go there. Since the times of slavery and the rubber genocide, the Matsés purposely avoided the large rivers where they might have encountered Peruvian nationals and enemy tribes. By then, the wheels of the whole world were literally rolling on the latex blood of Amazon rubber gatherers. Not even in the Congo did people suffer from industrial genocide as much as the tribes in that part of the Amazon. They were scarred like Hevea trees and cutdown like Castillas.

Tapping rubber for a few months at a time was incompatible with their way of life, so their crops suffered, people starved, and villages were abandoned. The early rubber years for the Matsés were characterized by purposeful avoidance of Peruvian and Brazilian nationals. Gradually, though, some Matsés started to tap rubber, "which usually ended in violent separation" according to Romanoff. Thus, during the hostilities of the "rubber boom," the Matsés lost their access to the Yavari River banks as well as to the oxbow lakes nearby, all rich in fish. They also suffered epidemics and diseases, slaving raids by Spanish, Portuguese, and Shipibos, and many tribal wars. They saw their numbers dwindle to about five hundred.

Since the 1920s, the Matsés have become famous for raids on settlements and other tribal communities, capturing women and children to augment their population. This worked successfully for a few decades, but it also caused many problems, the least of which was having to deal with many wives. In the late 1970s, captives from the decades before accounted for twenty-one percent of women and six percent of men in Matsés communities. According to Romanoff's research, however, captives made up sixty percent of those above the age of thirty. About forty-five percent of population have one or both parents who were captives. The Matsés had captives from at least ten different ethnic backgrounds, including Spanish-blooded women from Requena along the Ucayali, as well as Brazilians. Despite the obvious ethical questions which these kidnapping raids raise, they did serve to augment the Matsés population.

Although the kidnapping of Spanish and Brazilian women and children generated most of the attention, actually more of the Matsés captives were taken in raids on other tribes. The Matsés were enemies of almost every other Panoan tribe—they actually completely eliminated four of them. Old enemies such as the Kaxinawá, Sharanahua, and Amahuaca all suffered raids. Women and children were captured and the men were killed. What was left of the Remo and Capanahua tribes fled the area.

The easiest people left to raid were the nationals and the Matsés's cousins, the Marubo, who lived across the river in Brazil. These Matsés raids have caused their small tribe to become an amalgamation of people from at least ten different ethnic groups. In spite of this, and the fact that nearly every child today has a family member who was a captive, everyone is a proud Matsés.

The Matsés battled their riverine neighbors, the Yagua, who lived on the Amazon River, and the Shipibo, who lived along the Ucayali. The Shipibo also raided the Matsés to sell to rubber barons as slaves.

In an area of such tribal diversity and conflict, the Matsés sought refuge in narrow tributaries far up the embowered Yavari. Many anthropologists believe that if the Matsés had not made these raids for wives and children, they would have disappeared entirely or would now number only about two hundred. Though terrible, it seems that violence and polygamy associated with kidnapping wives and children saved the tribe. Strangely, Romanoff records that in the late seventies, the Matsés had a very high rate of infanticide despite their declining numbers. Some sixty-four percent of female deaths and twelve percent of male deaths were the result of infanticide.

According to David Fleck, an American linguist and zoologist who lived with his Matsés wife and sons in Estiron, only a few of these captive women and children are still alive, yet their legacy remains. Romanoff made reference to the fact that the Matsés "owners" considered boy captives as their "pets." Though eventually integrated into the tribe, they were always of secondary rank. Any resistance from them resulted in death. Also, because the tribe was polygamous, woman captives needed to establish themselves socially among the other wives of their new husband. Though Romanoff saw no justification for calling Matsés captives "slaves," using the shared poverty of the slave holder and slave as the reason, I doubt whether the captives would see things his way.

Because they are an interfluvial rather than riverine culture, the Matsés managed to escape much of the slaving and the reaches of the Hevea estates on the Yavari. Unfortunately, this did not stop the wandering, disease-bearing, caucheros from coming across the flat, stone-less jungle from the Ucayali River, looking for the next area full of *Castilla elastica* trees to plunder. After giving up the Yavari to the violence of slavers and Hevea estates, the Matsés did not take kindly to caucheros entering their interfluvial forests. Feeling pinched on one side by caucheros looking for rubber trees to kill and on the other by the death camp-like Hevea estates along the Yavari, the Matsés reacted by raiding the Peruvian settlements for wives and tools. It is said that their first few shotguns were used for raids and not for hunting.

The first Matsés attack on Requena was in 1924, and then again in 1927 and 1928, continuing some twenty times until the 1960s. Much to the grief of the people of Requena, which was a prime target for Matsés attacks, no help was forthcoming due to Peru's governmental dysfunction. The residents of Requena asked for help several times, to no avail. After raiding Requena for over forty-five years, the Matsés ceased hostilities in 1969. Until then, Peruvian nationals were afraid to go beyond the last houses in Requena, and three settlements nearby were abandoned in 1967. The tribe's dire demographic situation led to four decades of kidnapping raids, which though a nightmare for Requena residents, helped the Matsés survive.

A civilian/military expedition entered into Matsés territory in 1964, to seek vengeance for Matsés raids and to do reconnaissance for a road to Angamos. Requena's mayor and other dignitaries, including the lieutenant governor and a local priest, led a military patrol of a few dozen armed men. After crossing the Galvez River, they came to an empty Matsés village, cut down crops, and entered a longhouse. They set out an armed scouting party to search for the Matsés villagers. The Matsés responded by attacking the longhouse with bows and arrows, wounding six men and killing one. The besieged party radioed for help, but when it came, it was not from Peru, but rather from US Marine helicopters flown in from Panama. The armed party waited for Peruvian army reinforcements before going on to the Yaquerana River, where a naval vessel awaited to take them back.

At that point, the missionary group Summer Institute in Linguistics (SIL) intervened and made contact with the Matsés. They presented the situation as if the Matsés were an uncontacted tribe, which may have played well for those with evangelistic missionary zeal, but was not the reality. The Matsés were not an uncontacted tribe—they had been known for centuries, but had chosen to remain separate.

After a few years of missionary work with the Matsés, the SIL changed the name of God to Lord and a minor theological storm thundered. As missionaries have done repeatedly, SIL convinced the Matsés that they should live in separate houses consisting of nuclear families, instead of living with their extended family members in malocas, which sometimes housed up to one hundred people.

Like other Panoan tribes, the Matsés once had a variety of tribal ornamentations, including body paintings, coiffures, ornaments of labrets, facial tattoos, ear plugs with feathers, and spiny, cat-like whiskers inserted into holes made in the nose and lips. It is said that in the old days, both sexes were clothed only in red body paint made from the seeds of achiote (*Bixa orellana*). With their cat-like whiskers made from palm splinters, they must have been quite a sight. The Marubo, their cousins from across the river in Brazil, have tattooed lips—thus their appellative of "black lip people." These black-lipped people chased the white-lipped peccaries and thus were enemies of the Matsés.

Many of the traditional beautification styles are not being adopted by tribal youth today. Facial tattoos and palm splinter whiskers are going out of fashion. Where they once painted their bodies red with achiote, today a Lionel Messi football jersey is the preferred garb. A necklace of jaguar teeth had been replaced by flashy sunglasses, and facial tattoos, piercings, and a cord holding up the penis are superseded by a pair of Levis. Yet the Matsés are still adamantly Matsés.

It was said by Izaguirre, Tessman, and other early twentieth-century ethnologists, that in times past, amongst many other cultural idiosyncrasies, various Panoan tribes (including the Matsés) practiced parenticide and funerary endocannibalism, drinking dead relative's ashes mixed in fermented masato at their wakes. In 1904, the anthropologist Figueroa observed that "dying people for whom Christian burial was planned were greatly distressed at the prospect of being eaten by maggots instead of by their relatives. The bones were then ground, mixed with masato and drunk. The head was kept until filled with maggots, when the brains were spiced with aji (chili) and eaten with great relish." Hold the relish and mustard, I'll take an order to go, please.

Figueroa records that when the Matsés wanted to trade, they went to the Yavari River and blew bamboo trumpets to signal their enemies on the opposite side, who would cross in canoes. They would not land, but held the articles for exchange on the points of their spears. The Matsés would wade out and exchange parrots, hammocks woven from wild cotton, feather headdresses, and other items in exchange for knives and various small objects. The traders would separate, until at a certain distance, when they would then shoot arrows at each other.

At night sometimes in Puerto Alegre, a women's choir would sing. I have never heard sweeter music coming from a church. They sang their own songs, which Bach would have been proud to have written. The music was very quiet, extremely beautiful, and rivaled the famed huangana bird for angelic quality. To lay on my air mattress in the darkness of the house given me and hear them singing would transported me beyond any problems I might have.

In the Tupi language the name Yaquerana means, "People with lice." Thus, it appears that it was a pejorative term for the Panoan tribes living along the Yaquerana River. Yet today in Puerto Alegre, as in a multitude of indigenous villages, a favorite pastime for women and girls is picking lice and nits (lice eggs) from each other's hair. Humans and monkeys share this grooming trait in common. Both will pinch lice out of each other's hair, then pop them between their teeth and swallow them. From my room I could see a gaggle of giggly girls who stood in the shade of some mamey trees, all searching for predatory piojos, lice, in the heads of their friends. The men all have short hair and don't usually harbor lice, but every woman has more lice than mamey trees have fruits. I brought no lice shampoo in the buckets of medicine I took to the villages, since the Caritas partner in Lima had none. As had been the case with the Chama Indians, I wondered if I would have interfered with the natural order of things had I given away lice shampoo. These pestilent lice serve a function for promoting social intimacy through these women's grooming practices. Having lice shampoo would cause them to have no reason to hunt in each other's heads, breaking a chain of human dependency.

Though the Matsés live partly from horticulture, their crop production is very limited due to a lack of seeds. As Romanoff wrote in his thesis: "For most of the century, the continuity of garden production has been a more critical problem than has continuous production of meat by hunting." This is truer now than during the period of his research, due to the depletion of game. The wife raids of the Matsés actually increased the variety of their crops, because they sometimes took plant starts and seedlings from the people they raided. The Matsés still cultivate a certain reed which are used for their long arrow shafts. The seeds and fruit trees which I had brought were welcomed. What they valued most were the corn, watermelon, and onion seeds, and the avocado and citrus trees.

The village president and I scooped out seed corn from one of the twenty-five-pound sacks into plastic bags. Many of the villagers were eager to plant and gathered around to receive seeds. Most were women, which is normal with Amazonian tribes, since women do most of the planting. As always, I wished I had brought more than 200 pounds for each of the three villages. A dozen needy families were each given about two pounds of corn to plant. The other sack of seed corn for Puerto Alegre, a standard variety called Marginal 28, would be used for the village's collective garden. The same was done with the rice seed. For a couple of days following, I spent much of my time dividing the many other varieties of vegetable and fruit seeds into hundreds of small envelopes to be given to each village family.

In times past, my gifts of seeds and fruit trees would have caused young Matsés men to pierce their bodies in order to insure a good harvest. For lazy youth, the seeds would cause them to be given sapo, their famous toad secretion, to cure their indolence. As is the case with many tribes, corn planting has many rituals associated with it.

Sapo is a key identifier of the Matsés tribe. Though named "sapo," i.e. toad, it is actually an emetic and exudate of narcotic frog skin. It is scraped from the skin of a small nocturnal frog and dried on a piece of bamboo. Then it is applied to a deltoid muscle that has received a small burn to open the skin. Unlike ayahuasca, which is not used amongst the Matsés, it is not used as a shamanic medium for entrance into other realms. Instead, it is used for strengthening people before major hunting expeditions, or as a punishment for laziness, adultery, or eating prohibited foods.

Not long after I arrived in Puerto Alegre, a Matsés man of about fifty asked me a couple of different times for one of the shovels I had brought along. He seemed to expect to get it, but I told him they were for projects. Finally, after he asked me again and again in the following days, I relented. After I handed the shovel to him, he silently walked away. Then, a couple of days later, I wanted to take his photograph. Much to my surprise, he refused. I was incredulous and I thought that I might have offended him somehow, perhaps because of his facial tattoos. Like many Matsés he had a chain of T-like tattoos stretching down from his ear lobes and ringing his mouth. But it wasn't that; he just wanted money.

At first, I thought that he was joking, but then he got upset when I took out my camera and reached out to stop me. I stopped and looked him straight in the eyes then shamed him in front of some other people by saying, "Though I just gave you a thirty-sole shovel, now you want to charge me to take your photo?" He finally relented, but was not happy about it, as the photos later revealed. In addition to the shovel, this man also received a few different fruit trees for his family land, plus seeds, like all of the sixty homes in the village. His request for money from me to take his photo seemed very out of focus, a clear snapshot of ingratitude.

Though his tribal tattoos clearly marked this man as a Matsés, he did not look very indigenous. Rather, he looked more mestizo. No doubt he was one of those who had a parent or grandparent taken captive, or perhaps he had been taken captive himself as a child, which would perhaps explain his bellicose demeanor. I would never find out, though. This man was also illiterate, so my bringing books and writing materials might have caused some feelings of inadequacy to surface. The only ink he has ever experienced was that of his tattoos. Women and children captives were normally given facial tattoos as a Matsés signifier and mark of their passage into the tribe. These tattoos thus played a role in maintaining social cohesion. The ink for Matsés tattoos is made from mixing the soot from copal smoke with the black juice from the huito fruit (*Genipa americana*).

One day, a man who had gathered (or rather, plundered) three hundred Teracaya turtle eggs wanted to sell them to me. But do you think that he would give me even one? No! And he knew what I had brought for his village. I have usually found indigenous people, especially those in remote places, to be more generous. I wondered why the Matsés are so quick to ask for things, but show so little thanks and rarely reciprocate. I wondered if it was because of their history and lack of outside contact, especially positive contact, with "the other"? Perhaps living for centuries in the remote wilderness where their only neighbors were their enemies had left them insulated and somewhat selfish.

I later told these stories to two elderly mestizo women in Angamos who had lived for years among the Matsés. One was a teacher who spoke the Matsés language. She knew their word for thank-you, but confirmed that the Matsés seldom use it or show any signs of thanks. I had already experienced that on several occasions. When I purchased the airline tickets from Iquitos to Angamos for Emilio and Roberto, they never said a word, although neither could have gone there without my tickets. Emilio had never even seen his son, who was a year and a half old. And Roberto hadn't been back in four years. I found their silence and lack of any thanks quite odd. Later, their devious behavior was even harder to digest.

Perhaps Emilio was showing his village that he had not lost his virility and prowess as a hunter and gatherer, even after living in the big city for some time. They said that he once killed a jaguar, which earned him respect among his people. Now he seemed to be hunting and gathering my precious gasoline and other things I had brought with me. It was not until a few days after we arrived in Puerto Alegre that I found out that only fifteen of my sixty gallons of gasoline remained. I was shocked. Once I realized that the two young Matsés had recklessly wasted and "disappeared" most of my gasoline, I became disgusted, especially after everything I had done for them and their community. Emilio had given away seven gallons of gas to someone I didn't even know. They drained my plans of spending any time in the area, because there wasn't enough gasoline left to do anything other than return to Angamos. I had wanted to spend a few weeks there, but when the gasoline suddenly "disappeared," so did I.

When I told Santiago, the cordial president of the village, about the missing gasoline he shook his head, obviously upset by the behavior of my two Matsés helpers. I told him, "If they do not respect my things, then they do not respect me either. And if that is true, then what am I doing here?" But to avoid a confrontation, I only told Emilio that he had no right to take the gasoline. He was with his wife at the time and I did not want to argue or shame him in front of her. I knew that Santiago would shame the two young men later, so I left it up to him. Then I walked back to the place where I was staying and never saw Emilio or Ricardo again.

I asked Santiago to arrange a dugout back to Angamos and took eleven of the remaining fourteen gallons of my gas from Emilio's house, where it was stored. How Emilio would get the large boat back to Angamos was his problem. "Let him learn a good lesson," I told Santiago. The next morning at three-thirty, Santiago came to wake me up and I left rapidly with the two boatmen.

As we were leaving, a crocodile showed its red eyes in the dark and then dashed for the water just a few meters from the dugout. During that fourteen-hour journey, I also saw a nice capybara on the Brazilian side of the river, where the forest is most intact. It walked slowly up the bank like a giant guinea pig.

Later we stopped to see a hunter's fresh kill—a paca fish laying in his dugout. I asked the man about a gun, but he told me he had no gun. He pointed to his two dogs he then to an eight-foot-long spear lying in his dugout. Those were his weapons. I asked to see the spear and he handed it to me; the wood was light as a feather, but very strong. He usually used it for spearing the huge paiche fish, he said. I asked him if I could buy a piece of the paca, but he wanted too much money so I declined. I was again surprised by the money-mindedness of the Matsés, especially in the middle of nowhere. Somehow, he and his wife had also caught two large Teracaya turtles, laying on their backs with their legs tied together. I felt sorry for them, especially since it was the egging season. Though the Matsés are known to be ethical hunters, the call of hunger recognizes few rules.

As we neared Angamos, just above the confluence with the Galvez River, we passed the third dugout we had seen all day. It was about seventy meters away, going upriver. Suddenly, a man stood up and held up both of his arms, as if questioning. I immediately recognized him as the owner of the boat I had rented. Of course, he wanted to know about his boat. I just waved and laughed—it was my first laugh for awhile.

Soon we were in Angamos and I immediately went to the home of the elderly Dona Beatrice. Days before, she had asked me for one of my caimito trees (*Pouteria caimito*), which I happily gave her. She had offered me a room, so I had my first bed in a while. I was thankful that I didn't have to stay in the rat trap hotel again. Because the twice-weekly flight back to Iquitos was leaving in the morning, I went right over to the airline office to present my open ticket and reserve a seat. I was fourth on the list. The next morning, I again went to the airline office to check my bag. Coco, the agency owner, weighed it and told me to wait a little while, and then he disappeared out the door.

Meanwhile, I was entertained by his very smart five-year-old daughter Briana, who had seen me a few times around Angamos and somehow took a liking to me. Along with her seven-year-old brother, she was looking through a dictionary, but they didn't know how to use it. For the next hour I gave them a lesson. When Coco returned, there were several people waiting who also wanted to get on the flight, but most did not have tickets. Though I had already been waiting there for more than an hour for my boarding pass, Coco again told me to wait some more. Finally, after another hour, I realized that he had bumped me from the list and given my place to someone else, a Peruvian. We exchanged some harsh words for several minutes, but he wouldn't relent. I had to retrieve my bag and return to Dona Beatrice's house. After telling her the story, she told me to wait on her porch. I watched as she walked across the little plaza to the Angamos police station. Awhile later, I saw her and some police officers come out and walk around the corner to the airline office. Less than five minutes later, I heard my name on the village loudspeaker, telling me to go to the airport. With a smile on my face I thanked Dona Beatrice and walked over to the eight-passenger plane. There was Coco, who avoided any eye contact with me.

Juxtaposed against the grueling ten days it took to get to Angamos by river, the forty-five-minute flight back to Iquitos seemed like a joy ride. Soon the flat, seemingly endless expanse of the Amazon revealed things only seen from the air. The Yavari disappeared into the midst of the jungle like a giant boa, but the larger Ucayali slithered into sight on the horizon. Hidden oxbows and ancient river courses revealed themselves like old riverine footprints from ages past. They stood out by the texture and color of the plants now covering them. Below, the flat and expansive lowland jungle stretched beyond sight. In there, it is far easier to get lost than it is to be found. Within forty minutes, Iquitos revealed its parameters of poverty. I completed the circle as we passed closely above a sprawl of thatched shacks that sat among the knot of rivers.

In Iquitos, the Christian Brother priest there already knew that I did not want to give the rest of the things I had stored at RAL to three Ticuna villages. I had told him that I didn't want to help those villages, because they were known for making cocaine for the Colombian cartels. He was not happy to hear my words, because he had been helping those villages for many years. Either he was so naïve that he didn't know about the drugs, or he did know but just didn't care. He had already sent two untrustworthy Matsés to help me, so I realized that I had twice been mistaken in trusting his bad judgment.

I knew this was going to lead to a confrontation, so I decided to just go and get all the things I had stored at RAL and give it to more deserving villages. With a friend, I went there with two mototaxis, but we soon realized that everything was gone. Anticipating my move, the priest had intentionally given the $2000 worth of books, seeds, medicine, and other supplies to the three narco-villages before I could reclaim them. It was lucky for him that he was out when I came, because I was angry and the Iquitos jail is right next door to RAL.

Later I phoned him and he told me that he thought I wasn't coming back. I was incredulous and told him that he knew better than that and was wrong. I told him that I had come back early, after the Matsés he sent to help me had stolen my gasoline. He responded that he didn't want to talk about it, because he had hypertension. Some unprintable words then filled his ears and I hung up the phone on him. Just as with Emilio and Roberto, I never cared to associate with him again.

After spending nearly three months working on and spending lots of money on this project, and then traveling for seventeen days on four rivers, I felt betrayed. First, my gasoline was hunted down like a white-lipped peccary and divided up by a Matsés "hunting party." Then, acting as if he was the rightful owner, the priest helped himself to the rest of my supplies. I don't know who I was more disgusted with, the priest or the two Matsés "helpers." In truth, it was the priest.

Although a Matsés land reserve has been set up, it is legally tentative and not titled land, so all oil concessions continue to be awarded by the government of Peru. Just as the Matsés had dealt with Portuguese, Spanish, and Shipibo slavers, then later with the rubber barons and their industrial genocide, now they face more threats from oil companies. Even though Arco was once stopped from oil exploration, in 2011 the Canadian/Colombian Pacific Rubiales Oil Company gained a concession to explore for oil in the reserve. Perhaps Matsés kidnappings should start up again and the Seven Sisters of oil should be abducted and given tribal tattoos.

PART SIX:
BOLIVIA AND CHILE

Chapter 21

BOOKENDS WITHOUT BOOKS

"A room without books is like a body without a soul." – Cicero

It wasn't until I reached Arica that I realized Chilean law prohibits foreigners from taking vehicles, which they bought in Chile, out of the country. No one had ever said a word, and who would have suspected that such a law existed? The Chileans are trying to prevent the business of selling used vehicles from Chile in places like Bolivia, where they cost more. Chile is a land of laws which only generals are allowed to break.

The whole back of my pick-up truck was loaded with children's books which I had purchased in Santiago and Las Serena the week before. I was on my way to Bolivia with enough children's books for more than twenty remote primary schools. But I couldn't get out of Chile. I even paid for an agent to intervene for me, but it didn't help. Almost every day for two weeks, I visited the office of the head of Chilean Customs in Arica. I got nowhere. Certainly, the Customs boss was tired of seeing some bearded gringo and his big shaggy dog come to his office every day. I am sure he was very tired of telling me "No!" time after time. And it didn't help me any when my dog, Mr. Jeb, vomited on his office floor. But as the official more than realized, I wasn't going to take "no" for an answer.

Finally I decided to take another approach. I invited him out for lunch and as bait I used the best white-tablecloth seafood restaurant in Arica. Perhaps because of its reputation he decided to take along his secretary. I had met Lenin and Victor, the chef and head waiter at the restaurant a couple of weeks before and we had become friends. They soon knew my plan and Lenin, an authentic gourmet chef, said he would make something special.

Later the three of us would agree that it was Lenin's grilled sea bass covered in a white sauce, his salad with peeled tomatoes in the form of roses, and more than a couple bottles of fine wine which finally changed the Customs boss's mind.

After finishing the meal, the Customs man told me, "Ok, you can take your truck out of Chile, but only if you have a Chilean driver."

Right then Lenin approached the table in his stovepipe chef's hat and apron. He told the Customs man, "Sir, excuse me, but I heard what you said. I am also a professional driver and I have a chauffeur's license. I'll drive the truck."

Suddenly, just like that, there was a way out. The next day we went and got some papers for Lenin notarized and that cleared us to go. That same day he quit his poorly paid job. Realizing that his best friend was leaving, Victor also wanted to go. "Why not?" I thought. The restaurant had to close for a few days and the owner was not happy with me, but suddenly the three of us and my dog were going to Bolivia.

The day before we were ready to leave I had a new problem, this time with the Bolivian Customs. They told me that before entering Bolivia I would have to pay a one-thousand-dollar tax on my books.

"You've got to be joking!" I told the head of Bolivian Customs. "No, I refuse to pay a tax on a gift I am going to give to poor schools in your country. That is not right! "

Again, just like at the Chilean Customs, I was told there was nothing he could do. "The law is the law," I was told.

So first I could not get out of Chile and then I could not get into Bolivia. I decided to use the same plan of attack and go to the Bolivian Customs office every day with Mr. Jeb, my emissary dog. Startled to see such a large dog enter the office, the very proper Bolivian Customs secretary asked me, raising her voice, "Is he coming in?"

"Oh, yes, Señora, he is my secretary," I insisted. "I need him to take notes." Within a minute he was getting a cookie.

Though an understanding man, the head of Bolivian Customs became frustrated when I continually refused to pay the tax, so he sent me to their Bolivian Embassy in Arica. There, too, I was told, "I can do nothing!" But the Bolivian Ambassador finally suggested something: "Okay, do this: contact the Minister of Education. Tell him your situation. Maybe he will do something."

The next day I returned with my "secretary" to the Bolivian Customs office and convinced them to fax the Bolivian Minister of Education in La Paz for me. For the next ten days we returned every day to the Customs office to see if there was a reply, or at least to get a cup of coffee for me and a cookie for my "secretary."

We often waited besides Gustof Eiffel's filigree iron building, which blossoms in a tiny green park between the treeless Atacama and the flat Pacific.

Finally we got a response. They had received a fax with the all-important signature of the good Minister. The one paragraph response said that I could freely pass into Bolivia with my books without paying any taxes, but I must visit the Minister of Education's office in La Paz. Finally, I was not only free to go, but I had an "in" with the Minister.

Lenin, pleased at the news, told me, "Sometimes problems can turn into blessings. The thing is don't give up, don't succumb to the problem. Only because you persisted did you win."

As we were readying ourselves to leave the next morning, I found it strange when Lenin didn't show up. Both Victor and I knew something was wrong, but we had no idea what it was. After calling and visiting some of Lenin's friends, we finally decided to call the police.

"Yes," we were told, "there is a Lenin Ramos here." Luckily, we soon found out that it was a simple case of mistaken identity. Having a name like Lenin and growing up in the time of General Pinochet was a bit precarious. After the Allende coup, not far south of Arica, there were some actual concentration camps for "questionable" people.

Finally, we left Arica and passed below El Moro, the towering rocky fortress captured by Chile in the War of the Pacific. Along the Pacific Ocean the land and the water are much alike in their vast expanses of treeless horizons. A drop of the Pacific's water seems like a grain of sand in the Atacama. The salty sea smell and coastal morning fog dissipated as we drove inland into the bone-dry desert. Taking a short-cut, we followed a sandy track out of Arica which sooner or later would connect us with the paved road heading for Bolivia. It is not until one rises hundreds of meters that there is any change in the landscape. Eventually candalaria cacti peppered the rising mountains. Looking above us, we could see snowcapped peaks and the land turned somewhat greener.

The fax with the Minister's signature was put to good use several times in the next few months, although not always in the way it was intended. It got us out of speeding tickets, parking tickets, and some other minor infractions. We would just hand the letter to the Bolivian police and they would waive the fine. We made sure not to misplace the fax, and made a photocopy of it which was kept in the glovebox with the truck's papers.

When I got to La Paz, I went to see the Minister of Education. I found out that he was not only the Minister of Education, but also the Minister of Sports and Culture. Therefore he held a tripartite position, sharing his time with two other concerns. The fact that Bolivia did not even have a full time Minister of Education, but had him share his time with sports and culture, didn't say much for their commitment to education. Later I was assured that the Minister's real job was actually exporting cocaine. The title "Minister" is just a masquerade which facilitated making this enterprise easier. If Thomas Katari, the late eighteenth-century Macha Indian revolutionary who is credited with the introduction of schools in Bolivia, had been alive, he would have hung the good Minister from a light pole as had been done to a former president.

As we were entering the several stories tall Ministry of Education building in downtown La Paz, we noticed a green Mercedes limousine parked in front. A group of smartly dressed men were conversing in the front lobby. I suspected that one of them was the Minister.

We waited for them to finish their conversation and when the one I thought was the Minister walked outside to the waiting six-door limousine, we followed. The chauffeur was waiting with one of the rear doors open. Then the three of us and my four-footed "secretary" approached the limousine. The Minister seemed a bit put off by us as we walked up. Perhaps it was because the best dressed of us was my "secretary." I introduced us and thanked him for the fax.

Then Victor, who was holding my dog's leash, suddenly gave it a yank. All of us including the Minister looked over to see Mr. Jeb with his leg raised, pissing on the back tire. Saying that he was in a hurry, the good Minister told me to make an appointment with his secretary. I made an appointment, but it never worked out, both because of our travels and the Minister's schedule.

It turned out that they wanted us to take different Ministry workers along with us to the schools we were planning to visit. That was fine, except for the fact that my truck was already full. But we managed to do it. The first Ministry worker was a very nice man named Luis, who went with us to some forgotten little schools in the Altiplano. For some reason, he had with him the budget for Ministry, which I was curious to look at. I paged through the document trying to find out how much money was allocated for books and other school materials. None was discovered; not a cent was available for books. They spent money on posters telling kids to love their country and other posters telling them not to stick gum under their desks, but no money was spent on children's books. There were also many thousands of dollars allocated for various types of electronic gear such as tape recorders, radios, cameras, video cameras, computers, and other things. It seemed very strange to me that so much money was spent on electronic devices when a large percentage of the schools didn't even have electricity. I asked Luis about this, and he told me that these "electronic toys" were never meant for the schools. Instead, they were gifts which high-ranking Ministry workers bought for themselves. This was all done at the expense of the bookless schools. No wonder the schools were empty when the education budget was a gift list for the Ministry's unconscionable directors.

At about that same time an article appeared in a Bolivian newspaper revealing the deplorable situation of many primary schools. In La Paz young students were even required to buy their own chairs or else sit on the floor. Because of poverty many children had no choice except to sit on the cement floors, with only pieces of cardboard to insulate them from the cold concrete. After classes were over the chairs would be locked in a storeroom. At the same time, the Minister rides around in a chauffeur-driven Mercedes limousine.

Bolivia is the poorest country in South America and it also has the highest percentage of indigenous inhabitants. Many children never go to school at all. Instead, they tend the family's flocks, work as shoeshine boys, sell things on the street, and do a host of odd jobs. Of those who do go to school, many only go until the fifth grade. This is especially true in remote areas, where there are often no secondary schools. In order for many of these kids to go beyond primary school, they are required to commute to a larger village which has one, or else go to live in the other village. Very few families can afford this, so consequently their kids never go beyond fifth or sixth grade.

This is how feudalism and centuries of oppression are kept intact. This is why such places will always have a cheap pool of labor. This is why helping to educate children in remote primary schools is so important for them; for many it is the only education they will ever receive. But without books, who can learn to read? And without a pen and paper, who can ever learn to write?

Chapter 22

IN THE NAVEL OF CHUQUISACA

"I regard the library as a temple."—Sartre

Ethnically, the area around Sucre, Bolivia is very diverse. There are many different indigenous groups: the Jalq'a, Tarabuco, Ch'uta, Peana, Lamera, and several more. They are united by the Aymara language, but are distinguished by their particular cultural customs, in dress, weavings, festivals, and more.

Once the Jalq'a were part of the greater Yampara culture that was ultimately subservient to Cusco, the ancient capital of the Inca. That was, until the Spanish arrived in the 1530s. Quilla Quilla was their most important village and at the time of the Conquest it was allied with the chiefdom of Moro Moro and Quara Quara. Today, the twenty thousand Jalq'a living in over forty remote villages are a result of that alliance. None of these have a complex socio-political structure, even when compared to neighboring indigenous groups. Since the time of the Conquest, many Jalq'a villages have belonged to large haciendas and suffered perpetual poverty under a system of feudal exploitation. It wasn't until the Agrarian Reform of 1953 that steps were taken to liberate them. On the basis of their current situation, however, it is obvious that those steps failed; the Jalq'a are still some of the poorest people in Bolivia.

In March of 2001, accompanied by two Chileno friends, I set out to bring books and build a green house in the Jalq'a hamlet of

Irupampa, also known as "The Navel of Chuquisaca." About fifty kilometers from Sucre, in the barren Cordillera de los Frailes, is a huge caldera-like crater formed by the long extinct Moragua volcano. Inside this ancient volcano are three very small communities—one of them, Irupampa, was our destination.

We left Sucre eager to spend several days in Irupampa, but we got stuck in traffic due to a common occurrence in Bolivia: a demonstration by striking workers. We waited in my truck in front of a bank's ATM machine, just opposite Sucre's beautiful plaza. There, an elderly Jalq'a man sat begging beside the machine. His eclipsed eyes were not organs of sight, but of imprisoned passion imploring passersby to take pity. It seemed as if he was staring from behind bars. Besides being blind, his leprous fingers were stubs, like cigarettes consumed to their filters. Next to him sat a small boy who guided him around by clutching a corner of his old poncho.

Together, they sang a song of petition against their poverty. Meanwhile, a tourist couple came up to use the ATM. Waiting for them to turn his way, the Jalq'a boy held out the old man's felt hat. He reminded me of one of the many street dogs that beg for scraps in front of the market's meat shops. Though they could hear the song, the tourists declined to turn. It seemed that the old man's blindness meant that they didn't exist for him. It seemed to excuse their existence. But actually, it was he who didn't exist for them. I wondered who was really blind? Once their money was extracted from the ATM, they quickly moved on.

These illiterate and marginalized Jalq'a can be found begging on nearly every street corner and in front of every old church in Sucre's beautiful colonial center. Most are elderly—too old and frail to work the land anymore—and totally without any social security other than the alms they collect. There are also others who are single mothers who have no recourse but to beg.

There is something particularly sad about rural indigenes begging in a city. To me, it seems like it would be much better to be poor in the countryside than to be a beggar in the city. "How do they end up here?" I asked myself. Certainly, most have little choice. Sucre's colonial churches are places where alms can be received, though they offer little assistance. Jalq'a beggars flock to them like winter birds to a bird feeder.

With my Chilean friends Lenin and Victor, I had already spent weeks going to eighteen remote village schools with books and seeds, including the Jalq'a village Potolo. Now we wanted to hike back into this remote Chuquisaca region.

Lenin met Luis Polo, a Jalq'a Indian from Irupampa, while getting the truck washed one day. He ended up helping us load a large transport truck. In addition to books and supplies, we were also taking fifty long eucalyptus poles for the construction of two greenhouse frames. The Sucre city government had donated them and even provided a city worker who cut them with a chainsaw. While he worked the chainsaw, two of us stripped the branches off with machetes. Once the truck was loaded, we drove out to Quilla Quilla. I sat up front, but the others rode uncomfortably in the back along with my dog and twenty Jalq'a.

Not far outside of Sucre, we entered the Cordillera de los Frailes, a barren stretch of jagged mountains. The rocky road soon reached an overlook far above the San Juan River. One can look a few hundred meters below and see the river disappear into the dry, winding canyon. Looking toward where we were to ford the river, I could see large patches of red coloring the ground. A group of people were doing something, but it was too far away to tell exactly what. It wasn't until we had driven down a dozen switchbacks that we were close enough to see that they were drying chili peppers. On a flat, stony area beside the river, women were turning the chilis over one by one.

About two hours later we were in Quilla Quilla. Like many Bolivian villages, Quilla Quilla has only two dirt streets, lined with low adobe houses. It is literally the end of the road, and has more donkeys traffic than vehicle traffic. A very large adobe church dominates the place.

We drove the truck to the very end of the increasingly narrow road and stopped. Six Jalq'a men helped us unload. They stacked the fifty poles in a large pile next to a stone wall. Everything else—rolls of plastic, boxes of books, seeds, nails, hammers, food, dog food, water, three rabbits, and two chickens—was loaded onto six donkeys. We then started the three-hour hike to Irupampa.

The ancient trail from Quilla Quilla quickly rises up the rocky, nearly treeless slopes, often intersecting a stream that constantly dripped into turquoise-colored pools. Fossilized dinosaur prints let us know that this land had been trodden upon for a long time. Free of our packs, my Chilean friends and I all tried to keep pace with a young Jalq'a man. Approaching a series of long switchbacks, we decided to take a breather next to one of the many clear pools before starting the ascent.

By the pool sat three elderly Jalq'a, two women and a man. They all wore sandals made from old tires. Their feet, especially their heels, were deeply cracked and calloused, which made them seem like extensions of the eroded earth. Both of the women wore skirts of woven wool embroidered with birds and animals. The Jalq'a are among the world's finest weavers and are one of the only tribes known to use the difficult two-sided, two-colored twill technique. The little old man was mostly hidden beneath his black and red poncho. His down-turned face was partially obscured by his round, white felt hat. Beside him was a crooked walking stick.

We stopping only briefly and soon told them "Adiós" as we continued the ascent. After hiking for several minutes, we were nearly to the top when were quite bewildered and surprised to see that same little old man with his crooked walking stick looking down on us.

"How did he get to the top before us?" I asked Lenin. "I didn't see him pass, did you?"

"He must have walked straight up—amazing!" Lenin replied. He seemed to do it as a joke to surprise us. Looking at him, I detected a glint of amused satisfaction in his eyes. Charmed by his almost boy-like attitude and impressed by his endurance, I had to ask him his age. "Ninety!" he proudly told me.

He then told us that he had fought in the Chaco War from 1932 to 1935. That was when Bolivia fought Paraguay over the Chaco's oil and natural gas fields. Similar to Bolivia's 1880s War of the Pacific with Chile, the Chaco War was also instigated by foreign commercial interests. In the Chaco, two foreign oil companies were vying for territorial control. Standard Oil backed Bolivia and Shell supported Paraguay. Both companies spread rumors about potential oil and natural gas finds, knowing that it would cause turmoil and bloodshed. At least 100,000 soldiers died—most of them illiterate peasants who rarely used gas or oil.

It took three hours to get to Irupampa, and then we needed to wait for the donkeys. The community consisted of a run-down school with broken windows, surrounded by a dozen houses scattered in fields bordered by stone walls.

Luis Polo's family owned a couple of the houses. We stayed in one and pitched a tent next to it. For the next four days, five or six Jalq'a men carried the fifty poles, one by one, for three hours to the site of the proposed greenhouses. While we waited for the poles, I delivered books to four area schools. It would be hard to find schools in worse shape. The only thing they had was a desire to learn.

Historically, reading has been foreign to these Aymara cultures that are steeped in oral tradition. They have felt that writing robs narrative of its power and forcefulness. Today, however, they all want education for their children, though little is provided. Sadly, it is really no better for the rural poor than it was in 1780. At that time, Thomas Katari, the Macha Indian utopian pacifist, started public education in Bolivia, but it died with his execution.

Inside the rolling perimeter of the volcanic crater is Moragua, the largest of the four small Jalq'a communities. It is not much more than a collection of fifty crumbling adobe houses, many seemingly abandoned. Irupampa is about a mile away, on the rim of the crater. Lenin and I walked with my dog and a single donkey through the bucolic crater. Soon we were accosted by several local dogs that barked at us viciously. We had to resort to the only language they respect—the sharp sound of stone striking stone.

We walked through the center of the Jalq'a world—the Navel of Chuquisaca—the immense two-mile-wide Moragua crater. It looked like a huge unglazed ceramic bowl with colorful sides featuring a series of concentric stripes made from mineral deposits. It resembled a giant flower, with each petal layered with contoured colors.

In the crater's center, a conical hill rises abruptly from the surrounding fields of wheat, barley, fava beans, and potatoes. The top has been a cemetery for three centuries. Like a thick rash, goats and sheep grazed on its unplanted slopes. In the distance, on one edge of the crater's farmed floor, a cliff drops precipitously a hundred meters. Along the rim is another cemetery, an ancient pre-Colombian one, designated only by occasional exposed bone fragments. Along its side, a narrow waterfall clings to the cliffside as it drops into cold transparent pools far below. We followed the rim back to the Polo family house, tired from the hike.

There beside their humble house, Luis' mother sat weaving in front of her back-strap loom. Her long braids, almost reaching her waist, were tied together at their ends on her back. She was weaving what they call an aqsu. Though the Jalq'a had no books, they would sometimes relate information and stories through their weavings. Each part of the weaving was filled with intricately designed iconic figures. Included in the seemingly disordered space were griffins, hunchbacked animals, and an emblematic being with winged arms using a crooked walking stick. Immediately it made me think of the little old man we had met earlier.

In Jalq'a cosmology these beings are called khurus and saxras. Khurus are monstrous etheric beings inhabiting visions. They appear in frightening forms not subject to earthly laws. The deity-like saxras, the masters of the khuru world, also live in a parallel existence. They are the rulers of solitary spaces and linger in the shadows beside subterranean waters and caves. Sometimes they reveal themselves in the mists of lonely landscapes as a human being. By weaving them into sight from the unseen world through the semiotic threads spun from their flocks, the Jalq'a keep their memories close and their fears far away.